Ethnicities and Nations

Ethnicities and Nations

Processes of Interethnic
Relations in Latin America,
Southeast Asia, and the Pacific

Edited by
Remo Guidieri
Francesco Pellizzi
Stanley J. Tambiah

assisted by Rose Wax Hauer and Harris Rosenstein

A ROTHKO CHAPEL BOOK distributed by
UNIVERSITY OF TEXAS PRESS AUSTIN

© 1988 The Rothko Chapel, Houston, Texas
All rights reserved. First published in 1988.
Printed in the United States of America

Requests for
permission to reproduce material
from this work should be sent to
　Permissions
　University of Texas Press
　Box 7819
　Austin, Texas 78713–7819

Composition, editorial assistance: Geraldine Aramanda
Technical consultant: Arvin C. Conrad
Typesetting: TEXSource, Houston
Printing and binding: Edwards Brothers

Library of Congress Cataloging-in-Publication Data

Ethnicities and nations.

　Bibliography: p.
　1. Ethnicity–Cross-cultural studies. 2. Ethnic
relations. I. Guidieri, Remo. II. Pellizzi, Francesco, 1940–
III. Tambiah, Stanley Jeyaraja, 1929–
GN378.E84　1988　305.8　88–6471
ISBN 0–945472–01–3 (alk. paper)

Contents

SOUTHEAST ASIA

ERRATA

P. 56, n. 23: "Guadeloupe" should read "Guadalupe"

P. 145, line 28: "Maykuth" should read "Maykruth"

P. 147, line 4: "initated" should read "initiated"

P. 170, n. 1: "Dyptich" should read "Diptych"

P. 175, line 6: "are" should read "is"

P. 185, Section X, line 9: "sepent" should read "serpent"

P. 210, line 3: "spirts" should read "spirits"

P. 210, line 21: "organizating" should read "organizing"

P. 214, lines 12–13: "‡" should read "+"

P. 250, line 38: "ecoomic" should read "economic"

P. 295, line 33: "D. S. Senanayaka" should read "D. S. Senanayake"

P. 298, line 8: "Polonnarura" should read "Polonnaruva"

P. 301, line 8: "Vaviniya" should read "Vavuniya"

P. 304, line 16: "Mullaitiva" should read "Mullaitivu"

P. 307, line 5: "*Chelvanaygan*" should read "*Chelvanaygam*"

P. 392, line 17: "Cotobato" should read "Cotabato"

P. 397, n. 2: "Zamboango" should read "Zamboanga"

Foreword

STANLEY J. TAMBIAH

The issues surrounding ethnicity, nation, nation-state, interethnic conflict, tensions between majorities and minorities in the process of nation-building, are by no means new to scholars and politicians. They have already stimulated and generated both historical and contemporary studies in the humanities and in the social sciences. Yet they are inadequately understood and are of continuing and perennial interest. [1]

Because today there is an intensification and proliferation, a "heating up," of violence all over the world, there is special reason for it being urgent to take up these issues in serious discussion. Simultaneous explosions in different parts of the globe, mutually feeding upon one another, threaten to plunge us into another world war, this time perhaps fought with nuclear weapons. We cannot help feeling that we are on the brink of a global war that may be ignited by one or another of these conflicts that appear to be interethnic, or interclass, or intercommunity, exploding within polities that are pushed and pulled by divisive forces as well as integrative impulses. These conflicts are occurring in territories and demographic areas that claim to be "nation-states," which are assumed by everyone in both the North and the South, and in the First, Second, and Third Worlds, to be a necessary and fundamental condition of political existence in the modern world.

The present violent conflicts within countries that are pluralistic or mosaic in composition—in El Salvador, Nicaragua, Lebanon, India, Sri Lanka, and Cambodia, to name just a few—are themselves perhaps affected, distorted, and dislocated by "world historical processes." These processes, often labeled as "modernization" and "economic development," were expected, under the sponsorship and direction of Western and North American countries, to heap great benefits upon the rest of the world.

Although there have been successes in the push toward economic development and modernization, the deep disillusionment of the eighties consists in the disconcerting realization that these programs have generated—whether by collusion or reaction, in good faith but poor anticipation—massive civil war, repressive authoritarianism by military coteries fortified by Western weaponry, and gruesome interracial and interethnic bloodshed roused by fundamental religious bigotry and inflamed by flagrant misuse of mass media.   More often than not, development has produced steeper differences in wealth, income distribution, and education between, on one side, the multinational corporations and the local military and other elites feeding off them, and, on the other, the rural poor, whose subsistence agriculture increasingly became irrelevant to world trade, and the flood of migrants to cities foraging on the margins of poverty.

Moreover, the optimism of sociologists and political scientists who naively foretold the onset of the "integrative revolution" and the inevitable decline of "primordial loyalties" such as kinship, caste, and ethnicity in Third World countries, has now waned. The introduction of constitutions and democratic institutions, enshrining human rights, universal franchise, the party system, the elected legislature, majority rule, and so on, has often resulted in strange malformations that are far removed from the goals of liberty, justice, tolerance, and freedom that were the ideological supports of Western European and North American "liberal-democratic" syntheses. Something has gone gravely awry with the center-periphery relations throughout the world, and these seem to be bleak years for us all.

It is imperative, therefore, that we return to our libraries and our field notes, to our places of contemplation and constructive dialogue, like the Rothko Chapel, and reconsider our previous assumptions, suppositions, and interpretive schemes. Among others, two issues seem to me to have already become the foci of close critical study, and we may expect a colloquium such as ours to contribute to that venture. I will consider each in turn.

1. We have to study closely the last phases of the colonial era and the early decades of independence in Africa and Asia (and elsewhere), when what historians call the "transfer of power" took place from the British, Dutch, or French, to the local elites who emerged and consolidated under their aegis. This transfer of power was enacted in the idiom and rhetoric of "secular democratic politics" and the "secular nation-state."

The colonial forces brought together diverse groups, frequently within arbitrarily and accidentally defined and unified territorial spaces, and both subjected and enabled these groups to a greater degree of interaction and symbiosis than they had experienced before within the framework of colonial economic and administrative regimes. But with the transfer of power to local elites, their "primordial loyalties" have not withered away. Instead, competition for prizes and benefits of all kinds have intensified among ethnic groups, minorities, nationalities, and religious congregations, most visibly among the most vocal intelligentsia in their midst, the very social segments which it was hoped would lead the way to "progress." In many countries, a swelling, spiraling tornado has been unleashed by the dialectic between tradition and modernity, between religious fundamentalism and secularism, between an intensification of ancient populist sentiments and a transformation of traditional social bonds and forms, between the attraction of Western lifestyles and the preservation of classical moral codes. Let me give some examples:

a) In Nigeria we have recently seen an instance of a country arbitrarily created by British colonial rule, which later, in the midst of immense wealth flowing from oil revenues, was riven by the politics of alleged tribal loyalties labeled as Ibo, Hausa, Yoruba, and so on.

b) India, which after the Hindu-Muslim partition was viewed hopefully as having some kind of unity through its Hindu civilization, has progressively fragmented into linguistic states, a process that has threatened its federal unity. Yet, a few weeks before this was written, after three decades of constitutional democracy, violence flared up in the Punjab under the guise of Sikh nationalism, a violence that conflates and fuses religions with linguistic nationalism. Punjab, it is in'riguingly relevant to note, is India's best and most prosperous grain-producing area, and an important frontier state, having a border with Pakistan. The Sikhs now demand their own state with Chandigarh as their exclusive capital.

c) The Balkans have manifested throughout the last two centuries, and especially snce 1918, forms of ethnic, linguistic, and religious conflicts that seem to bear similarities to what we have recently witnessed in Asia and Africa. With the break up of the Ottoman Empire, the various Christian nationalities and minorities jockeyed in the nineteenth century to define themselves and realize their political presence. Thus the Roumanians, Bulgarians, and Serbs discovered and sharpened their linguistic separateness from the Greeks; and the Slovak nationalist movement activated a literary language to further its fight against the Hungarians.[2] These turmoils and ideological mainsprings in which emergent intelligentsias and bourgeois elites had a major role to play, may provide us with some clues to the understanding of the explosive ethnic and nationalistic conflicts of today.

2. A second issue which bears examination, in relation to the trajectory of events in Western Europe that were associated with the development of the "nation-state," is the extent that it was special to the West and

therefore nongeneralizable and nonexportable to the rest of the world.

To explain, at the cost of some simplification, it may be said that the "nation-state" and the concept of "nationalism," as understood for instance in France and Great Britain today, are developments that have occurred since the Enlightenment and since the French Revolution.[3] It is true that in Western Europe forms of "national consciousness" did exist before that time; they were the accompaniments or results of the play of various factors, such as the influence of a monarchical form of government and of a state structure, of religious fervor and linguistic patriotism, of historical memory and other cultural legacies. But only the first-mentioned developments produced that entity called the "nation-state" as a phenomenon both essentially *secular* and essentially *democratic* in its make up.

The transformations that occurred in Europe are commonly identified as follows:

a) A secular loyalty to the nation replaces as a primary ingredient loyalty to a religious community and loyalty to the ruler. The "legitimacy" of politics and the political life is grounded in some conception of the sovereignty of the people.

b) Such a collective integration and identity was accompanied by— some might say preceded by—that kind of economic transformation which, as an expansionary positive force, might be called "capitalism," creating movements of people and the labor market, dissolving parochial and regional trade barriers, developing interlocking market systems, and integrating diverse social segments in an encompassing enterprise. In other words, political integration and economic integration went together and had cumulative consequences.

c) The culture and literature of those nation-states were integrally linked to the development of languages—French, English, German— which replaced the lingua franca of medieval Europe, Latin, and became effective mediums and agencies for the exploration, shaping, and delineation of collective and personal self-consciousness, the sense of the past, and a forward-looking belief in a dynamic progress. Vital factors that contributed to these processes were the institution of changes in education that produced elites and intelligentsias, and the development of mass media of communication, the printing press in particular, which spread literacy and created reading publics.[4]

d) Christianity underwent a change in the face of the growth of positivist science. In Europe, especially, it became possible for many people to separate their lives into secular and sacred domains, to ground the "rationality" of spheres of action like politics and economics in self-sufficient secular motivations such as power, profit, etc., closely associated with possessive "individualism."

Since the metropolitan centers from which "modernization," "democratization," "secularization," and "industrialization" are brought to be transplanted in the Third World are principally located in Western Europe and North America, it is relevant to ask in what sense and to what degree it is meaningful and practicable for the West to expect a similar pattern and chain of events to recur in another part of the globe. Not only may we have to relinquish the idea that the Third World ought to or must follow the Western route, but also we are positively compelled to inquire whether "religion," "language," "history," "nationality," "territory" have connotations, resonances, impulsions, and implications for political action and nation-making in the Third World that have not been experienced before—and therefore are largely unsuspected today—in the countries of Western Europe and North America.

For example, Western Europe with its monarchical and Christian past has never felt except at its periphery the full impact of the Islamic experience and position that the code by which political authority rules cannot be divorced from religious law and injunction, or that education cannot be taken away from the imams and Koranic scholars and given over to secular bodies, or that to commit violence and die by the sword in a holy war (*jihad*) is rewarded by immortality. Similarly, little in Western European experience, whether in feudal or modern times, bears parallels to these Southeast Asian Buddhist Theravada religio-political formulations: that kingship and polity ought to be yoked with the order of Buddhist monks (*sangha*) in a paired relation of mutual support and symbiosis; that Buddhism as the special legacy of an ethnic or racial people speaking a distinctive language, whether they be Sinhalese, Burmans, or Thai, makes it axiomatic that Buddhism should be the religion of their state, whose duty is to protect and sponsor it. This same ideology of fusing religion and territory with a people, generates in Burma, Thailand, and Sri Lanka certain discriminatory attitudes and dominating actions toward minorities, whether they be the "hill tribes" (which are viewed as inferior groups to whom the morality of the true religion and the virtues of the special language of the majority have to be propagated) or they be minorities, Tamil-Hindu or Malay-Muslim, who have their own competing definitions, ideologies, and achievements of equal claims. Of the countries I have mentioned, Burma is the most "ethnically rebellious,"[5] as one scholar has put it, because of the presence of numerous minorities who demand their own political autonomy.

In the face of epidemic occurrences of violence in many places in the world today, in the face of conflicts that seem to be of an interethnic character that threaten to explode into international disasters, we as scholars should not merely scrutinize them from a dispassionate distance, but also deliberate as to whether we can offer normative valuations and prescriptive advice on how to alleviate them. For, scholars or not, we are ourselves historical actors participating in the events of the contemporary world, and our postures will have some bearing on their future outcome. Many of us here, participants and discussants, whether citizens or residents of the societies we describe, or, at a further remove, lifelong scholars of these societies, are touched by sentiments and loyalties, agonized by paradoxes and equivocations, which we might both confront and reveal in the course of our dialogue.

NOTES

1. The following, with minor variations, was delivered as the opening address at the colloquim *Ethnicities and Nations: Processes of Interethnic Relations in Latin America, Southeast Asia, and the Pacific*, held at the Rothko Chapel, in Houston, Texas, 28–30 October 1983. The work of organizing this colloquium, of defining the issues and inviting the participants, has been shouldered by Francesco Pellizzi and Remo Guidieri. We are thankful to Mrs. Dominique de Menil and to the directors and personnel of the Rothko Chapel for making this colloquium possible. The scholars assembled here are concerned with at least three major regions of our globe—Latin America, South and Southeast Asia, and the Pacific and Oceania. Francesco Pellizzi, with the assistance of Rose Hauer, has coordinated the editing of this volume.

2. See Hugh Seton-Watson, *Nationalism and Communism* (London: Methuen and Co. Ltd., 1964).

3. It is relevant to bear in mind that even in the Europe of today, many states have yet to complete the process of national integration, and that minorities continue to resist homogenization.

4. The role of "print capitalism" in the spread of nationalism has been developed by Benedict Anderson in *Imagined Communities: Reflections on the Origin and Spread of Nationalism* (London: Verso Editions, 1983). Also see Seton-Watson, op. cit.

5. This expression is used by Charles F. Keyes in his Introduction to a volume he edited entitled *Ethnic Adpatation and Identity, the Karen on the Thai Frontier with Burma* (Philadelphia: distributed for the Study of Human Issues, 1979).

Introduction:
"Smoking Mirrors"—
Modern Polity and Ethnicity

REMO GUIDIERI and FRANCESCO PELLIZZI

I

Today, the "theatre of the world", which ever more resembles a Grand Guignol, presents us with a striking paradox. The protagonists of our political plays are states with complex power structures, supported by sophisticated technology in weaponry and information, yet most of today's *overt* conflicts are at the infranational level.[1] With a few notable exceptions, war between nation-states has played a minor role in the politics of the last forty years, while civil wars, wars of attrition, guerrilla wars, cold wars, etc., have held center stage. These are postcolonial wars, whose primary aim is the internal and external manipulation of social *order* in regions that fall within given spheres of global hegemony. They are "balkanic," prestatehood wars (struggles over the composition and strength, the "independence" and final onset of incipient nation-states) or, for the first time in history, poststatehood wars, that have developed within the cracks of the economic and military "imperial" world order imposed by the great powers. In our new cosmopolitan environment, the nineteenth-century form of the idea of nation-state may be losing much of its significance, but there are vast regions where the struggle is still centered around it.[2] It is the framework within which individuals as well as local and ethnic communities are seeking room for greater autonomy and some measure of control over their own destiny.

"Ethnicities"—in the modern sense of distinct ideological constructs and more or less cohesive social entities bent on political action—are largely the product, rather than the foundation, of nation-states. It is essential to recognize this lest, ignoring anthropology and history, we fall into the naive belief that traditional, preindustrial groups could have expressed a *modern* conception of nationality and statehood without any direct experience of their preexisting, European-derived models. The ever more powerful structures of central state control— be they colonial or autochthonous, imperial or national—are what generate and motivate the new *need* for ethnic autonomy, and even, in many cases, the actual sense of ethnic identity on which the latter is predicated. In the modern era, regional, ethnic, and religious groups of the Third World quite often appropriate the ideologies that had legitimized the modern states; these then appear to fuel the struggle for autonomy from central authority in those very states that were created *from* the collapse of the colonies.

Following is a preliminary discussion of some of the historical themes and patterns in the relations between communities and states, in Europe and the colonial world, which underly the particular cases of ethnic strife treated in the present volume.

NATIONS AND STATES

The idea of nation-state has survived the corrosive enthusiasm of internationalists, the xenophobic excesses of the first half of this century, the wars and revolutions they unleashed, and the global power of multinational organizations and corporations. It continues to resurface forcefully, sometimes as a last resort, often chaotically. Frequently, as in Africa and Oceania, mosaics of different peoples have been coerced into a more or less hasty acceptance of this formula, in order to acquire the international legitimacy and financial standing (i.e., the "right" to contract debts) needed to tackle the problems brought on by the demise of the old colonial administrations.

There has also been, meanwhile, a resurgence of nationalist and separatist movements within well-established nation-states in Eastern and Western Europe. They have resurfaced through the constraints of world hegemony and industrial development, and have been spawned by interests more widespread (though less marked by ideological concerns) than those described by Lenin at the turn of the century. The stranglehold of monopolies and oligopolies—whose smooth functioning is in the interest of democratic and totalitarian regimes alike—has not limited these centrifugal tendencies. It is remarkable that when they occur in European states, these movements, no matter how turbulent or even violent, are considered to be far less threatening to world equilibrium than those which proliferate in non-Western regions.

It is legitimate to wonder, then, what the (Western) idea of nation can possibly mean today in the nonindustrial world—areas where the West is politically on the defensive but still maintains dominance by its technological superiority. Can the desire for international recognition further a unitary—if federative—order, and still avert centralist and authoritarian bureaucratizations? Can political reason govern when those who hold the cultural values develop the sense of the state only under duress and in response to fierce technological blackmail? In their new need for national recognition (or at least for some *real* measure of autonomy), these political bodies confront problems left behind by a colonial system that for centuries had quite successfully prevented "native" solutions from developing. In this new task, these ethnic communities must combine the traditional values which legitimize them *as a people* (though they may be the most antagonistic to the requirements of centralized statehood) with modern principles of organization. The latter, with all their apparatus of internationally sanctioned "laws" and "guarantees," are often the only forms, again paradoxically, through which traditional ideals of communal integration and harmony can change and still be preserved. This inherently conflictual dilemma reappears in several of the otherwise very different situations examined in this volume.

It is only recently that the idea of nation has become a political ideal in the West. The moral and political values of the eighteenth century, sanctioned by two revolutions, have fed all later social and philosophical thought concerning the potentially "harmonious" relations between authority and community, between liberty and power. Within its ideological climate, the theme of individual and collective freedom found a juridical definition and a political expression in democratic systems of various shades, and new principles were sought that would relegitimize the social contract while still retaining the basic fabric of Western society. The contribution of the idea of nation to strengthening the state was crucial in the development of modernity; conversely, the ideal of nation could only be fully implemented as the centralized structure of the bureaucratic state was developed. While states began to be centralized and strengthened long before any true ideology of nation was defined, their legitimacy was based ever more exclusively on their ideological adoption of this new concept of nationhood. This complementarity between nation and state is a necessary point of departure when describing the deep ambiguity of contemporary, infrastate nationalist (ethnic) claims. At the same time that the nation-states in Europe were developing, a *pluralist* model of administrative structure reemerged, such as that of the Germanic empire. In this alternative form, a configuration of multiple ethnic and even "national" entities, kept in more or less stable balance and requiring a strong central authority to manage and protect it, constitutes the core of the state. Any discussion of contemporary non-Western nationalisms must also examine the wide influence of this alternative, imperial model of an ethnically all-encompassing bureaucratic authority; for it is certain that in its attempt to deflect the disintegration of the state resulting from the rising alienation of autochthonous ethnic identities, the empire often succeeded (and in some parts of the world still succeeds) in offering an administrative solution to the problem of nationalities. Issues of political legitimacy stemming from cultural discreteness within a supranational context, and the contrast between local and global allocation of authority, are all of critical concern in the imperial model of statehood. Today, societies that have recently gained their independence confront similar issues as they seek to establish their identity within the framework of international power plays. This occurs both at a supranational level, because of the areas of global hegemony within which these weak nation-states find themselves struggling for survival, and at an infranational one. As to the latter, there is, for example, a striking analogy between the inner nationalist tensions within the plurinational nation-states of Europe, and those that can be found in many nation-states of the Third World that contain pluriethnic complexities.

Modern political thought—and even more important, political economy as it was formulated from the French Revolution onward—redefined the nation, that entity which emerged in the nineteenth century as a "historical necessity," by attributing to it prerogatives and goals which belonged to the "neutral" administrative functions of the imperial state. In the process, what was originally an idea became the ideological motor and justification of the modern nation-state. Unlike Hegel's, the Romantic definition of nations as "grand historic individualities" had fatally ignored the practical imperatives that the attempt to make nation and state coincide would impose on the idea of nation. At first, the nation represented "destiny," while the state merely stood for "management." Over time, as the nationalist (as opposed to "national") principle prevailed, the nation-states of Europe began to resemble one another more and more in upholding the pragmatic values of the new science of economics along with the conception of a managerial, "industrial" organization of the state. Thus the concept of the nation contained within itself the contradiction between an ideal, "mythical" representation of society and its "rational" counterpart, a new form of the old contrast between *communitas* and *societas*. Ever since its reemergence in the ideological debate of the nineteenth century, with thinkers such as Marx and Tocqueville, this age-old split has been reformulated as one between "society" and "culture." Today, we see the tension between these two concepts as one form that collective self-awareness takes in the multiple struggles of changing societies. It is in fact remarkable how these four parameters of nation, state, society, and culture mix and overlap in the multifaceted reality of changing geopolitical patterns today, both in regions long industrialized and in areas where modernity (as we shall have to argue in greater detail below) is still at the same time a daunting aspiration and an enemy to be feared.

NATION AND IMPERIUM

The modern, managerial nation-state had its conceptual roots in the principles on which the late medieval European monarchies were founded. Dynastic continuity and a reliance on the support of commoners (their rank still keeping them at a safe distance), gradually reinforced the secular rule of law and recentralized fiscal administration after the collapse of Rome. A communal identity based on something transcending solidarity with the township or feudal allegiance began to emerge; the king's subjects were coming to see themselves as *citizens* of a *kingdom*. Meanwhile, ever more rigid boundaries were being defined, although still in a dynastic rather than a strictly territorial sense. People still identified themselves by the places where they lived and died, places which were consecrated by ancestry and the agricultural bond, and by ultimate reference to the authority vested in the *person* of the king. Little by little, a new dimension was added: a belonging to a *country*, to a geopolitical entity whose physical limits few could experience directly, and at the same time the notion of being part of, in fact of *being*, a *people*. It is only much later that the more abstract conception developed of the nation as ideological space, concomitant to the drafting of the first "objective" (and scientific) geographical maps.

As the legitimacy of the absolute power of European kings came to be questioned (having long being balanced and challenged by other forces, such as the Church and the rising merchant class), a constant reevaluation of incompatible political alternatives began to develop— that ever-renewed and ever-frustrated quest for reliable principles, that peculiar mixture of fact and possibility that characterizes the definition of authority in modern times. After the secularization of the *rex*, legitimacy *itself* has become a question of definitions, and what constitutes political power a matter of opinion, of constant debate and conflict. It is this that explains the growing need for written national constitutions, and consequently for constitutional courts that might uphold and interpret them. It is moreover in the context of these charters that the very existence of separate ethnic entities with "equal rights" was first recognized, at least implicitly.[3]

What the late medieval king brought together was an often culturally heterogeneous grouping of social bodies: in the Indo-European perspective, this type of integration and organization ranges on a spectrum that goes from the extreme verticality of the Indian system of *varna*—within which, in theory at least, hierarchy can be graduated *ad infinitum*—to the premodern Eastern / Western *regnum* and its complex balance of social forces, which expresses an ideal of absolute power and concentric territorial and ethnic integration.[4] Once the king was no longer sacred, the manipulation of political elements (ethnic, cultural, castelike, even class) and the legitimation of power became increasingly pragmatic and contractual. Success was now measured by the ability to maintain the balance (*and* the tension) among all the parts, under the ever-present threat of total disintegration. For breaking apart would involve more than the inevitable ups and downs of the different groups' fortunes; it is also organically linked to an order now bereft of any consecrated—or metaphysical—"reason."[5]

The emergence of modern nations coincides with the decline of the traditional principles equating power and function. The figure of the *rex* and the structure of the *regnum* underwent gradual transformations and "contaminations" without altogether disappearing.[6] In the general secularization of power, Enlightenment also meant a *demythologizing* of the foundations that had given the sociopolitical context its meaning, and hence its legitimacy.[7] Without such cohesive principles, multiethnic environments no longer expressed an *eternal* sense of things, guaranteed by God for all. Principles seen in the perspective of their actualization as well as in their immanence as *modus operandi* then came to be perceived as intrinsically and chronically changeable. The Enlightenment reified charisma, dehumanizing it in the process. Accordingly, the center itself became *fixed* once and for all and urbanized in an unmovable *location* (the protoindustrial *metropolis* being in itself both a new symbol and a new modality of organization), the modern "seat of power." As for the ruler, whatever his dynastic claims, it is now *as an individual* that he exercises the power of which he is now no longer the embodiment, but the representative; eventually, he becomes just a "big man."[8] As the capital city constitutes the new permanent Center, seat of all administrative "knowledge" and ultimate authority—a maze of ever more impersonal decisions—the territory and all its inhabitants, whatever their cultural history and roots, are increasingly relegated to being mere satellites of this new and quite rigid apparatus.

The geopolitical entity, thus defined in a manner at once "natural" (in terms of its "rational" and *newly* symbolic boundaries) and historical (with respect to the inheritance of the area of earlier feudal allegiances), was now ideologically burdened by nationalistic programs that rather contradictorily revamped old dynastic expansionism, justifying it under the new guise of "manifest destiny." The self-containment and self-reliance of social entities which were partitioned by the rigid boundaries of new pluriethnic states, generated tensions at the newly sacralized borders. An ideological and military (rather than a dynastic and communal) conception of political authority, which accompanied a second wave of colonial expansion, this time effectively covered most of the non-Western world, redefining national territory and imbuing it with a sort of secular sacredness.

Nation, in the modern sense, implies a community not only in political but also in cultural and racial terms. Indeed, this tendency to equate the cultural with the specifically racial components of a social entity, so alien to traditional monarchic and imperial settings, is essential to a definition of the modern nation-state. Yet the great military and technological powers in the world today provide striking exceptions to this general modern tendency. Their very "pluralism" negates a unity of roots except in reference to a (written) constitutional, hence contractual and *conventional,* sense; thus today's Empires of the West and of the East are in some way heirs to the old Western imperial model of political organization, though in a secular and technological form. Certainly these modern political organisms seem to be controlled by opposing tensions: a centripetal versus a centrifugal one. The first tends towards ethnic homogenization; despite the lip service paid to cultural pluralism, the "melting pot" is an apt metaphor for its hidden nationalist and centralizing character. The second, which is perhaps more akin to the old regimes, combines all the traits of a modern bureaucratic and centralized state with a semiautonomous type of peripheral articulation, controlled by more or less *secret* means.

DEMOCRACY AND THE STATE

Democracy, considered as a legitimate political form, obviously cannot be reduced to a mere corollary of the rise of the bourgeoisie against the backdrop of the Enlightenment. In Plato's *Republic,* already, Glaucon's famous questions point to the principles of plurality, eligibility, and accountability in the formation and preservation of the *socius.* For almost two millennia, this ancient, classic model of democracy was little developed, with the possible exceptions of medieval Italian, German, and Flemish commercial townships with their corporative organizations, on the one hand, and the extreme and ephemeral visions of a few political and religious utopists (such as Cola di Rienzo and Savonarola). Strikingly enough, the idea of democracy reemerges with the Enlightenment and industrial society, becoming, irresistibly it must be said, the ultimate *summum bonum,* a last recourse for the "salvation" of the old Europe.[9]

The "mythical horror of myth" of the Enlightenment culminates in a materialistic and pragmatic interpretation of social utopia; that is, as rational and efficient social relations. We no longer have the *Civitas Dei*, but the Phalanstery, reduced to the organization of the working force—while "labor," as opposed to "work," makes its appearance as the basis of society. Absorbed into hyperrationality, myth becomes utopia and engenders a well-known and already fading chimera, the so-called "power-of-the-all." Here we have the ideological counterpart to that traditional type of society in which order was administered by a time-sanctioned authority endowed with a god-given charisma; nonutopian, it is this latter type, strangely enough, that might be called "realistic," while the new "enlightened" one is a leviathan which preserves the commonwealth by impersonal force. Political enlightenment can then be seen as a compromise of Practical Reason, according to which the common good becomes the result of the fulfillment of duty and not of the gifts of Redemption: it advocates Progress instead of material renunciation *and*, historically, it turns a "paganized" history into a theodicy. There is a link between Hobbes and Rousseau, and not the paradigmatic opposition that Jacobin distortions have asserted, just as there is a link between Enlightenment and Conservatism, progress and fundamentalism, innovation and reaction.[10]

The two extreme forms of this rationality, then, should be seen as fluctuating perspectives, sharing the same matrix.[11] Generally, though, the fusion of utopian and pragmatic forms reinforces the secular conception of hegemonic authority which Napoleon's attempt to establish a new "unified" European order initiated. But this radical questioning of traditional dynastic legitimacy also advocated new—or at least till then unidentified—national and territorial values. Thus the Napoleonic adventure had its own built-in contradiction: it extended, for a time, Jacobin internationalist revolutionary principles to the whole of Europe, but simultaneously furthered the formation of modern states with their nationalistic (and, at least implicitly, "racist") ideologies and rigid boundaries. Here we have the origin of a modern political paradox: "stability" is sought and cherished by all existing political systems as an absolute value, while "democracy" is also affirmed as a supreme virtue, or at least as the ultimate political goal.[12] Order is based on managing an often precarious balance that masks deep conflicts embedded within the systems themselves—conflicts that can seldom be acknowledged for what they really are, except in those moments of abrupt change when all order is in fact questioned and subverted.[13]

What emerges then as the defining contradiction of modern and paramodern systems—whether on the level of their actualization (as in the capitalist version where one who is exploited can only escape from his predicament by becoming, in turn, the exploiter), or on that of their teleological limits (as in the communist case, where the utopian goal is methodically postponed in the name of the more immediate "needs" of the state)—is the hypostasis of opposite principles, both of which imply a relentless absorption of the "other," of the alien, i.e., of the *imperfect*, in conjunction with an ever more rigidly defined structuring of authority. This is why one can say, with Hegel, that modern political practice—an art of managing tensions—expresses a *Machtpolitik* that can only be exercised against a permanent backdrop of crisis. Now, if these crises are both necessity and obstacle, dare one hope for an eventual integration of conflicting elements, for the traditional *Sakkima*—the Peace invoked by Ibn Arabi—which requires a faith *in* peace? The *Sakkima* entails *concordia*, not abundance. It becomes a matter of assessing whether the "management" of power, in the modern conception, though banning "anarchy," can still keep alive those dialectical tensions that are the substance of our political dialogue. [14] At a time when neoimperialist forces seem to dictate the fate of large, once-powerful or new and potentially powerful, states—not to mention the even newer and often smaller ones that have recently begun to place their hopes in this Hegelian conception—it is important to explore the current ethnic and national substance of these political visions.

CHURCH AND STATE

A critical assessment of the revival of nationalist and ethnic movements in our time must include their religious component, both as an expression of "spontaneous," fundamentalist *faiths* and as a remarkably vigorous, often controversial, commitment by venerable religious institutions.

The Church has always had to define what makes a community. Taken individually, the private experience of Faith as given by religion and guaranteed by the Church, is an attitude of surrender to a noncontingent will. Taken collectively, it is a way of grounding this surrender *in the community*, in the order that is expressed by the community, and in the enhancement of anything that might contribute to this order. This has been particularly evident in times of crisis, and the progress of the earth's technological "postindustrialization," with its still hazy goals, *does* constitute today's crisis. All Christian Churches have, of course, had to face the upheaval provoked by the industrial revolution of the eighteenth century, its new ways of organizing labor and of allocating capital, and the changes it brought about in the structure of the society; but essentially, what remains unconfronted by religion is the basic notion of Progress. This idea, since it derives from a principle of cumulative change—seen as the relentless and methodical transcending of the boundaries set by contingent circumstances—gives a new and secular twist to the traditional religious and philosophical conception of the Unlimited.

Such a new vision of infinity also evokes a new conception of "freedom." Traditionally, when expressed in terms of faith, particularly in Christian terms, freedom was set in the eschatological perspective of Redemption. As some have observed, the idea of Progress (perhaps the most flagrant and unequivocal expression of the secular and pragmatic orientation of the modern world) still belongs to the long tradition of Christian, perhaps even pre-Christian (Hebrew) teleology. That this is not a direct derivation but a distortion, "diabolical" or otherwise, has also been claimed, from a variety of different points of view. What we wish to call attention to here is that Redemption, while it offered an ultimate *transcending* of the world—implying a casting off, an abandonment and hence a renunciation—did not really intend to make the world "better": St. Francis's *laudes* praise Creation *as it is*. The modern compulsion to instantly devalue what has been attained, brought on by the demands of Progress, by the endless production of new *needs*, is inextricably linked to the processes of industrial and technological accumulation. Neither accepting nor casting off the world as it is, the modern compulsion purports to make the world transcend its limits *by its own means*. Afflicted by a task not unlike Sisyphus's, it is through accumulation, not renunciation, that the immanent power of transcendence is found. The position of the Western Churches on Progress—a question that is central to the ideological battles of the nineteenth- and early twentieth-century nation-states—thus remains important today, as witnessed by such phenomena as Working Priests, Liberation Theology, and other political, social, and religious movements, both in the industrial world and the Third World.

The crucial conflict between modern Christianity and Marxism, two mythological / ideological movements having a similar hegemonic thrust and a *telos* that finds its embodiment in human works, *preceded* the October Revolution. Their common utopian and messianic burden that condemns them to an almost fratricidal *agon* is still the one that the *lumières* had proclaimed as inevitable: the Progress-of-Enlightenment itself, through an abstract positing of Mankind (as opposed to the Son-of-Man), and of the *feats* of human Works, as absolute and ultimate. As "Church," all of historical Christianity resisted the Enlightenment, for the Church's conception of the nonintrinsic and transcendent value of Works is one that the Enlightenment was bound to perceive as pernicious. However, the issue here is not the incompatibility of faith with reason, but rather the new definition that must now be given to man's historicity: should it be in terms of Redemption or in terms of freedom? The Church now—reformed or unreformed—is constantly forced to look for areas of compatibility between opposing and even incompatible views. The compromise between faith and reason always consists of reincorporating reason within faith; as in the case of Thomism, this is a way of expanding faith by absorbing what reason generates—*doubt*, in particular the very doubt about the possible compatibility of reason with faith. There is a limit, though, to this capacity for inclusion, appropriation, and absorption: it is encountered when the Church, sensing a real threat, finds that both faith and reason must reclaim the ground that give them their legitimation and authority. In the end, the Church must always reclaim its primacy—which has perhaps deeper roots than historical Christianity itself—over any worldly authority, just as the Western political world, until modern times, has always needed a set of transcendental mediations ("the two bodies of the King"), which are precisely those that the eighteenth century radically, and it seems irreparably, questioned. [15]

Political authority is made responsible for the new salvation as the new *lumières* focus on the rationalization of work for profit. Social consensus, no matter how ephemeral, is now sought through pacts among the often contrasting forces that are metamorphosing the social body. These are all relentlessly, and successfully, dedicated to reducing their "demystified" vision to the costs and profits of their manufactured products. Perhaps one of the chief consequences of this secularization of work is the unhappy conscience of the times, well manifested by the repeated cropping up of the irrational in recent European and Third World history. But this modern necessity to impose ever new needs on the social order (and they are inexhaustible needs, because their source, profit, is the very epitome of the inexhaustible), this spirit that claims to embody the hard demands of a rationality identified with the *materially* pragmatic (while ignoring all the initiatory and experiential parameters of *pragma*), makes of rationalism the only possible "spiritual" discipline given to modern man. Hence, it paves the way—perhaps unwittingly, if it is true that men make history without knowing it—for religious authority to become hollow at its core, particularly in its traditional role of defining the foundations and limits of temporal authority.

MARXISM, CHURCH, AND UTOPIA

In the spiritual and political climate of the nineteenth century, Marxism's adherence to the principles of the Enlightenment was stronger than that of its "liberal" counterparts in developing not only a belief in technological progress but a rigorous consideration of its consequences; it also bent reason to its pragmatic imperatives and, most of all, proposed a subversive program—transcending the explosion of anarchic regicide and social insurgence—in which the view of worldly power became the reverse, literally, of the order traditionally proposed by Western utopias. Beyond its incidental anticlerical aspects, Marxism's atheism and its confrontation with Christianity are the logical and inevitable consequence of a need to clarify the ideological consequences of the Enlightenment. October 1917 showed that victory was possible. Now, seventy years later, it may be legitimate to ask whether this confrontation between faiths has the same meaning, or even whether it has had any meaning at all, especially in the form it has sometimes taken over the last twenty-five years.

The Leninist / Stalinist myth—the dream of a collectivity "liberated" *by* work, a collectivity made up of the first truly nonalienated individuals that mass socialism would produce, has itself turned into a Medusa, just another form (as a traditionalist sociologist from India once expressed it) of the cruel illusions of industrial society. It now appears that the hope for a strict Marxist alternative has considerably weakened everywhere and that it has come to be seen (by a sort of Manichean reversal) as an obstacle to modernity: no longer the motor of a daring social laboratory, but a grey mausoleum for embalmed wishful thoughts. Thus, once again, Russia today represents a form of anti-modern polarity—a polarity *within* the West, one could add—just as once (and again now) Islam embodied the anti-West. The current church opposition to this industrial "otherness," however—to this neo-Byzantine half of the Empire—is unlike the earlier reaction of Faith when Marxism lit fires throughout the world in the first half of the century. It has come about *in spite of* the current exploitation by the Western neo-Roman half of the Empire of the "threat" Marxism would represent—public opinion needing a scapegoat, a palliative to the fears and uncertainties generated by the economic and financial vagaries of the "free" capitalist system.

Old Marxist states, for their part, survive as static heritages: monuments whose glorious aura has vanished, without vitality despite efforts to keep them alive through a combination of ceremony and repression; sclerotic, yet held together by an oligarchic civil and military bureaucracy that is conservative more out of insecurity than conviction. Elsewhere, particularly in urban areas of the neocolonial world, overpopulated by the disinherited masses of what has now come to be called the "Fourth World" (postindustrial avatars of the lumpen of yore), the reactivation of Marxism often degenerates into syncretic phantasmagorias and is accompanied by slaughters and famines. At times it is a last resort in the face of encirclement. Whatever the ideological form of their regimes, technological and financial distance from the hegemonic centers keeps the political play within these societies from having any substantial impact on the determination of their destiny.

In the present world situation (with the Middle East in the lead) Marxism appears as no less fraudulent an intrusion than the now crumbling capitalist postcolonial regimes with their puppet leaders; it is just as truculently opportunistic and devoid of real authority, always subject to the same behind-the-scene manipulations by conflicting and sometimes "collaborating" secret services. The disorder of our time, which is uniformly exploitative and tragically bent on furthering blind "progress" (even in areas of the world already not "ready" for it), multiplies the crises that baffle armies of experts. The proposed remedies appear to be no more than *ad hoc* stratagems and patchwork palliatives, aimed at maintaining a situation (or at preventing it from exploding) rather than at really changing it. The financial chaos in which the world currently finds itself is dramatic proof of this impotence.

The churches are now even too timid, too fundamentally insecure to hold on to the principles of evangelical reason; they lend themselves to diversionary tactics—thus by similar maneuvering giving credit to the Powers that rule covertly without the authority to rule (this is another characteristic of modern world polity). Recent perspectives, particularly in Latin America, have created new conditions for political commitment within the Catholic Church. They arose out of a transitional period, when the enthusiastic belief in being finally liberated from the posthumous effects of the colonial system rapidly gave way to a rather pessimistic and conservative vision of what the times require. In most situations, however, political cosmetics could only disguise the heavy cost of the Church's lack of direction and of its difficulties in facing up to the new worldwide strategy of hegemonic forces, while recent official reactions to the challenge of the *teología de liberación* show that the Church's capacity for taking risks is still limited.

All this constitutes a *double* failure—the failure of both contestants. In less than a century, the incapacity of Marxism to provide an alternative to the *nemesis* (or *karma*) of the industrial revolution has been confirmed. The opposition of Marxism to the present order of the world is nothing more than tactical. Its reasons come from a *Realpolitik* of the Party and of the state. Its "victories," that claim to be political, in the best of cases are mere rationalizations of the *status quo*. At the national level, the only alternative open to Marxism, once it resigns itself to being only a party, is to take over a role which is functionally similar to that of all bourgeois oppositions. Internationally the only political cards Marxism can still play are local wars—wars of attrition and wars of position—and rebellions. (Capitalist powers today are of course similarly limited today in their international political action.)

Since it has not fulfilled its utopian promise, the credibility of Marxism is now at a very low ebb. Significantly, the utopian challenge today in the ex-colonial world shows up primarily in the resurgence of anti-Western feelings. This is not just a fleeting phenomenon, and cannot be summarily dismissed under the rubric of extreme and bloody experiments; examples are the collective purges that equate slaughter with salvation, the hecatombs perpetrated from opposite ideological positions, as in Indonesia in the sixties and in Cambodia in the seventies, or even the war between Iran and Iraq.[16] That horror should be the price to be paid; that the victims should be counted by the hundreds of thousands, even by the millions—nothing, alas, is more banal in this century. In the last two centuries, in fact, revolutions (and wars) have been characterized by a bloodiness matched in the past only by the catastrophic "conquest" of the New World that accompanied the Renaissance and inaugurated premodern times. Utopia, again, spoke through the voice of Isaiah: happiness and death respond to one another. And if utopia has become synonymous with revolution, the ultimate peace to which it aspires can only be conceived at present as an armed one.

Utopia originally implied harmony; it was not merely a dream of plenty. But Marxism would have us gauge its victories in the light of material things alone. Impatient to succeed in a world of production and merchandise, it has fallen into its own trap, with no conservative recourse, no way back. What might a return to utopian origins mean, in Marxist terms, when its adversaries—at the cost of spectacular crises, wars, and overwhelming social evils—are far more adept at exploiting the heritage of our *"règne de la quantité"*? The evidence provided by Russian dissidents is enough to show that the eschatological roots of Marxism have no way of reasserting themselves in the Marxist state. Utopia, at the close of this century, has reemerged as much *despite* Marxism as against the capitalist universe of merchandise. It has thrived within marginal situations: alternative cultural movements, cultures of global dissent, fundamentalisms, ethnic movements. Some of these movements even represent millenarian utopias, announcing a spiritual salvation *beyond* the boundaries of a world that only offers the puny achievements and rewards of social-democracy, middle-of-the-road Christianity, tired party-Marxism, media-conditioned "liberal" democracy, etc.

The dialectical relation that developed between Christianity and the new faith, Socialism, constitutes the thread of Ariadne through the maze of spiritual and political tensions of modern times. One aspect of this problematic rapport, which is at once ethical and political, and which in many cases deeply concerns ethnic groups, is the tension between faith (spiritual and secular) and freedom. It is a problem that state socialism has had to face, juggling Marxist principles and ultimate goals with the new powers that industrial technology gives the state. It is proclaimed that in order to bring about ultimate freedom—the supreme human good through which the authentic vocation of the man-of-progress is expressed—all obstacles in the way of socialism's full realization must first be removed. Religious faith is one such obstacle, as it prevents the advance of Reason ("reason" in the sense given to it by the Enlightenment—not just as an expression of "free will," but as validating a goal, or justifying a value). In general, all that predisposes man to the Divine Will and its intercessions, rather than to a collective effort aimed at furthering him in the *worldly* course that pursues ever-growing material goals—is also an obstacle. In the constant and *general* upheaval that is a key feature of the twentieth century, it may well be that the dynamics of industrial society have stripped "goal," "freedom", "progress"—the concepts that have become springboards for mobilizing modern masses—of all their traditional and metaphysical connotations and reduced them to merely relative, operational notions.

The opposition of socialism (Marxist or non-Marxist, communist or nationalist) to religion, centers on the implications inherent in this redefinition of values. But even if both the former seats of authority, the worldly and the spiritual, were invested with the new definition of liberty; even if

this need for absolute immanence (a perfect society in which all human needs are equally satisfied in an immanence of man to man himself) coincides with the dissolution of all that might prevent man, given his equality and determination, from positing himself as a pure individual reality, one that is all the more closed because it is open to all . . .[17]

it is certainly not simply in this "right to self-alienation" that the contrast between the *ancien* and the *nouveau régime* lies. Now that a single authority was no longer legitimized by traditional interests, a major new form of social control ("totalitarian" or not) emerged in socialist societies: the *Party*, which rises above all individual figures of authority and collective bodies. There is neither a Palace nor a Parliament, in reality, but rather a "bureau," a closed place, where the individuals called upon to exert the new power are selected. Gone are the dark undergrounds, masonic lodges, confraternities, once the breeding ground of *nihilism* and teeming with demons and damned, wanderers, hot heads, desperados, marginals of all sorts, *spretati*, hack philosophers, uprooted and ruined gentlemen, all sorts of *parvenus* of the spirit and floating rejects of industrialization, whose inner vacuum and humiliation had turned into an unremitting force of upheaval and destruction. The new masters, in business suits and uniforms (these are now equivalent), create new ceremonies, new conventions, and rely on a new form of legitimacy: an office of authority that proclaims the iron law of absolute *revocability*. The party's *Nomenklatura* and the social mechanisms that co-opt the *élites* into leadership in "democratic" regimes—hence reenlisting the principle of genealogical transmission in the interest of preserving the new order—resemble each other closely. The novelty, however, still lies in the factors that determined the difference between socialism and liberal democracy in the first place: the reification of work as *summum bonum*. Could this freedom *to work* currently advocated by socialism, in the end be the same liberty that the bourgeoisie had found absent from the socialist programs? A close look will show that the contrast is only superficial: in the process of industrialization there are no actual paradises, only advanced societies and backward ones. The process, which is everywhere the same, is the one that Simone Weil so lucidly described fifty years ago, when she stated that in all modern systems, the power that exploits and oppresses

the workers resides in the very formulations of our social life, and cannot be annihilated by any political or juridical transformation. This power is first and foremost the very *regime* of modern production, which is heavy industry.[18]

II

ETHNIC IDENTITY

The ideological and social movements discussed in the previous pages form the backdrop for the issue of ethnic identity, both within the industrial nation-states and in all that rest-of-the-world that has already been so deeply transformed by contact with the West and with modernity. The term "identity" has been used in many ways, but primarily as an operative notion, a concept having dynamic attributes, and an ideal tightly bound to individualist values. It is linked (with varying degrees of critical awareness) to the axioms and presuppositions on which the psychological disciplines—hallmark of this century—are founded. Though in psychology itself the applicability of the concept of identity may have declined, it has enjoyed remarkable extensions into other fields.[19] Its use in these areas points up a number of contradictions which are at the heart of the most pressing and tension-ridden ethnopolitical issues of our times.

The individualism of mass society is perceived as one of its most positive values. In fact, it epitomizes the extreme, if unavowed, solipsism of our time, especially as, more and more, "impersonal" managerial functions nullify the essence of the individual. But the term "identity," as applied to the individual, has not only acquired wide usage in everyday language, it has also become a seemingly indispensable tool in sociological description as well as food for the rhetoric of political revendication. Such commonplace expressions as "ethnic groups," "cultural minorities," "marginal cultures," "survival," "traditional (or archaic) cultures," and "neonationalisms," refer to situations whose origins go back a long way—some as much as a century and some much more—as well as to conditions that have recently and sometimes unexpectedly emerged. Caught as they are in a tangle of legitimate demands and chronic frustrations, it is hard to grasp the substance and complexity of these responses, and still avoid joining the ranks of those well-intentioned and, more often than not, self-appointed spokesmen who confuse ideology with reason. Since the realities encompassed by the notion of ethnic identity are in fact movements—processes of collective becoming—in contexts where the historical and cultural intelligibility of past and present can only be provisional—there is bound to be some haziness at any given time, both for the actors, who are often at the same time the victims of these processes, and for the observers.

The claims now being made in the name of cultural identity are no longer primarily based, as they once were, on culturalist (or para-anthropological) definitions and interpretations. They are inherently political: the concept of identity is a concise, though opaque, expression of aspirations that speak the universal language of contemporary politics—a language that is, above all, a strategic one, aimed at legitimizing specific international and intranational relations. These claims coincide with the emergence of a social self-awareness in which the "self" is doubtless an even more dynamically and ambiguously fraught term than its psychological counterpart. It is, in many cases, a "culture consciousness" of cultures on the wane—threatened cultures. In them, customs, beliefs, memories, and the traditional legitimacy that they carry with them, have undergone every colonial vicissitude, both economically (the politics of exploitation) and spiritually (the values of Christian morality and democratic *civitas*). Thus the spread of ethnic awareness is now based on a "negative" premise, on a "destiny of need" that all Western aspirations—i.e., progress, science, technology—share. The encouragement of cultural consciousness among the conquered peoples has not ranked high among Western priorities, probably because since the Renaissance the Western will-to-power—despite its recourse to the models of Antiquity—has negated both tradition and cultural continuity even at home. Still, the political affirmation of ethnic identity has been for quite some time the result of Western expansion. For the threat of cultural annihilation, whether real or perceived (a blurred distinction at best), stems precisely from this domination, even (and this is a complex issue we shall not tackle here) within the boundaries of European countries themselves, where internal historical rifts mirror those created by colonial conquest. The claims to identity came as a reaction to the threat to *delegitimize*, in Western (i.e., juridical) terms, any *communal* will towards self-preservation that would differ from the only definition acceptable to the new global system: the techno- or socio-economic definition. They are, therefore, primarily a defensive movement—as many of the studies in the present volume indicate—and thus, more often than not, an aggressive one, impelling cultures that are trapped in similar sets of circumstances to claim a communal identity that combines cultural particularity (which never before had to be affirmed) with modern political aspirations.

TERRITORY

In this perspective, the concept of cultural identity implies—indeed presupposes—a territorial dimension. Before modern administrative definitions came into use, i.e., those made possible by *writing*—which transformed territories into land tenures and landmarks into supports for legal holdings—the actual occupation and use of a given territory was all the base one needed for cultural affirmation. It was its true substance and at the same time its root, its arche—the origin of its legitimacy and its principle—but also its image and ideal expression. The territory, as an empirical given, was the image of a *space* through which a people's identity found its primary manifestation: our Land. The legal inscribing of a community within a given space determined its existence in the world at any given moment, but its traditional connection to the land also oriented it toward its permanence *as* itself through time, and thus defined communal legitimacy in terms of territorial continuity or loss. One could hardly speak of a diaspora—that is, of an ethnic memory carried over into exile—without the indelible image of a *place* providing both a ground for recollection and a reference for tradition.

In many instances, *landmarks* still serve to legitimize cultural identity, and the territory constitutes their stage-setting. They support the claims of the present and reactivate those which are deeply rooted in the culture, having marked its past and shielded it in the face of danger. There are undoubtedly cases where claims to ethnic identity appear altogether to ignore this spatial reference, where the recourse is not so much to knowledge, or memory, of land held, as to cultural traits, often long repressed and buried under hostile pressures. But if these no longer refer back to the knowledge and sanctity of an original territory, it is only because that place which the past evokes, and in whose memory it is fused with the present, has become mythical; it has retreated into the realm of the imaginary. Forced cultural contact jeopardizes this land base of identity. Often it negates the legitimacy of discrete cultural enclaves within the "national" territory, either by imposing discriminations of caste and class or through economic oppression, or again, not infrequently, by outright physical suppression. One can thus consider forced cultural contact—after any form of "conquest"—as an intrusion with a major stake in drawing up a new charter for overall territorial legitimacy. As long as there is any permanent settlement by intruders, the cultures intruded upon generally respond by profoundly altering their sense of identity. Having once "naturally" occupied a specific territory, which was studded with traditional *landmarks*, they now assert an ideological identity-to-be-recovered, by means of "legal" (i.e., Western) land titles—to provide newly needed international sanction for the occupation of their territories. This change in the validation of land occupancy is of crucial importance and often problematic, especially for those traditional (e.g., nomadic) cultures whose spatial base is most vulnerable to this new rigid, juridical, and administrative definition of territory. It should also be noted—and this is something of immediate relevance to present-day struggles—that space, once it is thus legally secured, becomes again, though in a new way, the last bastion of cultural survival and of the preservation of some form of cultural difference in the face of indiscriminate modernization.

MEMORY

Tradition, whether peaceful or aggressive, is a cultural memory. It is to identity what foundation myths are to rites of initiation, enthronement, and passage. Both as an intellective register and as the locus of meaning, it penetrates expressions, formulations, narratives—all of tradition is expressed in cultural identity. We know the forms that such mnemonic material can take, but the particular combination of universal and specific features that it reveals, and the reasons for its endurance remain unclear, despite attempts to relate it to what our century calls the Collective Unconscious. Ethnic memory has the same eidetic flexibility in all human cultures: in ours, which are haunted by change, as well as in those still more or less thoroughly entrenched in tradition. Its traces show remarkable resistance to circumstances that might alter them. It is these mnesic elements (at once cause and by-product of survivals) that help societies to resist change in acculturative situations: they often, in fact, provide a means of absorbing—and hence, to some extent, subduing—those very elements of change which, by virtue of their radical novelty, could seriously endanger cultural discreteness.

Today, with progressive homogenization taking over traditional cultures all over the world, the general consensus seems to be that any surviving aspect of culture is doomed to a quasi-biological extinction. Yet in many instances—precisely because it is by definition inalienable—ethnic memory seems capable of reconsolidating authenticity through *mutations* in form, so that the current task of traditional societies appears to be the recycling of ethnic memory through various forms of cultural reinterpretation. So, while a culture must appear to negate novelty in order to reassert the immemorial identity of the group, at the same time, through adaptation (even in its most ephemeral or paradoxical expressions) a culture comes to a new self-awareness, through a kind of "spontaneous" hermeneutics upon its own premises. What we refer to as acculturation (the "neutral"—hence "positive"—assessment of the effects of contact) or deculturation (the negative assessment of these same effects) consists in allowing cultural intrusion to take place while reevaluating its effects. Interpretation, by the culture, is an attempt at appropriating the event by presenting it as *compatible* with tradition. In turn, however, only what is acceptable to tradition can be reinterpreted, and tradition is selective since it is grounded in mnesic properties which are imperative, idiosyncratic, and for the most part nonconscious.

It should be stressed that all adaptive forms—such as the Christianization of the American Indians, the destruction of the surplus of goods created by the introduction of metal tools, the "neo-pagan" eschatology of Melanesian cargo cults, alcoholism and native neonationalisms—are examples of the interpretation (and appropriation) of "otherness" that is emphatically present in every phenomenon of cultural contact. As already stated, to adapt means to assimilate, but assimilation also implies the *prior* transformation of the "other" so that it becomes compatible with existing cultural configurations. If acculturation faces limits beyond which it cannot go, it is because there are limits to the reinterpretive potential of any threatened culture and, as the remarkable homogeneity of contemporary acculturative processes indicates, their range is far from infinite. There is a reason for this in today's world: agents of acculturation are themselves homogeneous with respect to both their means and their ends. Similar kinds of techno-economic intrusion and exploitation produce similar techno-economic results. Yet, although modern acculturation inevitably comes up against these limits, the great range and flexibility of these adaptations should make us wary of adopting a "catastrophic" view, in which traditional societies that are undergoing cultural contact must inevitably disappear. The events of this century, and especially those of the last two decades, demonstrate that traditional cultures are as resilient as they are permeable in the face of drastic change.

CYCLES

The Western evaluation of cultures, from both an ideological and a pragmatic perspective, is based chiefly on their capacity for assimilation, which really means, for *being assimilated*; conversely, the extent of their "survival" seems to be defined by what cannot be assimilated. As noted earlier, it would be an error to equate nonassimilation with an absence of cultural reinterpretation; absorption and incorporation of foreign and modern elements, but outright rejections, too, carry the mark of assimilation. Innovations that cannot be assimilated are those which threaten to render obsolete the rationale of what the culture perceives as necessary to its own preservation. [20]

In acculturative processes, most instances of radical rejection of exogenous elements are expressed—and this is crucial—in a "positive" way, often in the form of cults: these, through ritual, transform both what is rejected and (by a sort of catharsis) the act of negation itself into a reaffirmation of cultural identity. For any refusal, any forcing back, must affect the refuser. Thus, in traditional and transitional societies, exogenous elements are accepted and rejected through performative configurations of ritual that "new" cults articulate precisely to this end of reaffirmation. In most cases, in the cultic representation that dramatizes the process of contact, absorption and rejection is not limited to the religious sphere, nor separated from daily existence. Rather, when a culture is oriented towards adopting this form of "negative acculturation," it may become completely absorbed in its own endogenous cult practices and identify with them even more completely. There has been no dearth of revivalist syncretism throughout the world to illustrate this point.

However, in the rare cases where the process of adaptation actually results in a thorough transformation, the tendency is to obliterate the memory of the long historical phase of adaptation. The fruit of this obliteration is often described—in keeping with the evolutionist spirit of our time—as the birth of a *new* civilization. Our own North-European cultures are the result of such a process. Since the fourth century, they have continued to adopt values and customs which were completely foreign to them, among them Christianity.[21] Whether such an "absolute" transformation carries (over a very long time) the risk of retrogressions and unforeseeable resurgences (the force of these being almost proportional to their distance from the source) needs to be investigated. It is striking, for instance, that in recent times such European resurgences—actualized in movements that, in one way or another, are still embodiments of the Western will-to-power—have rarely, if ever, been marked by the dominance of their Judeo-Christian element. The paradoxically "successful" nature of this syncretism of ours, which has become the driving force in world history, has generally gone unrecognized by modern historical theory. This is largely due to a deeply rooted neo-Manichean bias that pits light against darkness, present against past, and, ultimately, Christianity against Paganism.[22]

All the relevant issues pertaining to national identity, tradition, and cultural memory, were raised by Nietzsche in *The Case of Wagner*. The finality which he attributed to art, a finality at once nationalistic and metahistorical—one of "destiny" and "saga," in the midst of the revolutionary fervor then prevalent—foreshadows all of the debates on nationalism in European culture. It was linked to the project (which, as was to be expected, turned out to have a liturgical, though secular, nature) of reviving a "strong" atavistic culture and of rediscovering, through a cult of the "sublime," the roots which preceded its Christian adaptation.[23] Many, indeed, have emphasized the timeliness of this return to the archaic. It is an unprecedented resurgence—both in the way that the discourse of modernity has seized upon it (fragmented, and therefore difficult to recycle, the myth resurfaces as a *text* rather than as trace of a submerged memory) and has made it into an instrument for its industrial triumph—Masses *and* Power. Through this "awakening" in the Fascist movements, the West experienced its progress in the century of technology—something neither wished for nor foreseen by Goethian reason—through a sort of ancestral nemesis which, at least temporarily, brought *civil* progress to a stop. In fact, it is the very ambiguity of the mass phenomenon that establishes its terrible and true modernity (as had been shown prophetically by Karl Kraus's *Die Letzten Tage der Menscheit*). In a "primitivity" that one had never expected to witness again, the modern found an unprecedented legitimation.[24]

TECHNOLOGIES

In the acculturative situation prevailing since World War II— particularly during the phase which is euphemistically referred to as "decolonization"—Western nations have reached the limits both of the geographical expansion of their influence and of their will (or need) to hide their hegemony behind "spiritual" justifications. Indeed, in the name of some future global wealth (a concept as vague as it is contradictory) a new form of techno-economic expansion has developed. This is supported by an ideology of reciprocal profit, which is now heralded as the only effective driving force of progress. One domain, however—that of political discourse—still generates an ideology legitimizing ends other than those of accumulation (for instance: imposition of "democracy" has become a stronger and stronger rationale for dominance). There is a kind of "political reason" that, in this new world climate, sanctions programs, strategies, alliances, and conflicts of all kinds, and which justifies both the management of corruption in "democratic" regimes and of oppression in "totalitarian" ones. It is called *"raison d'état."*

Surviving traditional cultures are confronted with the problem of assimilating new technologies. In many areas, it is only in the last fifty years, or even less, that people have had to deal with them. Now, the use and "consumption" of their products has become more and more widespread. Much more than the old unequal access to the financial means of production, the most recent forms of exploitation are based on an unequal access to the knowledge and *savoir faire* that produces the technology. What was originally an inequality (of classes and / or nations) with respect to property, is now an even greater difference in the acquisition and control of procedures, of forms of thinking and acting. To these the "traditional" world has less and less access and grows more impermeable as technology advances further into the electronic and postindustrial era. For the essence of modern technology is its potential for infinite innovation, generating an acceleration of change that is at the antipode of traditional cultural orientations, which are based on principles of duplication and *repetition.*

Present-day geopolitical exploitation is founded upon a calculated, i.e., strategic, use of technological distance. In this respect, not only does nonassimilation reflect a dependence on alien technologies, but the distribution of unassimilated technological innovation, to a great extent, matches the contemporary map of inequality between cultures. Now, in the last ten years, unassimilated innovation has acquired a faster pace. More than ever, it is the "price" and corollary of advanced technological development, because for technological innovation to succeed, new needs must be created independently of the conditions that made the new technology possible in the first place. This is obviously a new form of colonization; now the outlets for technological products are old, and new markets are in vast areas that will never be able to produce them themselves.

The general nonassimilation of the know-how of technology in the

Third World may be masked by those economic imperatives which regulate the flow of goods through world markets and form the substructure of international politics. The latter are well served by "universal" consumption—the generalized and passive pseudo-assimilation of innovation—which is founded on artificial needs (in their inception and in their relation to actual historical conditions) that nevertheless promptly acquire the force of cultural imperatives, and even come to mimic the urgency of autochthonously generated necessities. In the frantic consumption by nonindustrial peoples of those sophisticated postindustrial products that in the West are an integral and "organic" part of the productive technological process itself, one sees a perfect example of nonassimilated innovation. *Within* the West, of course, this phenomenon has been known by the name of cultural alienation since the beginning of industrial times. It is important to investigate exactly what happens when now, our new, highly technological forms are exported across ethnic and cultural boundaries. Today, in the electronic second-half of this century, the impact of postindustrial consumption and the "values" linked to the dramatic and paradoxical problems of acculturation, must be viewed in terms that are more complex than those that defined colonial and early postcolonial relations. [25]

RESIDUES

In acculturation, what cannot be assimilated becomes a residue. No innovation presents itself as a limited and isolated import; rather, it is accompanied by a body of principles and procedures, of beliefs or of ends, that constituted its context in its place of origin. A perfect assimilation should integrate all of these aspects. However, this is by and large impossible, often even for minorities and "marginalized" majorities *within* industrialized societies. In exotic cultures, one may copy Western tools without ever managing to reproduce their function (as one might adopt Catholicism, but stripping it of the dogma of the Immaculate Conception or without any grasp of the mystery of the Trinity), but this kind of residuality is very different from the initial resistance to dominant innovation on the part of subcultures that has frequently occurred within our own Western societies. In exogenous acculturative change, the real question is not a simple one of acceptance or rejection, but of cultural "combinations"—of the creation of irreducibly nonhomogeneous cultural hybrids.

In attempting to deal with this problem, a culture utilizes modes of adaptation often characterized by forms of "deviance"—which are a series of partially adequate responses. For the tendency is—and it is a widespread one—to mask the inadequacy, and to develop a superficial mimicry, instead of a genuine (but often impossible) assimilation. Thus an apparent adaptation will manifest itself as a make-believe, or *faux-semblant*. In what sense, though, can we speak of "inadequacy," of "imitation," or of "false-appearance"? In each acculturative situation that involves ethnic identity, to what degree can we apply *our* criteria for evaluating as "successful" the responses of other cultures to the intricate and perhaps insoluble problems that *we*, by our actions, or simply by our very existence, put in their way?

We do not even know whether, or under what conditions, complete assimilation might really be possible, or even conceivable, or whether *irreducible* residues are inevitably produced in any process of acculturation. Such residues are, in a sense, double: for every nonassimilable innovation must produce as its counterpart a core point of resistance (a sort of "anti-body" to that very innovation): this one can then be interpreted as a "survival." Cultural survival, as Aguirre Beltrán was one of the first to indicate, is made possible by sociopolitical resistance, even if mostly of a "passive" kind.[26] The breadth and persistence of these survivals in the postcolonial world confirms that the dialectic of the unassimilable, and its correlate, the indestructible, is prevalent in acculturative processes. It is a dialectic, however, that the West, by the evolutionary bias that justifies its position of dominance, negates and reaffirms at the same time. For industrial societies, the extreme poverty of ethnic (and "natural") cultures is a function of their clinging to the old ways and by upholding noneconomic and nonpragmatic values, while "folklore" alone is perceived as the "legitimate" (and touristically desirable) survival of tradition: The non-Western world can be said to to have become *Western*, to have succumbed to "progress," only to the extent to which it accepts and incorporates this alienating contradiction.

This issue is crucial today, when a nonlinear conception of history is perhaps gaining ground again, concerned both with the hazards of acculturation and with the inevitable course of innovations brought to the world by European culture. This means that unassimilable residues and survivals are likely to be conflictually reinforced whenever it is only the *products* of advanced technology that dominate in acculturative transferals. The West has imposed this particular type of intrusion almost exclusively upon other cultures in the last generation; it is a new kind of colonization—which is postmissionary and post-Marxist—as reflected in the spread of sophisticated weaponry and techniques of slaughter to areas of the world that appear otherwise quite impervious (or even violently antagonistic) to the lure of the "higher" manifestations of Western culture.

In situations of crossbreeding, the issues discussed above take on even more poignant connotations. Here, a traumatic ambiguity is *first* imposed from without, *then* experienced from within, as a sort of schizophrenic destiny in which two different races and cultures find themselves merged while yet remaining distinct. From a historical, as well as a phenomenological point of view, *métissage* is a condition of ambivalence and ambiguity. *Métissage* can be seen as an extra identity, or as bringing about a double identity. In either case, the dual component in the mixing of two races is almost never accompanied by a sense of equality between the two corresponding cultures: invariably, the heritages and, hence, the racial components that "carry" them, convey unequal symbolic connotations. Thus we have those long traumatic splits, which often cannot be resolved even over a span of many generations, that prevail in situations of *métissage*. The dramatic and paradoxical aspects of crossbreeding—in situations otherwise marked by well-defined ethnic belonging—derive from the superimposition of contrasting but asymmetrical attributes such as autochthonous versus foreign, "superior" versus "inferior," "civilized" versus "natural" (primitive, barbaric), master versus slave, etc. Thus, for instance, what is inferior, insofar as it is native (or "uncivilized"), is also ideally superior, inasmuch as it is autochthonous, with deeper and more ancient roots in the land. The same contradiction applies to "racial" and religious groups that have, for thousands of years, been mutely holding on to their spiritual privilege, to their "elected" condition, as national minorities within alien and "unenlightened" ethnic majorities. [27]

The cultural underpinnings of the genetic mix in *métissage* are manifest, first of all, in the historical self-awareness of the group which socializes the *half-breed*. In most cases (there have been exceptions, particularly in ancient times) the group which becomes more important symbolically has also been the conqueror of the other. While rejection by both cultural matrices has often been the destiny of the half-breed, the difficulties that result are far from symmetrical. Rejection by the "inferior" group, when it occurs, is certainly traumatic; yet integration into the "superior" group is a totally unfulfillable aspiration (as attested to by the case of the supposedly super-democratic United States), and so it comes to be the ultimate symbol of frustration where social status and ethnic definition are concerned. Such an integration, in fact, even if possible, would entail a nearly unimaginable suppression of basic components of the *persona* on the part of the protagonists themselves. The conflict—between wanting to belong and the impossibility, inner and outer, of actually belonging—is therefore insuperable. The result is frequently an aggressive, often self-destructive, assertion of the autochthonous (or in any event the "primitive") component of the half-breed identity against the one coming from the dominant group.

One individual and collective solution to this conflict is what we are calling the "extra identity." Here, the half-breed renounces both of his untenable identities, opting instead for one that is cultic and syncretistic (as the concept of *la Raza* expresses for postrevolutionary Mexicans, for example). This kind of mixed identity remains, however, unstable and highly problematic: the syncretic elements are not only borrowed, but reinterpreted. The issue is to understand what form this reinterpretation takes, and in exactly what sense it can constitute a lasting solution to the problem of ethnic identification: nationalist ideology has often concealed this sort of hybrid, surrogate ethnic identity behind a smoke screen of pseudo-historical claims of a dual heritage and of the reality of the cultural synthesis that purports to conciliate its opposite components.

The special kind of syncretism occurring in conjunction with *métissage* is often associated with the creation of new cults. In postcolonial situations these cults can combine a pre- (or anti-)Christian basis with practices inherited from Christianity; their use of trance and visions, and especially of sacrifice, is widespread. These particular forms of syncretism seem to exploit and liturgize "asocial" behavior. Perhaps this is an attempt at mastering and redirecting the unfocused deviance, typical of many culturally mixed groups, which so often expresses itself through violence, alcoholism, and other anomic forms of drug-taking. These collective symptoms might be compared to the individual ones of psychosis—insofar as the latter can also be seen as an effective (if distinctive) "solution" to an individual's actual difficulty in adapting to reality. From the "objective," or "normal," viewpoint, the psychotic solution is an illness; but for the psychotic who is overcoming limitations and reinterpreting assumptions, it may be part of an effort towards a more extreme—and sometimes rather creative—form of personal readaptation. This may also be the case for much collective behavior that is nonadaptive in appearance.

Syncretic cults, in fact, are neither more nor less pathological than other cults. For us they have the peculiarity of being the only ones of which we can actually witness the beginnings. Consequently, their nature as potential solutions to deep-rooted conflicts can appear more clearly than in the case of older, well-established and more "respectable" religious movements. One can only conjecture whether the origin of all cults is in anomic or conflictual situations, whether they have always constituted attempts to find "answers," or rather to reflect "questions" to which "rational" existential answers could not be found.

In any event, it appears that amid all the possible contrasting outlets for the half-breed's situation of impasse, the cultic-ecstatic and sacrificial ones do allow for projection and catharsis, liberation and oblivion. It is also conceivable that, through sublimation, the mestizo may be able to experience a transcendence that radically obliterates the inner relation between dominance and inferiority that constitutes his dual heritage.

National aspiration, in its present non-Western versions, is fraught with ambiguity. It upholds autochthony, while developing a new "modern" image of the collectivity that, ultimately, is bound to transcend the limitations of land and country. In Western Europe, the nationalist idea has had many ups and downs, and a universalist (and internationalist) representation of the community offers a persistent alternative. Today, national interest is enjoying a considerable revival, often kindled by economic anxieties that are expressed as political xenophobia and chauvinism of the most virulent kind. But considering general tendencies, while the statehood principles of Western nations are beginning to show signs of wear, in the Third World they seem to be increasingly effective as expressions of vital local needs, even as necessary—if perhaps temporary—prerequisites to survival. In the process, however, conflicts arise that are not unlike those that occurred in Europe in the formative period of its nation-states: the redefinition and political instrumentalization of ethnic identities *within* these younger statehoods are at the root of many of today's bloodiest conflicts. Through the tensions between particularist and universalist discourses, a new postimperial *and* postnational order of the world is painfully being sought.

NOTES

1. Parts of this introduction were written as a position paper (1980), entitled: "Ethnicities and Nations: Contemporary Reinterpretations of the Problematic of Identity (Ten Themes of Reflection for a Colloquium)" for the colloquium *Ethnicities and Nations: Processes of Interethnic Relations in Latin America, Southeast Asia, and the Pacific*, held at the Rothko Chapel, in Houston, Texas, 28-30 October 1983. Other sections were developed from themes brought up at the conference itself, and from more general reflections on the development of the ethnic issue in the history of the West. We would like to thank Gini Alhadeff for her assistance on the revision of this text.

2. Even where conflicts *appear* to be "national" wars, as in the Middle East, often the ideological undercurrents are primarily of a religious, "pre-Enlightenment," nature. It is paradoxical that the Palestinian cause in the Middle East, with all its externally manipulated sectarian strife, should have

taken the form of a *positive* (i.e., *modern*, "enlightened" and anti-imperial) struggle for state-nationhood, against the opposition of a "religious" state (that was actually conceived in the late nineteenth-century Europe of positivism).

3. The precedent for such a recognition, however, must be sought in the Greco-Roman foundations of individual and family citizenship rights. The old centripetal order of authority achieved integration, i.e., the political joining of "naturally" separate cultural entities, through chains of allegiance. In Rome's republic—at least in the first centuries—the *communitas* was a more or less homogeneous social unit, defined by the bonds that held it together *from the inside*: what would one day become an "ethnic group" had originally been the *gens*, or family, having values, customs, and obligations shared by all. Nothing more concrete than that conglomeration of values—"our land, our names, *our dead...*"—defined the old *communitas*. Premodern centralized models of political organization, however, could no longer rest on these traditional principles alone. They were by now devoid of their experiential, initiatory and sacrificial foundations (the *pater familias* was, above all, the *sacrificer*) and it is only *metaphorically* that they could claim to restore the order that these principles had implied.

The feudal model, for instance, operated on this kind of metaphorization of proto-ethnic values and relational modes. There is at least a superficial analogy here with the extended application of broad kinship categories (as well as with some widespread archaic modes of "adoption") in societies having kinship systems that, for this very reason, are called "classificatory"; but even a cursory analysis of the similarities and differences would take us too far afield.

4. While the West did not finally opt for a true caste system, it should also be noted that the empire itself was not truly a "European" form: it was rather an Asiatic one, transmitted across the Mediterranean sea.

Again, the resemblance is only superficial between what Durkheim called the "spontaneous and organic solutions" of archaic segmentary societies (with their functional and acephalous distribution of power, a power in fact so *pervasive* in its multileveled manifestations, that it can certainly not be thought of as incarnated, much less as "vested") and the modern principles of alternating power.

5. Thus, if the Roman ambiguity concerning the status of political power had indeed been a consequence of clanlike patterns being extended to larger social and territorial bodies (an extension that later resurfaced in the hierarchy of the feudal system), the altered modern conception of the nation calls for a totally new idea and an organizational structure in keeping with it. This idea would have the state itself as a *disembodied and abstract* entity (or "external necessity," in Hegel's terms), and as a *community-state* (in which the later concept of the welfare state originated). Again, the ideological contamination of traditional principles came as a result of the Enlightenment: eschatology became a matter of destiny (manifest or otherwise), temporal order fashioned itself into the organizational integration of individuals with groups, subjectivity turned into individualism, and education was reduced to the experimentation of pedagogical systems. For a vast and penetrating treatment, from a somewhat

different view, of these changes which constitute modernity, and some of their more pervasive consequences, see R. Calasso, *La Rovina di Kash* (Milan, 1983).

6. Crucial to the king's prerogatives, for instance, had been the identification of the Center with his *persona*; as the king moved about within the often uncertain and shifting boundaries of the land (which he needed to do constantly in order to renew feudal bonds), the focal point of power and administration always remained *with him*.

The King's main stops in his cyclical itineraries were rather like *stations* (in the specific sense given this term by the Christian and Islamic traditions), as he constantly renewed these sites as centers and invested them with the "sacredness" attached to his person. The inhabitants at such visitations were themselves touched by the king's "grace," which was often even blessed by thaumaturgical qualities. Thus, even without ethnic closeness, the bond to the ruler was reaffirmed all along the feudal ladder. (There was in fact a tendency to fix the seat of *imperium* so as to intensify its effect, but this was a metacultural tendency, not one, that is to say, that was intrinsically part of the kind of power embodied by the *rex*, which in fact bore resemblance to forms of absolute authority in the great Asiatic civilizations, as in parts of Africa and the New World and in Polynesia).

7. "Man, becoming responsible for meaning, this one in turn becomes problematic" (D. Van de Velde, "La grande lessive," *L'Homme*, XXIII, no. 1[1983] : 142).

8. In the sense first given to this concept by the ethnographic literature on the social organization of Melanesian societies. "Big-men" come and go, they are disposable and replaceable according to "nonorganic" principles; their standing, no matter how high, is *precarious* (as expressed in Napoleon's mother's anxious and prophetic exclamation, on being told of her son's extraordinary rise to power: "If only it could last!").

9. Adorno and Horkheimer actually saw in democracy as supreme value the mark of utopian aspirations deeply embedded in the Western mythological (and ideological) tradition. Persisting despite all the apparent denial, these yearnings were progressively shaped into ideological programs which could be assimilated by the new "enlightened" consciousness of Europe and transformed into new "operative" principles so pervasive that even the most authoritarian and despotic regimes today would not dare not to call themselves "democratic."

10. This corroborates the fact that the two nations which were the stage for this debate in the eighteenth century actually advanced towards similar ethico-political solutions, as if deeply driven by analogous forces. These were represented precisely by the ideologies that spoke of a *nova rationalis civitas*.

11. In its nineteenth-century aspect, for instance, colonial expansion tried, to an extreme degree and with consequences still apparent today, to make the material and the spiritual coincide, and this is expressed in the key concept of Welfare.

12. Democracy defined only in terms of *certain* existing forms: as in today's convenient support of authoritarian systems simply because they are "reversible," unlike supposedly "irreversible" "totalitarian" ones, or a support

of authoritarian "classless" systems, as opposed to "bourgeois" ones.

13. The more general ideological context, however, within which this new conception of a radically secular political order was developed antedates the resuscitation of the democratic model after the Enlightenment. Machiavelli might in fact be considered both a symptom and the "author" of this *prise de conscience*, as he was the first to establish an *empirical* and operational basis to the exercise of power.

14. Hegel adumbrated a "solution" that was both a statement of faith and a blueprint for the constitution of nineteenth-century statehoods: "The blind mutterings of pretended freedom have suffocated the concept of the State . . . [to the point] that all the misery that has come upon Germany in the Seven Years progress of reason and experience deriving from the convulsions undergone by French liberty, no longer justify that the following belief be imposed either as a faith for the people or as a principle of political science: that liberty is only possible where a people has been united under the rule of law, into a State." (*Constitution of Germany [Notes on Machiavelli]*, Italian ed., [Turin, 1972], 101–8).

15. The atheism of the Enlightenment gave rise to compensatory spiritualist (and spiritist) outbursts, similar to those set in motion by the Reformation and again by the positivist and anticlerical climate of the last third of the nineteenth century. The Spirit of Protestantism, which has been interpreted as "the regime that expects ever-increasing profits from a durable and successful enterprise" (M. Merleau-Ponty, *Les Aventures de la Dialectique* [Paris, 1955], 18), despite the apparent causes of the schism that originated it, does not abrogate religious authority while secularizing it. The example of the peasant revolts that broke out at the beginning of the Reformation in France, forcefully demonstrates the stern, even fierce vision that Lutheranism had of the new pact of alliance between secular and spiritual authority. Protestantism, be it Lutheran, Calvinist, or Anglican, was bent on affecting political function at least as much as on rendering obsolete the universality and ultimate political arbitrage and legitimation formerly attributed to Roman Christianity. "Called upon to break the vital alliance that we entertain with the times, with others, and with the world, the Calvinist brings about a full demystification, which is also a depoeticization and a disenchantment (*Entzauberung*): the sacraments, the Church as the social context of salvation, the images that are always on the verge of depicting finite creatures as divine to the point of idolatry, are all rejected as 'magic.' Absolute anguish cannot find solace in a fraternal bond with the created: the created is rather the basic material within which one works, that one manipulates, that one transforms and organizes to celebrate the glory of God" (op. cit., 23).

16. A former U. S. Secretary of State recently said: "Ideally, we would like them *both* to lose," which is of course what has been happening.

17. M. Blanchot, *Le Communauté Inavouable* (Paris, 1983), 11.

18. *Reflexions sur les Causes de la Liberté et de l'Oppression Sociale* (1935), 15.

19. The current inflated use of the concept of identity in the social sciences does not derive from the actual distillation of a precise sociological concept,

as was true of psychology. Until its most recent sociological application, as "cultural identity," anthropology (especially the American variety) contributed a great deal to its development through its study of cultural enclaves on the verge of extinction. The concept, however, remains hampered both by its ideological claims and implications and by the practical imperatives supporting them—which international crises make more urgent every day.

20. Even within our own criteria, it is almost impossible to gauge the extent of success versus failure in the processes of "assimilation"; for example, in the case of syncretism, solutions invented to reduce the distance between the old and the new, and to master the ever-present threat of the unassimilable, are fundamentally of an eidetic and ideological nature, so that there can be no possible tangible *measure* of their effectiveness.

21. Hegel, in his *Jugendschriften*, contemplated at length the religious conversion that set the foundations of Germany.

22. Despite appearances, which derive from the Marxist option that has profoundly influenced it, this sort of bias is *not* Hegelian.

23. Still, insofar as they combine "traditional" sources with a radically reinterpreted Christian spirituality, with the aim of achieving an ethnic reawakening, the *Nibelungen* depart from the *Trauerspiel*.

24. "One more time, the ancient Dionysian rites of the holocaust. Western ceremonies. Feasts of shipwreck. The ultimate revival of distant myths such as offering of blood and the sacrifice of the son in order to accede to God. Europe's last attempt at maintaining its hegemony of old in the new era of masses" (Syberberg, *Hitler, ein Film aus Deutschland*, [1976]).

25. A group of Melanesians invited to an Australian factory in order to observe the "origin of Western goods," replied to their hosts "that they had not been able to perceive the fundamental cause of the productive cycle itself, because it was *invisible*" (quoted by K. Burridge). A Western philosopher would not have responded very differently; but present-day positivism "which has lost track of Being," sees a philosopher the way it sees a Melanesian, as a paradoxical and outdated creature.

26. A. Beltrán, *Regiones de Refugio, El Desarrollo de la Comunidad y el Proceso Dominical en Mestizoamérica* (Mexico, 1967).

27. All these conditions, because of the inherent splits and contradictions they entail, could be described—in Bateson's terms—as marked by a "double-bind." In crossbreeding, this double-bind operates simultaneously on the collective (and hence political) level as well as on the individual plane of *interiority*, but a discussion of this last aspect and of what the West may have contributed to it, would lead us too far afield.

The Net Torn Apart: Ethnic Identities and Westernization in Colonial Mexico, Sixteenth–Nineteenth Century

SERGE GRUZINSKI

At the dawn of the seventeenth century, in 1604, in the Otomi village of Amanalco, an Indian began his testament with these words: "I, Miguel de Santiago, state that I am an Indian of genuine stock because it pleased my Lord and God to make me an Indian, for which I am infinitely grateful . . . ."[1]

It may come as a surprise that less than a century after the conquest of Mexico, one can already find native people thanking the Heavens for having been born Indian. In the form of a profession of faith without reference to a specific ethnic group or community—the Otomí one— the statement reveals the early internalization of an identity that was "exotic" both in its origins and in its religious foundations.

This leads one to wonder just how the people of the central Mexican plateau accepted the identity which the Spaniards foisted upon them in making them *Indians*. At first a vaguely geographical label, the colonists gave the term juridical content, religious significance, and the weight of a stereotype marked by ever stronger racism.[2] The "Indian"— we hardly need to be reminded—was first and foremost a Western invention, and so it continues to be. It summarizes in a word the slow process of Westernization set in motion by Spanish colonization, a process that continued even after independence.

When speaking about ethnicity and ethnic identity in Amerindia today, it is useful to examine the colonial transformations that occurred and to bring together whatever indigenous testimony has been preserved on the subject. Were the aborigines conscious of becoming "Indian"? Did the transmutation take place, and at what price? I shall try here, with the use of some examples, to clarify a number of indigenous transformations that led to the shaping of one, or several, types of indigenous identity and to relate them to the corresponding processes of acculturation and Westernization.

THE CONQUEST AND THE DISLOCATION OF NATIVE
REALITY: SIXTEENTH CENTURY

The first West to conquer America—the empire of Charles V—was a conglomerate of ethnic groups and languages, a stranger to the ideas of state and nation that we hold today. Although it used in America a reductionist, homogenizing term—"Indian"—it was far from being a "colonialist, totalitarian state"; rather, it sponsored a penetration that was often chaotic and uncontrolled, carried out in the name of contradictory interests, with limited possibilities of action. We forget that for a long time the Spanish were only a tiny minority drowning in an ocean of native populations, and that their one consistent, coherent acculturation project—Christianization— depended on human resources that were utterly insignificant. I make these remarks in order to qualify, from the start, the broadly "apocalyptic" picture generally referred to as the "traumatism of the Conquest." While it certainly was traumatic, the Conquest at first affected only certain narrowly circumscribed social elements; later, in successive waves, it reached the mass of the population and the peripheries. Although under the weight of the stereotype we often forget it, we know quite well that Mesoamerican societies were as complex and as stratified as those in the Old World, and that the cultural and intellectual distance between the painters of the Codices and the native country folk was probably as great as that which separated sixteenth-century European clergy from the masses.

The first groups to be touched by Westernization were those most directly exposed to it—the indigenous nobility. By opposing this dominant class, and especially by doing its utmost to inculcate its own approach to reality, the Spanish conquest shook the entire complex of frames of reference, implicit and explicit certitudes, and identities that buoyed the ruling class's existence. It is this that distinguishes the *Conquista* from the numerous conquering ventures that had preceded it into Mesoamerican territory.

The Church's execration and prohibition of "idolatry" signified something very different from the confrontation of cults with one another; that was an old experience for the Indians. By denying the authenticity of the native gods ("their gods were not true ones") the Spaniards, as the Indian priests themselves asserted, called into question their "norms of living," the "tradition of their ancestors," and their entire legacy from the past—to the point of depriving their life of meaning and reality, and reducing it to death and nothingness. By annihilating the structures that gave the indigenous world its plausibility—the clergy, the temples, the sacrifices, the calendar— Christian preaching disrupted the course of a routine, orderly world in which men and gods were jointly responsible forever. In effect, it attacked the foundations of every prior identity, dislocating them while substituting for their ancestral patrimony—ethnic, communal, lineal— a "net full of holes."[3]

The hopelessness of the vanquished priests reveals how deep was the rupture brought about by the Spanish conquest. But it would be wrong to assume that this was a uniform reaction. Part of the priestly caste, among those who survived the wars and the massacres, chose the path of refusal and of the clandestine: that of idolatry, to use the Spanish, Christian term. To preserve the integrity of the ancient world—which guaranteed their essential identity as "servants of the gods" and legitimized the ethnic, religious, and historical origin of their power—these Indians opposed Christianity. Paradoxically, however, these upholders of continuity and tradition came to acquire a borrowed identity, that of idolators. Endowed with an acute awareness of their difference and their uniqueness, often understanding clearly the significance of the Christian enterprise and the impossibility of reconciling their ancestral beliefs and practices with it, they were drawn, despite themselves, into debates unprecedented in their own past, and took to utilizing Western arguments to denounce the Christian god.[4]

For some, this new reflection even led to an early form of cultural relativism. Noting that at the heart of the Spanish clergy—for example, between Franciscans, Dominicans, and Augustinians—there were divergences in practices, in clothing, they asserted their own right to be different: "Each one must live according to the law that pleases him and as he pleases."[5]

Thus one did not remain an idolator, one *became* one. And this new, colonial identity was only one of the many repercussions of a Christianization that produced an irremediable rupture in the religious homogeneity of the Mesoamerican world. Within the context of this first colonization—which was, above all, religious in nature—it was the Christian / idolator schism, more than the Spanish / Indian one, that affected the indigenous elites, shattered the ancient consensus, and favored the emergence of a counteridentity, that of idolator.

Thirty years after the conquest, around 1550, the ranks of idolatry began to thin out. New generations came to power. This time, their massive rallying around the Spanish Crown dismantled Mesoamerican societies definitively—decapitating them, depriving them of elites who, until then, had been the guarantors of the survival of the world and of the gods, while the vast majority of the population had been but superficially touched by Christianization.

Following the conquest, young nobles began to receive a Franciscan education; this resulted in conversion and collaboration. In an effort to regain power, in trying to join a system that they now saw as firmly rooted and irreversible, they succumbed to opportunism. Unquestionably, however, this rallying must also be seen as an existential necessity to fill the void—the "net full of holes"—created by the conquest, the need to adapt to the new rules of the game while salvaging what was essential: the wealth, memory, and privileges of the former ruling class. Because, although vanquished, these classes were far from being stripped of authority. They knew they were indispensable as intermediaries, and they enjoyed the support of religious orders which, we must remember, constituted a major force in sixteenth-century Mexico.

It is within this context that the Indian nobility undertook to fashion a suitable identity for themselves, reconciling their vision of the world with the colonial reality they themselves confronted and as the Other—the Spanish—might see it. They learned to conform to the model which the Spanish Crown held out to them, that of the Iberian hidalgo, adopting its garments and emblems: weaponry, coats of arms, the horse. They saw (and situated) themselves at the center of the vast political arena surrounding the vice-royalty and the Spanish monarchy. Undoubtedly this was a comedown for the old reigning families fallen from sovereignty; but it also meant a freer hand for those lords who in the past had been subordinate to them.

The Christian nobility nevertheless found itself facing the same difficulty as the idolatrous nobility: what to do about the pre-Conquest past? For it was impossible for them to make a clean slate of it without affecting the "origin, foundation, and genesis of the fiefdoms." They relegated this "before the Conquest" to the "past"—in the Western sense of the word—using the European model to give it a linear, providentialist structure and expurgating its pagan aspects. This led them to alternate constantly between understatement and alienation, mixing self-censure with the reshaping of events. Thus emerged a recomposed past which, occasionally, they even attempted to fit into the Procrustean bed of biblical and Greco-Latin chronologies.

For the Indian nobles, this was definitely a new memory for a new identity, but also bringing new modes of expression which combined the traditional pillars: the Codex and the glyphs; the oral tradition and the new, exotic prestige of alphabetic writing. Typography, Gregorian chants, Renaissance painting, etching, Latin, and European accounting practices fertilized a cultural mix scarcely equaled in modern Western history.[6] As long as it remained a precious, indispensable channel for the colonial power structure, this literate aristocracy was able to insert, in judicious dosages, a part of the pre-Hispanic heritage into the Christian, Spanish, colonized framework. This dual indigenous-Christian identity can be seen in the names chosen by Indians, combining the old and the new. Let us consider, for example, that historian of the Valley of Mexico, Don Domingo Francisco de San Antón Muñón Chimalpahin Cuauhtlehaunitzin. The *don*, a Spanish title, indicated that he was a man of standing; Domingo Francisco were his baptismal names; San Antón conjured up San Antonio Abad, the chapel to which Indians belonged; Muñón, the name of his Spanish protectors; and Chimalpahin Cuauhtlehuanitzin, the names of his paternal and maternal ancestors.[7]

This double-faced identity concealed additional facets that went beyond the ethnic ancestry. First, it opened out onto a universalist, Christian vision of humanity: "In the beginning of the world we had but one first father, Adam, and one little mother, Eve: it is from them that we come, even though today our bodies look different from one another."[8] This identity also coexisted, then, albeit not without contradictions, with an awareness of the natives' impoverished condition. Thus, in the mid-sixteenth century, it adopted the criticism of Las Casas, the Indians' protector, with denouncements of "the numerous trials and injustices that we receive from the Spanish who find themselves amongst us and amongst whom we find ourselves."[9]

Between the memory of ancestry and Christian universalism there developed a major antagonism (us / them, *nosotros / ellos*) which gave rise to a collective identification ("we the Indians"). From the start it was laden with ambiguity because the lamentation of lords and princes was also, above all, a class stance. And it was a class which, with its new forms of thinking and new modes of expression, removed itself even farther from the bulk of the native population.

IDENTITY AND IDENTIFICATION OF THE OTHER: THE OTOMÍ IMPASSE

The transformations in the seventeenth-century colonial scene generally led to the aborting of such attempts at survival by the Indian nobility. The catastrophic drop in the native population, the continual reinforcement of the Spanish presence, the unforeseen appearance of mestizos, and the Church's new concerns often dealt a fatal blow to the authority of the aboriginal nobility.

An Otomí text dating from the mid-seventeenth century illustrates the impasse in which former ruling circles could find themselves. At that time, the Otomí caciques in the town of Querétaro (some 200 km northwest of Mexico City) were suffering an irreparable decline. Though they had founded Querétaro a century earlier and sometimes even accumulated considerable wealth, they now occupied only an obscure position in a town that was no longer a frontier station, and which had fallen into the hands of Spanish stock breeders and merchants. The Otomís had become an ethnic minority lost among other minorities: Nahuas, Tarascans, mestizos, blacks, mulattos. Their identity shrank to the dimensions of a shriveled, urban subculture held together, essentially, by language and kinship ties. On all of them, populace and caciques alike, weighed the crushing stereotypes forged by a new and most unbridled racism: "These Otomís are considered to be the most boorish, the most inept, and the most savage Indians in the entire country." [10]

Despite this, and in the absence of an acceptable present condition, the caciques built a glorious past which they furnished with a fictitious identity. They created an almost exclusively indigenous history [11] of the origins of Querétaro in which the major figures were solely Indians—Otomís or Chichimecas. The Spanish vanished from the stage of events and even from the Mexican scene—with the exception of the far-off viceroy and an obscure clergyman—even when in reality they had closely supervised and in some cases accompanied the expeditions led by their native assistants. The picture given is one of a colony without Spaniards and, even more disconcerting, one without Otomí Indians, to the extent that the latter appear only as "Catholics." No mention was made of the country's military conquest, as if the *Conquista* had never taken place. The date used to locate the events—1502—actually seventeen years before the arrival of the Spaniards and several decades prior to the founding of Querétaro, completed this grandiose attempt at historical fakery.

In the middle of the seventeenth century, Otomí collective imagination invented a posthumous, fictitious identity for itself, transforming past generations into Catholics and Conquistadors, laden with privileges and prerogatives, divided up into long, bedecked corteges out to evangelize their Chichimec adversaries. An idyllic, baroque tableau of a Mexico without Spaniards, Christianized by its own natives, it was a world apart from the real, precarious, perilous conditions under which the raids on the north were in fact carried out. It hardly matters that it was "historically" false; the narrative denotes a desperate will to identify with the conqueror by becoming Catholic, to reproduce the colonizer to the point of taking his place.

By associating the fruits of assimilation with those of a preserved autonomy, this mirror-identity merely developed the promises of royal, colonial, and Christian ideology to the point of absurdity: Christianized and subject to the Spanish Crown, shouldn't the Indians have kept a sphere for themselves—an "Indian Republic"—distinct from that of the Spanish? Reality would contradict this program; but we must conclude that the Otomí caciques borrowed its features for the reconstruction of their own identity from Spanish discourse, and that the Christian reference provided the keystone.

In the face of the idolators' irreducibility and of the viable, sometimes brilliant compromise of sixteenth-century Christian nobles, the seventeenth-century Otomí identity fiction demonstrated the impasse of a declining sector that was prey to what may well be called a second identity crisis. Nor is the case of Querétaro unique.[12] Rather, it is representative of the difficulties and contradictions through which the indigenous nobility had to struggle. And it illuminates sharply the complex movements of ethnic identities under the colonial regime.

ENLIGHTENED ELITES AND INDIANS: THE EIGHTEENTH CENTURY

A class in crisis, perpetually drained of its vitality, the Indian nobility managed nonetheless to maintain an honorable position within Mexican society until the eve of independence. Although during the sixteenth and early seventeenth centuries they defended their privileges and their identity essentially by relying on their history of princely lineages, by the eighteenth century they seem to have shifted the orientation of their discourse noticeably. It was as if they had a presentiment that the safekeeping of their rights would require a global reference to the Indian world, the "Indian nation" or the "American nation." In the face of new European colonists who did not discriminate between caciques and populace in their general scorn, the native nobility deplored how the "Indians" had been neglected in "their own country"; they spoke for the populace, and in their name demanded an education that would release them from the "ignorance and barbarism" in which they had been stagnating for two and a half centuries: "Is it because, and only because, he is an Indian that he should not receive an education comparable to the one that all peoples have instituted in order to correct their errors?"[13] They even exalted the crucial role that they played internationally: "[The Indians] are, without a doubt, the strongest member of the monarchy upon whom the subsistence of these lands and of many of those in Europe depends . . . ."[14]

These stances undeniably attest to the fact that the core of the Indian elites was aware of having to endorse the overall interests of indigenous people, the "Nación de los Indios." They indicate that an indigenist, humanist discourse inspired by the criticisms of a Las Casas had been taken up again *by Indians*. They infused it with a new virulence, a ruthless acuity in drawing up the negative balance sheet of two and a half centuries of colonization and in masterfully dismantling the underpinnings of anti-Indian racism: "The sophistic perversity with which the Spanish negated the rationality of the Indians after having known them resulted solely in hindering its utilization."[15] Eventually these Indian analyses were included in the debate on the "noble savage" conducted by the Enlightenment that criticized "the literary journals of Rome, the memoires of Trévoux, the Journal des Savants of Paris, the Royal Societies of Science of Upsala, London, Berlin, Bologna . . . ." for the image of Indians that they portrayed. "One reads in these monuments," wrote the caciques of Mexico in 1770, "passages which—to our great consternation—deem us to be idolators, dunces, incompetents, ingrates, and incorrigibles, and this conception of us—without any distinction whatsoever—is all the more regrettable and injurious because it strips us of the talents and qualities with which God created us as He did other men . . . ."[16]

Indian and indigenist rhetoric, however, could not conceal the chasm that separated these educated elites from the rest of the Indian population. The essential Westernization of the discourse was accompanied by a Westernization of perception in which the logic, beliefs, and syncretisms of the masses were denigrated to the level of barbarism and ignorance, of superstition and idolatry. The gap between the two groups became so wide that in the eighteenth century, Indian priests were the ones pursuing the "obtuse idolatry" of their poor parishioners. Just as in the sixteenth century, the identity of *indio*—the consciousness of an Indianness that would transcend ethnic distinctions—barely camouflaged the still powerful class interests. We see here an enlightened Indian intelligentsia capable of posing the Indian question in global terms without having to rely on Europeans. Remarkably, the question ceased being one of the favorite objects, or rather foils, of the West's bad conscience. Thus in the course of three centuries of colonial rule, the native nobility developed, managed, and promoted an Indian identity that oscillated between reference to lineage and to tribal loyalty, between a Christian view of human nature and a feeling of Indianness, of an "Indian condition" which it could neither renounce nor fully adhere to. And yet, these were far from being the only manifestations of ethnic identity in the indigenous world of the Colony.

While the native nobility entered a long decline which would not end until the mid-nineteenth century, as early as the first decades of the colonization, upstart commoners—made rich by trade and strengthened by the support of clerics and colonists—invaded the ranks of the petty village leaders who held the destiny of peasant communities in their hands. They went about forging an identity that split with the pre-Hispanic past and brushed aside the image that the old nobility was forming for itself. One discovers the written trail of this in the Primordial Titles jealously preserved by these Indians and presented by them to the authorities whenever they had to defend community rights, privileges, or lands.

These Titles do not reflect historical reality factually as we conceive of it. They express what Nahua Indians, from the seventeenth century on, imagined to be the emergence of their pueblo, their community, their territory, and the identity associated with them. The Titles cannot be dated with any precision; nor did their authors care to, for they hoped to endow them with the prestige of time immemorial. And so they remain anonymous, even if we can pinpoint their social origin.

The Titles describe the conquest and founding of the pueblo, or, more precisely, its reconquest and refounding during the colonial period, as if it had been necessary to restart on new foundations. To mark the Christian birth of the pueblo, indigenous memory retained two crucial events which are invariably associated with one another: the granting of lands by the Spanish Crown, and the construction of the church and its dedication to a patron saint. The church was seized upon as the symbol of the coming of a new era, the "Time of the Very Holy Trinity." It was the receptacle for the new divinity— the Holy Sacrament—and the home of a series of rituals designed to reprovide a rhythm for the passage of time and the reproduction of the community (baptisms, marriages, funerals). Along with the building of the sanctuary, the selection of a patron saint grew out of native initiative: a saint appeared before the leading citizens and let it be known that he wished to be the pueblo's patron, to become lord of the lands and master of the community.

It is true that a pueblo's attachment to a particular divine being has nothing specifically Christian or colonial about it. According to very ancient, pre-Hispanic traditions, when founders settled on a site, there were often miraculous apparitions signifying that "the god was ceding the farmland to the immigrants."[17] The Primordial Titles repeated, in a "Christian version," the story of the pact linking the tutelary god— the *calpulteotl*—with the pueblo. Just as before the patron god "went to dwell on a nearby mountain," the saint was received in his church.

Every time that their images were worshipped by the community, they also represented the founding bond which lent strength and cohesion to the collectivity.

The Spanish, who until then had been unobtrusive, became highly visible once the new local administration—seen as the logical outcome of Christianization—was installed. Was it not Charles V, Cortez, or some viceroy who appointed the first native governors, the alcaldes and fiscales? An institutional genesis that doubled as a veritable shaping of the pueblo, for the space and habitat were remodeled after the grid layout—the *traza*—of the Spanish, the finishing touch being the creation of different neighborhoods. There still remained the project of regrouping the dispersed population and nearby pagans within this space. That was the raison d'être of the congregation. Far from being perceived as a brutal measure imposed by the Spanish—which it actually was—the congregation is remembered as the capturing and restriction of "idolatrous" Indians, the triumph of the Christian faith, and the definitive foundation of the pueblo.

The church, the patron saint, communal duties, the *traza*, the congregation . . . Through a paradoxical inversion, in their effort to underscore the uniqueness of the pueblo, these Indians seized upon the very traits that embodied the penetration of Spanish colonization. It is true that they offered a coherent alternative to the thenceforth outlawed pre-Hispanic institutions, and that they installed a ready-made structure which allowed a rethinking of the community, giving it an identity, assuring its survival. What undoubtedly remained as essential, was the territory.

It is the appropriation of the land by the defining of its boundaries that is the focal point of the Titles. It is presented unmistakably as a ritual, sacred step: "We have marked our boundaries so that from this moment forth, we may serve God."[18] The operation conducted by the village elders consisted of an exhausting succession of climbs and descents during which they "marked the boundaries" by making piles of rocks and staking out their route with small stone images. Carried out to the sound of trumpets, amidst exchanges of flowers and countryside banquets, the survey was finished only when the circuit had been completed and they had returned to their point of departure. The group was thus defined by marking out the territory on which it was grounded, tracing a vast circle—or quadrilateral—that had the church as its ideal center.

To stake out the perimeter also means to close in on oneself. In addition to signifying a reclaiming, the Titles express a concern for protecting oneself from the outside: from the nomads with their devastating raids; from the conquering Mexica; and later, from the neighboring pueblo and especially from the Spaniards whose deceitful offers and incessant encroachments were an object of dread.

In this small world entrenched behind its borders, rare were the references to any larger ethnic or linguistic entity. No use of the term *indio* nor an equivalent in the native tongue. These Indians preferred to refer to themselves and to their neighbors by the name of their locality. One was "someone from Cuixingo" or "the people from Cuixingo." [19] No longer any reference to a humanity of which the Indians were one of the branches. But let us not conclude that these natives were ignorant of the fact that, in the eyes of the Spanish, they were nothing more than *indios* and, at best, human beings *almost* like the rest. These vaster, ironclad identities, lacking any relation to territory, probably remained rather abstract, whereas for the native nobility their relevance corresponded to their own social and cultural uprooting.

While the identity of the nobility was rooted in the ancestral past, the communal microidentity was, above all else, spatial. It coincided with a litany of place names, an enumeration of toponyms with infinite connotations. It took form in a map, or rather in a "picture," to use the Spanish *and* indigenous term—to the point where the Titles and the map constituted for their holders a priceless, inalienable object, as if they had become the precise equivalent of the land and of the being of the pueblo. These are the "Royal Papers to be Preserved," the "Written Papers of God." [20]

Let us take note in passing, once more, of the correlation between identity and writing. Western writing was not the prerogative only of nobles, who recorded in it their genealogies and their rights. It was also the favorite form of expression of communal identities, the indispensable vehicle for the collective memory of the elders. The instrument for colonial domination now became the graphic support for an affirmation of autonomy, the bearer of a right, of an identity. This matter of writing, then, is inseparable from the establishing of a memory in which—we cannot help but note—a high degree of acculturation is present. Unlike the nostalgic nobility, however, the leading citizens of the pueblo felt free to reinterpret the past; they granted the colonial period a privileged position at the expense of pre-Hispanic events of no consequence, which they relegated to the role of prerequisites or antecedents. One can attribute this shifting of focus to the workings of forgetfulness, to the hazards of a pictographic and oral tradition, to the continual assaults of deadly plagues. But one can also see in it the quest for a Christian and colonial legitimacy indispensable for the community's survival.

This change in emphasis, this different chronological highlighting, corresponds to the process of contraction and regrouping noted earlier, for it voided the record of larger territorial and ethnic aggregates to which the community may have belonged prior to the Spanish conquest. Is it, though, a question of a totally acculturated memory, one forced to pay the high price of Westernization in order to safeguard a local identity? Our evidence rules out such a simplified view. The pueblo, using its elders as intermediaries, establishes an identity that is a compromise between the imperatives of evangelization, the weight of colonial domination, the will to survive of a group attached to its territory and the memory that it develops. So too, there operates another compromise between the linear-time orientation of the conquerors and the indigenous sense of time, which was traditionally both cyclical and linear.[21] Hence, all along the Primordial Titles, there appears this confusing permeability between pagan and Christian eras—filtering into each other, overlapping, and responding to one another—as if, for these Indians, the notion of a unidimensional, irreversible flow were as difficult to admit and grasp as that of an irreducible opposition between Christianity and paganism. This is why—to the great confusion of the Western reader—from one period to the next the same events are repeated, the same actors appear and move about. And hence the impression of an elusive magma, of a chronological chaos which, in fact, is congruent with the workings of an indigenous memory that organizes historical matter according to specific criteria still partially autochthonous.

At the risk of overstating the case, let us say that the memory of the nobles and of the community are diametrically opposed to one another: the former varnished Westernized structures with an ancient content; the latter subordinated a colonial and Christian factual history to an Amerindian construct.

Perhaps we can now better understand in just what way the ethnic identities set up by these two sectors of seventeenth-century native society diverged so radically. There is one point, however, where they meet inexorably: their subjugation to colonial power. Despite maintaining their own temporality and a preserved, closed space, the Titles could not conceal the unavoidable presence of the Spanish Crown and of the colonial system. It was the priest and his vicars in the pueblo, the alcalde mayor in the circumscription (later "municipality") who guaranteed the insertion of this unit into the larger, nonindigenous one. Not only was the communal identity "on probation"; it was cut off from the bonds that had integrated it into larger political and ethnic movements before the Conquest. Hence the splintered appearance of colonial history, generally reduced to the history of the relations between each pueblo and its neighbors—restless hamlets, adjacent pueblos, Spanish hacendados.[22]

SUBIDENTITY TO MACROIDENTITY: CONFRATERNITY TO MESSIANISM

Community and noble identity were not the only manifestations of indigenous ethnic identity within colonial society, as a historiography overly focused on the pueblo might suggest. The proliferation of other institutions within the pueblo—also borrowed from Christianity— served to establish an array of group and kinship identities, and one wonders whether they did not end up playing a preponderant role in the experience of those who took them on. This is the case, for example, of the religious confraternities introduced and imposed by missionaries beginning in the sixteenth century.

Created at the start according to the established procedures, equipped with written constitutions that placed them under Spanish ecclesiastical control, the confraternities multiplied throughout the seventeenth century. The usual process of appropriation and deflection, with which we are now familiar, manifested itself in this case as well. Leading citizens, neighborhoods, hamlets, as well as simple, pious Indians, all decided to consecrate part of their resources to the cult of the saint of their choosing. By providing new frames of reference for the group's members, the tightly knit web of these obligations and groupings soon provided the structure for what was essential to collective living and sociability. One other institution should also be mentioned here: ritual godparenthood, or compadrazgo, which enjoyed equal success. Let us simply take note of the emergence of these subidentities and of their flourishing during the seventeenth and eighteenth centuries. They corresponded to the growing autonomy of small areas of life upon which colonial power had little hold.

Should one conclude, then, that Christianity contributed strongly toward crushing Indian identity by confining it to the sphere of the pueblo or to even smaller units? To do so would be to suggest that there generally existed an awareness of ethnicity during the pre-Hispanic era which was dissolved by the Spanish conquest. We must stress that we have no idea how a pre-Cortez man from the countryside perceived his own identity, and that attempts at guessing it often confuse the discourse of sixteenth-century Christianized elites with pre-Hispanic reality!

Nor should one forget that Christianity—misappropriated, reinterpreted, locally adapted—did help to create, and undoubtedly maintain, vast social units by regrouping one or more ethnic groups. Pilgrimages furnished one of the supports for this common consciousness extending beyond the tight confines of town and countryside. Often rich in pre-Hispanic antecedents, these movements of devotion and of populations developed during the seventeenth century around miraculous images whose worship was largely encouraged, if not instigated, by the baroque Church. The more famous ones are familiar to us: the Virgin of Guadalupe near Mexico City; the Virgin of Ocotlán in Tlaxcala; the Christ of Chalma.[23] The fairs and holidays inspired by these cults periodically brought together people belonging to one or more ethnic groups. Unfortunately, it is difficult to know how these participants perceived each other or conceived of the potential macroidentity thus brought up. We know all too well, however, the historic role of the worship of the Virgin of Guadalupe in foreshadowing the birth of a Mexican national consciousness, to underestimate the importance of these "transethnic" gatherings.

On the other hand, we do have precise evidence of some popular movements which, during the second half of the eighteenth century, took hold of these baroque structures and made them overflow with new contents. Messianic movements, blending indigenous Christianity with millenarianism, like the one led by the shepherd Antonio Pérez (whom we have studied in detail elsewhere).[24] At the outset, the worship of an image and the growing reputation of a healer named Antonio. Then a resounding fervor region-wide, well beyond the community borders, suddenly rejected by the Church and thrust into clandestinity and dissidence. As the movement took on a more openly messianic and millenarian tone, the intensified consciousness of an Indian identity, in the fullest sense of the term, came into view: "Everything must revert to the native. . . . They alone should remain, but the Spaniards and the people of reason should be burned. . . . All wealth should remain in the hands of the natives."[25]

It all sounds as though the encounter between a native Christianity and a much older substratum—among other things, an Indian interpretation of the charismatic leader in the form of a "man-god"—gave rise to an overall rejection of colonial society, choosing the paths of messianism and millenarianism. But unlike the criticisms formulated by the native elites, millenarianism demanded a reversal of the colonial situation: punishment of the exploiters—the Spanish and their acculturated collaborators, the "people of reason"—and the crowning of an Indian king who would reign over Mexico and the world. Two identities overlap here: that of the *natives*—the term "Indian" is not used, but rather this equivalent of it—in opposition to the Spanish, the mestizos, the blacks, and the mulattos; and that of *Christians*, referring to the movement's followers, in opposition this time to nonbelievers. The indigenous group was thus included in its totality, but in terms entirely different from those held by the enlightened elites when they evoked the "Indian nation."

Furthermore, the millenarian identity broke with the past—whether that of the noble lineages clutching onto their genealogies or that of the pueblo's elders—to inscribe itself into the future opened up by the eschatology drawn from Christian millenarianism. With no past and no land, and cut off from both town nobility and local elders, the countryfolk involved in these movements saw in an apocalyptic future the hope to put an end to colonial domination, to the power of the state and to that of the Church.

Thus, during the same period (the second half of the eighteenth century) and within one ethnic group (the Nahuas), two disparate social groups—one belonging to the nobility, the other to a peasantry in crisis—asserted their identity as *Indians* or *natives* (*naturales*) in the face of the state of Enlightenment, independently of their specific ethnic or community affiliations. An intellectual and political movement based on the Las Casas tradition on the one hand, and the convoluted twists of a millenarian faith on the other, culminated in a parallel acquisition of a sense of "ethnic" self-awareness.

FALSE IDENTITIES AND IDENTITY LOSS

Needless to say, what we have been dealing with here are extreme cases and situations that constitute spectacular examples of the extraordinary indigenous ability, at every level, to assimilate and adapt Western ideology in its most diverse forms. At each turn it is the borrowing of a Christian and Western matrix that allows Indians to consider the native world in its totality and to devise an identity that situates them within the universe that they perceive.

But that is the exception. Far from the self-defense of the nobility and the messianic movements, the alternative to the tight circle of communal identity ordinarily lacked luster. Ultimately, it signified the dissolution of all Indian identity. For complex and contradictory dynamics continually cracked the pueblo's strong communal façade, too long identified with its leaders, spokesmen, elders, governors, and alcaldes, parvenus to whom we owe the Primordial Titles and the identity they convey. The community itself—that is to say, the dominant faction—could take it upon itself to remove members whom it deemed undesirable by, for example, accusing them of witchcraft. But of their own accord, too, Indians would decide to leave the pueblo: sometimes to escape from overly burdensome communal obligations; sometimes in the hope of finding better land elsewhere or making a living on nearby haciendas; sometimes to remarry illegally, since Christian marriages were indissoluble.[26] In each case, the communal identity faded with the land left behind, to be replaced on occasion by a new and equivalent one when, for instance, installation on the hacienda's land was made official by the construction of a new parish church and thus by the establishment of a new collective bond.

The obliteration of Indian identities is a complex process that will not be discussed here, other than to point out that it runs counter to the evidence that we have presented and foreshadows, from the colonial period onward, what in the course of time would become widespread. Thus, ethnic or communal affiliation quickly dimmed when Indians in town mingled with the Spanish and mestizo people in whose employ they served. They now changed their way of dressing, spoke Spanish, and did not hesitate, when it was in their interest, to try to pass as mestizos or even as Spaniards. They were thus able to elude the gaze of the Indians' parish priests and to avoid the duty of paying tribute in their home communities. They were also free to assert their position as Indians whenever they wished: Indians paid lower church tithes, were not subject to the jurisdiction of the Inquisition, etc. A common practice in the large colonial towns, these identity shifts were part of a larger process of cultural miscegenation and of individual strategies— often successful—in opposition to colonial domination.[27]

Nevertheless, renunciation of ethnic identity often took on more sordid aspects, which we shall only note in passing. It is true that they still call to mind situations of deculturation that are already sad portents of the future. We are reminded of the world of the tavern—the Mexican pulquería—which sheltered an interethnic and shady sort of sociability where delinquency, prostitution, and alcoholism rubbed elbows; or the world of the already concentration-camplike *obrajes*, those workshop-prisons where races, sexes, and generations were packed together; where promiscuity, forced indebtedness, and brutality were common currency. It was within these subcultures that Indians were molded to conform to the colonial and modern stereotype that makes them into ignorant, lazy, brutish drunkards. Still minorities in the eighteenth century, these marginal sectors grew dramatically, in the following century—along with urbanization, demographic growth, economic transformations, and deculturation of every sort.

The evidence so sketchily evoked here brings everything back to the protean process of Westernization that, since the sixteenth century, has transformed natives into *Indians* and Indians into faceless half-breeds. Rising in the face of this challenge—this hold that is in turn brutal and insidious, of which we have been able to glimpse some of the ideological, political and intellectual transformations—are Indian responses and movements that the historian can only very partially reconstruct. At least, however, he can bring out their multiplicity, coherence, and inventiveness, even if—in the long or short run— these Indian identities are in any case doomed to failure, to folkloric diversion, or to ethnological preservation. In following the thoughts and actions of those who, each in their own way, attempted to patch up the "torn net" of their identity, one has the perhaps illusory feeling of grasping an otherness that would be something more than, and different from, the sum of our discourses, our phantoms, and our ignorance.

Translation by Annabel Sherk

NOTES

1. Archivo General de la Nación, Mexico, Ramo Tierras, vol. 2554, expediente 14.

2. See among others: Lewis Hanke, *El prejuicio racial en el Nuevo Mundo*, Sepsetentas, 156 (Mexico: Secretaría de Educación Pública, l974); Magnus Mörner, *Estado, razas y cambio social en la Hispanoamérica colonial*, SepSetentas, 128 (Mexico: Secretaría de Educación Pública, l974); Anthony Pagden, *The Fall of Natural Man, the American Indian and the Origins of Comparative Ethnology* (Cambridge: Cambridge University Press, 1982).

3. "Una red de agujeros." "Anales históricos de la nación mexicana (Anónimo de Tlatelolco)," facsimile edition by Ernst Mengin in *Corpus Codicum Americanorum Medii Aevi*, vol. II, fol. 34 (Copenhagen, 1945), quoted in Miguel León-Portilla, *Culturas en peligro* (Mexico: Alianza Editorial Mexicana, 1976), 108.

4. Regarding their reactions, see León-Portilla, *Culturas en peligro*, 105–29.

5. *Proceso criminal . . . contra Don Carlos, indio principal de Tezcuco* (Mexico: Gómez de la Puente, 1910), 45.

6. Regarding some of the members of this educated aristocracy, see the "Prologue" of the Franciscan Juan Bautista to his *Sermonario en lengua mexicana* (Mexico, 1606).

7. Francisco Domingo Chimalpahin, Cuauhtlehuanitzin, *Relaciones originales de Chalco Amaquemecan* (Mexico: Fondo de Cultura Económica, 1965).

8. Chimalpahin Cuauhtlehuanitzin, *Séptima Relación*, Bibliothèque Nationale, Paris, ms. Mexicain 74, fol. 213r-v.

9. León-Portilla (1976), 98: letter of May 2, 1556 from the "lords and eminences of *pueblos* in this New Spain" addressed to King Philip II.

10. Felix Zubillage, S. J., *Monumenta Mexicana* (Rome: Institutum Historicum Societatis Jesu, 1959), 416 (late sixteenth-century Jesuit testimony).

11. About this text, see Serge Gruzinski, "La memoria mutilada: construcción del pasado y mecanismos de la memoria en un grupo otomí de la mitad del siglo XVII," presented at the II° Simposio de Historia de las Mentalidades, Mexico, I. N. A. H., October 1983 (in press).

12. On the Otomís of Querétero, see John C. Super, *La vida en Querétero durante la colonia, 1531–1810* (Mexico: Fondo de Cultura Económica, 1983.

13. Archivo General de Indias, Seville, Mexico, 1937, "Memorial de Don Juan Cirilo de Castilla, Indio cacique de Tlaxcala", ca. 1778.

14. Ibid.

15. Ibid., after 1770.

16. Ibid., "Los indios caciques gobernadores de Tenochtitlán y Tlatelolco al rey," Mexico, 11 April 1770.

17. On the Primordial Titles, see James Lockhart, "Views of Corporate Self and History in Some Valley of Mexico Towns: Late Seventeenth and Eighteenth Centuries" in *The Inca and Aztec States 1400–1800. Anthropology and History*, edited by George A. Collier, Remato I. Rosaldo, John D. Wirth (New York: Academic Press, 1982), 367–93.

18. Alfredo López Austin, *Hombre Dios. Religión y política en el mundo náhuatl* (Mexico: U. N. A. M., 1973); *Cuerpo humano e ideología. Las concepciones de los natiguos Nahuas* (Mexico: U. N. A. M., 1980), vol. 1, 78.

19. Archivo General de la Nación, Mexico, Ramo Tierras, vol. 3032, expediente 3, fol. 197v.

20. Ibid., Ramo Tierras, vol. 2819, expediente 9.

21. Ibid., Ramo Tierras, vol. 3032, expediente 3, fol. 199; Ramo Tierras, vol. 2674, expediente 1, fol. 13v.

22. The communal identity that we have attempted to reconstruct here based on the Primordial Titles is applicable to the Nahuas in the Valley of Mexico; but with certain corrections, which would be too long to examine here, it could also be extrapolated to other groups and other regions in the Mexican altiplano.

23. On the cult of the Virgin of Guadeloupe, see Francisco de la Maza, *El guadalupanismo mexicano* (Mexico: Fondo de Cultura Económica, 1953).

24. In *Les Hommes-Dieux du Mexique. Pouvoir indien et société coloniale* (in press).

25. Ibid.

26. On leaving communities, see Nancy M. Farris, *Maya Society under Colonial Rule. The Collective Enterprise of Survival* (Princeton: Princeton University Press, 1984).

27. Ecclesiastical literature from eighteenth-century Mexico provides numerous illustrations of these identity games; for example, Manuel Pérez, *Farol indiano y guía curas de indios* (Mexico: Francisco de Rivera Calderón, 1713), passim.

Multiethnicity and Hegemonic Construction: Indian Plans and the Future

STEFANO VARESE

AN ALMOST PERSONAL PROLOGUE

Today, as I begin to write these lines, two photographs have fallen into my hands. They synthesize ideas and ideals that I, along with a number of Latin American friends and colleagues, have been involved with. One, in black and white, shows perfectly drawn designs made with a long palm-leaf fiber impregnated with "huito" paint and black soot. The vision is of the expert hand of a Matsés man inscribing the Worm clan's symbols on my chest with the indelible paint of the Amazonian *huito*. It transports me back to the beginnings of a social and political experiment that, in addition to putting Peru at the forefront of a socialist project of self-management for workers, peasants, and native peoples, proposed multiethnicity as a precondition for a planned and conscious restructuring of the nation and its state.

In the second photograph are the faces of Zapotec peasants from the Oaxacan *sierra* in Mexico. They are seated beneath the roof tiles and adobe arches of a locale given by the community to the native cultural organization; above them is a large placard of V. I. Lenin, published and distributed by an agency subordinate to the Presidency of Mexico. Peasants, Zapotecs Indians, bilingual cultural extension workers who, punctually each month, receive a modest salary from the state so that, in relative freedom, they can think and take actions concerning their culture and a possible ethnic plan. Those who know Mexico will argue that this is simply another example of the innumerable contradictions in the complex, difficult, and delicate balance of a post-revolutionary government which has kept most sectors of the country calm, especially during periods of economic crisis. One should also observe, however that this balancing act is very close to being an open social dialectic in which, despite an inequality of conditions, the various social forces compete, expressing their own levels of consciousness and their own abilities to organize.

Those, on the other hand, who closely followed the Peruvian revolutionary process during the seventies and took a critical (or, I should say, a prudent, leftist, abstentionist) position, will argue that these indigenist measures raining down from heaven upon the ingenuous and unprepared heads of Indian ethnic groups could only lead to a certain passivity among native peoples in terms of their political consciousness and, ultimately, to a kind of demobilization. True only in part. There arose during those years in Peru some of the most militant native organizations in the recent history of Latin American ethnopolitical movements: to cite only a few, the Campa Congress, the Amuesha Congress, the Aguaruna-Huambiza Federation, the Shipibo Federation. There was a great deal of ferment during that period, and substantial progress was made in terms of the social consciousness of the Indian ethnic groups.

I see the Matsés and Zapotec ethnic groups as symbolizing and synthesizing two cultural, and therefore ethnopolitical, extremes. The first, a tribal, diminutive, Amazonian group, composed of a few subgroups living on both sides of the Peruvian-Brazilian border, represents the "ethnic plan" in an implicit, nonideological form: that of the spontaneous cultural expression of an Indian people's social and historical project, articulated not as a program or as a political platform but as a "normal" trend of development. An ethnic group, in short, producing and reproducing its own culture in initial confrontation with the surrounding, dominant society, but still essentially master of its own civilizational project. A relatively autonomous expression, a structure that, at least from appearances, is not based on a doubtful confrontation, on an identity that is questioned by the "other"—the subjugator, but is rather an affirmation of their own cultural and biological superiority. I am a Matsés, I am a human being, we are people, I am a citizen of my own world.*

---

* These people, as is well known, have for decades been the subjects of ethnological description and reflection. The development of an anthropological consciousness which recognizes that the inevitable preconditions for any reflection on the "other," on the cultural alternative, is found in colonialism, in recolonization and in class analysis, is only relatively recent, however, and its genesis and growth have received a substantive contribution from Indian thought in the Americas. At Barbados I (1971), Latin American ethnologists spoke for the Indians and called for superseding a science that was cloistered by academic thinking and aspirations. We demanded a commitment to con-

The other picture, of the Zapotecs gathered at their community center, seems to me to symbolize something different: the halting beginning of the political and cultural synthesis necessary if the Indian ethnopolitical plan is to go beyond the ideological blinders of vindication, petty chauvinism, and identity defined more by opposition than by self-affirmation. Only thus can it become articulated with a larger, more encompassing program involving the well thought-out construction of a pluralist future both for the entire country and for Latin America as a whole. I see there a group of native peasants and intellectuals who are debating their social and cultural plan with urban intellectuals, in a joint search to find some compatibility between the cultural and political aspirations and vocations of both sectors within the nation. I see the dialectical relation in which each project becomes more viable, more likely to succeed, the more it becomes the comple-

_____

structing a national space that was politically and culturally democratic, plural, and multiethnic. We demanded it of ourselves as part of our civil, intellectual struggle, and we proposed it for the Indian ethnicities of our countries who had no voice or who were silenced. Six years later, in 1977, the Indian half of the participants in Barbados II took the floor and decried the colonial character of the scientific enterprise that was controlled by the non-Indian sector of our countries (cf. Dostal 1972; Grupo de Barbados 1979).

Some of us left that second meeting with a bitter taste in our mouths; as anthropologists, we had experienced, in a concrete confrontation, what we had been stating for years in our writings: that the deeply colonial, class-structured, racist situation in our countries had masterfully alienated us from our own peoples, situating us, despite ourselves, in the ambiguous position of tactical allies. We were involved in a struggle that was not ours, constantly in need of legitimizing our participation in the Indians' liberation movement, overwhelmed by the sense of political solitude that one feels when organic militancy is absent.

The Indian half at Barbados II had abruptly faced us with the "explicit" Indian ethnopolitical project that we had been supporting. At the same time, and even more serious for us, they confronted us with the absence and neglect of an overall plan that could involve the Indian and non-Indian sectors our our countries. We were both, Indians and non-Indians, the outcome of a colonialist ideology that had managed successfully to divide us, fragment us, and make us assume that our respective historical projects were mutually incompatible. The anthropologist found himself committed to the cause of the Indian peoples' liberation more out of a sense of political activism tinged with a social-worker mentality than out of any detailed thinking about the overall future of society itself and of the countries in the region. And the indigenous intellectual community accepted that support as a form of technical assistance, advice that in no way compromised their objective of a future Indian society nor their strategy for achieving it. A misencounter between inadvertence and mistrust.

ment and alternate for the other: its respectful, necessary counterpart.

It is a matter of beginnings, and of a maturation that is occurring in other Indian regions in the hemisphere and in other liberational enterprises as well. Having gone through the necessary period of radicalization and of a Manichaean vision of the world, they are addressing one of the most critical points of the process of national liberation in our countries. And that is the recognition that national decolonization, as an objective that is still sought after, is essentially a task of cultural construction. It implies reflecting on and searching for the profound roots of all the peoples that make up our countries. And this collective search, which must confront inertia, contradictory interests, and differing images of society in the future, can be for nothing less than a shared, rational, explicit, global program based on an open consensus. The consensus must continue to attract social forces through struggles for common interests, through debate, and through cultural definitions, until that shared accumulation of cultural ideals is converted into a political bloc within the actual field of planned reconstruction of our national societies. It is in this Gramscian sense that I view the role of the Indian struggles for liberation and of our own solidarity and individual, ethnic, and class involvement as intellectuals, as we attempt to overcome the remaining links to our "traditional function" and become, increasingly, "harmonious."

INDIAN ETHNICITIES AND CIVIL SOCIETY UNDERGROUND

From the beginning, the initial fracture of the European invasion and of colonial submission left the countries and peoples of the Mesoamerican and Andean area marked by a trauma of culture and identity which, to this day, permeates the imagination of the entire society. "All of Peru," states J. Ortega (1977), "is [a] direct manifestation of the Conquest." His statement can be extended to every Andean and Mesoamerican country in which the Indian presence inevitably defines its national and cultural character. The cultural and cosmological rupture that the conquest and invasion signified did not end with the definitive establishment of a colonial administration, for it continues into the present and is lodged in every single expression of the life of our societies. "The events themselves occurred at the origin, but the transformations unleashed by them have not ceased. . . . We are living through the change itself, the drama of its madness that has no dénouement" (ibid.). Ortega claims that for this reason we live in the imminent condition of a country that is still being created, in which some standards are favored and others devalued, alternating in their exclusivity; that is, a country in which the search for a legitimate administration has met with successive failures: elites legislating on the island of a state, a form with no capacity for articulating with the country's real nations. The national states of Peru, Ecuador, Bolivia, Guatemala, and Mexico were, from the start, mirages of the desires of a few. These were of a privileged sector who built their own phantasmagoria, and have been trying to bring it to life in a continual effort to legitimize and impose a culture, a history, a language, a world-view, and a daily lifestyle which have nothing or very little to do with the various "deep-rooted peoples" that inhabit that space called a country.

Guamán Puma de Ayala, the Indian chronicler of Peru and author of the *Nueva Corónica y Buen Gobierno*, is the first witness and analyst of of the displacement experienced by the Indian nations that were invaded and ravaged by European colonialism. In that sense, he is the founder of the critical Amerindian discourse on the false and illusory nature of the forms of government and administration, and of the social order implanted in the Americas. The universal order, and its corresponding social order ("Good Government"), has been shattered. It is the start of the New Chronicle: the Indian nation begins its long and tragic history of peoples without a history, of subjugated peoples. Simultaneously, an uprooted minority, incapable of comprehending the world of their subjugation, undertakes the project of building and legitimizing an illusory, constantly counterfeit world—a more or less extemporaneous copy of the workings of ruling metropolises. A plural social whole, on which attempts—frustrated from the start—have been made to impose a single (colonial) code and (political and cultural) discourse since the rupturing moment of the invasion, has declared its dissidence and taken refuge in a culture of resistance.

Guamán Puma, Inca Garcilaso, Santa Cruz Pachacuti, and the *Popol Vuh* of the Mayans: theirs are the first arguments that, using the former order as a basis for comparison, are critical of the cultural, political, and economic regime imposed by the invaders. At the same time, they are the last manifest expressions of the Indian consciousness that had been invaded and occupied by the outsiders. After them, that critical consciousness becomes concealed and practically impenetrable. More than four centuries after the invasion, a Quechua states, "You are not Peruvians. You're Spaniards or mixed-bloods. You are members of Pizarro's family. I am Reyes, from the family of the Inkarey" (Ortiz, quoted in Pease 1973).

A tremendous civilizational rupture ensued, which the colonial regime articulated with bureaucratic precision. From the moment that the European colonial apparatus established itself in these areas of the Americas, there began the process of repressing the peoples who were subject to the ruling classes and cancelling out their history. To abolish the history and to suppress the collective memory of a people, means to veto their future, to split their consciousness of unity, to impede them from formulating their social project, to cut the roots of their collective imagination. The colonial society cleverly used repression and violence to achieve all this. Not only did they "decapitate" the native intelligentsia and co-opt those remaining members of the elite who could function as depositories and transmitters of knowledge and culture, but they also systematically tried to destroy and alter those cultural symbols that might give the subjugated peoples a sense of continuity and identity. This secular task of annulling and reinterpreting Indian history and legend was later taken up by the colonizer's heirs, the creole aristocracy and quasi-bourgeoisie that founded and tried to sustain their republics.

The official intellectual community centered itself around the miniscule minority of the ruling class that could manipulate the very definition of culture to exclude the dominated cultures. Beginning in the nineteenth century, they tried to create a national unity and connect the various collectivities, cultures, and ethnicities in a single discourse. The territory inhabited economically and politically by these diverse groups became an administrative space, the nation-state—a concept and a reality constantly remaining to be achieved (Monsiváis 1976). This is a post-, neo-, endocolonial formula for organizing lands and peoples that signifies and synthesizes the eventual triumph of mercantile relations and the consolidation and establishment of peripheral capitalism and its national class. The typical capitalist state is the market-nation-state. In postcolonial countries, however, nationality was not formed through feudal disjunction, by confining homogeneous ethnolinguistic groups within defined territorial borders, or by setting up a system of mercantile production that involved the bourgeoisie's conquest of an internal market and the political unification of territories whose populations spoke the same language. Rather, the state was erected on the foundation of an artificial national independence that, in effect, reconstructs the heterogeneous social and territorial space of the ex-colonial country to the benefit of the small, dependent ruling class that finds itself under the effective control of the central countries. And, as is well known, this external control becomes increasingly enveloping and exacting, not simply in terms of the neocolonial country's economic development, but its political, social, and cultural structure as well.

The process whereby a minority—lacking any autonomous cultural and political plan but capable of bringing people together—conceals and confuses the peoples and cultures that make up our countries, has never, in the strictest sense, resulted in the hegemony of one class. Instead, it has led only to a system of domination and repression carried out, in most cases, with naked brutality. Since the sixteenth century, our countries' neo- and endocolonial islands of government have been located exclusively within the realm of brute force, never managing to overcome it and subordinate it to an ideological consensus. In other words, they have not been able to establish any real hegemony. Since it lacks full economic and political control of the country and its administrative and governmental apparatus (the state), the servile bourgeoisie cannot exercise any cultural or moral leadership. Cultural and moral direction comes from the imperial center. Meanwhile, the subservient national elites play a vicarious, alienated role; and— except during fleeting moments of threatened patriotism or, as in the case of Mexico, during periods of revolutionary recomposition— they never take on actual moral and cultural leadership. On the contrary, given the bourgeoisie's lack of autonomy and the poverty of their program, the state, in all its authoritarian and repressive power, occupies, or at least aspires to occupy, every area of social life. To such an extent that, despite the traditionally liberal statements made by the official spokespeople for our countries, the actual, objective structure projects the image of societies occupied by an authoritarian, repressive apparatus extremely active in economic and cultural fields (education and mass communication), in which civil society is shrunken and constantly threatened. Thus there is the constant doubt in one's mind about the actual capitalist character of our societies, if by capitalism one understands the bourgeoisie's historical project par excellence.

The result of all of this is an apparent absence or clandestinization of civil society—or rather, the civil societies that make up the "deep" country. I suggest the plural term—civil societies—precisely in order to underscore the nonintegration and disarticulation of our societies, in which a complex of peoples or ethnic groups carry out parallel cultural and political lives and come into contact with the mestizo, national sectors of the country through the labor market and through weak attempts at regional markets, which, quite obviously, should comprise the actual structural skeleton for integrating the national state within capitalist development or the modern nation-state.

I use the concept of civil society here in the wide Hegelian sense and in the more specific Marxian and Gramscian senses. As N. Bobbio (1977) has shown, the latter two differ from one another. For Marx, it is "the entire complex of material relations . . . the true home, the stage of history"; that is to say, the structural moment. For A. Gramsci, on the other hand, civil society is essentially the superstructural moment, the complex of ideological-cultural relations (ibid., 34–35). Civil society (both in its structural moment: Marx; and in its superstructural moment: Gramsci) represents the active, positive field of historical development and not the state, or political society, as Hegel maintained. Within this framework, it must be understood that the Indian ethnic groups are subjugated through economic domination, and not through any full, accomplished hegemony of political society, i.e., the state. The neo- and endocolonial bourgeoisies have failed, totally or in part (as in the case of Mexico), to create first a true nation-state and secondly a class hegemony which would allow them ideological and cultural control (and not merely the use of repression) over the peoples of the nation. This leaves the ethnic groups with a fairly wide margin of cultural and political autonomy, which they have been utilizing to produce and reproduce their own "implicit" ethnic projects. The creole and mestizo bourgeoisies' ineffectiveness in constructing plans suitable for autonomous national states becomes a positive factor in the resistance and disagreement of the different social groups and their projects—"long-term" cultural projects that resist and reproduce themselves through encapsulation, that are felt and experienced rather than reasoned through. They persist beyond the reach of all those personal wills that disown them within the ethnic group, declaring the uselessness of their own language and culture and the superiority of their subjugators. These last are signs of the subordinate position of the Indian ethnic group's culture, a subordination that will end once the ethnic groups win their independence and autonomy. Because what does subordinate culture mean in this case, if not the fact that, for historical reasons, the Indian ethnic groups' potentialities and civilizational projects have been forestalled and that they themselves have been kept submissive and deprived?

CULTURE AND PRODUCTION

Nevertheless, where the "national" ruling class—the dependent bourgeoisie—fails, the transnationalized sector of the same class may have a degree of success. As deputy for the imperial project, it may achieve a consensus on lifestyle and daily living by spreading and imposing a uniform world-view, homogenized culture, planned aspirations and, above all, patterns of consumption that seep into every crack of the social mechanisms of cultural reproduction. Elsewhere I have taken Marx's statements on consumption (especially Varese 1982) and applied them to the question of cultural penetration and resistance and the reproduction of ethnic groups as particular, differentiated sociocultural entities. In brief, following the Marx of the *Grundrisse* (1972, passim), I stated that in producing an object for a subject, every society, every ethnic and cultural group also produces a specific subject for the consumption, the use of that object. The product is realized only through consumption; this gives rise to needs for a new production which, therefore, does not simply produce an object, but a given "style" of object that is to be used and consumed in a given (one might say "ethnic") manner. As a result, production objectively and subjectively produces a specific mode of consumption, so that "production not only produces an object for the subject, but a subject for the object as well" (Marx, ibid.). As social groups, ethnic groups, and national societies lose autonomy and control over the productive process, and as they further the process of alienation of labor, becoming "workers" in productive processes planned wholly from the outside and articulated like a sum of fragments without any apparent sense, the object produced produces an alienated subject, a "user," a consumer who has been preconditioned from outside his own society and cultural patterning. The organic link between mode of production and mode of consumption—that is to say, between the cultural object produced by and for a specific cultural subject, and a subject that is located again and reproduced in its own production—is broken and destroyed by the mass, transnationalized process of preconditioned, anonymous production and consumption. It cannot be identified as part of one's own culture and of the symbols that synthesize it and give meaning to life, to work, and to the consumption of the product of labor.

This process radically affects the specific ethnic culture and identity (indigenous, mestizo, and creole) in our countries. They are made uniform, homogenized, emptied of any autonomous specificity, will, or creativity. Not so much through the cultural hegemony of the ruling classes and the servile bourgeoisies, but rather through the global process of expanding and implanting a transnationalized, imperial economy, our countries and peoples have been divided into differentiated, unequal, and apparently unarticulated sections, distinct pockets of production. It must be pointed out here that the political and cultural aspects are not separate from the economic: the distinction we make between economic and political orders is not an organic one, but is merely an analytic tool (Portantiero 1980, 5). Culture is production (and mode of consumption), and production is culture; and any alteration made in the world of labor and productive relations is substantially reflected in culture. The opposite is true, as well: cultural, scientific, and technological innovations, changes, and losses, affect and modify production. Thus when we speak of economic dependency, penetration, neocolonialism, we are referring to a far-reaching phenomenon that profoundly affects a subordinate people's culture: it causes that people to lose their cultural and civilizational autonomy, and transforms them from cultural creator to passive user, consumer, and alienated reproducer of a foreign culture.

Today in southeastern Mexico, in Oaxaca, of the hundreds of

varieties of corn that this Indian region produced during centuries of cultural creativity, there remain only a few dozen in use; and the region, subjected to production plans arising out of the international division of labor, must now import corn in order to satisfy its basic food needs. Naturally, it produces coffee and sugarcane to feed remote industries. In his increasing genericness, the Zapotec or Chinantec peasant who does his own labor bears an increasing resemblance to any Páez, Amuesha, or Chiriguano peasant of Colombia, Peru, or Bolivia. He is more and more a subject produced for an object that has little or nothing to do with his real needs—an object which is the "insumption"—the proffering of absorption—of an industrial pattern that is alien to his life and to the cultural trajectory of his ever more ethnic group. He himself is a simple product of absorption who demonstrates the temporary victory of the whole system as he exploits himself and identifies less and less with the specificity of his culture, his environment and, consequently, the possibility of structuring an autonomous social project that would really suit his aspirations.

The question of cultural independence and autonomy, therefore, cannot be divorced from the concrete level of production. I think we can expand on the separation that N. Bobbio (ibid.) points out between a civil society belonging to the structural moment in its relations of production (Marx) and a civil society belonging to the superstructural moment (Gramsci). For we can see culture and analyze it as an integral phenomenon, a process that emerges from the structure and submerges itself in that structure, modifying it through constant interaction in which one cannot isolate, separate, and freeze two moments, one structural and the other superstructural. The culture of a people is its production, its objects, its works, the specific mode in which they are used, the style contained in the work from the very moment of its production. The culture of a people includes decisions about production (producing an object for a subject and a subject for the object), consumption, ideas about both moments of social reproduction, and decisions and fundamental definitions concerning surplus. For every people and every historical moment has defined surplus differently, assigning it a qualitatively different use, which in the end has also defined, through its uniqueness, the group and its civilization. Surplus can be accumulated or not; it can be spent lavishly to increase the "prestige fund" (Godelier 1977), or authority; it can be extracted through physical or ideological violence, designated for the construction of temples, monuments, aesthetic works, for concerts. It can also be burned systematically and obsessively, so as to avoid its being used as a basis for differences between people. Or, as those who have lived among pre-peasant peoples, Amazonian horticulturalists and hunters, know, one of the principal axes that defines a society of this type is, precisely, the nonproduction of surpluses—unless we include in our understanding of surplus the abundant free time thus obtained, giving rise to the creative leisure that manifests itself, among other things, in marvelous creations, mythical fantasies, ethics and aesthetics. A spiritual culture that gives to the transformation of material—as a civilizational activity—only secondary, tenuous importance compared to feather arts, body painting, or even the periodic ritual construction and destruction of magnificent ceramics, confirms that laborious material production is only one of the faces of creative power.

CULTURE AND CONSCIOUSNESS

It is within this perspective that I consider the cultural question as a total, encompassing extension of any reflection on ethnicity and nation-building. Consequently, I see culture as a field of political formulation and action—because culture includes the structural moment (relations of production, distribution, and mode of consumption) as well as the superstructural moment (representations, symbols, ideas about production, the definition and destination of surplus). At the same time it is potentially the sphere in which a people's individual and collective consciousness can be fashioned and expressed: the concrete, specific framework in which there is on-going synthesis and symbolization (in a particular language, an exclusive semantic world belonging to each ethnic group) of both the past and the present. To recognize this law is to affirm culture's encompassing nature, the primacy of the spiritual aspect over its concrete material manifestations. It also affirms that a people can become conscious of their creative capacity and potential and, further, give form to a social plan as they critically examine their culture—the total complex of their social life. Thus, I identify culture as a dimension of consciousness that is the reflection of objective reality through physical, neural, and mental mechanisms. Consciousness includes reason, emotion, will, imagination. It is the loftiest, most promising expression of the organized matter in that complex phenomenon that we call man. But consciousness is, by definition, a social phenomenon with a biological foundation: it originates and develops as an integral part of people's social activity. It is constructed within a given historical, spatial, social, cultural, and linguistic framework. As Marx said, language not only expresses consciousness, it is consciousness itself. The connection between consciousness and culture, therefore, is linguistic. In every society's language, specific to each as a secularly accumulated, condensed praxis (Schaff 1975), "individual consciousness" is expressed as a social product which each person manifests; a spiritual world that expresses the social (historical, cultural) through the unique life of each individual.

But the social aspect is not an indistinct, undifferentiated whole. It includes groups, interests, cultural forms, which is to say that there are classes, ethnic groups, subcultures. To state that consciousness is social is to maintain that it is formed within a given sector, class, or ethnic group. Consciousness is, therefore, class, group, or ethnic consciousness, which can be expressed as "consciousness itself," "real consciousness," or as "consciousness for itself," "possible consciousness" (to paraphrase and quote Marx and L. Goldmann, respectively). It is only through critically examining ethnic consciousness (realization of its own, unique, civilizational tradition and vocation) and class consciousness (socially shared knowledge and understanding of the fact that their interests as a group, on the economic and social plane, are in opposition to those of another group, and that that opposition is expressed as a struggle to suppress relations of domination) that a group can truly become master of its own culture and make it into the means for transforming and rebuilding society.

CONSCIOUSNESS AND HEGEMONY

This reflective, programmatic search implies an organizational dimension, for it obviously cannot be left to the random chance of occasional, individual initiatives. We enter here the area of hegemony-building, which is always the product of a clear social consciousness and its application. A people cannot create a hegemony without developing institutions and apparatus, without a structured application of political, cultural, and ideological struggle. The theory of hegemony is part of the basis for the theory of organization (Gramsci, quoted in Portantiero 1980). It is therefore important to avoid the simplification of attributing to it an exclusively superstructural character, confusing it with the state apparatus and its ideology; or reducing the state itself to an entity separate from civil society. Instead, the state should be understood as the dynamic product of correlating forces that comprise and envelop all of society: a complex of articulations, contradictory relations, and mediations (Portantiero 1980, 2). The state in this regard is a field of forces (Kaplan 1984), and every crisis within it signifies a change in the relation between the subordinate classes (and ethnicities) and the administrative apparatus of the ruling classes. Thus, a crisis always offers a possibility for the subordinate classes and ethnicities to further counter-hegemonic action, that is, to reconstitute *themselves* into a hegemony (Portantiero 1980, passim).

I see here certain essential questions that need to be clarified. In the majority of Andean and Mesoamerican countries, or in certain regions of those countries, the "retainers of the nation" (Mariátegui, quoted in Franco n. d.) are principally Indians. The ethno-cultural, historical, and civilizational background of this specific characteristic is obviously important, but it does not exclude it from class analysis and praxis. And therefore, as Mariátegui realized in the case of Peru, the national question for these countries is the Indian question. This Indian question, however, is a problem of class and culture; of relations of production and superstructure; of relations of production and political behavior—all mediated by the culture(s) not merely of one subordinate people (one popular class), but rather of many peoples, many ethnic groups, many popular classes.

Thus, in our countries the construction of a popular hegemony, a counter-hegemony to civil society, is a plural enterprise: it is the hegemonic construction of subordinate ethnic groups (and classes) who together comprise the majority "retainers" of the nation. Therefore, the construction or reconstitution of a set of hegemonies is a prior, inevitable step. This, of course, implies the formation of a clear ethnic and class consciousness that will serve as a basis for transforming ethnicities with implicit economic and cultural aims into ethnicities with explicit political ones, or "corporative ethnicities" into "hegemonic ethnicities" (I am using here an adaptation of the Gramscian concept).

The step is from a corporative consciousness bent on limited vindication, that only aims to acquire those benefits that the ruling class and its state are willing to yield, to a hegemonic field of struggle. The difference is between corporative and political action, between an ethnic consciousness that focuses on the immediate present and ethno-national and class consciousness. The process of forming an ethno-national consciousness that clearly identifies the ethnic group's historical role on the national scene and in the overall social plan must of necessity go through the arduous tasks of demystifying one's own history and culture; of rejecting ethnocentric, chauvinistic positions; of recognizing the advantages of a dialectic between opposites; and of knowing, therefore, how to appropriate—and transform—the culture of the subjugator. Corporative ethnic consciousness is generic: it develops through perceiving and experiencing cultural differences and diversity, the singularity of one's own traditions as opposed to those of the other, dominant society. It is a consciousness which, originating from an initial cultural focus and from the relationship between expressions of diversity and specificity, can become transformed into a class consciousness which is also ethno-national. This occurs upon the realization that, in many cases, cultural specificity is simply a manifestation of colonial mutilations, shortcomings, and submission. In this regard, the moment of corporative ethnic consciousness is important in the political and cultural development of every people.

It precedes ethno-national class consciousness; but the latter, once it forms, does not eliminate it upon surpassing it, but rather expresses itself through it. It is the particular (ethnic, national) mode for expressing the class consciousness of a people and, consequently, the revolutionary social thrust of an Indian ethnic type.

Within this creative task of Indian ethnic groups, historical memory and consciousness play a fundamental role. The historical consciousness of an ethnic group, of a people, must be distinguished from its historical memory. For the latter comprises a nostalgic respect for one's own collective, cultural past, viewed generically and indeterminately, in which cultural heroes, events, and feats are placed in single, indiscriminate, and homogeneous past time. Rescuing and re-valuing a people's historic memory is of fundamental importance for its institutions, its intellectuals and the Indian people themselves, but it is not sufficient. Rather, it should be seen as a necessary step in the cultural and political liberation of native peoples that will contribute towards building a critical and clear historic consciousness.

None of these cultural and deeply political tasks is easy. Several centuries of social, economic, cultural, linguistic, and political fragmentation and submission have created serious obstacles. To critically retrieve one's history, to elucidate one's cultural consciousness and construct a social plan that is at once viable and compatible with the project of greater national liberation, is not simply a matter of political will. It requires long and exhausting concrete study and analysis, reflection and proposals. It entails hegemonic—and therefore organizational—theory and practice.

These applications of theory, in effect, give the civil society its contours and substance, causing it to emerge once again from underground. There it had been long cloistered with no aspiration to reoccupy the total field of struggle. And it is in this civil society, a social space in which the relations of forces are expressed, debated, and reconciled, that the ethnic group with hegemonic consciousness comes into being and grows—a process whereby the Indian ethnic group produces itself as an historical subject and ceases to be the object of neocolonial relations. And as it does so, the Indian ethnic group retrieves, incorporates, and develops a multiplicity of cultural and political applications, actions, and principles. It reconstructs its unity as a political subject based on a multiplicity and diversity that, to a large extent, were also produced through colonial fragmentation and disarticulation.

I turn here to the thoughts of J. C. Mariátegui, as analyzed by the Peruvian author C. Franco. All the retainers of a nation—Indians and non-Indians alike—must come together autonomously through their own organizations, means of expression, cultural strategies, vindications, and political mobilization, in a political and cultural act of convergence and national formation (reformulation). It is therefore necessary to lend suport to the process of forming and institutionalizing all of the nation's social actors, seeking, said Mariátegui, a cultural and poltical consensus. In other words, a hegemonic plan (again, in the almost modern Gramscian expression).

Only a very broad, pluralistic conception of the production of a hegemonic bloc of national unity, in which the different hegemonic spaces can play their political and historical roles in democratic equality, can lead to establishing a kind of socialism that is truly responsive to the culturally diverse, multiethnic nature of our countries. The formation of a hegemony (process and strategy) thus entails constructing new elements for the national society and putting them into play even before power is transferred. Because, in this line of thinking, it is evident that revolution and national reformulation are processes, not moments; and that the struggle for power is the struggle for hegemony. It cannot be diminished, or confused with pro-coup positions, courtier, high-level victories that occur at the apex of the institutional superstructure and the political society, but remain alien to the civil society, the peoples of the country. Without necessarily taking a "gradualist" position, it is therefore clear that hegemony-building is in the political and cultural long-run, and not in the trade guild short-run of the "counter-class class." Qualitatively and not necessarily quantitatively long-run, for we know that cultural time and times of awareness are heterogeneous, cumulative and erratic, and therefore progress and become pressing in spurts. And during these moments when consciousness is being stirred and revolutionized, these festive times of the spirit granted so that the people can show their will, debate should be initiated: always prior to, and not following the program (Mariátegui).

These are disputes which gradually define the great cultural themes of the society that is being intentionally rebuilt, disputes in which the Indian ethnic groups, as traditional, collective dissidents, are in a better position to question the models and alternatives that are being chosen. Their historical distance, in most cases, from the logic of the exchange value, along with their link to forms and structures of reciprocity, bring them close to the truly socialist ideal, in which the profit principle is not a precondition nor a primary element in the whole productive and labor system. It is an undertaking that must question the industrialist ideology that is presented as enveloping and homologous to "progress," and instead must propose the issue of the quality of life as the fundamental indicator of development, focusing on cultural factors rather than the simple components of economic indices.

In this perspective of a multiethnic, national confluence centered around a project of national construction that radically questions quantitative development models, the Indian ethnic groups in our countries perform an essential role as a reservoir and bearer of alternative civilizational forms and patrimonies. This does not mean that one should take populist or Rousseauian positions, attributing to the masses of Indian ethnic groups a precapitalist "purity" which, in the great majority of the cases, has clearly been radically altered over the centuries of colonialism and of integration with peripheral capitalism. In the first place, it must be recognized that while social thinking has accepted cultural relativity, the same is not true concerning possible societal models and development. There is no established school of thought regarding the relativity of development. Also, it becomes a question of identifying the qualitative distance between Indian ethnic groups, in all their phases and modes of articulation, and the other national groups that comprise our countries.

INDIAN MODES OF PRODUCTION AND HEGEMONIC PLANS

Elsewhere (cf. Varese 1982, 153–55) I have noted the principal characteristics of this qualitative distance. Here I shall summarize those ideas. Out of the vast, complex panorama of the continent's nationalities and ethnicities, it is possible to distinguish an elementary typology concerning the mode of producing essential material goods. This typology consists of two basic modes: a) the domestic mode of production according to M. Sahlins' initial definition and the later elaborations made by C. Meillassoux; and b) the simple mercantile mode of production. In other words, all of the indigenous ethnic groups of Latin America, as collectivities, belong in one or the other of these two modes. Which means that the numerous tribal microethnic groups in the so-called marginal and tropical areas, according to the classical definition by A. Métraux and J. Steward (1946–59), constitute pre-peasant societies; while the macroethnic groups and nationalities in Andean and Mesoamerican regions are peasant societies. We are defining peasant society here as one governed by an economc system in which part of the production satisfies subsistence needs, while the rest, the "surplus," enters the circuit of commercial exchange through the capitalist market.

It is obvious that today, among the ethnic groups in Latin America, these two modes of production have undergone considerable change, depending upon the extent to which the surrounding, dominant capitalist mode has penetrated and dominated; in this respect, one can speak of "modes of production in transition," as P. P. Rey put it. Nevertheless, what I would like to point out here with regard to indigenous ethnicities is that in both modes there is the objective of producing use values. Among tribal ethnicities that have a domestic mode of production, the production of use values is the principal economic and social objective. On the other hand, among indigenous peasant ethnicities that have a simple mercantile economy, the production of use values (the area of subsistence and reciprocity) is in constant competitive tension with the production of exchange values, and this competition becomes more acute as the capitalist economy penetrates further.

Why focus on this aspect of the production of use values in relation to the modes of production and economies of Indian ethnic groups? Because, in essence, a style of civilization, a culture, a given ethnicity can be defined through the way in which the society has organized historically, and in the present, the utilization of use values and the definition and consignment of surpluses, as we have seen. To the extent that an Indian ethnic group autonomously and collectively manages this aspect of its cultural life, its ideology and world-view, without allowing itself to be enslaved by the hegemony of the capitalist culture—that is, by the primacy of exchange value—it can be said that there is some cultural independence and, consequently, the potential for an autonomous decision with regard to plans for the future.

To summarize:

a) *Use value* dominates the internal social relations of pre-peasant Indian ethnicities that have a domestic economy (domestic mode of production). The vast majority of (tribal) microethnicities located in geographical zones that are still marginal, or that have been marginalized by the expansion of the capitalist frontier, fall into this category. Historically, these ethnic groups have not experienced social-class differentiation, centralization of power, urbanization, accumulation of surplus (although they may have produced it). There appear to be two basic principles underlying these ethnic groups' social relations: (1) symmetrical reciprocity; and (2) the amassing of authority (not power) based on one's ability to expend, on social and ritual occasions, any surplus produced. Both principles keep the social group equalized and undifferentiated in terms of the emergence of possible classes, or segments of social classes.

b) *Exchange value* is present in the internal and external relations of peasant macroethnicities. It is in constant tension with use value, which tends to govern relations within the community but which is constantly threatened and displaced by exchange value, whose scope increases as surrounding capitalist relations predominate. Under this heading fall all the large Indian ethnic groups of Mesoamerica and the Andean region, the peasant macroethnic groups. As descendants of agrarian civilizations, these groups historically have had social experiences of decided importance: a social class structure; a state apparatus at different levels and modes of development; a centralization of power; urbanization; accumulation of surplus; development of a system of exchange via the market; the notion and implementation of tribute.

The logic of the social relations of these ethnic groups can be generalized as the opposition between use value and exchange value. In other words, between, on the one hand, those principles governing reciprocity, symmetrical and nonmonetary exchange, the attainment of authority through lavish, wasteful spending and the successive fulfillment of social duties (the "*cargos*" of authority), and the obligatory economic leveling achieved by this control on accumulation; and, on the other hand, the whole set of opposite principles: accumulation and savings, investment, denial and abandonment of reciprocity, accumulation of power through economic means; substitution of the criterion of authority founded on the accumulation of hierarchical community services by criteria of power and force.

This constant tension in which the peasant ethnic communities live and that, we repeat, intensifies and increases as the enveloping capitalist system is introduced within the ethnic structure, defines in a general way the cultural style of these ethnic groups; at the same time it sets the framework for their aspirations and social goals. The issue here, obviously, is not to postulate a mechanistic position, but to identify general tendencies within social processes which apparently are highly diversified and irreducible to general interpretative schemes.

The above outline can be condensed into a formula even more daring. The logic behind both capitalist productive and financial organization, and the industrialist and productivist solutions of historical socialism, is *accumulation*. The logic of Indian ethnic economies, both in the domestic and small mercantile modes of production, is anti-accumulation; in the latter, lavish expenditure is the foundation of each person's social legitimacy and the basis for prestige and authority.

Once this qualitative difference is recognized, the hegemonic plan must be to recover these attributes and give them a significant role in the overall national model. This means discarding economic determinism (vulgar Marxism) and technological optimism (a bourgeois conception of progress), both of which serve to sustain the illusion of a unilinear, homogenizing, exclusive evolutionism. But once again the concept of culture comes into play as the pivot of analytical discussion and praxis: culture is not simply the accumulation of achievements; it is what makes possible and gives meaning to the relations between the individuals who share it. By opening up and multiplying the various cultural expressions and constructs, hegemonic confluence and concurrence creates a broadened, intensified arena for cultural reformulation. And by including different peoples and their cultures and different geographic spaces which have been humanized (defined culturally), it points towards what the Yugoslavs call "geopolitical civilization": a multinational, multiethnic configuration in constant dialectical tension towards progressive syntheses achieved through open dialogue in an open society.

Therefore, culture, as the critical dimension of the overriding consciousness and synthesis of the entire social process, must be the center of articulation in the goal of constructing a plural, multiethnic, socialist nation. A project which in no way can be limited to a paltry administrative decision to socialize the means of production, it is, rather, the continuation of the dialectical process of hegemonic construction in which the most important, most fundamental socialization is that of people who, "fully conscious of the contradictions," develop a free social behavior characterized by solidarity, unhampered by the external apparatus that may be imposed (Hobsbawm, 1978, passim). In this way a multiethnic, pluralist socialism identifies with the process of building a popular and national collective will that involves all of the peoples, all of the nations of the nation-to-be. This political art of merging all the propensities and contributions, according to J. C. Mariátegui, is precisely the fulfillment of the nation within socialism. It is also, quite obviously, the affirmation of a multiple dialectic in which there is no thesis or antithesis to be eliminated and suppressed. Because one minus one is always and inevitably zero, that is, destruction, disappearance, and death—just as the impoverishment of the antithesis ends in reformism, and the weakness of the thesis in the immature voluntarism of the left.

The challenge that I see in this dialectic of a hegemonic merging is an enormous one for each and every one of the sectors and ethnicities, bearers of the nation-to-be. This is because it assumes that, in the face of the most easily and comfortably selected, incontrovertible truths, dialogue and reason will ensue; because it supports the critical rescuing of the very objectives of the civilization (what is to be discarded or preserved, and why), making them the subject of collective debate. It is a challenge that is presented to the collectivity and the individual, one that engages the "intellectual," the militant, the cultural reproducer; that implies the absence of any right to grant certificates or degrees that will guarantee one's revolutionary commitment or theoretical infallibility. But even more complex is the problem of the democracy that must regulate relations within the organizations generated by our civil societies (both Indian and non-Indian), and the balance that must be struck among the combination of organizations representing different—although objectively complementary—cultural and political interests, aspirations, and vocations.

The obstacles that must be overcome bear the same colonial and authoritarian weight for all the members of our civil societies. Historically, none of the sectors has tended to the development and functioning of its own political and cultural institutions. Instead, the latter, in their obsolete forms, have dragged undiscriminatingly behind programs and initiatives proclaiming a substitution of the opposite, not realizing that another enemy was harbored within.

AFTERWORD

Today, I learn of the death of seven native Colombian Paéz men, members of the Regional Indigenous Council of Cauca (CRIC), at the hands of the Sixth Front of the Revolutionary Armed Forces of Colombia (FARC), which claims to have "executed" them on the grounds of their being "counterrevolutionary" and "divisive" elements. I add these victims to the thousands, the millions of Indians and Latin Americans uselessly sacrificed out of the brutal ignorance of reaction and reaction in the revolution. And I recall with anguish that mixture of authority and authoritiarianism, of verticality and submission, of the domestication of the imagination that one witnesses, in surprising and repeated similarity, in some of the native communal assemblies in southern Mexico and then inevitably compares with similar experiences in other arenas of our societies. Colonial—and perhaps even precolonial—inheritances. Ancient, internal beasts locked up at the end of the labyrinth spoken about in the cosmology of the Papago Indians on the U.S.-Mexico border, which awaits a renewed cultural hero who cyclically, generation after generation, will be victorious in an old and new effort to establish, in the negation and affirmation of the past, the present of future society.

REFERENCES

Bobbio, Norberto. 1977. *Gramsci y la concepción de la sociedad civil*. Barcelona: Editorial Avance.

Dostal, Walter, ed. 1972. *The situation of the Indian in South America*. Geneva: World Council of Churches.

Franco, Carlos. n.d. "Sobre la idea de nación en José Carlos Mariátegui." Manuscript.

Garcilaso de la Vega, Inca. 1609. *Comentarios reales de los incas*. Buenos Aires: Emecé Editores, 1943.

Godelier, Maurice. 1977. *Perspectives in Marxist Anthropology*. Cambridge: Cambridge University Press.

Goldmann, Lucien. 1970. *Marxisme et sciences humaines*. Paris: Gallimard.

Grupo de Barbados. 1979. *Indianidad y descolonización en América Latina*. Mexico: Editorial Nueva Imagen.

Guamán Poma de Ayala, Felipe. fl. 1613. *Nueva Corónica y Buen Gobierno* (Codex péruvien illustré), Paris: Institut d'ethnologie, 1936 (English version: *Letters to the King*, edited by Christopher Dilke, [New York: Dutton, 1978]).

Hobsbawm, Eric J. et al. 1978a. "La ciencia política de Gramsci." In *El pensamiento revolucionario de Gramsci*. Mexico: Editorial de la Universidad Autonoma de Puebla.

_____ 1978b. "Gramsci y la teoría política." In *El pensamiento revolucionario de Gramsci*. Mexico: Editorial de la Universidad Autonoma de Puebla.

Kaplan, Marcos. 1984. *Estado y sociedad en América Latina*. Mexico: Oasis.

Libro de Chilam Balam de Chumayel. 1941. Mexico: Universidad Nacional Autonoma.

Marx, Karl. 1972. *Elementos fundamentales para la critica de la economía política, 1857–1858. (Borrador)*. Vol. I. Mexico: Siglo XXI Editores.

Meillassoux, Claude. 1981. *Maidens, Meals and Money: Capitalism and the Domestic Community*. Cambridge and New York: Cambridge University Press.

Monsivaís, Carlos. 1976. "La nación de unos cuantos y las esperanzas románticas." In *En torno a la cultura nacional*, edited by Hector Aguilar Camín, J. J. Blanco, N. Girón, C. Monsivaís, J. E. Pacheco, and S. Varese. Colección SEP-INI, 51. Mexico: Instituto Nacional Indigenista: Secretaría de Educación Pública.

Ortega, Julio. 1977. "La cultura peruana: experiencia y carencia." *Escritura* 11, no. 3 (January-June).

Ortiz, Alejandro in Franklin Pease. 1973. *El dios creador andino*. Lima: Mosca Azul Editores.

Popol Vuh. Ca. 1554–58. (Advertencia, versión y vocabulario de Albertina Saravia). Mexico: Editorial Porrua, 1975.

Portantiero, Juan Carlos. 1980. "Notas sobre la crises y producción de acción hegemónica." Paper presented at the Seminario sobre Hegemonía y Alternativas Políticas en America Latina, Instituto de Investigaciones Sociales, de la UNAM. Morelia, Michoacán, February.

Rey, P. P. 1975. "The Lineage Mode of Production." *Critique of Anthropology* 3.

Sahlins, Marshal. 1972. *Stone Age Economics*. Chicago: Aldine-Atherton.

Santa Cruz Pachacuti Yamqui, Joan. 1613. *Relación de antiquedades deste reyno del Perú*. Madrid: Biblioteca de Autores Españoles, 1968.

Schaff, Adam. 1975. *Lenguaje y conocimiento*. Mexico: Grijalvo.

Steward, Julian, ed. 1946–59. *Handbook of South American Indians*. 7 vols. Washington: Smithsonian Institution.

Varese, Stefano. 1982. "Limites y posibilidades del desarrolio de las etnias indias en el marco del estado nacional." In *America Latina: Etnodesarrollo y Etnocidio*, edited by G. Bonfil, M. Ibarra, S. Varese, D. Veríssimo et al. San Jose, Costa Rica: Ediciones FLACSO.

Agrarian Structure and Ethnic Resistance: the Indian in Guatemalan and Salvadoran National Politics

SHELTON H. DAVIS

INTRODUCTION

In 1892, to mark the fourth centenary of Columbus's discovery of America, the government of José María Reyna Barrios in Guatemala awarded a prize for the best essay on the history of the Mayan Indians, as well as the "most adequate and economic methods of civilizing them." The winner of this prize was Antonio Batres Jáuregui, a well-known Guatemalan lawyer and intellectual and one of the major defenders of late nineteenth-century Central American liberalism. In his essay, Batres Jáuregui noted that while the Indian population of Guatemala had nearly tripled since the beginning of the century, it still lacked the economic dynamism of the non-Indian, or ladino, sector of the population. Citing John Stuart Mill's *Principles of Political Economy*, Batres Jáuregui argued that the infamous *mandamientos* or forced labor laws, reintroduced under the regime of Justo Rufino Barrios in 1877 as a way of mobilizing Indian labor for the nascent Guatemalan coffee industry, held the Indian population in a condition of virtual slavery and prevented its members from experiencing individual liberty. According to Batres Jáuregui, these laws explained the low level of productivity in the Indian sector of the agricultural economy and the fact that the Republic failed to produce sufficient food crops and basic grains.[1]

Batres Jáuregui also attacked the continuing existence of Indian systems of land tenure and the ineffectiveness of Spanish land laws. He claimed that even those laws which were instituted following the Reform Period in 1871 to promote commercial agriculture, benefited only the large landowners and the ladino sector of the population. The Indian, he wrote, continued "to live under a primitive system of communal property ownership, which represents epochs of poverty and backwardness."[2]

After surveying the general backwardness of several Indian townships, including the famous Mayan ceremonial center of Chichicastenango, Batres Jáuregui suggested that the government should follow the examples of Chile and Argentina, introducing a Rural Code which would integrate Indians into the wider political economy. Such a code, he said, should abolish Indian communal lands, regulate the contracting of rural laborers, and prepare Indians to become members of modern society through the teaching of Spanish and the introduction of new agricultural and industrial arts. "It is necessary," Batres Jáuregui wrote, "that the agrarian laws, along with fomenting the development of agriculture, should bring the aborigines along the road of civilization."[3] Civilization, he asserted, "is contagious and it expands and infiltrates those people who are closest to centers of culture and commerce."[4]

Antonio Batres Jáuregui's essay is one of the clearest statements by a late nineteenth-century liberal intellectual on the fate of Central America's large indigenous population. Throughout the final quarter of the last century, all of the Central American republics—following the example of Mexico—passed laws calling for the private titling of communal and *ejido* lands and the eventual dissolution of the Indian community, which they saw as an obstacle to national progress and economic growth. As Octavio Paz has written of Mexico, the protagonists of the Reform Law "projected the founding of a new society. That is to say, the historical project of the liberals was to replace the colonial tradition, based on Catholic doctrine, with an affirmation equally universal, the freedom of the individual."[5]

This essay follows the Indian communities of two Central American countries— Guatemala and El Salvador—in the wake of the agrarian laws of the late nineteenth century. While the political, economic, and legislative changes of the Reform Period caused widespread social dislocation, Indians responded by protecting their communal institutions and reaffirming their right to exist as distinct ethnic groups. At first, they clung tenaciously to native religious traditions. Later, they responded by participating more actively in national political movements. Since the 1930s, their role in national politics has been an enormously important one.

A major thesis of this essay is that the native communities of Guatemala and El Salvador, along with being the main victims of capitalist agricultural development and repressive state policies, have also been among the most active proponents of a new and more just society. This activism was certainly present in El Salvador in 1932, when the Pipil-speaking Indian communities of the southwestern part of the country rose up in revolt against the newly imposed government of General Maximiliano Hernández Martínez. More recently, it has been present in Guatemala, where large parts of the country's 3.5 million Mayan Indians joined forces with a revolutionary guerrilla movement to try to overthrow the military regimes which held power since 1954.

The long, and often tragic, struggles of Indians to participate in national society is a vital but little understood feature of the current Central American crisis.

INDIANS AND THE COFFEE REPUBLIC

In at least three of the Central American countries, the process of capitalist agricultural development—what the Guatemalan sociologist Edelberto Torres Rivas describes as the "definitive insertion [of Central America] in the world market economy"—began with the late nineteenth-century production and export of coffee. By the mid-1880s, coffee comprised 75 percent of the value of all exports in Costa Rica, 85 percent in Guatemala, and 53 percent in El Salvador. Yet there were vital differences in the domestic effects that coffee production had on the social structures of these countries.

In Costa Rica, where the crop was first planted, coffee was produced on relatively small estates owned by immigrant farmers, and with a salaried, non-Indian labor force. In Guatemala and El Salvador, on the other hand, the expansion of coffee production depended upon the private expropriation of Indian communal lands and the mobilization of Indian labor.[6]

Guatemala, with a population of 1.5 million Indians at the end of the nineteenth century, led the way in preparing the legal groundwork for coffee production. In the 1870s, Justo Rufino Barrios, the architect of the Guatemalan Liberal Reform, promulgated a series of decrees promoting the early development of coffee production in the Alta Verapaz and the Pacific Piedmont regions. Between 1871 and 1883, the Barrios government sold over 397,000 hectares of public lands to coffee planters in what are today the richest and most productive areas of the country. Many of these lowland coffee areas, such as the famous Costa Cuca, had previously been cultivated by highland Indian subsistence farmers.[7]

Barrios also reinstated the colonial institution of the *mandamiento*, which forced Indians to work for the new coffee planters. His 1876 decree to his *jefes políticos*, or regional political bosses, stated:

If we abandon the farmers to their own resources and do not give them strong and energetic aid, they will be unable to make progess, for all their efforts will be doomed to failure due to the deceit of the Indians. [Therefore], you should see to it: First, that the Indian villages in your jurisdiction be forced to give the number of hands to the farmers that the latter ask for, even to the number of 50 and a 100 to a single farmer if his enterprise warrants this number. Second, when one set of Indians has not been able to finish the work in hand in a period of two weeks, a second set should be sent to relieve the first, so that work may not be delayed. Third, the two weeks work shall be paid for ahead of time by the mayor of the Indian town, thus avoiding the loss of time involved in paying every day. Fourth, above all else see to it that any Indian who seeks to evade this duty is punished to the full extent of the law, that the farmers are fully protected and that each Indian is forced to do a full day's work while in service.[8]

A special rural labor law in 1877 forced all rural workers to carry a document showing their labor obligations, legalized the system of *mozos colonos*, or resident workers and sharecroppers on coffee plantations, and regulated the flow of Indian laborers from the highland townships to the coastal coffee farms.[9]

The national government also called for the registration and titling of all municipal and communal lands. Table 1 shows the amount of land granted by Presidential decree in seven Indian departments between 1896 and 1918.

Forty-five percent of the land grants were given to individuals, mainly Spanish- or European-surnamed individuals who had migrated into the Indian highlands at the turn of the century and who were trying to profit from the national coffee boom as local merchants, liquor salesmen, and labor contractors.

Despite this process of land expropriation, 55 percent of the lands granted by presidential decree between 1896 and 1918 were either given to highland townships, and then parcelled out among Indian or ladino residents, or titled in the names of Indian communities. Indians knew that their traditional lands were threatened by the Reform Period agrarian laws, and collectively responded by competing with non-Indians for presidential land grants. In departments such al El Quiché and Huehuetenango, where ladino encroachments did not begin until the last two decades of the nineteenth century, Indian communities raised funds, sought out attorneys, and petitioned the national government for municipal and communal lands.[10]

Although the Spanish *encomienda* and *repartimiento* placed the Indian population in a state of subjugation, it was not until the land and labor laws associated with the rise of coffee production that Indians began to assimilate with the non-Indian population. Thus, Dana G. Munro, a North American who conducted a survey for the Carnegie Endowment for International Peace in 1918 on the political and economic conditions

Table 1

Amount of Land Granted by Presidential Decree
In Guatemalan Indian Departments, 1896-1918
(in caballerías)*

| | Type of Title Grant | | | |
Department	Municipal	Communal	Individual	Totals
Chimaltenango	10	6	242	258
El Quiché	153	493	736	1382
Huehuetenango	1675	974	1285	3934
Quetzaltenango	10	41	261	312
San Marcos	43	10	127	180
Sololá	7	7	228	242
Totonicapán	—	123	7	130
Totals	1898	1654	2886	6438
Percent	29%	26%	45%	

Source: Julio César Méndez Montenegro, *444 años de legislación agraria, 1513–1957* (Guatemala: Imprinta Universitaria, 1960), 259–397.

* A *caballería* is a Spanish land measure equal to approximately 45.1 hectares or 111.4 acres.

in the five Central American republics, noted that Guatemala was "the only one of the Central American countries where the aboriginal population still maintained its identity as a distinct race."[11] Here too, however, the loss of native lands was great and Indians were forced to migrate as seasonal laborers to the lowland coffee estates. Munro described how Indian *jornaleros*, or day laborers, theoretically free to contract wherever and with whom they pleased, were in fact tied to the plantations under a peonage system. The *jornalero* on the average plantation received a limited amount of food and a wage of from two to three pesos (from five to eight cents in U.S. currency) per day. Plantation wages were four to eight times greater in El Salvador and Costa Rica, where farms were worked by mestizo or ladino laborers.

Munro also described the conditions of the thousands of so-called "free Indians," who were not tied to the plantations, but who maintained small parcels of land in the "less developed" parts of the country and conducted a lively trade in foodstuffs and locally manufactured products. According to Munro, the number of these "free Indians" was constantly diminishing. He wrote:

As the extension of the coffee plantations had made the demand for laborers more and more insistent, it has become increasingly difficult for the Indians to escape from the snares of the *habilitadores* (labor contractors) and the pressure exerted by the local officials, so that those in the more developed agricultural districts have with few exceptions been persuaded or forced into service on the plantations. [12]

Munro was one of the first observers to note the deteriorating effects that the coffee plantation system was having on Indian community life; with the peonage system, he wrote, the situation of the Indians was worse than it had been fifty years earlier, and worse than that of the lowest classes in the other republics:

The native municipalities have been powerless to protect [their] members from the operations of the *habilitadores* and the tyranny of the representatives of the central government. Many of the Indian villages which once enjoyed a sort of independence of their white neighbors are now completely at the mercy of brutal local officials, who are not content to exact money from the people under them by every conceivable pretext, but even make a regular practice of virtually selling into slavery those who are entrusted to their government. [13]

Many anthropologists who did fieldwork in Guatemala during the interwar years also recognized how the coffee plantation system was intruding upon Indian community life. One of these anthropologists was the German ethnologist Franz Termer, who did research in both the highland and plantation zones. During the 1921 harvest season, Termer reported that in the plantation township of San Andrés Asuna there were workers from twenty-two different Indian towns; they had traveled a distance of twenty-two to ninety-nine kilometers, mostly by foot, and were accompanied by their families. Alcoholism was one of the major social problems of these migratory Indian workers, and many returned to their homes with illnesses they contracted on the plantations. During the harvest season, Termer said, the highland Indian towns gave the impression of being "dead and abandoned." [14]

Ruth Bunzel, who conducted research in Chichicastenango in the early 1930s, paints a similar picture. Bunzel noted that the plantation, although theoretically "outside of the circle of Indian life," stands at the gates of the Indian community "like some multiple Circe, waiting to lure men to their destruction." In the 1920s, when coffee was selling for high prices in the European markets of Bremen and Hamburg, the planters sent thousands of Indians from Chichicastenango and neighboring towns to work in the coffee plantations of the Pacific Coast. [15]

Bunzel described how all of the large coffee plantations maintained labor contractors (what one German planter and banker called "slave catchers") in the most important Indian population centers. These agents were supplied with liberal amounts of cash which they would distribute to local Indian *capitanes* who, in turn, would go into the mountain villages and lend money to poorer Indians. Once the mountain Indians accepted the money, they would be asked to put their signatures or thumb prints on a receipt, promising to work off their debts on the coffee plantations. Then, when the harvest arrived, the *capitanes* would round up the indebted people in the villages, bring them to the town center where they would be housed in sheds, and take them off to the coastal plantations in gangs. On the coast, the Indian workers would contract malaria and dysentery and accrue further debts. "So effectual are the familiar devices of colonial exploitation, alcoholism, easy credit, debt indenture, and liability for debts to the third generation," Bunzel wrote, "that once caught in the system escape is difficult." [16]

Numerous anthropologists who did research in Guatemala during the 1920s and 1930s recognized the profound effects that the coffee plantation system was having on the Indian population. Yet, these scholars also discovered that the Indians still maintained a fairly vibrant and cohesive community culture and a strong sense of local ethnic identity. Each highland Indian community, for example, had a unique style of dress and dialect, practiced local village or township endogamy, specialized in the production of certain crafts or agricultural commodities, and maintained a rich ceremonial life based on Mayan calendrics and community worship of the Catholic saints. Indian culture and ethnic identity, in other words, had persisted despite strong pressures for acculturation from the plantation system and Guatemalan national society. [17]

In 1941, anthropologist Sol Tax, who had just completed several years of research in the Indian townships surrounding Lake Atitlan, tried to explain why there was so little ethnic passage, or ladinoization, of the Guatemalan Indian population. Tax noted that the low degree of acculturation of Guatemala's Indians could not be explained simply by social barriers to ethnic passage or a lack of physical proximity beween the Indian and ladino populations. For although ladinos comprised less than 10 percent of the population in highland Indian townships, they lived in almost every town where there were major Indian social, religious, and marketing centers, and they were in almost continuous interpersonal contact with the Indian population. Yet, despite this intense, day-to-day personal contact, there was very little passage of Indians to the ladino class, demonstrating that it was possible for a people "to live in continued physical contact with suburbs of modern urban civilization" and still maintain a strong sense of ethnic identity and a highly traditional, religiously based, community culture. [18]

Although Tax and his contemporaries never phrased the phenomenon in these terms, it is fairly clear that a movement of ethnic resistance and revitalization arose among the Mayan Indians of Guatemala during the period that historians call the *siglo de café* or "century of coffee." Anthropological studies conducted during this period show that indigenous peoples do not necessarily vanish or disappear in the face of sustained contact with what is today called the "modern world system." To the contrary, these studies indicate that Indians have often tended to reaffirm their native ethnic identities and cultural traditions, as a collective defense mechanism, when faced with the loss of large amounts of communal lands and the transformation of large numbers of people into a seasonal rural proletariat for capitalist agricultural estates. [19]

Three aspects of this ethnic affirmation process among Guatemala's Indians are noteworthy. First, as Tax pointed out, traditional ethnic identity in Guatemala is locally based and focuses on the township or municipal unit, rather than on a larger language or ethnic group. Second, the major organizational way in which ethnicity is expressed is through participation in religious brotherhoods (*cofradías*) or other organizations dedicated to the worship of Mayan gods and Catholic saints. And third, the social ideology of traditional Indian ethnic identity supports, rather than challenges, the ethnic division-of-labor upon which the national economy is based. Although traditional Indian ideology might reverse the terms of social domination in humor and ritual drama, it tends to accept the fact that ladinos are patrons and Indians are workers. [20]

In summary, the persistence of traditional Indian ethnic identity in Guatemala demonstrates the failure of the liberal state to assimilate Indians to its own vision—that of a modern capitalist society, where all men and women sell their labor as individuals and where land is a commodity to be freely bought, sold, and exchanged. This identity does not pose a threat to the capitalist agrarian order as long as it remains locally based, and expresses itself in religious rather than political terms. Only when Indian ethnic identity changed from a local, community-based religious phenomenon to a regional or national political movement did it threaten the liberal Central American state— an important social transformation that, as we shall see, first appeared in neighboring El Salvador in the early 1930s and in Guatemala in more recent years. [21]

Numerous commentators have pointed to the 1932 Indian peasant revolt as a major turning point in the political history of El Salvador. On January 22, 1932, after a series of heated municipal elections in which candidates carrying the banner of the Salvadoran Communist Party were denied victories, Nahuatl-speaking peasants from the towns of Izalco, Juayúa, and Nahuizalco in southwestern El Salvador rose up in revolt against the newly installed government of General Maximiliano Hernández Martínez. For three days, the Indian rebels, led by their own leaders, cut the telegraph lines leading into their towns, sacked the homes and stores of local ladino merchants and landowners, publicly executed some of the worst exploiters, and, with red flags in their hands, marched on the larger regional centers of Ahuachapán and Sonsonate. The national government, which had already cut the Indians off from the supposed provocateurs of the revolt by jailing Salvadorean Communist Party leader Agustín Farabundo Martí and his two student comrades, Mario Zapata and Alfonso Luna, responded quickly to the peasant uprising. In less than two days, army troops, members of the feared rural *Guardia*, and recently formed civilian militias were mobilized to suppress the revolt. Over the next days and weeks, perhaps as many as thirty thousand Indians were killed in what has been labelled the *matanza*, or massacre, of 1932. Historian Thomas P. Anderson writes of the significance of these events:

The revolt was no mere *jacquerie*, no sudden impulse on the part of Indian *campesinos*. It was, on the contrary, the result of a long chain of events both within the country of El Salvador and outside it. Further, it has the distinction of being the first Latin American revolutionary movement in which men who were avowed international communists played a major part. It marks, therefore, the beginning of a significant new phase in the history of the region. The age of ideologies had come to Latin America.[22]

Like so many other events in the modern political history of Central America, the roots of the 1932 Indian peasant revolt lie in the social dislocations caused by the rise of coffee production. Although commercial coffee production came to dominate the national economy of El Salvador somewhat later than it did in Guatemala, it had a much more violent effect on the fabric of rural society.

As late as 1879, over 25 percent of the lands of El Salvador were still held under some form of communal (*tierras comunales*) or municipal (*ejido*) title. Most of these lands were located in the western or southwestern sections of the country, which also had the most appropriate ecological conditions for coffee production and the largest concentration of surviving Indian populations. In 1881, the liberal government of Rafael Zaldívar abolished all *tierras comunales*, on the grounds that "the existence of lands under the ownership of *Comunidades* impedes agricultural development, obstructs the circulation of wealth, and weakens family bonds and the independence of the individual." A year later, in March 1882, the national government passed another decree abolishing all *ejido* lands. Both of these decrees set in motion a large-scale process of private land appropriation and titling, especially in the rich coffee zone of western and southwestern El Salvador.[23]

The late nineteenth-century agrarian laws intensified the competition between subsistence and commercial farmers and created a large, permanent class of mobile, landless workers. The dislocating effects of these measures were so great that local peasant revolts broke out throughout the coffee-growing areas at periodic intervals during the final decades of the nineteenth century. The federal government responded to this rural violence by assigning "agricultural judges" to regulate the movements of rural workers, by permitting landowners to evict squatters from their estates, and by establishing a mounted rural police force in the departments of Ahuachapán, Sonsonate, and Santa Ana. Finally, in 1907, the federal government combined all of its measures to regulate and control rural life in a comprehensive *Ley Agraria* and, in 1912, it established a *Guardia Civil* to protect rural properties and patrol rural roads.[24]

By the turn of the century, coffee dominated the agricultural landscape of western El Salvador. From the point of view of El Salvador's Indian population, the expansion of coffee production not only led to the expropriation of large amounts of Indian communal lands, but set in motion a major process of cultural change. By then, most of the Indian townships had been transformed from traditional communities, which spoke Indian languages and still wore distinctive Indian dress, to modified or ladinoized communities, which spoke Spanish and actively participated in the national economy. Nevertheless, reports from this period indicate that Indians still comprised nearly half of the population in the departments of La Paz, Sonsonate, and Ahuachapán, and had a strong presence in the towns of Panchimalco, Izalco, and Nahuizalco. Most important, Indians still maintained a strong sense of ethnic identity and, in those towns where they predominated, actively supported their own religious brotherhoods.[25]

Following World War I, another coffee boom took place which again threatened the integrity of these Indian communities. From 1912 through 1916, the average annual production of coffee in El Salvador was 345,000 quintal; between 1917 and 1921, average annual production rose to 413,000 quintal and, in 1924, it reached 750,000 quintal per year.

As a result, the proportion of coffee to total exports rose by 1931 to 95.5 percent. By the early 1930s, El Salvador surpassed Guatemala as the major coffee producer in Central America, contributing over one-third of the total coffee exports for the region.[26] Once again, coffee production increased at the expense of Indian lands. The area of land cultivated in coffee nearly doubled, from 57,000 hectares in 1921 to 106,000 hectares in 1934. Several writers noted the parasitic relationship between coffee cultivation and indigenous subsistence farming.[27]

By this time, the rural population of El Salvador was increasing at an average annual rate of 2.5 percent. The non-Indian rural population began to migrate to Honduras in search of work. The Indians, however, remained in their communities and either became tenants on newly acquired coffee estates or cut down the remaining forests on the steep slopes of volcanos in order to plant their subsistence crops. They also became much more dependent on markets for the purchase of foods. Between 1922 and 1926, a serious inflation occurred: corn prices rose by 100 percent, bean prices increased by 225 percent, and rice prices rose by 300 percent. In 1929, for the first time in its history, El Salvador was forced to import large quantities of corn and rice.[28]

In 1927, at the height of the economic euphoria created by the postwar coffee boom, there was a brief democratic opening in El Salvador under the leadership of President Pío Romero Bosque (1927–30). Factors directly affecting the political mobilization of the country's indigenous peasant population were: (1) A political space was provided for trade union organizing; this was immediately filled by the Regional Federation of Workers of El Salvador (FRTS), which turned from organizing local unions among mechanics, electricians, and other craftsmen to organizing rural workers in the western coffee department. (2) A major discussion took place among the urban and more educated sector of the Salvadoran population concerning the so-called "social problem" in the countryside. Led by the social publicist and philosopher Alberto Masferrer, Salvadoran intellectuals began to question the premises of the liberal state, calling for a new social order which recognized the basic needs of the country's dispossessed rural population. Among the issues raised by Masferrer and his collaborators was the need for a fundamental change in the country's agrarian structure, including the reintroduction of the *ejido* and other indigenous forms of land ownership. (3) At the end of his term of office, Romero Bosque called for the first free presidential election in the history of El Salvador.

Of the six candidates running in this election of 1931, an urban reformer named Arturo Araujo won, running on a party platform that combined the social ideas of Masferrer and of the British Labour

Party.[29] Most of the Indian communities voted for Araujo, based on his populist platform and vague call for agrarian reform. Economic conditions, however, had changed dramatically in El Salvador. In late 1929, the leading coffee growers of El Salvador established the Society for the Defense of Coffee—later renamed the Coffee Growers' Association of El Salvador—to represent their interests before the national government formally. At the same time, the world economic crisis pulled the international market out from under coffee production. Coffee which sold for 39 *colonos* per quintal in 1928 dropped to 18 *colonos* per quintal in 1931; the value of the *colono* also dropped from 2.04 to the dollar in 1929 to 2.54 in 1932. By 1931, the national income of El Salvador was only 50 percent of what it had been in 1928 and the wages of rural workers fell from fifty to twenty cents per day.[30]

Given these conditions, it is hardly surprising that rural El Salvador provided fertile ground for more radical political organizing. In 1930, a small Salvadorean Communist Party was secretly organized. Led by Agustín Farabundo Martí, a peripatetic revolutionary who had become frustrated with the nationalist aims of the guerrilla movement led by Augusto César Sandino in Nicaragua, the Salvadorean Communist Party began to organize strikes and land take-overs in rural areas. Much of the success of the communists came from the groundwork laid by the Mexican rural organizer Jorge Fernández Anaya, who had played a key role in the establishment of the Aztec Farm Workers Union in Mexico. Fernández Anaya—Nahuatl-speaking and with Indian features—came to the coffee zone to help the FRTS with its union organizing and, it is said, organized as many as eight thousand farmworkers in his three months there in 1930.

In the final months of the Romero Bosque regime and during the early months of the Araujo presidency, the federal government cracked down on the activities of these militant rural organizers. Farabundo Martí and his collaborators nevertheless continued to work in the countryside, especially in the Indian towns. One of the methods used to mobilize Indian peasants into rural organizations was the "people's university," whereby urban university students went out into the countryside to lecture peasants and workers about economics, agriculture, history, and politics. Organizers working under the umbrella of the FRTS, the Salvadoran Communist Party, and the newly formed Socorro Rojo International (SRI), traveled throughout the country as itinerant peddlers, carrying out mass propaganda. Often, rural school teachers were mobilized to propagate the communist cause, or organizers appeared at religious gatherings, such as the miraculous appearance of the "Vírgen del Adelanto" near Ahuachapán, to preach their more secular political message.

Thomas Anderson, in his excellent description of what occurred in rural areas just prior to the January 1932 uprising, notes that Indianism and Indian *caciques* also played their part in spreading radical ideas among the Indian population.[31]

In December 1931, a group of young army officers carried out a coup which unseated Araujo from office. In a surprise move, the new president, General Maximiliano Hernández Martínez, announced that the municipal elections promised by Araujo would be held and that the Communist Party would be allowed to participate. However, when a number of communists actually did win the local town elections of January 1932, Martínez would not let them take office. Seemingly, he made the election promise to find out who the communist leaders and sympathizers were. Following this abortive election campaign, the call for a general insurrection by the Salvadoran Communist Party, as well as a planned barracks revolt, were discovered, and Martínez's security forces placed Farabundo Martí and his co-conspirators in jail. At the last minute, the remaining leaders of the Communist Party tried to call off the insurrection, but their pleas came too late. On the evening of 22 January, large sectors of the peasantry in the western part of El Salvador rose up in revolt.

The uprising was mainly, but not entirely, centered in the Indian townships, covering a fifty-mile area from Santa Tecla to the town of Tacuba, near the Guatemalan frontier. Cut off from central leadership, the rebel activity proved ineffective. Mostly, it took the form of sacking the homes and stores of rich people and distributing their goods to the local peasant population. The rebels possessed only machetes and old rifles, no match for the Thompson machine guns the Martínez government sent to the region. Thus on 25 January 1932, just seventy-two hours after it began, the peasant revolt came to a halt, with an estimated one hundred people killed by the rebels and all of the western coffee towns again in government hands.[32]

A North American Protestant missionary named A. Roy MacNaught was in the town of Juayuá throughout the three days of the revolt and witnessed what happened when the soldiers arrived. According to MacNaught, many of the citizens of the town who were previously wearing red arm bands to show their support for the rebels, put on blue-and-white ribbons (the colors of El Salvador) after the soldiers entered the town. The government, however, had commanded the soldiers to "exterminate completely" the "Communist enemy" in the town. In a communication from Juayuá to the mission headquarters in the United States, MacNaught wrote:

The soldiers searched the houses of Juayuá and whenever stolen goods were found, the man of the house was taken out and shot. After finishing with

Juayuá, the soldiers went out into the country and started bringing in the poor folks. The commander and his staff had taken up their quarters in the town hall. They had in their possession a list of those who were communists. The men were brought before these officers and, if their name was on the list, they were taken to the place of execution . . . . All day long (and this lasted for several days), we could hear the shots in the plaza as the work of execution went on.[33]

In the aftermath of the insurrection, the Martínez government organized a campaign to totally wipe out the "Communist threat" in the countryside and to test the loyalty of the civilian population. Martínez's Minister of War, General Joaquín Valdéz, asked for a doubling of the size of the National Guard, and General José Tomás Calderón, the Commander-in-Charge of the Army, called for the creation of a Committee for National Defense. The national elite responded to the government's call by forming a Patriotic Association in San Salvador, which in five days collected four hundred thousand *colonos* to help suppress the Indian peasant revolt. Meanwhile, in the rural areas, where the insurrection actually occurred, local landowners and storekeepers formed civilian militias and defense leagues in order to insure that another rebellion would not recur.[34]

Again, the eyewitness testimony of the North American missionary MacNaught provides insight into what took place in the weeks immediately following the revolt. On 24 February 1932, MacNaught reported that trouble broke out in the town of Nahuizalco when the Indian men were called into the plaza to get identification cards and tried to overpower some of the guards. The soldiers opened fire on the men with their machine guns and three hundred Indians were killed. "The Indians," he wrote:

are hated now as never before. In Nahuizalco there is a defense league comprised of the Ladino element. These Ladinos have rounded up all the male believers they can find and had them shot. Pedro's brother and father (a local evangelical family) are safe. The remainder of the Indian men in Nahuizalco have either been killed or are in hiding. This Ladino defense league went into our chapel there, burned all the Bibles, carried off the benches, the gasoline lamp, the gasoline, a woolen blanket of mine, the table, all of Pedro's personal things; in fact, they cleaned out the chapel. Thus, in one single blow, the work which was going along so nicely has been practically ruined.[35]

About ten days later, MacNaught reports from Cojutepeque, El Salvador:

We have word that there have been executed in Nahuizalco alone, 2,500 men. One day they lined up 400 boys and shot them. They have tortured the women to make them tell where their husbands and brothers are. In that town, there is scarcely a man to be seen now. It would seem that they are going to exterminate the Indians.

Two general points are important to make about the 1932 peasant revolt for the light which they cast on contemporary events in Central America. First, as Thomas Anderson argues, the 1932 Indian peasant revolt in El Salvador was not a mere *jacquerie*, like so many of the local and even regional Indian uprisings that arose throughout Central America during the colonial and early independence periods. Nor was the 1932 revolt an archaic social movement with religious or millenarian overtones, like those movements which historian Eric Hobsbawm has described for parts of southern Europe in the late nineteenth and early twentieth centuries. To the contrary, the 1932 peasant revolt in El Salvador had all of the elements of a modern social movement. The revolt showed, perhaps more clearly than any other social movement in Central America before it, that indigenous peoples which have been uprooted and dislocated by capitalist agricultural production have the will and the capacity to participate in modern movements for radical social change.[36]

The Salvadoran peasant revolt also demonstrates that indigenous peoples are extremely open to the revolutionary message of urban political organizers. In fact, one of the main reasons that the Indians of southwestern El Salvador were so readily mobilized for radical social action was precisely their strong sense of ethnic identity and a well-defined set of historic grievances concerning the restoration of communal lands. Although their own view of a new society might not have been the same as that of the communist organizers with whom they allied themselves, the Nahuatl-speaking peasants from such towns as Izalco, Nahuizalco, and Juayuá showed themselves remarkably able to understand and participate in modern political movements for social change.

The Salvadoran experience also provides important insights into attitudes toward Indians in Central America. To truly understand the scope of violence and repression which followed the 1932 revolt (i.e., the genocidal proportions of the Salvadoran *matanza*), it is necessary to recognize the essentially colonial position that Indians have been forced to assume in modern Central American societies. Although race is defined culturally in Central America (i.e., in terms of one's language, dress, customs, etc.), it still plays a vital role in the attitudes toward Indians held by the national oligarchies, the military, and local rural elites. While Indians are granted citizenship and their heritage often looked upon with great national pride, as persons they are looked down upon, discriminated against, and oppressed.

In his book on the subject, Thomas Anderson tries to assess how much of the 1932 revolt and the massacre that followed can be explained by the racial antagonism between Indians and ladinos in Salvadoran society. Anderson cites a book by a Salvadoran journalist which contains the following quote from an interview with a ladino survivor of the rebellion immediately following the revolt:

We'd like this race of the plague to be exterminated. . . . It is necessary for the government to use a strong hand. They did it right in North America, having done with them by shooting them in the first place before they could impede the progress of the nation. They killed the Indians because they will never be pacified. Here we are, treating them like part of the family, and you see the result! They have fierce instincts. [37]

From the point of view of the government and the national elites it represented, the Indian rebellion in the western part of the country was doubly subversive. Not only did Indians rebel against the premises of the colonial order, but they also allied themselves with an alien ideology that questioned the entire basis of agricultural capitalism and the liberal state. As one Salvadoran landowner, cited in Anderson's book (p. 17), wrote in the newspaper *La Prensa* soon after the revolt, "There was not an Indian who was not afflicted with devastating communism . . . . We committed a grave error in making them citizens."

As many observers have noted, the *matanza* which followed the 1932 peasant revolt was a major factor in undermining regional Indian culture and ethnic identity in southwestern El Salvador. In neighboring Guatemala, however, a local and regionally based Indian cultural presence continued into the second half of the twentieth century. During the democratically elected governments of Juan José Arevalo and Jacobo Arbenz Guzmán, populist political party and agrarian organizers went to the countryside to mobilize Guatemala's rural Indian masses. The military coup led by Carlos Castillo Armias and sponsored by the U.S. Central Intelligence Agency in June 1954 brought an end to this period of Indian social mobilization. As we shall see in the following section, Indians were again mobilized in the past decade; this time, though, under radically changed circumstances in Guatemala and throughout the Central American region.

THE INDIAN PEASANT WAR IN GUATEMALA: 1978–82

In the late 1970s, a great deal of international attention focused on Indian participation in the revolutionary guerrilla movement in Guatemala. Dating back to the early 1960s, armed guerrilla activities took the form of kidnappings in urban areas or small *foco* actions in non-Indian, rural parts of the country. Following a brutal counter-insurgency campaign in the late 1960s, in which the revolutionary guerrilla organizations were thought to be destroyed, and after a decade of violence, in which more than thirty thousand people were either killed or disappeared, four guerrilla organizations reappeared on the political landscape of Guatemala. Two of these organizations—the Guerrilla Army of the Poor (EGP) and the Revolutionary Organization of the People in Arms (ORPA)—were particularly active in Indian areas of Guatemala.

The EGP and ORPA had perfected a tactic of armed propaganda meetings, whereby small bands of armed guerrillas would take over Indian towns for brief periods, drape their flags or banners over the town hall, and lecture the town inhabitants in the Indian languages about the people's war against the national army and the rich landowners. During 1980 alone, the EGP and ORPA occupied over seventy towns in the western and central highlands. The EGP was particularly active in the far northern departments of Huehuetenango, El Quiché, and Alta Verapaz, as well as along the southern coast where Guatemala's large coffee, sugar, and cotton plantations are located. ORPA was active in the midwestern highlands, having gained some notoriety in the summer of 1980 by occupying several towns around picturesque Lake Atitlan and lecturing the Indian inhabitants along with a number of foreign tourists. [38]

Alan Riding, then the *New York Times* correspondent for Mexico and Central America, was one of the first foreign journalists to recognize and describe the signficance of these guerrilla actions for the country's large Indian population. The historic exploitation of Guatemala's Indians, as well as more recent acts of repression, had made the Indian population more sympathetic to the guerrilla cause. In an article published in August 1980, Riding wrote:

Throughout the highlands, the Indians are beginning to stir. On May Day this year, Indians in traditional costumes carried defiant banners past the National Palace in Guatemala City. Entire villages now sympathize with—and feed and shelter—the guerrilla. And when the army arrives after rebel occupations, it can find no one who has seen a thing. "There are places where guerrillas have executed all Government informers," a priest said. "There, they feel entirely safe." [39]

Many Guatemalan conservatives—as well as foreign businessmen and diplomats—refused to see the indigenous sentiment for the guerrilla movement, arguing instead that such actions were carried out by small, vocal bands of extremists financed and directed from outside of Central America. But, according to Riding, the converse was true. "The Indians," he wrote:

may be fighting more against repression and the theft of communal lands than for the socialism espoused by the guerrillas, but they are nevertheless beginning to fight. Priests in the region say that about one-quarter of the guerrillas are now Indians.[40]

There were clear historical and sociological reasons for Guatemala's Indians to seek alliances with radical political movements. Perhaps the most fundamental reason was the serious crisis in the peasant sector of the Guatemalan agricultural economy. Although the basic structure of the Guatemalan agrarian economy has remained the same since 1950, the poverty and misery of the country's large rural and indigenous population have increased. First, there has been the sheer vegetative growth, through population increase and inheritance fragmentation, in the number of *minifundios*, or farm units which are too small to support a peasant family, from 308,073 in 1950 to 468,461 in 1979. And second, there has been a significant increase in the number of large, multifamily farms, from 7,553 to 13,659 units controlling over 62 percent of the best agricultural land.

At the same time, there has been a significant increase in the number of landless persons in rural Guatemala. Between 1965 and 1980, for example, the number of landless persons increased from 310,440 to 419,620. Currently, 32 percent of the economically active population engaged in agriculture are estimated to be landless, and 57 percent are estimated to have parcels of land which are too small for a family to subsist on.[41]

Government agrarian policies of recent years have exacerbated, rather than resolved, these serious land-distribution problems in the countryside. Between 1952 and 1954, the Arbenz government instituted an agrarian reform program which did distribute hundreds of thousands of acres of unused lands expropriated from foreign- and national-owned plantations to poor tenant and subsistence farmers. The military coup of 1954, however, returned these lands to their former owners. Subsequent governments have promoted various ineffective resettlement and colonization schemes, while paying lip service to agrarian reform. An assessment by the U.S. Agency for International Development of government land reform efforts in the post-Arbenz period noted that the impact of these colonization schemes on the country's land-tenure structure has been negligible.[42]

Despite this dire economic picture, one fundamental change has had a profound effect on the welfare and social outlook of the country's indigenous population. This is the extraordinary growth and the tremendous social and cultural influence of clergy and lay leaders of the Roman Catholic Church. Between 1950 and 1965, the number of Catholic priests in Guatemala increased from 132 to 483, while the number of sisters increased from 96 to 354. Most of this growth in religious personnel, an increase of 266 percent in fifteen years, came primarily from foreign orders sending missionaries to Guatemala. Initially, they conducted fairly conventional missionary activities, aimed at converting traditional Mayan religious believers (i.e., members of the *cofradías* or religious brotherhoods) to a reformed Catholicism based on ritual participation in the sacramental life of the Church. Through the training of Indian catechists or lay religious leaders in a program called *Acción Católica*, or Catholic Action, the clergy began to transform the social and political outlook of Indians, while at the same time going through radical ideological changes themselves. [43]

Catholic Action was an extremely paradoxical movement. Its roots, which go back to the late 1940s, were very much tied to the institutional Church in Guatemala, attempting to assure that the "evils of Communism" and other forms of "secular humanism" did not ideologically pollute the rural, indigenous population. On the other hand, the clergy and lay leaders who helped to establish Catholic Action went through an ideological transformation themselves. This led them to break from the institutional Church and, under the influence of Vatican II and the new Liberation Theology, to establish a "people's Church" in the Guatemalan countryside. [44]

The place where Catholic Action took hold most firmly and was ideologically transformed most completely was in the department of El Quiché, where Spanish priests from the Sacred Heart Order have been active since the late 1950s. Throughout the 1960s and 1970s, the Sacred Heart missionaries not only converted large numbers of Indians to the new Catholicism, but also organized numerous peasant leagues, agricultural cooperatives, and pioneer resettlement schemes. Not surprisingly, it was mainly in this area, and especially in the Ixil-speaking region of northern El Quiché, where guerrilla organizing among Indians initially occurred. [45]

Following the earthquake which struck Guatemala in 1976, new alliances began to form between progressive Catholic clergy and lay leaders, peasant communities threatened by land-title disputes with large landowners, and the labor movement which was active again in Guatemala City. The key event in the forging of these alliances was the massacre that took place in the town of Panzós in Alta Verapaz in May 1978. Throughout the 1970s, the entire Alta Verapaz region had been embroiled in land conflicts, as large landowners, mineral and petroleum companies, and government hydroelectric schemes dispossessed thousands of Kekchí-speaking Indians of their lands. When the government refused to give land titles, as promised, to a group of Kekchí from the villages of Cahaboncito and Chichipaté, the Indians marched on the town of Panzós in protest. There, the

Indian protestors were met by a heavily armed special-forces unit of the Guatemalan Army. Over one hundred people were killed, including several women and children who drowned trying to escape. The government denied responsibility for the Panzós massacre, blaming it on "subversive elements" which had encouraged Indian peasants to take over private lands, and refused to let the International Red Cross or reporters into the area. On 8 June 1978, over eighty thousand people—including university students, slum-dweller associations, and members of the recently formed Justice and Peace Commission of the Roman Catholic Church—marched through the streets of Guatemala City protesting the increasing military repression in the countryside.[46]

A month before the Panzós massacre, a group of Indians had formed the Committee for Peasant Unity (CUC). This organization played a major role in linking up popular struggles in the countryside with those in the city, and eventually with the small guerrilla movement which then existed in the hills. From its inception, CUC, the Quiché word for "squirrel," saw itself as a broad-based organization which would eventually include all of the peasants and workers of Guatemala. At the beginning, CUC organizers—who were mostly Indians—focused their attention on providing support to local Indian communities threatened by large landowners and the army. They would advise local Indian leaders on ways of protecting their communities from land and resource robbery, exploitation on the large farms, indebtedness to the state agricultural bank, the drafting of young men into the army, and kidnappings and assassinations. Behind this program there was a more general moral and religious message arising out of the new Liberation Theology in Latin America and the experience of rural social change movements in neighboring El Salvador.[47]

Throughout 1978 and 1979, CUC organizers worked closely with Quiché catechists and community leaders under attack from large landowners and the army. Since 1975, sixty-eight leaders of cooperatives had disappeared in the Ixcán region of El Quiché, forty in Chajul, twenty-eight in Cotzal, and thirty-two in Nebaj. In one community, the presidents of Catholic Action, Caritas (the Catholic food-assistance program), and the local cooperative and community development committee, as well as five sacristans and four bilingual school teachers, were killed. The army had also set up bases throughout the region and, recognizing that northern El Quiché was becoming a stronghold for the guerrilla activities of the EGP, it began to terrorize the local civilian population.[48]

As army actions in northern El Quiché became intolerable, the Indians began to seek support from the popular organizations in Guatemala City. In September 1979, a group of one hundred peasants from San Miguel Uspantán marched through the streets of Guatemala City carrying white flowers and distributing petitions denouncing the kidnapping of seven persons by the army during the previous month. Then, in January 1980, residents from the towns of Nebaj, Chajul, and San Miguel Uspantán returned to Guatemala City, this time calling for the establishment of a national commission to investigate the recent killings and militarization of the region. When no response to their petition came from the national government or congress, the Indian peasants—joined by a small number of students and representatives of popular organizations—peacefully occupied the Spanish embassy. Despite protests from the Spanish ambassador, government security forces surrounded the embassy building and, within view of Guatemalan television crews, set it on fire. In this incident, thirty-nine people were killed, including twenty-three peasants, a former vice president, and a former foreign minister of Guatemala.[49]

Two weeks after the Spanish embassy massacre, a group of some two hundred people, representing fifteen of Guatemala's twenty-two Indian language groups, met secretly at the ruins of Iximché, the ancient capital of the Cakchiquel Indians. From there they released a declaration calling for the unity of Indians and poor ladinos to liberate themselves from the violence of the rich landowners and the army. During the same month, CUC organized a strike of more than seventy-five thousand farm workers, paralyzing the large sugar and cotton plantations along Guatemala's southern coast. The strike, which for the first time brought together permanent ladino farmworkers and Indian migrant laborers, affected more than sixty farms, sugar mills, and cotton-processing plants. While the government responded to part of the strikers' demands by increasing the legal rural minimum wage from $1.12 to $3.20 per day, it also increased the amount of repression in the countryside. Not only did the Guatemalan Army and paramilitary forces jail, kidnap, and kill strike leaders, they also began a rampage in which no one involved in rural organizing, educational, or development activities was safe.[50]

The government, headed by General Romeo Lucas García, considered the Church to be the most "subversive element" in the countryside. Whether there was an actual plan by the Lucas García government to wipe out the "people's Church" is unknown; what *is* known, as Phillip Berryman has written, is that "for the first time, there was a systematic and virtually indiscriminate attack on church pastoral agents." This was particularly true in the El Quiché province, where throughout the first six months of 1980 several parish houses were bombed, numerous death threats were made against pastoral agents, two priests were killed, and the life of the bishop was threatened. Finally, in July 1980, Bishop John Gerardi of El Quiché told his priests and other religious workers that he had decided to leave the diocese, asking them to join him as an act of protest. By this date, the only possible response for the Indian community leaders was to either abandon their communities or join the guerrilla movement as a means of defense.[51]

Recently, several revealing personal accounts have appeared by Indians who were involved in the organizing activities of the late 1970s and who experienced the repressive actions of the army and paramilitary groups.[52] As one reads these accounts, it is clear that the Mayan Indians were among the main protagonists in a revolutionary peasant war which gripped that country between 1978 and 1982. Eric Wolf—who has written the major anthropological study of modern peasant wars—provides ample documentation that peasants who have been dislocated by agricultural commercialization but who still maintain close ties to their lands are often mobilized into revolutionary armies when the appropriate national conditions exist. Wolf also demonstrates that when these peasantries live in peripheral areas and possess distinct languages and ethnic identities, they often have the "tactical mobility" and autonomous "systems of communication" to make their mobilization by revolutionary political parties a significant political threat.[53]

It is obvious that many of the conditions isolated by Wolf existed in Guatemala in the period between 1978 and 1982. Wolf's study, however, deals with those cases of modern peasant wars where revolutionary parties, claiming to represent peasants, have been successful in capturing state power (e.g., Mexico, Cuba, China, Vietnam, etc.). What, though, of cases such as Guatemala, where peasants are mobilized for revolution and where the revolutionary program or political-military strategy fails?

Today, as we get further away from the euphoria which gripped some analysts of Central America in the early 1980s, we see that not only were Indians the main protagonists in the popular uprising, they were also the main victims of the Guatemalan Army's brutal counter-insurgency campaign. Thousands of Indians were killed during this period; more than a hundred thousand sought refuge in Mexico and other countries; and perhaps as many as a million people were uprooted from their ancestral villages and became displaced persons in their native land. Meanwhile, at the height of the counter-insurgency campaign, the Guatemalan Army started to reorganize rural society, forcing over nine hundred thousand men to join civilian militias and creating a network of "model villages" (i.e., Army-controlled hamlets) to ensure that the Indians would not again fall under guerrilla control.[54]

Recently, a group of anthropologists have attempted to assess the effects of the past decade of political mobilization and violence on a number of Guatemalan Indian communities. Perhaps the major finding of these studies is the great amount of terror and fear that was instilled in the Guatemalan Indian population as a result of the Army's brutal counter-insurgency campaign. The Guatemalan Army was not content with wiping out the guerrilla movement; it also wanted, and apparently was successful in doing so, to pacify and create a "culture of fear" among the Indian population. Although it is difficult to assess whether this culture of fear will have a permanent effect on Indian political attitudes and behavior, there is little doubt that it has psychologically and culturally scarred the Guatemalan Indian population.[55]

CONCLUSION

In conclusion, three general points can be made about the important role that Indians have played in the national politics of El Salvador and Guatemala. First, the political struggles of Central American Indians are deeply rooted in the agrarian structures of the countries of the region. Not only did the introduction of coffee production at the end of the nineteenth century integrate El Salvador, Guatemala, and the other countries into the expanding world economy for agricultural commodities, but it also transformed the social relations of production within these countries themselves. Indian communities lost large amounts of communal lands following the introduction of coffee production; Indian labor was mobilized to satisfy the needs of the new coffee estates; and Indian culture was looked down upon because nineteenth-century liberals thought of it as an obstacle to national progress and growth. From the late nineteenthth century onward, Indian communities were at the mercy of the international market for coffee, bananas, sugar, cotton, and other commercial agricultural crops. The rise and fall in prices for these commodities determined the levels of poverty and misery, and played an important role in defining both the strength of indigenous ethnic identity and indigenous reactions to the state. These agrarian processes continue to determine the strength and direction of Indian ethnic identity today.

Second, since at least the 1930s, Indians have shown an interest in participating in national politics in order to better their life chances and regain their lands. The peasant war that occurred in Guatemala between 1978 and 1982 led a number of observers who were unfamiliar with this history to assume that Indians had only recently awakened from centuries of political slumber and that they were only now, under the influence of a revolutionary guerrilla movement, making demands on the state. In fact, there is a long history of Indian attempts to participate in national politics—including the 1932 Indian peasant revolt in El Salvador, the peasant mobilization under the Arbenz agrarian reform program in Guatemala between 1952 and 1954, and the consciousness-raising and mobilization of Indians by progressive Catholic clergy that took place following the Guatemalan military coup of 1954. Indians, in other words, have a history of seeking access to national politics in both El Salvador and Guatemala. They also have a history of being denied such access and turning to more radical forms of political action in order to defend their communities and provide some reason for hope.

Finally, no discussion of the role of Indians in the national politics of El Salvador and Guatemala can overlook the effects that state violence has had on their ethnic identities, community structures, psychological outlooks, and ways of life. The Salvadoran *matanza*, with its slaughter of ten to thirty thousand Indians, and the Guatemalan Army's "holy war" against subversion, with its burning of scores of Indian villages and its legacy of thousands of Indian widows and orphans, are the modern Central American equivalents of the Wounded Knee massacre in the United States. These horrible acts of genocide instill fear in a people, force them to submit psychologically and culturally to a more powerful military force, and lead them to find salvation in religious, rather than political, means. In some sense, the past experience of state-directed political violence, as symbolized by the Spanish Conquest, lives on in the collective memory of the Indians of Central America: for these people know that by struggling for their ancient birthright to land and cultural freedom, they always run the risk of being denied the collective right as a people to exist.

NOTES

1. Antonio Batres Jáuregui, *Los Indios, Su Historia, y Su Civilización* (Guatemala: Tipográfico La Union, 1893), 160–62.
2. Ibid., 172.
3. Ibid., 159.
4. Ibid., 178.
5. Octavio Paz, *The Labyrinth of Solitude: Life and Thought in Mexico* (New York: Grove Press, 1961), 126. More detailed descriptions of the social ideology behind the late nineteenth-century liberal project in Central America are contained in Ralph Lee Woodward, Jr., *Central America: A Nation Divided* (New York: Oxford University Press, 1976); and Mario Rodríguez, *Central America* (Englewood Cliffs, New Jersey: Prentice-Hall, 1965).
6. Edelberto Torres Rivas, *Interpretación del Desarrollo Social Centroameri-cano: Procesos y Estructuras de Una Sociedad Dependiente* (San José, Costa Rica:

Editorial Universitaria Centroamericana, 1971), chap. 2. On the history and social consequences of coffee production in Central America, see also Ciro Flamarion Santana Cardoso, "Historia económica del café en Centroamérica (Siglo XIX)," *Estudios Sociales Centroamericanos* (Costa Rica) 4, no. 10 (1975): 9–55.

7. Histories of the growth of coffee production in Guatemala are contained in Sanford A. Mosk, "The Coffee Economy of Guatemala, 1850–1918, Development and Signs of Instability," *Inter-American Economic Affairs* 9, no. 3 (1955): 6–20; and Julio Castellanos Cámbranes, *Coffee and Peasants: The Origins of the Modern Plantation Economy in Guatemala, 1853–1897* (Stockholm: Institute of Latin American Studies, 1985).

8. Jorge Skinner-Klee, *Legislación Indigenista de Guatemala* (Mexico: Instituto Indigenista Interamericano, 1954), 34.

9. For a discussion of the persistent pressures that coffee planters placed on the Guatemalan state to mobilize Indian labor, see David J. McCreery, "Coffee and Class: The Structure of Development in Liberal Guatemala," *Hispanic American Historical Review* 56, no. 3 (1976): 438–60.

10. For detailed description of land titling and ladino expropriation of Indian lands in the northern Huehuetenango region during this period, see my doctoral thesis, "Land of Our Ancestors: A Study of Land Tenure and Inheritance in the Highlands of Guatemala" (Ph.D. diss., Harvard University, 1970).

11. Dana G. Munro, *The Five Republics of Central America: Their Political and Economic Development and Their Relations with the United States* (New York: Oxford University Press, 1918), 58.

12. Ibid., 65.

13. Ibid., 65–66.

14. Franz Termer, *Etnología y Etnografía de Guatemala* (Guatemala: Seminario de Integración Social Guatemalteca, 1957), 43–47.

15. Ruth Bunzel, *Chichicastenango: A Guatemalan Village* (Seattle: University of Washington Press, 1952), 9.

16. Ibid., 11. For more general descriptions of the effects of the coffee plantation system on indigenous economy and society, see Sanford A. Mosk, "Indigenous Economy in Latin America," *Inter-American Economic Affairs* 8 (1954): 3–25; and Alain Y. Dessaint, "Effects of the Hacienda and Plantation systems on Guatemalan Indians," *América Indígena* 12, no. 4 (1962): 323–54.

17. Sol Tax, "The Municipios of the Midwestern Highlands of Guatemala," *American Anthropologist* 39 (1937): 423–44.

18. Sol Tax, "World View and Social Relations in Guatemala," *American Antrhopologist* 43 (1941): 27–42. Tax argued that one of the major reasons for the persistence of Indian ethnic identity and culture was that Guatemalan Indians viewed cultural differences between themselves and other Indians, as well as between themselves and non-Indians, as "cultural specialties" among interacting but independent groups, rather than as "cultural alternatives" requiring choices. He also claimed that the Mayan Indians of Guatemala had a particularly sophisticated way of separating their highly individualistic and impersonal social relations from their essentially "sacred" and "traditional" world views and religious beliefs.

19. The collective responses that indigenous peoples make in the face of sustained contacts with colonialism and modern capitalism were first described in Eric R. Wolf, "Closed Corporate Peasant Communities in Mesoamerica and Java," *Southwestern Journal of Anthropology* 13, no. 1 (1957): 1–18. See also Rodolfo Stavenhagen, "Classes, Colonialism, and Acculturation: A System of Inter-Ethnic Relations in Mesoamerica," in Irving Louis Horowitz, ed., *Masses in Latin America* (New York: Oxford University Press, 1970), 235–88.

20. Excellent contemporary descriptions of traditional Mayan religious beliefs and social ideology are contained in Ruben E. Reina, *The Law of the Saints: A Pokomam Pueblo and Its Community Culture* (New York: The Bobbs-Merrill Co., 1966); and Kay B. Warren, *The Symbolism of Subordination: Indian Identity in a Guatemalan Town* (Austin: University of Texas Press, 1978).

21. In distinguishing between passive forms of ethnic resistance, such as those practiced by traditional Mayan religious believers, and more active forms of political resistance, such as those which occur among Mayan Indians today, I am not making any judgment about the ultimate value or worth of one form or another of indigenous response to colonialism and ethnic domination. Nor am I assuming that the domains of "politics" and "religion" are necessarily separate realities in indigenous social action and thought. To the contrary, the distinctions being made here are merely analytic ones, similar to those made by other students of indigenous and peasant social movements, such as Eric Hobsbawm, Eric Wolf, and Peter Worsley. In fact, in the two cases of indigenous social movements that follow, politics and religion are intermixed.

22. Thomas P. Anderson, *Matanza: El Salvador's Communist Revolt of 1932* (Lincoln: University of Nebraska Press, 1971), 1, 2.

23. Salvadoran sociologist Alejandro Marroquín, who studied this process in the Indian community of San Pedro Nonualco, writes, "In less than thirty years, the pattern of land tenure was radically altered; a few privileged people enriched themselves by the purchase of good lands at low prices and the majority of the centers of population sank into misery." See David Browning, *El Salvador: Landscape and Society* (Oxford: Clarendon Press, 1971), 212, 213.

24. Ibid., 212–21.

25. Richard N. Adams, *Cultural Surveys of Panama, Nicaragua, Guatemala, El Salvador, and Honduras* (Washington, D. C.: Pan American Sanitation Society, 1957), 485–500. This monograph still remains the major source on the contemporary Salvadoran Indian population. See also Alejandro Marroquín, "El Problema Indígena en El Salvador", *América Indígena* 35, no. 4 (1975): 747–71.

26. Figures cited in Edelberto Torres Rivas, *Interpretación del Desarrollo Social Centroamericano*, 283–89.

27. Writing in the Salvadoran magazine *Patria* in 1928, one commentator claimed: "The conquest of territory by the coffee industry is alarming. It has already occupied all the high ground and is now descending to the valleys, displacing maize, rice, and beans. It goes in the manner of the conquistador, spreading hunger and misery, reducing the former proprietors to the worst conditions—woe to those who sell out!" Another observer writing in the same

magazine stated: "Now there is nothing but coffee. In the great hacienda named California that covers the flanks of the volcano Alegría,where I visited last year, I did not find a single fruit tree. On that *finca* (farm) that extends for many *caballerías*, there were formerly a hundred or more properties planted in maize, rice, beans, and fruit. Now, there is nothing but coffee in the highlands, and pasture in the lowlands, which go on displacing the forests and the *milpas*." Cited in Everett A. Wilson, "The Crisis of National Integration in El Salvador, 1919–1935" (Ph.D. diss., Stanford University, 1970), 122, 123.

28. A much more detailed discussion of these relations between demographic growth, migration, and resource competition between commercial and subsistence agriculture is contained in William H. Durham, *Scarcity and Survival in Central America: Ecological Origins of the Soccer War* (Stanford: Stanford University Press, 1979).

29. A good discussion of the populist politics of this period is contained in Alastair White, *El Salvador* (New York: Praeger Publishers, 1973), 93–101.

30. These figures are cited in Anderson, *Matanza*, 12, 24–25, 67–68.

31. Ibid., 69, 70. Anderson writes: "While Indianism may not have played a large part in the success of the communist propaganda throughout all of the western zone, in the intensely Indian districts of Sonsonate it was extremely important. That was why one of the most important converts to the new doctrine was the cacique of Izalco, José Feliciano Ama. Ama had a strong hold over the barrio of Asunción, the Indian barrio of the town, through his chieftainship and through his leadership in the *cofradía*. He had inherited his position of power from his father-in-law, Patricio Shupan. Shupan had long looked after the external affairs of the Indian community and was a definite force in Salvadoran politics. He had been wooed by Quiñónez Molina (a three-term Salvadoran president in the postwar period) and had aided the crafty leader of Liga Roja in his election campaign. For this Shupan had been rewarded with even greater authority."

32. Ibid., 134–37. Anderson's description of the revolt, as well as his calculations of the number of people that the rebels killed, come from a survey of contemporary newspaper reports and personal interviews with a number of Salvadorans involved in the events.

33. A. Roy MacNaught, "Horrors of Communism in Central America," *The Central American Bulletin* (Dallas), no. 181 (March 1932):10. I am indebted to David Stoll, a student of North American Protestant missionary orders in Latin America, for bringing this important reference to my attention. To my knowledge, MacNaught and his wife were the only foreigners to actually witness the revolt and its aftermath. Interestingly, the title of their article is deceiving, as they describe more of the horror which followed the brief rebellion than the depredations caused by the Indians themselves.

34. Wilson, "The Crisis of National Integration in El Salvador," 230.

35. MacNaught, "Horrors of Communism in Central America," 27.

36. The distinction made here between archaic and modern social movements is from Eric Hobsbawm, *Primitive Rebels: Studies in Archaic Forms of Social Movement in the Nineteenth and Twentieth Centuries* (New York: Praeger, 1959).

37. Cited by Thomas Anderson, *Matanza*, 17. The quote is from Joaquín Méndez, Jr., *Los Sucesos Comunistas en El Salvador* (San Salvador, 1932), 105.

38. See "Guatemala: Re-enter the Guerrillas," *Latin America Political Report* 7 (January 1977) : 4; and "Guerrillas Put the Military in a Sweat," *Latin America Regional Reports: Mexico and Central America* 9 (January 1981) : 5.

39. Alan Riding, "Guatemala: State of Siege," *The New York Times Magazine*, 24 August 1980, 24.

40. Ibid., 24. Riding was not the only North American correspondent to recognize the sudden participation of Indians in the Guatemalan guerrilla movement. See also Marlise Simons, "Indians Resist Military Service: Guatemalan Army's Contempt for their Culture Breeds Spirit of Revolt," *The Washington Post*, 28 March 1980, section A, 21; Juan M. Vásquez, "Guerrillas Focus on Guatemala's Indians," *Los Angeles Times*, 13 July 1980, 26; and Daniel Sutherland, "Guatemala Repression Breeds New Rebels," *The Christian Science Monitor*, 21 April 1981, 1.

41. For a discussion of these trends, see my article, "State Violence and Agrarian Crisis in Guatemala: The Roots of the Indian Peasant Rebellion", in Martin Diskin, ed., *Trouble in Our Backyard: Central America and the United States in the Eighties* (New York: Pantheon Books, 1983), 155–71. These agrarian trends are also discussed in Alfredo Guerra-Borges, "La Cuestión Agraria, Cuestión Clave de la Crisis en Guatemala," *Polémica* no. 13 (1983) : 51–57.

42. See U.S. Agency for International Development, *Land and Labor in Guatemala: An Assessment* (Washington, 1982) for a recent evaluation of government agrarian policies. The best single source on the Arbenz agrarian reform program is José Luis Paredes Moreira, *Reforma Agraria: Una Experiencia en Guatemala* (Guatemala: Editora Universitaria, 1963). On the role of Indians in the agrarian reform, see Robert Wasserstrom, "Revolution in Guatemala: Peasants and Politics under the Arbenz Government," *Comparative Studies in Society and History* 17 (1975) : 443–78.

43. On the growth and influence of the Roman Catholic Church in Guatemala today, see Phillip Berryman, *The Religious Roots of Rebellion: Christians in Central American Revolutions* (New York: Orbis Books, 1984), chap. 6.

44. For anthropological studies of the role of the Catholic Action movement in Indian communities, see Warren, *The Symbolism of Subordination*; and Ricardo Falla, *Quiché Rebelde* (Guatemala: Editora Universitaria, 1978).

45. On the radicalization of the Catholic Action Movement in El Quiché, see: "A Priest Among the People: An Interview with Father Celso," in Jonathan L. Fried, Marvin E. Gettleman, Deborah T. Levenson, and Nancy Peckenham, eds., *Guatemala in Rebellion: Unfinished History* (New York: Grove Press, 1983).

46. See "Guatemala: Peasant Massacre," *Latin America Political Report* 9 (June 1978) : 175; and Gabriel Aguilera Peralta, "The Massacre at Panzós and Capitalist Development in Guatemala," *Monthly Review* 31, no. 7 (1979) : 13–23.

47. As one of the leaders of CUC related in an interview soon after its founding ("Interview with Committee for Peasant Unity," *Guatemala News and Information Bureau* 1, no. 3 [1978] : 8–9): "Most of us have been catechists and

we still are. Almost all of us practice religion in our communities. But just like we organize ourselves in churches to practice the Word of God, we should organize ourselves to fight for our rights. One thing doesn't exclude the other, but rather they go hand in hand. We hope for all the support of religious groups in our just struggles. Jesus came to teach us justice, that we are all brothers and sisters, and there shouldn't be exploiters or exploited; he came to teach us equality without discrimination, to bring us liberation.. As one *compañero* says, religion should be like the *chile* of our organization, and "organized struggle is the road which God has left his people for their liberation." Several commentators have noted the important influence that the Christian Peasant Movement in El Salvador (FECCAS) had on the formation of CUC. For an analysis of this movement, see Carlos Rafael Cabarrús, *Génesis de una Revolución: Análisis del Surgimiento y Desarrollo de la Organización Campesina en El Salvador* (Mexico: Ediciones de la Casa Chata, 1983).

48. A detailed history of events in northern el Quiché is contained in an anonymous mimeographed account, seemingly by a local priest, titled, "La Iglesia en El Quiché: Martirio y Esperanza de un Pueblo" (Guatemala, 1980).

49. "Guatemala: International Outcry over Embassy Deaths Pushes Regime into Isolation," *Latin America Weekly Report*, 8 February 1980, 4, 5.

50. Shelton H. Davis and Julie Hodson, *Witnesses to Political Violence in Guatemala: The Suppression of a Rural Development Movement* (Boston: Oxfam America, 1982). See also the Amnesty International Report, *Guatemala: A Government Program of Political Murder* (London, 1981).

51. Phillip Berryman, *The Religious Roots of Rebellion*, 200–206.

52. See statements by Quiché catechists in "Guatemalan Indians, Beyond the Myth," (in Special Edition of *Guatemalan Church in Exile* 4, no. 2 (1984):19. See also the autobiographical account, published in a German translation, *Rigoberta Menchu*, Elizabeth Burgos, ed. (Bornheim, BRD: Lamuv Verlag, 1984).

53. Eric R. Wolf, *Peasant Wars of the Twentieth Century* (New York: Harper and Row, 1969).

54. The New York-based human rights organization Americas Watch, among others, has been systematically documenting the effects of the Guatemalan Army's rural counter-insurgency campaign on the country's indigenous population. See for example, their report: *Guatemala: A Nation of Prisoners* (New York: Americas Watch, 1984) and *Human Rights in Guatemala During President Cerezo's First Year* (New York: Americas Watch and British Parliamentary Human Rights Group, 1987). Also, Amnesty International, *Guatemala: The Human Rights Record* (London, 1987).

55. The studies referred to in this paragraph are collected in a forthcoming book edited by Robert M. Carmack, *Harvest of Violence: The Maya Indians and the Guatemalan Crisis* (Norman: University of Oklahoma Press, 1988).

The Moral Economy of the Miskito Indians: Local Roots of a Geopolitical Conflict

THEODORE MACDONALD

The Miskito Indians' conflict with Nicaragua's Sandinista government made them the most highly publicized indigenous people in the Americas. But fame produced little understanding of either the people or their situation. Misinterpretation and misinformation more often supported other interests or motives. Concerned primarily with the political symbolism of the Nicaraguan revolution, many observers chose to portray the Indians as either dupes of imperialist advances or victims of communist totalitarianism; their perceptions were influenced more by their image of the Nicaraguan revolution than by any analysis of the Indians' actual condition. But, with increasing accounts of human rights violations by the Sandinistas, progressive political parties, national governments, and human rights organizations questioned the Nicaraguan government's Indian policies and actions. More important still, the Miskitos were able guerilla fighters supported by a sympathetic regional population. By late 1984 their image, both in and outside of Nicaragua, had shifted from that of a faceless mass with a few maverick spokesmen to an independent political and military force with legitimate complaints and representative leadership.

Specifically, the Indian organization MISURASATA (an acronym for Miskito, Sumo, Rama, and Sandinistas working together), and its general coordinator, Brooklyn Rivera, were no longer labeled as counterrevolutionaries; the cause of their anger was recognized, by some, as analogous to that voiced by Indians from the Arctic to Patagonia. This allowed MISURASATA to shed an imposed geopolitical cloak; to emphasize that the conflict concerned rights to land, natural resources, and self-determination; and to explain that peace required only negotiation and resolution of these rights.

Clarification, however, did not resolve the conflict. Obfuscation, misrepresentation and manipulation consistently forced the Indians to define their condition, outline its remedies, and act independently. In Europe and the Americas they spoke to public forums and to influential individuals, where many initially refused to listen. In the swamps and on the shores and plains of the Caribbean coast they waged a guerilla war, often accepting arms from governments and agencies whose motives, they knew, were unrelated to Indian interests.

Many critics of the Sandinista regime, however, tended to ignore the broader questions of Miskito rights. Instead many—most noticeably the Reagan administration, several of whose representatives earlier had railed at some of the Sandinistas' human rights violations—actively impeded peace negotiations while supplying and financing those Miskitos who proclaimed irreconcilable opposition to the Nicaraguan government. Likewise, despite an expressed willingness to negotiate a peace agreement, the Sandinistas rejected MISURASATA's claims, perceiving them as threats to the development of their concept of the new Nicaraguan state; eventually they proposed a unilateral resolution to the "Indian problem" through a government-initiated autonomy program.

This paper first explores the historical roots of this conflict. This is followed by a review and four critical phases of the post-revolutionary period. Finally, it considers the possibility of reconciliation.

INTRODUCTION

The Miskito-Sandinista conflict arose somewhat as a surprise for many observers, about eighteen months after the fall of the Somoza family dynasty in July 1979. By the first anniversary of the revolution, Miskito Indians had obtained impressive rights and opportunities: a multilingual literacy campaign; official status for their Indian organization, MISURASATA; and representation for that organization on the quasi-legislative Council of State and in government offices. But seven months later MISURASATA's entire leadership was suddenly jailed without formal charges. The arrests provoked a confrontation in the coastal village of Prinzapolka in which four Miskitos and four soldiers were killed. Fearing more widespread arrests, about three thousand young Miskitos fled to Honduras.

In late 1981 violent confrontations between Miskitos and Sandinista soldiers increased along the Nicaragua-Honduras border. In February 1982, about eight thousand Miskitos were suddenly and forcibly relocated from their homes along the Coco River border with Honduras to resettlement camps (Tasba Pri) about sixty kilometers to the south, while about ten thousand others fled to Honduras: their numbers quickly increased to about twenty-five thousand as forced resettlement and violence increased. With about 40 percent of their population displaced and angry, the Indians increasingly took up arms. Armed conflict peaked in 1983, continued to 1984, slowly abated after peace negotiations began in late 1984, and increased again in early 1986. Consequently, Miskito refugees in Honduras numbered about thirty-five thousand in May 1986 even though the government, after July 1985, permitted residents of Tasba Pri to return to their home settlements along the Rio Coco. At the same time Miskito military units controlled large sections of Nicaragua's northern Caribbean coast.

What happened? The conflict, as many have noted, arose amidst great historical and cultural differences. Geography and history cleave Nicaragua into Atlantic and Pacific regions; suspicion and racism have always characterized relations between their populations. But if such factors alone were the source of the conflict, roads and education might be its resolution. More profound differences actually sparked the violence. The Miskitos and the Sandinistas held contrasting perceptions and interpretations of the region's history and present condition. This, in turn, produced conflicting goals for the future.

The Nicaraguan government, like that of many recently "decolonized" countries, proclaims the need to build a state and instill a feeling of national identity, particularly for an area such as the Atlantic Coast where distinct peoples became "Nicaraguans" largely by nineteenth-century government decrees. Many government officials regard nation-building and expansion of the dominant FSLN party as an inseparable complementary process; since each responds to the needs of the people, they argue, it is their duty to promote both. In 1981, Daniel Ortega, then coordinator of the Junta of the Nicaraguan Government of National Reconstruction (JGRN) and now president, stated:

We have to integrate them [the people of the Atlantic Coast] totally, so that the Miskito of Waspam, Puerto Cabezas, Siuna, and Bonanza, as well as the Rama, the Sumu, the Blacks from Bluefields . . . become united with the Sandinista Front, with the Nicaraguan people and with the Nicaraguan Revolution. (Barricada 20 July 1981, emphasis added)

And four years later, Tomas Borge, Minister of the Interior, expressed a similar concern:

Here [on the Atlantic Coast] there are no Whites, Blacks, Miskitos or Creoles. Here there are only revolutionary and counterrevolutionary Nicaraguans, regardless of the color of their skin. The only thing that differentiates us is the attitude we assume toward the nation. (*New York Times* 26 April 1985; see also Ohland and Schneider 1983, 189–92)

But such notions of nation-building threaten Indians and other segments of Nicaragua's plural society. Thus, MISURASATA's general principles state that "we . . . consider [as] our enemies all those who deny our ethnic values, way of life and solidarity. . . ." (MISURASATA 1982). Such differences reveal more about the root causes of their conflict with the Sandinistas than broad geopolitical explanations. They are, therefore, the focus of this paper.

Contrasting images of an ideal society and the actual programs and policies they engendered, produced the conflict between the Sandinistas and the Indians, but the *extent* of this conflict and the *amount* of world attention focused on it reveals that the problem is not simply one of a state versus an Indian nation. Individuals, organizations, and governments fueled animosities and thus drew Indians, both as symbols and actors, into a global geopolitical arena where they were viewed as either pawns or caricatures. Such maneuvers prevented, or at least delayed, any efforts to negotiate solutions to the underlying causes of the conflict. Foreign influence, particularly the threat posed by U.S. government declarations and actions, is a critical feature in the history of Miskito and Sandinista fighting; the use and abuse of Miskitos in plots against the Sandinistas has been amply documented and fully substantiated (Abrams 1985, 1986; Americas Watch 1982, 1986; Constable 1986; Lernoux 1985a, 1985b, 1985c; McAward and Macdonald 1984; Maier 1985, 1986; Mohawk and Davis 1982; Muravchik 1984; *Newsweek* 8 November 1982; Rivera 1985, 1986 (personal communication); Sharkey 1985). Here, however, we focus on the roots of the conflict internal to Nicaragua, the only place where any lasting solution to the conflict can be found, since neither the removal of the Sandinista government, nor the subsiding of the "imperialist threat" to that government will necessarily eliminate its roots. By viewing the situation in terms of its fundamental causes, interpretation shifts from a focus on specific actors, particular events, and hasty generalizations to a perspective which takes into account the situation of indigenous groups within many other modern states. Nicaragua then stands out in high—but not singular— relief, and its peculiarity is that it represents a "socialist" regime facing a pluri-ethnic situation within the Western postcolonial world.

The root conflict is largely one of priorities. For the Sandinista government, national consolidation in both a political sense and an economic sense is the primary goal. To justify their aims they cite their understanding of national and regional history, and, by extension, validate their solution to problems created by that history. In this scheme the FSLN is the vehicle for change. Consequently national sovereignty often is invoked when there is a perceived threat to the FSLN's plans for nation-building. The Sandinistas' interpretation of history and their goals for the future, however, frequently contrast with those of the Miskitos. Although these Indians have maintained contact, to varying extents, with the world economy and non-Indian societies since the seventeenth century, they nevertheless have a different understanding of their past and somewhat divergent aspirations for the future. This basic dissimilarity has become obscured by the portrayal of both antagonists through a series of caricatures, or through projections of genuine leaders as either putty or puppets, molded or manipulated by outside interests.

HISTORY AND THE CONCEPT OF EXPLOITATION

Any understanding of the conflict begins with history, or more precisely, its various interpretations. Until late 1984 the Sandinistas maintained that the government's role on the Atlantic Coast was to expose and eliminate the economic forces that had engendered racial discrimination. Rather than considering social and political mechanisms for sustaining pluralism, official statements and government-supported research interpreted ethnicity mainly in a folkloristic sense (e.g., Borge 1981); their main concern was with the etiology and dissolution of ethnic inequality.

To illustrate, in 1981 a United Nations seminar on recourse procedures available to the victims of racial discrimination was held in Managua. While representatives from such countries as Brazil and Bolivia denied the existence of racism in their nations, the Nicaraguans acknowledged their history of racial discrimination, arguing that:

centuries of oppression and exploitation [have] created a structure of classes and an ideological regime of racial discrimination which has aided imperialism in the domination of the native forces of production through a dominant class, while exalting the supposed virtues of one ethnic group to the detriment of the rest. (Ramirez 1981, 4)

At the same seminar, a background paper prepared by members of CIDCA, a Nicaraguan social research institute, stated that "on the American continent and especially in Latin America, racism is based on the material conditions of life and on specific social and economic relations" (Vanegas, et al. 1981, 3) and added that "the future defense of Indian territories becomes a part of the struggle of all destitute people, such as peasants and workers, to obtain freedom within a State which respects their interests" (ibid., 8; see also CIDCA 1981a, 1981b).

Miskito leaders, too, recognize their links with peasants and workers, as well as the importance of the past in producing present circumstances.

We maintain that the purpose of the Sandinista revolution is to liberate all the oppressed and exploited of the country. We are part of this group. Fundamentally, the revolution is for the workers and the campesinos. We are part of those national groups. . . . Our entire history demonstrates to us that from the onset of contact with outsiders (conquistadores, pirates and missionaries), our ethnic groups have been marginalized and subjected to various forms of exploitation. (MISURASATA 1980)

The Indians, however, perceive class formation and ethnic relations differently from the Sandinistas. The MISURASATA's general principles emphasize that "ethnic identity is historically *prior* to the formation and consolidation of national class structure, and it casts itself *well beyond* their demise" (ibid., emphasis added). They insist that ethnic plurality and differentiation

constitute the basis for any revolutionary process which seeks the suppression of class-stratified society and the intentional building of a pluralist and self-determining society, and as such, one which is capable of offering a true alternative to [most forms of] human coexistence, one which is historically different. (Ibid.)

For them, a revolution is not only an opportunity to achieve economic equality but, equally important, one for exercising their unique identity.

This aspiration extends well beyond Nicaragua's Atlantic Coast. Thus Bonfil's *Utopia y revolucion* (1981), distinguishes a general status, *indio*, from a particular position, that of ethnic group: "Specific Indian communities, ethnic groups, are all *indios* in that one can assign them the status of colonized people, but at an ethnic level they are all distinguishable and separate—e.g., Nahuas, Quechuas, Shuars" (ibid., 20). He emphasizes that decolonization and the subsequent disappearance of the generic *indio* will allow the distinct ethnic groups to exercise their individuality.[1] Understood thus, ethnicity is not simply the cause of racism and discrimination, it is also the source of a unique, vital self-identity; it is something that Indians will not relinquish simply on the promise of improved social and economic conditions.

EXPLOITATION

These different perceptions of ethnicity are particularly significant as leaders attempt to negotiate a resolution to the conflict. Reconciliation and mutual acceptance, however, are further complicated by the fact that even if the Sandinistas begin to accept ethnic identity in anything more than folkloristic terms, many Indians may not embrace a regime that promises to eliminate exploitation as the Sandinistas define it. Moreover, the analytical category of *indio* and the experience of colonialist exploitation, while ideologically recognized by some leaders, is poorly understood by members of the actual communities involved in the struggle.

The Sandinistas claim a clear understanding of the region's economic history, and become frustrated when the residents do not see it the same way (Borge 1981; Ramirez 1981; CIDCA 1981b). The Indians' "political backwardness," they insist, has blinded them to foreign exploitation, which not only pillaged resources and abused workers, but even caused ethnic differentiation and racism.[2] Their "political backwardness" is said to be demonstrated by racial antagonism toward Spanish-speakers rather than by anger at exploitation. While MISURASATA's leadership agrees that Atlantic Coast Indians have been exploited historically by external forces, many community members do not conceive of themselves as *indios* in the sense described by Bonfil, nor do they reject or despise those defined as colonialist exploiters. On the contrary, many coastal Indians have historically welcomed numerous outside economic interests. Why?

Much of the explanation lies in the definition and perception of exploitation. Scholars agree that since the seventeenth century, Indians of the Mosquitia have been linked to outside political forces and the world market economy. But they differ on the question of what has been the nature of these links. Some see the Miskitos as subjects of British colonization or North American imperialism (Wheelock 1981, 11; CIERA 1981, 35–62; MISURASATA 1981); others view them as occasional allies or adventurers alongside the British (Floyd 1967; Ramirez 1981); others portray them as subjects of an indigenous or imposed royalty (Dennis 1981; Olien 1983; Dennis and Olien 1984); others regard the Miskitos as only occasional actors in larger political and economic arenas (Helms 1969, 1971; Nietschmann 1973; Parsons 1955). None, however, explains why lopsided economic relations were not rejected or challenged.

Rephrasing the initial question provides a more useful perspective. Rather than ask in what way the Miskitos were involved with outside forces, which produces an answer in which all authors are more or less correct, one might ask to what extent they—and by extension, their land and resources—were involved. This forces a look at the Miskitos' perceptions of exploitation and thus helps to explain not only their view of local economic history but also their unenthusiastic response to many initiatives on the part of the Sandinistas.

The Sandinistas focus largely on expropriation as the basis for determining exploitation. Some residents on the other hand regard the colonialist presence as a sort of "golden age" (Helms 1969). Are they blind to exploitation? Probably not. The work of Barrington Moore (1966), Scott (1976) and Godelier (1977) suggest an interpretation of exploitation which extends beyond actual expropriation of labor and resources to feelings of exploitation. According to Scott (1966, 7), one of the peasant's critical tests for exploitation is the subsistence test: that is, " 'What is left?' rather than 'How much is taken?' " [3]

Miskito economic patterns and their relation to the broader economic history of the Atlantic Coast support, in part, a "subsistence test" concept of exploitation. Since the conquest, subsistence-based production has periodically shared time and space with market-oriented activities either in the form of production for the market, harvesting for the market, or wage labor. Godelier characterizes societies such as this as "mixed economies . . . specific ways and *dominated by one*" (Godelier 1977, 18, emphasis added). However, for most Miskito individuals, families, and communities, no single set of activities consistently dominated. The primacy of the market economy ebbed and flowed as markets boomed and busted; subsistence agriculture dominated during the troughs but never disappeared during the peaks. Subsistence security was never threatened. So, despite periods of undeniably intensive expropriation, feelings of exploitation were not particularly strong.

Second, and equally important, for the Miskito as with Indians throughout the Americas, land transcends mere subsistence. There is a spiritual, religious link to the territory from which their ancestors emerged and to which they see their destiny closely tied. Throughout the prerevolutionary period, with only one exception, there was no perceived general threat to the Indians' land tenure or challenge to their rights over resources; despite periodic expropriation of resources, no one was viewed as having challenged the Miskitos' aboriginal claims to their land and resources. A brief historical review illustrates that such perceptions are not mystification imposed upon ignorance.

The "colonial" economic history of the Caribbean coast can be divided into two periods: 1633–1894, when England dominated trade; and 1894–1979, when U.S. companies, often in close collaboration with the Somoza government, predominated on the Atlantic Coast.

I. BRITISH INFLUENCE ON THE ATLANTIC COAST: 1633–1894

The Sandinistas tend to regard post-Columbian Nicaragua as an area totally colonized by Europeans (Ramirez 1981, 2; Wheelock 1974, 47, 1981, 11). They also tend to regard British and Spanish presence as analogous when in fact these nations maintained qualitatively different motives. In sixteenth-century Central America, Spain's interests lay in colonization and the utilization of the indigenous population as the colonists' labor force. Spain "failed" to colonize the Atlantic Coast, but their efforts were few and half-hearted at best. The Atlantic Coast Indians were simply not the sort of sedentary agriculturalists organized into hierarchically ordered societies which offered useful sources of labor. They were a dispersed community of relatively independent, subsistence swidden-horticulturalists, hunters, and fishers. These Indians, nevertheless, undoubtedly were aware of the Spaniards' brutal and decimating treatment of Pacific Coast Indians (Radell 1976), and repelled even sporadic incursions (Floyd 1967).

England's interests on the Atlantic Coast, by contrast, began in the seventeenth century and were almost entirely mercantile; they worked to establish a dominant trading position in the Caribbean, rather than to create a permanent colony that used Indian labor as the Spanish did. The Miskito served these ends ideally. British buccaneers and, later, merchants visited or set up temporary residence in coves along the coast. Anchorages evolved into permanent trading posts where manufactured goods were exchanged for local raw materials, principally hardwoods such as mahogany.

The most important of the manufactured items was the musket. Helms (1969, 78) writes:

Armed with these new weapons, the Miskito, as a population, gradually extended their influence over their now less powerful neighbors, who either became culturally extinct or retreated to the headwaters of the numerous rivers crossing the coast.

The regional hegemony of the Miskitos was validated when the British proclaimed a Miskito king.[4]

The Miskito "kingdom" has generated considerable recent research (Dennis 1981; Dennis and Olien 1984; Olien n.d.; Helms 1969, 1975). Most of this, however, has focused on establishing or questioning the existence of a royal lineage, and debunking the idea that the Miskito king was little more than a drunken buffoon and a political puppet. Relatively little new information exists regarding the impact of the king on local political, economic, and social life. The evidence that has been assembled indicates that, on some occasions, the king exercised authority as if the Mosquitia were his kingdom. But overall, the role of the Miskito monarch seems to have been more ceremonial than political. Seen from outside the Mosquitia, the British-appointed king established a close imperial link between the British and the Miskito, and consequently a further distance between the Indians and the Spaniards, and to have unified a Miskito polity. For the British, the king's principal role was to justify an English protectorate in the eyes of other European nations (CIDCA 1984). For some Miskitos, the king provided legitimization for attacks on neighbors or demands for tribute. But for most Indians the king mattered little. Although appointed by the crown, kings rarely exercised authority without first consulting with a council of elders, and, Helms (1969, 79) writes, "even then their directions were followed only if their constituents felt inclined to do so." She adds, "actual political decisions within Miskito society seem to have been made by village headmen and regional chiefs—a practice more in keeping with the traditional decentralized nature of the indigenous political organization" (ibid.).

What role, then, did the Miskito "kingdom" play for the British? Compared to activities in the rest of the Caribbean, the Miskito coast was relatively insignificant; nonetheless it was representative of the general pattern. In the early seventeenth century buccaneers roamed and plundered Spanish colonial outposts along the Caribbean coast— even extending their Nicaraguan raids up the Rio San Juan to the cities of Leon and Grenada—and sacking the Spanish settlements. The buccaneers' relations with the Miskito were minimal; the coastal lagoons served as safe anchorages and the population provided some food and occasional crew members. But later in the century, as Spain became a progressively weaker European (and by extension, Caribbean) power, the crown was unable to supply sufficient goods to Spanish America, yet demanded strict controls on all imports and exports in an effort to strengthen a weakening world position (Wallerstein 1980, 160). This redirected the nature of non-Spanish mercantile activities; the British and others shifted from plundering to "illegitimate trade." On the Miskito coast this involved contraband, "smuggling . . . became a way of life that linked the merchants of the core countries to the producers of peripheral countries they did not directly control" (ibid.). The Mosquitia thus became as much, if not more, an avenue of illicit exchange as it was a source of raw materials. The "warfare" that occasionally broke out was usually little more than attacks on the forts (*presidios*) constructed by the crown to prevent such exchanges (Wallerstein 1980; Floyd 1967). Everyone else benefited from the contraband trade. On the shore and coastal rivers, up to the end of the eighteenth century European presence was characterized by a few small settlements of logwood and mahogany cutters, and by the traders in contraband as well (Helms 1975, 215).

In brief, friendly alliances with the British were based on economic links characterized by occasional contract labor and exchange of trade goods. Payments and exchanges were lopsided, undoubtedly, in favor of those who provided the manufactured goods, but such inequity was not the Indians' major concern. What was expropriated mattered less than what was left, which, in turn, was considerable—subsistence security and territorial security. The Miskito labor expended to provide goods for exchange was only occasional and did not force the Indians to alter an economic pattern in which subsistence horticulture dominated. Equally important, these economic relations did not threaten the Indians' land base; British presence was limited to a few trading posts. Thus, although the Miskito maintained close contact with market economies and powerful nation-states, they, unlike the peasants and Indians of Nicaragua's Pacific Coast, were dominated by neither. As such, up to the end of the nineteenth century, exploitation was not a major concern and did not provoke resistance to outsiders.

II. U.S. INTERESTS ON THE ATLANTIC COAST: POST-1894

In the late 1800s the sphere of geopolitical interest shifted. Both the U.S. and Britain became increasingly concerned with an interoceanic canal, which each nation hoped to control, and Nicaragua, with its series of rivers and lakes, became a focus of interest.[5]

In early 1894, Nicaraguan troops, under orders from President Jose Santos Zelaya, occupied cities along the Atlantic Coast and repelled British attempts to stop them (Millett 1977, 20–21). Nicaragua subsequently annexed the disputed territory and abolished the Miskito Reserve while guaranteeing minimal land rights to the Indians through the Harrison-Altamirano Treaty of 1905. When Zelaya was elected president (1893), he initially supported U.S. presence, but later, as he began to oppose its increasing influence, he was perceived as entirely too nationalistic. He was overthrown in 1909 with U.S. support.

Access to a potential canal route was not the only U.S. concern in Nicaragua. By the turn of the century modest mercantile exchange on the Atlantic Coast was replaced by more intensive production of market-oriented resources, and the flow of these goods had shifted from Britain to North America. In 1911 the U.S. received 28 percent of Nicaragua's exports; by 1918, this had increased to 51 percent (CIERA 1981, 43).

Briefly, when England was the principal market, hardwood extraction provided the main source of cash to the Miskitos. Around 1860, rubber tapping started. Near the turn of the century American companies began mining gold and silver (Parsons 1955, 51). At the same time, exploitation of hardwoods increased and initial cropping of extensive pine forests in northeastern Zelaya gradually expanded exports of resin, turpentine and board lumber. Along the rivers, Standard Fruit Company and other smaller companies began to encourage banana production. By 1890 U.S. investments in such activities totalled $10 million (CIDCA 1984, 8). By the 1930s, commercial production of rice and beans was also well under way along the major rivers. And by the 1960s, coastal fishing for green and hawkbill turtle increased rapidly to meet a rising world demand. With this came wage labor and goods purchased from local stores or company commissaries.

The general shift in economic activities can be divided into periods marked by the predominance of particular commodities. A brief review illustrates no major disruption of Indian life.

RUBBER

From about 1860 to 1878, Nicaragua, more than any other Central American nation, reacted to the world demand for rubber. Along with ladinos from the Pacific Coast, Miskitos tapped rubber trees on the eastern slopes of the central highlands and in the forests of the San Juan River basin (West and Augelli 1976, 445). In 1867 Nicaragua exported 401,476 pounds; in 1871 754,886 pounds; and by 1878, production reached a peak of 3,693,000 pounds (CIERA 1981, 47). By 1900, Nicaragua's Atlantic Coast had exported more rubber than any region except the Amazon basin. Production, however, decreased sharply when Indonesian rubber plantations were established in 1912, rendering uncompetitive the gathering techniques of the Americas.

World War II again stimulated production of rubber in the Americas. In 1942 the Rubber Reserve Corporation was established on the Atlantic Coast. In April 1945, Nicaragua exported 557,760 pounds of rubber to U.S. markets (Parsons 1955, 62). Forty commissaries were established "to supply 5,000 Indian and Creole tappers and a salaried staff of 165 persons" (ibid.; see also CIERA 1981, 47). As the forests became depleted of high-quality rubber, tappers began to mix latex from chicle (*tuno*), found in large quantities in the upper Coco River. Demand diminished sharply with the post–World War II reopening of trade routes to Southeast Asia. More importantly, following the development of synthetic rubber, only about two thousand gatherers extracted chicle for chewing gum in the mid-1950s.

What was the composition of this labor force? In the Americas there were no rubber plantations. Tappers generally worked a section of forest assigned to them by an individual who had received a concession to exploit a broad area. The classic image of labor conditions during the rubber boom is from the Amazon basin, where Indians worked under extremely oppressive circumstances—forced recruitment, dispersal, and even murder (Hardenburg 1912; Casement 1912). However, this was the extreme; most rubber workers were contributors rather than laborers.[6]

Individual occasional contributors, as opposed to a full-time labor force, also seem to have characterized those of the Atlantic Coast (CIERA 1981, 66). Consequently, although rubber traders expropriated resources and labor, they did not introduce production patterns which dominated or transformed local economic life. The indigenous subsistence economy remained largely intact.

BANANAS

About 1880, banana production began on Nicaragua's southern coast. By 1883, thirty thousand stems were being exported to New Orleans. Ten years later, the Bluefields-Rama Company established about twenty small plantations near the south coastal port of Bluefields, and set up purchase agreements with about five hundred producers (CIERA 1981, 52). Exports were small until several firms established themselves in the early 1920s, the two largest being the Cuyamel Fruit Company (Cuyamel was purchased by the United Fruit Company in 1924) and the Standard Fruit Company. The largest plantation contained five thousand hectares and paid three thousand salaried workers in the area of Rio Grande de Matagalpa, while maintaining contract agreements with a number of independent producers.

In 1925, the Standard Fruit Company in collaboration with the Bragman's Bluff Lumber Company, established port facilities on the north coast and expanded the settlement, Bragman's Bluff, later named Puerto Cabezas. The company maintained a few small plantations, but most bananas were purchased from independent producers, to whom traders extended credit and provided technical assistance. By the early 1930s, the banks of the Rio Coco and other rivers of Northern Zelaya were lined with bananas planted by Miskito families, each of whom maintained several plots on their land (Helms 1971). Company-managed plantations in northern Zelaya were rare; Augusto C. Sandino and his troops were a major impediment.

From 1927 to 1933, Sandino's forces effectively controlled much of the provinces of Nueva Segovia and Jinotega, and were raiding in areas of northwestern Zelaya when banana production was peaking in other areas of the lowland Caribbean. Beginning in April 1931,

Sandino's troops launched a series of attacks along the Atlantic Coast. Such actions, compounded by frequent attacks on interior settlements, forced Standard Fruit to abandon its few plantations in the area, and to rely on individual producers. This had a significant impact on labor conditions. As Torres Rivas (1971) indicates, an economically viable banana economy requires nearly self-contained enclaves and a monopoly of all phases of production.[7] Such conditions existed at various United Fruit plantations in Costa Rica, Panama, Guatemala, and Honduras. To a lesser extent, they also characterized United Fruit's operations in southern Zelaya. Such inversions of capital and infrastructural expansion can cause significant changes in indigenous social and economic life (Gudeman 1978). Moreover, when large banana plantations close or transfer their activities, the effect on a subsistence population converted to wage earners can be devastating (Helms 1975, 254; Torres Rivas 1971, 90–108). Conditions in northern Zelaya, however—such as plant disease and political violence—made it difficult to establish extensive enclaves. Standard Fruit Company's activities there, although productive up to the 1930s, were never the sort of hermetically sealed, economic estates which existed in other areas. In some areas of Central America, when banana production came to a halt it removed the economic base of a rural proletariat. But in northern Zelaya, the decline simply meant that opportunities for market-oriented banana production disappeared and subsistence agriculture reemerged as the dominant economic activity.

While banana production and rubber gathering in northern Zelaya were, by and large, activities that were easily accommodated within a subsistence-based economy, Indian involvement in lumbering and mining required a shift to wage labor. By 1926, three thousand salaried employees worked for the Bragman's Bluff Lumber Company headquartered in Puerto Cabezas. Mining near the present-day settlements of Siuna and Bonanza began near the turn of the century, and by 1940 about twenty-four hundred workers were employed at mines there. With the collapse of banana production, lumbering and mining were almost the only source of cash. More importantly, they were activities which, it would appear, could not easily be accommodated into the cycle of subsistence agriculture. Those who worked for lumber or mining companies were full-time employees whose subsistence had to be purchased rather than cultivated.

Such a change in the allocation of time and resources would appear to signal a major shift in the mode of production. However, the activity per se did not alter coastal economic patterns. Again, the critical feature was not whether the population was involved in such activities but to what extent.[8] Most employees were either short-term laborers (heads of households in need of quick cash) or unmarried adolescent males who traditionally traveled and sought employment outside their natal community for a period before settling as "responsible adults." Neither the mines nor the forestry companies precluded regular maintenance of agricultural plots. Subsistence agriculture, with the security and economic independence it guaranteed, continued amidst a regional economy noticeably linked to wage labor.

Perhaps the most significant impact of these new extractive economies was the threat they posed to Indian claims to natural resources. Following World War II, the American-owned Nicaragua Longleaf Pine Lumber Company (NIPCO) opened large-scale lumbering activities on extensive pine forests in northeast Nicaragua. Although NIPCO is said to have developed a reforestation plan, Somoza accepted a higher export tax instead. As a result, the forests of northeastern Zelaya were denuded and unreplenished. Production declined in the early 1960s and NIPCO departed in 1966. To revive the industry Somoza initiated a massive reforestation project directed by the Instituto de Fomento Nacional (INFONAC) and the United Nations Food and Agricultural Organization (FAO). Large tracts of land used by the Miskitos were "nationalized" and the Miskito were prohibited from extracting lumber.[9] For the first time, the state and market economies were seen as a threat to the Miskitos' claim to land and natural resources. The first regional Indian organization, ALPROMISU (the Alianza para el progreso Miskito y Sumo), was formed, in part, to protest such actions and to protect Indian rights to land and natural resources.

This response is not surprising. Permanent state claims to land and resource rights, unlike previous forms of occasional external expropriation, violated what Scott (1976, 3) calls the moral economy:

[a group's] notion of economic justice and their working definition of exploitation—their view of which claims on their product were tolerable and which intolerable, . . . [is] socially experienced as a pattern of moral rights and expectations. Barrington Moore [1966] has captured the normative tone of these expectations: "This experience [of sharing risks within the community] provides the soil out of which grew . . . mores and moral standards by which they judge their own behavior and that of others. The essence of these standards is a . . . notion of equality, stressing the justice and necessity of a minimum of land [resources] for the perfomance of essential social tasks. These standards usually have some sort of religious sanction, and it is likely to be in their stress that these points [their religious view of the land] differ from that of other social classes." The violation of these standards could be expected to provoke resentment and resistance—not only because needs were unmet but because [perceived] rights were violated.

Broad, religious concepts of land are not unique to Miskito Indians;

they run through Indian communities throughout the Americas. The Miskitos' moral economy included both subsistence rights and deep emotional concerns regarding land and resource rights. The cycles of several boom-and-bust economies on Nicaragua's Atlantic Coast, while exploitative in other people's minds, generally did not violate that moral economy and so did not cause resentment or violence.

POST-1979: THE SANDINISTAS AND THE ATLANTIC COAST

Post-revolutionary national development, by contrast, did violate the Miskito's moral economy. For the Sandinistas, national reconstruction was the creation and consolidation of a state; economic development was, in part, a means to strengthen the state as an all-inclusive entity. The Miskito by contrast, focused on economic and political self-determination. The period can be divided into four, relatively distinct phases: (1) November 1979 through mid-1980—the initial efforts at state consolidation; (2) mid-1980 to October 1981—the Indian's open resistance (referred to as the *Lucha Cívica*); (3) November 1981 to August 1984—the Indian uprising (referred to as the *Lucha Armada*); (4) August 1984 to present—the peace initiatives (as interpreted by either the Indians or the Sandinistas).

PHASE 1: INITIAL EFFORTS AT STATE CONSOLIDATION

Shortly after July 1979, the Nicaraguan Government of National Reconstruction (JGRN) began its political and economic reorganization. Throughout Nicaragua, the government established and empowered a series of political and occupational interest groups, referred to as mass organizations. Some were continuations of existing groups such as COSEP (High Council of Private Enterprise). Others, such as the Sandinista Youth and the Sandinista Workers Central (CST), were postrevolutionary creations. From the government's standpoint, the crucial mass organizations for the reconstruction of the Atlantic Coast were the Association of Rural Workers (Asociacion de Trabajadores Campesinos, or ATC) and the Sandinista Defense Committees (Comites para la Defensa Sandinista, or CDS). The ATCs were formed to organize production and other economic activities, mainly through the establishment of cooperatives; the CDSs were charged with political organization, education, and local social control. These mass organizations, the government hoped, would provide the sort of institutional structures that would link Atlantic Coast groups to their national counterparts.

To establish these organizations on the Atlantic Coast, Ernesto Cardenal, the Minister of Culture, and Daniel Ortega, then member of the governing junta, traveled to Puerto Cabezas in November 1979 to meet with representatives of 185 Indian communities at the annual congress of ALPROMISU. Ortega explained the general outline of national reconstruction, particularly the role of the ATCs and CDSs. These organizations, he stated, would respond to the needs around which ALPROMISU had originally formed: an ethnic organization, therefore, was no longer necessary. From the government's standpoint this may have been true. Locally, however the new order aroused considerable doubt and suspicion. First, the government representatives sent into the region to set up the new organizations were generally from the Pacific Coast, and thus were perceived as alien. Second, their claim that Nicaragua was now "free" did not have the same impact as it did on the Pacific Coast; Somoza's rule had not violently affected the Miskito, and the U.S. companies were not perceived as particularly exploitative. And the insurrection itself hardly touched the Atlantic Coast. Finally, and far more significant, was the fact that, locally, self-proclaimed "Sandinistas" (mainly non-Miskitos) began to occupy most positions of authority within the mass organization and in government offices. There was, therefore, no noticeable change, as far as the Indians were concerned, in the local power elite. These new officials also circulated rumors that the Indian organization was at best conservative and reactionary or, even worse, counterrevolutionary.

Brooklyn Rivera, in an October 1979 interview, outlined the problem:

Those on the Atlantic Coast who speak Spanish [as their first language, i.e., non-Indians, non-creoles] are the dominant class. They have held and still hold the civil and political authority here. Added to this is racial discrimination, in which the Miskitos are at the bottom. The "Spanish," taking advantage of their language identity have been able to identify themselves with the new regime, and have retained the political structure that they controlled under the Somocistas. With the revolution, the most brutal of the Somocistas escaped. But others have remained; they are the ones who now are in control. These people want to maintain a social hierarchy in which they are always on top, meddling with everything that goes on here. But it is the people, the Miskitos, who are the majority here and should be in such positions. Since we [the Indians] are fighting for the breakdown of this structure, up comes the accusation "the Miskitos want to throw all the Spanish speakers out of here; they [the Miskitos] are racists. They want to kick us out of the Atlantic Coast." You have to look and see where these accusations of Indian racism and separatism are coming from—the same dominant circles which have and still maintain local economic power. This is what we have to fight against.

Bourgouis and Grunberg's government-commissioned report (1980, 91; heavily edited and reprinted in CIERA 1981) similarly observed:

The Spanish-speaking bourgeoisie frequently presented itself after the revolution, as "Sandinista," trying to offset the just claims of the coastal people. This is how one can explain the sometimes hostile reaction of the coastal campesinos and workers in the face of the "Spanish" who with displays of power, vacuous rhetoric, attitudes of discrimination and often racism, try to assert themselves as officials of the GRN and as representatives of mass organizations.

This political dynamic was set in motion during the first months of national reconstruction, and the accusations seemed to have the support of Sandinista officials sent from Managua. Moreover, the Indians perceived the Sandinistas' great pride with regard to their military defeat of Somoza as a veiled arrogance toward the the Atlantic Coast, as if having participated minimally in military actions its residents were undeserving of any special treatment.

In light of such actions and attitudes, and to assure the functioning of an organization which represented majority interests in the region, the November 1979 ALPROMISU congress rejected the elimination of a distinct Indian organization and, following a series of debates and alternative suggestions, formed MISURASATA. MISURASATA then became an officially recognized mass organization and, like all others, obtained a seat in the Council of State when it opened in May 1980.

Thus, in terms of designing and implementing any sort of development program or project on the Atlantic Coast, two lines of authority were officially recognized—the government-sponsored ATCs and CDSs on one hand and MISURASATA on the other. MISURASATA was expected to fade as the programs evolved and obtained the confidence of the communities. Instead MISURASATA gained considerable strength during its first year, due directly to its own efforts and indirectly to government errors.

MISURASATA, initially, was not a strong organization; replacing ALPROMISU simply meant that it inherited a set of organizational goals and a structure of village representation. So, as with many incipient, pan-community Indian federations, MISURASATA's first objective was to strengthen the organization itself and increase community participation; while economic development was a concern, actual projects were virtually nonexistent. In the past, non-governmental economic assistance programs had been linked to church groups or other non-Indian private initiatives (Bourgouis and Grunberg 1980, 60; Adams 1981). Now, most new services and development projects for the Atlantic Coast were in the hands of government agencies whose overall program was to: (1) increase production; (2) increase local participation; and (3) "decolonize" the Atlantic Coast (CIERA 1981, 137–42).

Many government officials considered the Atlantic Coast as an area capable of greatly increased production, able to provide not only for regional but also for larger national consumption. Low agricultural production was regarded as a problem directly related to exploitative control over marketing and purchasing (Bourgouis and Grunberg 1980). In contrast to the Pacific Coast, where class conflict was manifested in the relations between large landowners and peasant workers, on the Atlantic Coast economic dominance was exercised by local shop owners and riverine traders, who were regarded, therefore, as the main exploiters. Government agencies were expected to replace these intermediaries, establishing more equitable exchange and thereby to promote greater productivity.

A perceived "ethnic" feature of marketing patterns, however, complicated these plans. Even though most community merchants were Indians, many, particularly those in large communities such as Puerto Cabezas and Waspam, were ethnic Chinese or ladino. Purveyors and purchasers were thus regarded as "different" and, therefore, outside of the community; Indian farmers distinguished between "we the Miskito, the poor farmers, and they the merchants, the millionaires" (CIERA 1981, 123). These tensions plagued the government's overall program. On the one hand, the local population distrusted the non-Indian representatives of government agencies who promised better conditions. Also, as mentioned earlier, many local officials were part of the previous non-Indian economic elite, which, with a better understanding of political maneuvering and government bureaucracies, suddenly "became Sandinistas" and manipulated its way into positions of authority in many development programs, often working to promote or perpetuate its own interests. On the other hand, government initiatives, however well intentioned and managed, were complicated by local merchants. Although exploitative, these individuals were, for the Indians, dependable patrons who could provide essential services. Faced with threatening competition, many simply closed their doors and refused to sell to those who cooperated with the government (Bourgouis and Grunberg 1980, 30). Acceptance of untested government programs was therefore risky.

Indian caution and hesitation were reinforced by government inefficiency. Utilizing funds from the Nicaraguan Central Bank, agencies— mainly ENABAS (National Corporation for Basic Foods) and INRA (National Agrarian Reform Agency)—hoped to extend credit for seed, fertilizer, and storage facilities. They also promised to purchase any surplus from the harvest at significantly higher prices. But, however well-meaning the aims, many of the agricultural programs failed during the first year. Flooding was blamed for the failure (INNICA 1982), but inefficiency was the perceived problem (Bourgouis and Grunberg 1980;

David Rodriguez 1986: personal communication). In settlements close to such urban areas as Puerto Cabezas, credit was available, seed was efficiently distributed, and crops were quickly marketed. But in more isolated areas many farmers, as recommended by government agencies, prepared larger plots that they were subsequently unable to sow because either the credit or the seed failed to arrive on time, if at all. In some areas where seed and other items were efficiently distributed, large subsequent harvests rotted while waiting for government vehicles or boats to transport them to market. As such, government loans, however appealing in terms of their low interest rates, were difficult to repay. Added to this were threats from local merchants who, aware that any successful government initiatives could eliminate their livelihood, sometimes cut off supplies to local ATC and CDS officials or simply closed their stores temporarily, leaving many farmers with little or no access to essential resources or goods. Thus, when faced with the choice of obtaining loans for seed and other materials from exploitative merchants and later marketing their production through the same channels, or alternatively, risking collaboration with inexperienced and, as it turned out, uncoordinated government agencies, many Indian farmers chose the security of familar agents over the promise of higher returns from untested agencies.

The GRN's[10] plan to increase supplies of marine resources was somewhat different. Coastal fishing was not as strongly linked to local elites as was riverine agricultural production. CIERA (1981) reported that the problem regarding marine resources was not local exploitation but rather the absence of a controlled system of obtaining, storing, and transporting items such as prawns, lobsters, turtles, and fish. Most of the produce had been either distributed and consumed locally, or shipped to U.S. and other foreign markets. After 1979, these markets diminished or disappeared. The establishment of a state-run fishing industry was placed in the hands of the National Fishing Institute, INPESCA. But INPESCA's "rationalization" of artisanal fishing was planned and undertaken with little local participation and was seen as a threat to village social and economic life.[11]

In summary, the Sandinistas' plan was for government agencies to reorganize a local economy by: (1) replacing those who had controlled and exploited agricultural production; and (2) converting other aspects of the economy into more productive and equitable systems. The assumption was that government-managed programs combined with sensitive public relations would not only increase production but create stronger community ties with national-level institutions. However, popular participation was understood by the Sandinistas as incorporation into government programs. And since there was no perceived contradiction between participation and incorporation, "decolonization," the GRN assumed, would logically follow. The first year's efforts to implement this plan under Sandinista control were largely unsuccessful both economically and socially. MISURASATA, not involved in its designing or implementing, was not considered responsible for the problems associated with agricultural production and personnel. Nor was the organization held to blame for the strict controls on fishermen accustomed to working in a complex ecosystem where tides, weather, and currents influence decisions, not government plans. Thus MISURASATA benefited indirectly.

At a more active level, MISURASATA established two initial goals: (1) to revitalize and support Indian culture; and (2) to meet local economic needs by paying special attention to the production and distribution of essential goods (MISURASATA 1980). For the government, involvement in cultural revitalization was the logical role for an Indian organization. The second goal, economic development of the Atlantic Coast, could either coincide or conflict with government programs. Since the government saw its role as managing and increasing production on the Atlantic Coast, eventually integrating the Indians into a series of national institutions, some officials felt that MISURASATA should function as an intermediary to facilitate government programs. MISURASATA, however, was unwilling to play the minimal political and economic role assigned to it; the organization outlined several economic development programs but was unable to implement them, due largely to lack of funds. Consequently MISURASATA officials worked mainly to strengthen the organization's ties to the communities, to promote the literacy campaign in native languages, and to develop other education programs.

Although not involved in government agricultural and fishing programs, MISURASATA's direct intervention in the third major regional economic activity–mining–directly raised the organization's prestige with the Indians and demonstrated their authority to the government. In the mines, Indians had always labored underground while non-Indians acted as administrators and managers. This did not change after the revolution. As U.S. managers departed, other foreigners, often Chilean exiles, took their place. Despite government promises of higher salaries, improved housing, and health care, Indian workers did not see immediate relief; so, in August 1980 they went on strike at the mines in Bonanza and Siuna. The government, unable to persuade the Indians to return to work, asked MISURASATA to negotiate a settlement. MISURASATA leaders persuaded the workers to return and, to establish a mechanism for working out a settlement, helped form an Indian mine workers' union.

At about the same time Indian communities again became concerned over logging rights on the Atlantic Coast, an issue that had aroused them during the 1960s when the Somoza regime imposed the INFONAC/FAO project in the region. Aware of such fears, MISURASATA, in collaboration with the Ministry of the Atlantic Coast (INNICA) and the Institute for Ecology and Natural Resources (IRENA), established an agreement (5 August 1980) through which communities would receive 80 percent of the value of felled timber on community timber; this was to be deposited in an account in the Nicaraguan Central Bank and could be drawn upon for community development programs.

This agreement concerning natural resources was linked to the broader issue of Indian land rights. Much of the lumbering was to take place on "so-called disputed lands, which are those claimed by communities, but for which they have no legal title" (Ramirez, Rivera, and Jenkins 1981). [12] The formal GRN agreement stated that MISURASATA would be directly involved in the negotiation of land and resource rights on the Atlantic Coast; funds to undertake the demarcation study were provided by Cultural Survival, a support group for Indian human rights and self-determination. In light of MISURASATA's successful role in both resource disputes, the Latin American Regional Reports (19 September 1980, RA-80-08) stated: "Hope for the development of better relationships between the miners, fishermen, timber workers, and agricultural laborers of the Atlantic Coast rests mainly on the ethnic organization MISURASATA." [13]

Thus, with regard to both labor relations and community resource rights, MISURASATA's prestige increased. Moreover, the organization had obtained a formal government agreement to include the Indians in discussions regarding the principal tenets of their moral economy. In late 1980, however, these advances were challenged by two government announcements. This led to Phase 2 of the postrevolutionary period on the Atlantic Coast.

PHASE 2: THE INDIAN'S OPEN RESISTANCE

The first problem was the creation of the Bosawas Forest Reserve. In August 1980, shortly after signing the lumbering agreement, IRENA unilaterally announced its plans for a forest reserve in a dense tropical rain-forest area in northwestern Zelaya. Hale (1982, 21) stated that:

the justification for the reserve derives from its ecology. Steep slopes, heavy rainfall, and thin, easily eroded topsoils make Bosawas especially susceptible to serious ecological damage, both from intensive agriculture and from lumbering. Indigenous peoples are to be granted titles to the lands they occupy which lie within the reserve. However, the project proposes a moratorium on lumbering and a prohibition on immigration of "colonos" from the Pacific until questions of resource management can be studied thoroughly.

He also added that, "after careful study, the Nicaraguan and Mexican governments agreed to a joint investment of 56 million dollars to cut and process lumber from the pine savannah west of Puerto Cabezas."

MISURASATA denounced the Bosawas agreement as "nationalization" of Indian lands and, when the Mexican lumbering agreement was announced, demanded a moratorium on cutting until land and resource rights were defined. The projects provoked a sharp response from MISURASATA, not so much because of what was actually planned but for the precedent it appeared to set. Neither project directly or immediately threatened a particular community, yet both appeared to place the government squarely and solely in control of land and natural resources. This appeared to contradict signed agreements, challenge MISURASATA's role in negotiations over land and resource rights, and, by extension, violated the Miskito's moral economy.

The government had already accepted MISURASATA's proposal for a survey which would detail land and resource rights and subsequently serve as a basis for negotiating rights and providing legal titles when they were lacking. The study was to be handed over to the government on 5 December 1980, but MISURASATA hoped to discuss the issue at a general congress planned to conclude the literacy campaign on the Atlantic Coast. They requested and received an extension for submission of the research project until March 1981, when they also planned to flesh out an outline entitled "General Lines of Action for 1981," elaborated by MISURASATA's executive committee in late December (MISURASATA 1981a).

MISURASATA's outline for activities in 1981 was prepared both as a formal response to needs perceived and problems encountered during the first year and a half of Sandinista rule, and as an effort to strengthen the authority of the organization. There were plans to organize the communities for both political and economic activities (e.g., an indigenous training center and the establishment of Indian cooperatives and trade unions). These were understood as mechanisms essential to realizing the sorts of programs established but poorly managed by government agencies the year before. To improve MISURASATA's political status, they planned to request a seat on the national Junta and to establish official and public communication with the national directorate of the FSLN. MISURASATA considered that a genuine Indian organization, with its understanding of the social and physical aspects of the region, was the most effective way to administer development projects and establish a representative political structure.

MISURASATA's program, however, alarmed the government, particularly as it related to land claims. After indicating the nature of the land study to be presented to the government, the brief outline added four tasks: (1) an intensive "consciousness-raising" campaign at the community level, to establish the appropriate political climate for handing over the documents to the authorities; (2) preparations for mass demonstrations when deemed necessary; (3) an appeal to the representatives of each community to sign the documents before delivering them to the government; (4) an appeal for moral support from other sectors and organizations.

On 19 February 1981, the entire leadership of MISURASATA was arrested. Although they were never formally charged, unofficially the arrests were said to be justified because various aspects of the 1981 "Plan of Activities" were considered to be a separatist plot and, by extension, a virtual declaration of war against the government. The government's head of security, Lenin Cerna, said, "Although on the surface the document did not reveal anything, at the base of it was a well-defined separatist plot"; he labeled it "Plan 1981" (*Barricada* 21 February 1981; *La Prensa* 24 February 1981). Government officials feared that if the MISURASATA leadership presented the outline (promoted to a virtual manifesto by the press) to a general congress and it was accepted against the will of the government, it would be extremely difficult to negotiate terms with the Indians later. Government fears were based largely on the statements of Steadman Fagoth, MISURASATA's representative to the Council of State and an outspoken critic of the government, who indicated that he planned to use the congress to make strong demands on the government. But other MISURASATA leaders stressed that obtaining broad, indeed signed support for the "plan" was an effort to demonstrate that the projected activities actually reflected community needs and were not simply the independent creation of MISURASATA's leadership (David Rodriquez [MISURASATA comandante] 1986: personal communication).

As the arrests continued, a government security patrol entered the coastal village of Prinzapolka and attempted to arrest MISURASATA leader Elmer Prado while the community was gathered in the Moravian Church celebrating an official end of the literacy campaign. Outraged by the event and the insensitive manner in which it was carried out, a fight broke out, Indians grabbed army weapons and in a matter of minutes four Miskito and four Sandinista soldiers were killed. The incident, the first armed conflict between Indians and the government, produced acrimony and accusations on both sides; and fear of expanded arrests prompted the exodus to Honduras of about three thousand young Miskito men.

While most MISURASATA leaders were released after about two weeks, Fagoth remained in jail under accusations that he had been an agent of Somoza's secret police prior to 1979 (*Barricada* 22 February 1981). Mass demonstrations in coastal communities for over a week prompted Fagoth's "conditional" release; he would be freed if he agreed to study in Bulgaria for an extended period. Upon release, Fagoth traveled to the Atlantic Coast and then fled to Honduras where he immediately began to broadcast anti-government statements, publicly declaring "open warfare on the Sandinistas" and encouraging Miskitos to either leave Nicaragua or actively oppose the government. Since the broadcasts were transmitted from the station operated by the counterrevolutionary group "Legion 15 de septiembre" (later to become the Nicaraguan Democratic Force, the FDN), Fagoth was linked with them by association and, as it turned out later, by choice. Other MISURASATA leaders, principally Education Coordinator Hazel Lau and General Coordinator Brooklyn Rivera, remained in Nicaragua, hoping to negotiate a settlement with the government. In June, accompanied by Moravian church leaders, Rivera traveled to Honduras where he tried to persuade the refugees to return. But his efforts were frustrated by the actions of both the Sandinistas and the counterrevolutionaries. Fagoth's regular broadcasts denounced Rivera as a government collaborator willing to sell out the Indian cause. The FSLN in turn, suspicious of the political loyalty of MISURASATA, refused to empower the organization further through any bilateral agreements or negotiations on land or resource rights.

In June 1981, the FSLN and the JGRN published the "Declaration of Principles of the Sandinist Popular Revolution with Regard to the Indigenous Communities of the Atlantic Coast" (FSLN and JGRN 1981). Regarding natural resources, the declaration (article 6) states:

The natural resources of our territory are the properties of the Nicaraguan people. The Revolutionary State, representative of the popular will, is the only entity empowered to establish a rational and efficient system of utilization of said resources. The Revolutionary State recognizes the right of the indigenous communities to receive a portion of the benefits to be derived from the exploitation of forestal resources in the region; these benefits must be invested in programs of community and municipal development in accordance with national plans.

With regard to land rights in general, the next month (23 July 1981) new agrarian reform laws (JGRN Decree No. 782, article 30) declared that:

the *State* can make available the amount of land necessary in order that the Miskito, Sumo, and Rama communities can work it individually or collectively and in order that they benefit from the natural resources, with the aim that their inhabitants improve their standard of living and *contribute to the social and economic development of the Nicaraguan nation.* (emphasis added)

Despite public statements that the Declaration of Principles outlined the most revolutionary Indian policy in the Americas, both documents to a large extent declared government hegemony over land and resource rights. *Barricada* (2 September 1981) writes:

The eight points in the Declaration reflect an attempt to realize the legitimate demands of the indigenous peoples, while *simultaneously strengthening the principle of territorial and political integrity of the nation.* It rejects any secessionist or separatist aim that might arise, *framing the whole problem of indigenous peoples within the wider concept of national unity.* (emphasis added)

MISURASATA responded (28 July 1981) with its "Proposal on Land Holding in the Indigenous and Creole communities of the Atlantic Coast," which stated at the onset that, "The right of the indigenous nations over the territory of their communities exceeds (*es preferencial*) the right over the territory of states" (MISURASATA 1981b), and included a map of Indian and Creole land equal to 45,407.806 km^2 to be considered as legally recognized territory. In brief, the issue of land and resource rights suddenly shifted tenor from that of a negotiating table to a political arena, with both the FSLN and MISURASATA making public announcements of their strongest claims.

At the same time the Sandinistas offered Rivera the position of vice-minister of the Atlantic Coast. This made his position even more difficult. To accept the offer would have fueled Fagoth's accusations of capitulation and thus produced suspicion among those whom Rivera represented; to refuse would increase government mistrust of MISURASATA and add further obstacles to any possibility of a negotiated settlement. To compound matters, non-Indian Nicaraguan counterrevolutionaries in Honduras (Legion 15 de septiembre) announced that Rivera's attempts to obtain a peaceful settlement with their declared enemy made him a target for political assassination. In turn, when Rivera refused the vice-minister's position, government officials indicated that they could no longer be responsible for his safety.

PHASE 3: THE INDIAN UPRISING

In October 1981, Rivera left Nicaragua for Honduras where he was immediately placed under arrest and questioned extensively; his attitude and actions were still suspect. His departure nonetheless effectively marked the beginning of the third phase of events on the Atlantic Coast—the Indian uprising.

Prior to this, military action against the Sandinistas had been limited to occasional forays into Nicaragua from Honduras, mainly by ex–National Guardsmen who had fled into Honduras in 1979, and a few raids by Miskito refugees. But by the time Rivera arrived there were over three thousand young Nicaraguan Miskitos in Honduras. A number of these had been recruited by Fagoth, who then was working in close collaboration with anti-government forces established there. These Indians were trained by a combination of Nicaraguan exiles and Argentine and Guatemalan military advisors (U.S. military advisors first arrived in 1983 [David Rodriquez 1986, personal communication]). Many of the Miskitos, however, resented the racist treatment accorded them by the non-Indian combatants. They therefore began to work independently, forming separate units (e.g., the Astros) and undertaking independent military actions. In late 1981, they attacked the Sandinista army detachments in Raiti, San Carlos, Asang, and Suksayeri. Although initially such actions were considered limited border raids, they represent an early and significant shift in the objectives of the Miskito. At first the young men who crossed the border regarded their military activities solely as revenge. They were, therefore, willing to accept collaboration with the Legion 15 de septiembre forces for tactical reasons. But, compounding the racist treatment the Indians received, their community elders still in Nicaragua disapproved of the alliance. They not only encouraged separation but helped the fighters recognize legitimate motives for these actions. Land, resource rights, and self-determination replaced simple revenge (David Rodriquez 1986: personal communication). Fagoth, hoping to establish a united opposition, sent Rivera to persuade the Indian troops. But when they explained the reasons for their "rebellion," Rivera refused to collaborate in the unification. This led to his second arrest and a subsequent death threat (Rivera 1982: personal communication). The late 1981 Indian attacks escalated to a guerrilla civil war which eventually ran the entire length and breadth of the Atlantic Coast and had the support of most Indian communities.

The nature and impact of the Indian insurrection has been poorly documented and much debated. This is due, in part, to government reluctance to acknowledge the popular nature of the conflict, to the limiting of public access to the region and, in part, a certain willingness on the part of potential witnesses to regard many government actions in Indian communities as justifiable in the face of increased and open efforts by the U.S. government to overthrow the Sandinista regime. Therefore, the military chronology of this period, roughly November 1981 to mid-1985, has yet to be broadly detailed and substantiated. Nevertheless, a widely publicized and debated series of events—the incidents in the Rio Coco communities of San Carlos and Leimius and the so-called "Red Christmas" of 1981–82—are pivotal to any understanding of the post-1981 escalation of violence, for they illustrate the nature of the conflict and the sentiments it provoked.

The events at Leimius and San Carlos have prompted considerable concern by human rights organizations, particularly the Inter-American Commission on Human Rights (IACHR 1984), Americas Watch (1982, 1983, 1984) and the International League of Human Rights (1983). Briefly, on 21 December 1981, a helicopter with soldiers of the Sandinista armed forces attempted to land in San Carlos to investigate reports that rebels had occupied the town. They were met with gunfire, and six Sandinistas from the helicopter died. On 23 December, reports the IACHR, "between thirty-five and forty Miskitos were detained in Leimius by military forces—and . . . an as yet undetermined number of Miskito, all unarmed, were summarily executed. . . . possibly in retaliation for the events that had taken place a few days before in San Carlos. . . ." (IACHR 1984, 95).

Regarding the Leimius incident, Americas Watch writes: "Rather than direct answers to specific events, the government focused on what it called 'Operation Red Christmas.'" Luis Carrion, Vice-Minister of the Interior, stated:

This plan had as its objective a general uprising of the Miskito population in North Zelaya following a military take-over of the settlements along the Rio Coco by the counterrevolutionary bands. The general uprising would permit the intervention of foreign forces, or international organizations who would support and give recognition to the insurrectionist forces, and in this fashion finalize the separatist plan. (Ohland and Schneider 1983, 259–60)

Government reports (e.g., *Barricada* 6 November 1981 to 21 December 1981) listed at least fourteen raids in a two-month period. They stated that the events at San Carlos and Leimius were not isolated incidents but parts of a broad offensive to cut off the Atlantic Coast and thus threaten the entire nation.

The Indians, by contrast, argued that the San Carlos shootings were in retaliation for killings by government troops of Miskito Indians in numerous villages. They agreed that many incidents had indeed occurred along the upper Rio Coco (i.e., Raiti to Waspam), but the attacks were a series of local Indian responses to intolerable conditions and actions, not a grand plan to topple the government (*Akwesasne Notes* 1982; Brooklyn Rivera 1982: personal communication; David Rodriquez 1986: personal communication).

One year after the San Carlos/Leimius events, the *National Catholic Reporter* wrote:

Nearly five months of research into the relationship between the Miskito Indians and the Sandinista government . . . produced no evidence to substantiate the Nicaraguan government's claim of the plot ["Operation Red Christmas"]. . . . It appears [that] the government used the allegation to justify moving the Indians, and to stop a more serious challenge: an indigenous insurrection among the Miskito Indians. (Evans and Epstein 1982)

Such reports, by and large, were few and went largely unnoticed because in 1982 the Miskitos were flung into a larger geopolitical arena.

Fighting increased to such an extent in early 1982 that the government decided to undertake the most dramatic action of the period—the forced relocation of all communities along the lower Rio Coco, and the total destruction of houses, crops, and livestock in that area.

Indians were relocated to camps called Tasba Pri ("Free Land"), about sixty kilometers to the south. Three explanations for the move were offered, the first two military. The government (JGRN 1982) argued that: (1) it was essential to protect the population; (2) potentially insurrectional or even just supportive civilians had to be removed from an area where they could inform and supply Miskito rebels. World attention focused on the relocation. Detractors of the revolution used the event to decry gross human rights violations, often through use of false information and exaggeration. Nicaragua's defenders accepted the rationale for the move and defended the forced march of internal refugees and the conversion of hastily constructed camps into permanent communities.

The focus on the military justifications for relocation and the subsequent treatment of the refugees allowed the third, less dramatic, motive for the move to go relatively unnoticed. However, in terms of its relation to the root causes of the conflict, the third explanation is perhaps the most significant. The official government document, Tasba Pri, stated that the move had been planned at least two years earlier.

The Tasba Pri program is neither new nor improvised. It has as its immediate antecedent a feasibility study conducted by the Revolutionary Government through the Nicaraguan Institute of the Atlantic Coast (INNICA) in November 1980 for the purpose of improving and dignifying the living conditions of the Miskitos that inhabit the Nicaraguan side of the Coco River. (JGRN 1982, 46)

Thus even before violence erupted, the government had planned to relocate the Miskitos. Tasba Pri was situated on what was defined as the largest section of arable land in Northern Zelaya and alongside a route which was to become the first and only all-weather road connecting Nicaragua's capital to the Atlantic Coast (the same road along which Somoza's "coronels" laid claim to large tracts in the 1960s [David Rodriquez 1986: personal communication]). So the relocation was, in part at least, a massive program for national economic development and demographic change designed by the government. It was an effort to take a highly dispersed and, in the government's opinion, relatively unproductive population and place it where the products of their labor could be more efficiently marketed. Tasba Pri was, therefore, an effort to draw Miskitos more closely and permanently into the national economy. Americas Watch (1982, 681) writes: "The project's technicians maintain that the soil and techniques in use will produce enough food to meet all the nutritional needs of the community and, *eventually, will contribute to the national agricultural market*" (emphasis added). Official government reports reinforce the technicians' statements.[14]

For the same expressed reasons—safety and border control—the government, from 22 November to 22 December 1982, evacuated 685 Sumu and 506 Miskitos from communities near the headwaters of the Rio Coco. This time, however, the relocation was from riverine communities to state-run coffee and cattle estates (Unidad de Produccion Estatal, or UPE) in the departments of Jinotega and Matagalpa, over 150 km to the southwest and into high, cool, coffee-growing regions. As of late 1984 (when the author visited the camps), the Indians permanently occupied cramped, dark barracks built by previous landlords to house seasonal laborers who worked on the surrounding coffee plantations. These communities were being transferred slowly to government-constructed settlements similar to those of Tasba Pri. Eventually the residents were to obtain title to lands from the surrounding UPEs for cooperative-based coffee production and cattle raising.

Residents of Tasba Pri and the Matagalpa-Jinotega resettlement areas stressed that their foremost desire was to return to their homes on the Rio Coco, and, in 1984, government officials said that they would be free to do so when the current military threat disappeared. When pressed on the issue, however, officials indicated that even if the current fighting ended, a latent threat would remain as long as Nicaragua feared an invasion from across the border. There was, therefore, no immediate plan to return the population to the Rio Coco. Quite the contrary, all efforts were being made to create permanent, high population-density communities organized into production cooperatives geared toward market-oriented economic activities. Permanent housing, health centers, and schools had been established. In late 1984, government publications no longer even referred to Tasba Pri as a temporary camp; the settlements were regarded as "communities" on a par with other production centers in the area. The population of Tasba Pri was already the fifth largest in Zelaya Norte, and over 83 percent of the land titled in Zelaya Norte since July 1979 (approximately fifteen thousand hectares) had been awarded to residents of Tasba Pri. Only five other communities, mainly cooperatives, had obtained land titles to holdings, totaling about three thousand hectares. Moreover, with an agricultural storage capacity of twenty thousand quintals, Tasba Pri was second only to Puerto Cabezas, the capital and hub of the region. Four hundred hectares had already been cleared for production, and, in rice alone, the 1985 harvest was expected to yield over ten thousand quintals (INNICA 1982).

Such dramatic changes in the Indians' livelihood, land tenure, settlement patterns, and participation in the national economy are the dream of many national planners. Almost overnight, groups regarded as isolated, relatively unproductive populations were drawn into the state and became objects of state planning, regardless of their own desires. The government had a clear idea of how land and labor should be organized; it was outlined in the Declaration of Principles (1981) and the 1981 Agrarian Reform Laws. Although Indians were not to be deprived of access to land and resources, the government would decide where they would obtain that access and determine how Indians obtained benefits from resource exploitation. For the Indians, developers' dreams became nightmares; communities became labor camps.

Nevertheless, from mid-1982 until September 1984, any notice focused on one of two dominant themes: the activities of the "contras," and living conditions in Tasba Pri. Little or no attention was given to the demographic and economic reorganization of the region, or to what was undoubtedly the major event—the area's transformation into one pockmarked, if not controlled entirely, by Indian military units supported by local communities, and drawing numerous recruits from them. The local nature of the units was hardly acknowledged; whenever mention was made of these actions, it was largely to explain them away in terms of the political factions which had greater access to the media. It was either "MISURA forces, under the command of Steadman Fagoth" and linked to the Honduras-based FDN, or "MISURASATA forces under the command of Brooklyn Rivera" and linked with the Costa Rican-based ARDE. Indians were assumed to be just troops, led by whoever had recruited or drafted them. However, interviews with rebel fighters revealed a clearly angry group, with well-defined complaints. [15]

These men and women were not fighting simply as members of a party or faction: they were involved in what for them was an Indian war for land rights, access to national resources and self-determination. In fact, MISURA and MISURASATA Indian forces merged in August 1984 to form the Internal Indian Front (Frente Interno Indigena), thereby illustrating their concern with specific local issues rather than geopolitically aligned factions. Affiliation then became a logistical rather than a political consideration; since FDN-affiliated MISURA had easier access to U.S.-supplied guns, ammunition, and uniforms, their numbers were larger. Inside Nicaragua, however, equipment moved easily from one person to another. MISURA armed MISURASATA and they sometimes undertook joint operations.

They were also quite successful in battle. Indian war accounts hold that they never lost a battle and that their losses were always negligible. The fighting, however, did produce heavy losses for the Sandinistas, not only militarily but in terms of international support. Many European progressives now protested U.S. threats of intervention and other efforts to topple the Sandinistas, while also criticizing Nicaragua's treatment of the Miskitos. This combination of military and diplomatic challenges led the FSLN first to declare a general amnesty in December 1983; when that led only to a trickle of returnees, the government made a more significant peace overture in mid-1984—an expression of willingness to open discussion with MISURASATA.

PHASE 4: PEACE NEGOTIATIONS

Previously, both MISURASATA and the Nicaraguan government had requested negotiated or mediated peace settlements, specifically through the OAS Inter-American Commission on Human Rights (IACHR). Yet no progress had been made since the fighting erupted; on the contrary, relations consisted largely of acrimonious and often vitriolic accusations by both MISURASATA and the FSLN. The IACHR originally agreed to Nicaragua's request to act as mediator in a "friendly settlement." But two years later IACHR terminated this role, giving, as a principal reason, Nicaragua's refusal to negotiate with certain MISURASATA leaders (IACHR 1984, 74).

Despite public refusals to negotiate with MISURASATA, initial peace overtures on behalf of the government were extended quietly to Rivera when Moravian church leaders visited Costa Rica in July 1984. Later, at a rally in Puerto Cabezas, Daniel Ortega stated that Rivera was welcome to return under the 1983 general amnesty (those regarded as leaders in any attempt to overthrow the government had been excluded from the amnesty decree). Rivera responded with a statement expressing a willingness to return if the government agreed to free imprisoned Indians, recognize MISURASATA, and discuss regional autonomy and land rights. Although no formal response was received, various external authorities, among them U.S. Senator Edward M. Kennedy, John McAward of the Unitarian Universalist Service Committee and Cultural Survival, brought Rivera to a 3 October private meeting with Mr. Ortega, while the latter was in

New York addressing the United Nations. The meeting was successful; an invitation to return to Nicaragua was extended and accepted.

On 20 October 1984, Brooklyn Rivera, MISURASATA's General Coordinator, and several other Indian leaders flew from Costa Rica to Managua, entering Nicaragua officially after more than three-years absence. His arrival marked the beginning of efforts aimed at ending Indian guerilla fighting and reestablishing MISURASATA's role. A twelve-day trip allowed Rivera to observe conditions on the Atlantic Coast and to reestablish direct contacts with government officials and Indian communities. Despite two incidents of heckling by leaders of MISATAN, a newly-formed and, at that time, strongly pro-Sandinista Indian organization, the trip produced a warm welcome and, more important, vocal support for Rivera's argument that while peace was the primary concern it could only come about with acceptance of the Indians' basic rights.

On one level—that of most immediate concern to the Nicaraguan government and most noticeable to recent observers in Central America—the trip appeared to signal the beginning of an end to Miskito guerrilla warfare. Although MISURASATA fighters were neither the only nor the most numerous rebel force active in the area, its expressed aims—peace with dignity—reflected local concerns and thus obtained broad support among coastal communities. In addition, unlike other forces battling the Sandinistas, MISURASATA received attention and support from international human-rights organizations. Other, truly counterrevolutionary organizations had sought, unsuccessfully, to establish formal alliances with MISURASATA and thus capitalize on its positive image. MISURASATA's independent peace initiative further diminished the political imagery of these other forces and highlighted the difference between the Indian civil war and the counterrevolution. Understandably, the non-Indian opposition and their international backers (including the U.S. State Department) made numerous and open efforts to dissuade Rivera from traveling to Nicaragua, and subsequently worked to diminish the trip's significance. The most noticeable of these efforts was the forced expulsion by Honduran authorities, in November 1985, of a MISURASATA delegation which traveled from Costa Rica to Honduras to discuss the nature and progress of the peace initiative with representatives of the over twenty-five thousand Indian refugees in the Honduran section of the Mosquitia. No reasonable government explanation for the expulsion was ever presented. Rivera, however, indicated that the FDN's powerful presence within Honduras and the group's expressed hostility to the peace initiative undoubtedly influenced, possibly determined the Honduran government's actions.

Despite such setbacks, a major outcome of Rivera's trip was the opening of formal negotiations, initiated in December 1984 in Bogota through an invitation from Colombia's President, Belisario Betancur. As a result of negotiations in Mexico City, on 28 April 1985, the Nicaraguan Government released fourteen prisoners who had been charged with participation or association with MISURASATA and MISURA. The Mexico City agreement (22 April 1985) also committed the government, in collaboration with MISURASATA, to provide food and medical supplies to Indian communities affected by recent violence, and allowed community members to resume normal subsistence activities (hunting, fishing, and marketing). MISURASATA and government security forces also agreed to avoid all offensive actions against each other and continue negotiations concerning the fundamental complaints—land and natural resource rights, local self-determination, and recognition of MISURASATA.

Failure to reach any mutual understanding, let alone to implement an agreement, had stalled two previous negotiating sessions in Bogota. Again, it was an issue of priorities: state consolidation in conflict with ethnic self-determination. Although both parties always agreed that an end to the violence was essential, the Nicaraguan Government's goal was to obtain a total cease-fire. MISURASATA, reflecting the opinion of most combatants and non-combatants, emphasized that until rights to land, natural resources, and self-determination were recognized, fighting would remain endemic and widespread. Without at least a commitment to negotiate such rights the Indians would have equated a cease-fire with a surrender of their aboriginal rights, and would not have complied with the agreement.

Invited observers at the 26–27 March 1985 Bogota meetings included leaders of Indian organizations from Peru, Ecuador, Colombia, Costa Rica, Canada, the U.S., and the Six Nations Iroquois Confederacy. Although participating only as concerned observers, these Indian representatives unanimously expressed agreement with the basic goals of MISURASATA (see *Cultural Survival Quarterly* 9, no. 2 (1985), 40–41).

Equally significant in shifting the context to basic Indian rights was the presence at the Mexico City negotiating table of a Miskito comandante associated with MISURA, the Honduras-based group often characterized, inappropriately, as those troops commanded by and loyal to Steadman Fagoth. By association, they were assumed to be controlled by those contras mostly steadfastly committed to the overthrow of the Sandinista Government (i.e., the Democratic Revolutionary Front [FDN] and its international supporters, including the U.S. Central Intelligence Agency). However, the presence and support of MISURA leaders demonstrated that most Indians inside Nicaragua agreed on the causes of the conflict and supported the terms of a detailed peace proposal submitted by MISURASATA at the December 1984 Bogota meeting (see Macdonald 1984). For the Indians, the only advantages of MISURA were the easily obtained arms and other equipment; there was no loyalty expressed to Fagoth or his political allies. Inside Nicaragua the MISURA/MISURASATA distinction was relatively meaningless; Indians had fought in close coordination for several years, as illustrated by the August 1984 meeting of Indian commanders on the Atlantic Coast which led to the formation of the Frente Interno Indigena (Internal Indian Front). Any agreement with MISURASATA would therefore affect Indian fighters throughout the Atlantic Coast.

Eventually, the Nicaraguan Government publicly recognized the local genesis of the violence. Most noticeably, there was a shift in vocabulary; MISURASATA members were no longer labeled contras (counterrevolutionaries). This can be partly explained by Rivera's willingness to negotiate, and his public statements that the Sandinistas were not simply "evil villains" whose elimination would produce fair treatment for the Indians. [16]

However, while the Mexico City meetings produced feelings of optimism, the *Latin America Weekly Report* (5 April 1985) accurately observed that "a [permanent] solution may depend on the resolution of tensions within the Nicaraguan Government between President Daniel Ortega, who is believed to want a settlement, and the hardliners grouped around Tomas Borge."

The peace initiative was promoted, supported, and negotiated by those perceived as the more moderate elements within the FSLN, President Daniel Ortega and Comandante Luis Carrion. However, two days after the Mexico City agreement was signed, the Nicaraguan Government announced that Tomas Borge had been named to head the negotiating team and oversee government policies on the Atlantic Coast. His first statements (*New York Times*, 26 April 1985, cited earlier) cast doubt on the likelihood of attaining MISURASATA's goals.

Subsequent actions reinforced MISURASATA's suspicions that the hardliners would dominate. At the next (May 1985) meetings in Bogota, the attitude of the Sandinista negotiating team changed considerably. Rather than pursue discussion of the substantive issues (land and natural resources) whose resolution was essential for a lasting peace, the Sandinistas focused on perceived violations of the Mexico Agreement and refused to negotiate any other items until MISURASATA provided an explanation. The talks deteriorated and ended suddenly, each side blaming the other's intransigence. Although both sides expressed a willingness to continue, as of mid-1986 no formal negotiations had been reinitiated, despite formal requests by President Betancur and the World Council of Indigenous Peoples. Instead, the Nicaraguan government pushed forward on its unilateral autonomy program, which was to become part of the new constitution.

The autonomy concept was presented as a revolutionary recognition of the rights of the ethnic groups which comprised eastern Nicaragua. A formal commission composed of government officials and local representatives was established, and a rough outline, to be fleshed out through community participation, was prepared (Autonomy Commission 1985, 7–11). This outline closely paralleled the 1981 Declaration of Principles, particularly with regard to the priority of national unity and government control over security and major development planning. As outlined, autonomy more closely resembled local participation in minor decision-making than broad regional self-determination. Thus Francisco Campbell, Consular Minister at the Nicaraguan Embassy in Washington, stated, "Obviously, the overall economic activities of the Atlantic Coast will form part of national planning as a whole" (1986, unpublished interview). Nevertheless, the Commission stressed that "This is your project. Let's all participate. Make your point of view known" (Autonomy Commission 1985, 22). Local discussions continued and the final autonomy statute was anticipated for late 1986 (Diskin et al. 1986, 18). As discussions continued, debate hardened; MISATAN changed leadership and shifted its posture from that of a strongly pro-Sandinista group to one whose goals more closely paralleled those expressed by MISURASATA (*El Nuevo Diario* [Managua] 2 October 1985). MISURASATA was invited to consult with the Commission, but Rivera refused, arguing that such participation would serve only to legitimize, not alter, a document in which the basic premises were in total conflict with MISURASATA's goals. Meanwhile, the government attempted to establish peace treaties with individual rebel leaders working from bases inside Nicaragua, successfully in several cases. In part to stimulate support for both the autonomy project and the individual cease-fire negotiation, President Daniel Ortega, on 29 May 1985, announced that those Indians resettled in Tasba Pri would be allowed to return to the Rio Coco, thereby prompting a huge exodus from the unpopular experiment in national socio-economic reorganization.

Meanwhile, as a relative calm and cautious optimism appeared to be setting in on the Atlantic Coast, the U.S. Congress approved 27 million dollars in "humanitarian aid" to those rebel groups which, combined, form the United Nicaraguan Opposition (UNO). With approximately $25 million in private unrestricted support, and hopes for $100 million in additional U.S. funds, the contras expected to wage a more effective war. One of the conditions for U.S. economic support was political consolidation of the opposition forces. Consequently the FDN-dominated UNO created a new Indian-Organization, KISAN, and formally recognized it as the Nicaraguan Indian Organization. As such, KISAN would become the potential recipient of U.S. government and private funds administered through UNO. Rivera and others from MISURASATA, because of their continuing efforts to negotiate a peace settlement with the Sandinista government, were excluded from participation in KISAN.

Where then did MISURASATA stand? Both within Nicaragua and outside, there were efforts to marginalize the organization, or at least to neutralize its perceived authority. But to assume that such efforts would be successful would be a gross misinterpretation of the nature of a legitimate Indian organization and the ideas and goals it represented. The violence began with widely perceived violations to basic rights to land and natural resources, something which had rarely occurred earlier on the Atlantic Coast. MISURASATA repeatedly stated that national political issues or ideology were secondary to the basic tenets of their moral economy—land, resource rights, and genuine self-determination. Throughout the violence and the subsequent negotiations, these priorities never changed. This should have indicated something to the Nicaraguan government. And it should have made some impression on those who hoped to use the Indians to topple the Sandinistas.

But perhaps it did not. Rivera, in a December 1985 letter to the President of the World Council of Indigenous Peoples, stated that the Nicaraguan government consistently avoided negotiations on the basic issues which sparked the violence, and, despite changes in tactics and terminology, searched only for ways to incorporate the Indians into state-determined policy without ever seriously considering the idea of independent Indian self-determination. The same was true for those seeking to depose the Sandinistas. [17]

When Rivera, through the offices of Senator Edward M. Kennedy, tried to explain this situation to Assistant Secretary of State for Inter-American Affairs Elliot Abrams, Abrams refused to meet with him, stating that "we do not believe that receiving Rivera, in the absence of indications that is willing to address the concerns of [KISAN], would be helpful to promoting a solution to the problem" (Abrams 1985).

The solution, as perceived by the U.S. Administration, was a unified opposition. However, in a 7 March 1986 letter declining acceptance of a formal invitation by Secretary of State George Shultz to attend a broad opposition (UNO) meeting, Rivera made his position clear:

We have experienced serious threats to our Indian rights not only from the leftist Sandinistas but also from rightist elements and others. We are the victims of anti-Indian racism which is not neatly confined to one part of the political spectrum. Accordingly, we have learned from experience to make alliances carefully and to avoid situations where adversaries of Indian rights would seek to exploit the plight of our Indian peoples for political ends which ultimately will threaten us. . . . We have repeatedly expressed our belief that the dominant forces within the UNO organization present a threat to our rights.

In brief, as of mid-1986, neither the Sandinistas nor their opposition demonstrated a willingness to respond to the fundamental stimulus of the Indian conflict. Rather, they attempted to incorporate anger into agendas of their own creation. The human consequences of such insensitivity, particularly from 1981 to 1984, were severe, and failure to confront the basic complaints threatened the fragile peace that followed the Mexico City Agreement. In early 1986 violence again erupted near and along the Rio Coco, prompting about ten thousand Miskito recently resettled there to flee into Honduras. These events, once again, depersonalized the Indians and hurled them into the geopolitical arena as symbols. Americas Watch (1986) and Constable (1986) indicate that the exodus did not appear to be the result of abuse but rather a KISAN-FDN orchestrated media event to promote pending U.S. congressional support for the contras. While dramatic public relations manipulations were an undeniable result of the move, reports from inside Nicaragua supported fears that the government had indeed taken aggressive actions against Miskito military units inside Nicaragua (Americas Watch 1986, 18–20).

Although the violence is lamentable, it is not yet tragic, for the emotive power of tragedy is its inevitability. Destiny did not produce the conflict; decisions did. As such, they can be altered or reversed. In response to renewed violence, on 14 April 1986 a meeting in the Moravian Church in Puerto Cabezas led to the formation of the Commission for Justice, Peace and Unity on the Atlantic Coast. The Commission stated that "peace should be the product of justice and unity, not vice versa," and suggested an analysis of why negotiations between the Nicaraguan government and MISURASATA had broken down. It requested a change in government priorities and a willingness to actually confront, not simply reword, basic differences; this has been MISURASATA's consistent and, in the largest sense, only demand. The Sandinistas thus were given another opportunity to avoid a tragedy and provide an opening for reconciliation, with Nicaragua serving as a testing ground of the prospects for plural societies. Peace in Indian communities is everyone's expressed desire. The violence, however, arose as a protest to violations of a distinct group's rights and resources. As long as basic rights remain an issue, Indians on Nicaragua's Caribbean coast will fight to obtain them, regardless of anyone else's political or ideological agenda.

POSTSCRIPT: FEBRUARY 1988

Following the May 1985 breakdown of negotiations between the Sandinistas and MISURASATA, the root issues of the Indians' dispute were again submerged by concerns with the violence. The Sandinistas worked to end the fighting, while the "contras" and their U.S. supporters sought to perpetuate Indian participation.

KISAN, although created and armed by Nicaragua's opposition, became the principal focus of both sides. The Sandinistas, as they worked to formulate and promote their autonomy program on the Miskito coast, courted KISAN field commanders in hopes of establishing individual peace agreements. The arrival in Puerto Cabazas (3 October 1987) of several dozen armed KISAN fighters under the command of Uriel Vanegas and the subsequent cease-fire agreement which they negotiated, produced drama and high expectations for more such agreements. Some observers even began to speak of KISAN and "KISAN Pro-Paz" (pro-peace). These distinctions and hopes, however, were premature. Although some visitors to the area wrote that a series of such cease-fires had pacified much of the region and permitted the departure of many government troops (Carrigan 1988), a government researcher working directly with the Miskitos wrote that the numerous local attempts at dialogue "had at least one major setback, and [have] yet to produce a major break-through" (Hale 1987, 121). And numerous observers noted an increased military presence in northern Zelaya.

At the same time, despite some government officials' optimistic appraisals of the popular acceptance of the government's regional autonomy program, many residents remained skeptical and other government officials acknowledged its limited local support (Maykuth 1987). Parenthetically or directly, many inside Nicaragua acknowledged that peace and a widely accepted autonomy program would probably follow with the return of Rivera and MISURASATA (Hale 1987; Kinzer 1987).

Neither that end nor that means interested the Sandinistas' opposition. Their goals, recognized throughout the conflict, became more pronounced as the details of the Iran-Contra scandal unfolded. KISAN was recognized by the "contras" and the CIA as *the* Indian fighting force. At the same time they continued unsuccessfully to force the long-sought Indian alliance by drawing MISURASATA into their program. When this failed, "contra," leaders and their supporters worked to diminish the position and status of MISURASATA and were able to prohibit Rivera from entering Honduras to meet with Indian refugees and fighters.

Many of the Indians in Honduras, however, were upset with the role assigned them by the CIA. In early 1987, abuse and forced conscription of Indians by the CIA, the Honduran army, and the contras, and the Indians' resultant anger was documented and widely circulated to the public and to U.S. government officials (Anaya 1987). Appearing amidst the exposure of Nicaragua, this information allowed the U.S. Department of State to override the CIA and permit Rivera's travel to Honduras where he organized an assembly of leaders in the coastal settlement of Rus Rus (11–16 June 1987). Although the U.S. actors changed for this meeting, the play they envisioned remained much the same: unification of the Indians and their entrance into the United Nicaraguan Opposition (LeMoyne 1987).

Unification occurred, but the Indians remained independent. Their new organization, YATAMA, elected a tripartite leadership—Brooklyn Rivera, Steadman Fagoth, and Wycliffe Diego. Although Fagoth and Diego had worked openly with UNO's dominant party, the FDN, YATAMA did not join UNO. Like MISURASATA, YATAMA's initial statements stressed that their dispute was over the policies and plans of the Nicaraguan government, not its existence. YATAMA also expressed support for the regional peace plan promoted by Costa Rica's President Oscar Arias Sanchez.

As a result, in September and October of 1987, Rivera and other representatives of YATAMA began direct communication with Tomas Borge, Minister of the Interior and coordinator of activities on the Atlantic Coast. They agreed to reopen peace negotiations and, to facilitate this, the Sandinistas were ready to permit the Indians entrance without their accepting amnesty or any of the other conditions previously laid down by the Sandinistas but deemed unacceptable by the Indians. As the Indians were preparing to travel in late October, "contra" leaders announced their plans to enter Nicaragua. Unwilling to grant the "contras" entrance without amnesty, the Sandinistas decided that they could not set a precedent with the Miskito leaders and thus ended the opportunity for negotiation.

In late January 1988, following discussions between presidents Arias and Ortega, Rivera was again invited to return to Nicaragua without any conditions. Negotiations took place in Managua from 23 January to 2 February 1988. These were terminated with a formal agreement, signed by Borge and Rivera, which outlined a basic agreement on Indian autonomy, land and natural resource rights, and an agreement to avoid all offensive military actions during the process of negotiations

(Borge and Rivera 1988). Terms for a full cease-fire were to be discussed at the next negotiating session, which began on 28 February 1988.

This agreement is the most substantive since negotiations were initated in 1984. However, it was signed on the day before the contra-aid bill failed in the U.S. House of Representatives. Genuine and continuing willingness to negotiate issues related to the root causes of the Indian unrest, therefore, will be demonstrated in future talks. If successful and unencumbered by external threats, the talks could put an end to a sad chapter of recent history, and permit truly revolutionary change on Nicaragua's Caribbean coast.

NOTES

1. Bonfil (1981, 20) writes: "The disappearance of the *indio* as one who is the product of colonization will result from the suppression of their colonial situation, but this does not imply the disappearance of unique ethnic groups; on the contrary, the disappearance of the *indio* as a colonial category is one of the essential conditions for the resurgence of each and every one of the subordinate ethnic groups."

2. One of the first Sandinista officials in northern Zelaya, Manuel Calderon, stated, "the people of the Coast, because of their political backwardness, did not see that they were being abused by the [foreign] companies. The truth is that imperialism exploited this area even more cruelly than other areas" (1981).

3. Scott (1976, 7) contends that "the subsistence test offers a very different perspective on exploitation than theories which rely only on the criterion of surplus value expropriated. While the latter may be useful in classifying modes of expropriation, it is my contention that they are less likely to be an adequate guide to the phenomenology of peasant experience than the subsistence test."

4. Helms (1969, 78) writes: "To give Britain a legal foothold on territory claimed by Spain, a Miskito Indian was taken to Jamaica about 1687 to place his country under British protection. He was given a piece of writing and a cocked hat, and duly proclaimed 'king of Mosquitia' by the English authorities. This man was the first in a line of 'kings,' the last of whom ended his office in 1894."

5. CIDCA (1984, 8) writes: "By 1843, twenty-two years after Nicaraguan independence, Great Britain had maneuvered itself into a position as the legal 'protector' of the Mosquitia. But its declining power could not stand up to U.S. advances in the region. . . . In 1860, it signaled the end of its territorial aspirations by signing the Treaty of Managua with the Nicaraguan government. This treaty created a Miskito Reserve under Nicaraguan sovereignty, with powers of local self-government granted to the Miskito monarchy. In 1880 the Miskito king was granting concessions to U.S. lumber and banana operations throughout the region."

6. Hardenburg (1912, 143–44) describes several, small scale Upper-Amazonian operations: "Rubber was collected by the Indians in the company's service

who came periodically with what they had collected and exchanged it for merchandise sold them at rather exorbitant prices. These aborigines . . . lived in villages of their own in the heart of the forest."

7. Torres Rivas (1971, 91–92) writes: "In order for banana production to achieve optimal marketing conditions it is essential that there be an immediate transition from purchasing from local producers to control over production (i.e., a plantation) itself; beyond that, marketing must include management of all strategic economic aspects related, directly or indirectly, to the plantation; the railroads, the docks, and other port facilities and maritime transport such that all aspects of production and marketing move in a closed circuit around the banana plantation."

8. Parsons (1955) notes that mine administrators complained about their inability to maintain a regular labor force; Indians came and went to work in the mines irregularly. CIERA (1981, 67) similarly notes that "Many of the workers worked only for short periods and then returned to their communities until economic pressures obligated them to return to the mines or lumbering firms."

9. Despite this so-called nationalization, FDN leader and former Guardia Nacional Coronel Enrique Bermudez told Miskito leaders that he and others had been granted large tracts of Indian land on either side of the road under construction from Managua to Puerto Cabezas (David Rodriguez 1986: personal communication).

10. The acronym GRN initially (post-1979, immediately after the revolution) stood for the Nicaraguan Government of National Reconstruction. The same acronym, GRN, was retained to stand subsequently for the Government of the Republic of Nicaragua.

11. One Indian, who later joined the MISURASATA fighters, related his frustration: "Before, you could look for things. We used to use the little dory and go and catch shrimps and other things in the lagoon. When the Sandinistas come in they pressure you. They start to order you around and you can't catch nothing. Earlier you could go out in the river any hour you wanted. And then they start to pressure you and say you can't go out. You have to take out a license to go fishing and all that thing. Before, without any license, you could go out in the dory and get any amount of shrimp you want. And when you come in, if someone no have to eat they come and ask you. And you give them something" (1984, personal communication).

12. Regarding such land, Item (d) of the agreement states: "MISURASATA is obliged to deliver [by March 1981] a juridical map—in order to begin negotiations with the government on the demarcation of community lands" (ibid., 98).

13. Bourgouis and Grunberg (1980, 59) expressed similar sentiments.

14. "The location of the project, with access to the highway that runs from the Rosita mine to Puerto Cabezas offers the conditions necessary for agricultural and socio-economic development, while at the same time it reproduces the traditional jungle habitat of the Coco basin. The area of influence of the project is 53,543 hectares of arable land of a quality far superior to the land they used to inhabit. This makes possible the planting of corn, rice, bananas,

yucca, and beans, the basic food stuffs of the Miskitos" (JGRN 1982, 46).

15. One man explained: "The Sandinistas they want to find out how we live. They want to give us a [volunteer labor] job, and want to know why we don't accept it. All of the time we dress. All of the time we have money. But we never work for them and them not see us work, and them would like to know how Blacks and Indians live because all the time they expect me to let them take my strength and let me work voluntary for them. They think I'm gonna work voluntary in a kind of work could make the next man win bread for his children. We go and work voluntary and then look around next Sunday and there's your children staring at you. That's wrong. You can't put me to work voluntary when everyone needs jobs to mind their children. We respect the government and tell the government respect me too, because the town is where the government take the law. The government can't give strict law to the town, saying that the town deserves it. Often the town is what support the government. Without the town the government can't live. All the law men livin' off the sweat of the town, but they're walkin' up and down sayin' 'Keep this town in a cool way.' Then they come up to me with a gun runnin' me from the place where I am talking to my friends. They don't let you do it. And if you do it, they grab you and put you in jail" (anonymous personal communication 1984).

16. *Latin America Weekly Report* (5 April 1985) writes: "Noting that the Sandinistas had accused the Indians of being CIA dupes to smokescreen their determination to 'integrate' the tribes into the revolution, Rivera said the U.S. government was just as hypocritical in using the Miskitos to claim the Sandinistas were totalitarian, without ever showing any interest in the Indians' real complaints. As for the contras in ARDE and FDN, he said, 'They have told us that they would never give us Indians autonomy if they were in power.'"

17. On 8 October 1985, Rivera stated: "The Reagan administration has given short-sighted political support to the forces of the past who seek a return of Somocismo with a new Somoza—Adolfo Calero head of the FDN. . . . UNO is a mask of the FDN and of the interests of the [Reagan] administration. . . . The FDN made it appear that KISAN had been created by an assembly of Nicaraguan refugees in Honduras. In fact, this was a maneuver by Calero who was trying to strengthen his position in relation to Arturo Cruz, one of the UNO leaders" (Rivera 1985, 2).

REFERENCES

Abrams, E. 1985. Letter to Senator Edward M. Kennedy, United States Senate. Washington: U.S. Department of State.

_____ 1986. "Keeping Pressure on the Sandinistas." *New York Times*, 13 January.

Adams, R. N. 1981. "The Sandinistas and the Indians: The 'Problem' of the Indians in Nicaragua." *Caribbean Review* 10, no. 1: 23–25.

Akwesasne Notes. 1982. "Miskito Nation: Interview with Brooklyn Rivera."

Americas Watch. 1982. *On Human Rights in Nicaragua (May 1982).* New York:

Americas Watch.

_____ 1983. *Human Rights in Central American (October 1983).* New York: Americas Watch.

_____ 1984. *Human Rights in Central America (June 1984).* New York: Americas Watch.

_____ 1986. *With the Miskitos in Honduras.* New York: Americas Watch.

Anaya, S. James. 1987. "The CIA with the Honduran Army in the Mosquitia: Taking the Freedom Out of the Fight in the Name of Accountability. A Report on a Visit to the Honduran Mosquitia during April 1987." Albuquerque. Manuscript.

Autonomy Commission. n.d. (1986). *Autonomy.* Managua. Pamphlet.

Bonfil Batalla, G., ed. 1981. *Utopia y Revolucion: El pensamiento politico contemporaneo de los indios en America Latina.* Mexico: Nueva Imagen, S.A.

Borge, Tomas. 1981. "It Is Difficult to Fight Against Backwardness." *Por Esto,* no. 8 (20 August). Reprinted in *National Revolution and Indigenous Identity: The Conflict between Sandinistas and Miskito Indians on Nicaragua's Atlantic Coast,* edited by Klaudine Ohland and Robin Schneider, 189–92. IWGIA Document 47. Copenhagen: IWGIA, 1983.

_____ and Booklyn Rivera. 1986. "Acuerdos basicos preliminares entre el Gobierno de Nicaragua y la organizacion YATAMA en ronda de conversaciones del 25 de enero al 2 de febrero de 1988." Managua. Manuscript.

Bourgouis, P. and G. Grunberg. 1980. "La Mosquitia y la Revolucion: Informe de una investigacion rural en la costa Atlantica Norte." Managua. Manuscript.

Calderon, M. 1981. "We have a Job of Forging Class Consciousness." *Intercontinental Press,* June 29. Reprinted in *National Revolution and Indigenous Identity: The Conflict between Sandinistas and Miskito Indians on Nicaragua's Atlantic Coast,* edited by Klaudine Ohland and Robin Schneider, 142–43. IWGIA Document 47. Copenhagen: IWGIA, 1983.

Carrigan, Ana. 1988. "Ending the Other War in Nicaragua." *The Nation,* February, 152–54.

Casement, R. 1912. *Correspondence Reflecting the Treatment of British Colonial Subjects and Native Indians Employed in the Collection of Rubber in the Putumayo District.* Miscellaneous Publication 8, published by His Majesty's Stationary House. London: Harrison and Sons.

Chaliand, G., ed. 1980. *People Without a Country.* London: Zed Press.

CIDCA (Centro de Investigaciones y Documentacion de la Costa Atlantica). 1981a. "Encuesta a los trabajadores de la Costa Atlantica." Managua. Manuscript.

_____ 1981b. "A proposal for Research: The Impact on Human Communities of Environmental Degradation in the Atlantic Coast Region of Nicaragua." Managua. Manuscript.

_____ 1984. *Trabil Nani: History and Current Situation in Nicaragua's Atlantic Coast.* Managua: CIDCA.

CIERA (Centro de Investigacion y Estudias de la Reform Agraria). 1981. *La*

Mosquitia en la revolucion. Managua: Coleccion Blas Real Espinales.

Constable, P. 1986. "Nicaraguan Indians Move to Honduras." *Boston Globe*, 7 April 1986.

Dennis, P. A. 1981. "The Costeños and the Revolution in Nicaragua." *Journal of Interamerican Studies and World Affairs* 23, no. 3:271–96.

Dennis, P. A. and M. D. Olien. 1984. "Kingship Among the Miskito." *American Ethnologist* 12.

Diskin, Martin, Thomas Bossert, Salomon Nahmad S., and Stefano Varese. 1986. "Peace and Autonomy on the Atlantic Coast of Nicaragua." *LASA Forum* 16, no. 4:1–19.

Evans, J. H. and Jack Epstein. 1982. "Nicaragua's Miskito Move Based on False Allegations." *National Catholic Reporter*, 24 December.

_____ 1983. "A Revolution Fighting to Survive: Nicaragua." *In These Times* 7, no. 6:12–22.

Floyd, T. S. 1967. *The Anglo-Spanish Struggle for the Mosquitia.* Alburquerque: University of New Mexico Press.

Geertz, C. 1983. "The Integrative Revolution: Primordial Sentiments and Civil Politics in the New States." In *The Interpretation of Cultures*, edited by Clifford Geertz, 255–310. New York: Basic Books.

Godelier, M. 1977. *Perspectives in Marxist Anthropology.* New York: Cambridge University Press.

Gudeman, S. 1978. *The Demise of a Rural Economy: From Subsistence to Capitalism a Latin American Village.* Boston: Routledge and Kegan Paul Ltd.

Hale, Charles 1982. "Nicaragua—Responses." *Cultural Survival Quarterly* 6, no. 1:19–23.

_____ 1987. "Institutional Struggle, Conflict and Resolution: Miskito Indians and the Nicaraguan State (1979–1985)." In CIDCA/Development Study Unit, *Ethnic Groups and the Nation State: The Case of the Atlantic Coast in Nicaragua.* Stockholm: University of Sweden.

Hardenburg, W. E. 1912. *The Putumayo: the Devil's Paradise.* London: T. Fisher Unwin.

Helms, M. W. 1969. "The Cultural Ecology of a Colonial Tribe." *Ethnology* 8, no. 1:76–84.

_____ 1971. *Asang: Adaptations to Cultural Contact in a Miskito Community.* Gainesville: University of Florida Press.

_____ 1975. *Middle America: A Culture History of Heartland and Frontiers.* Englewood Cliffs: Prentice Hall.

IACHR (Inter-American Commission on Human Rights). 1984. *Report on the Situation of Human Rights of a Segment of the Nicaraguan Population of Miskito Origin.* Washington, D. C.: General Secretariat, Organization of American States.

INNICA (Instituto Nicaraquense de la Costa Atlantica). 1982. *Tasba Pri: A Seis Meses de Trabajo.*

International League for Human Rights. 1983. *Nicaragua's Human Rights Record.* New York: International League for Human Rights.

JGRN (Junta del Gobierno de Reconstruccion Nacional). 1982. *Tasba Pri: Free*

Land, Tierra Libre. Managua: Direccion de Divulgacion y Prensa.

Kinzer, Stephen. 1987. "Nicaragua Indians Agree to Accord." *New York Times,* 6 October.

LeMoyne, James. 1987. "U.S. Hopes a Miskito Parley Will Bolster Fight Against Sandinistas." *New York Times,* 7 June.

Lernoux, Penny. 1985a. "Strangers in a Familiar Land." *The Nation,* 14 September.

_____ 1985b. "The Indians and the Comandantes." *The Nation,* 28 September.

_____ 1985c. "Sandinista Treatment of Miskitos a Betrayal of Revolution Ideals." *National Catholic Reporter,* 26 April.

McAward, J. and T. Macdonald. 1984. "Missing Explanations in Miskito Problem." *New York Times,* 14 December.

Macdonald, Theodore, Jr. 1984. "MISURASATA Goes Home." *Cultural Survival Quarterly* 8, no. 4 : 42–49.

Maier, K. 1985. "Nicaragua: Contras Trying to Undermine Miskito Rebels" (interview with Brookyn Rivera 13 December). San Jose, Costa Rica: Inter Press Service Feature.

_____ 1986. "Miskito Hold to an Uneasy Peace." *Newsday,* 6 January.

Maykruth, Andrew. 1987. "Sandinistas Cope with Discontent on the East Coast." *Philadelphia Inquirer,* 4 January.

Millet, R. 1977. *Guardians of the Dynasty: A History of the U.S. Created Nacional de Nicaragua and Somoza Family.* New York: Orbis Books.

MISURASATA. 1980. *Lineamientos Generales De MISURASATA.* Managua.

_____ 1981a. "Lineas generales de accion de MISURASATA en 1981." Managua. Manuscript.

_____ 1981b. *Propuesta de la tenencia de la tierra de las comidades indigenas y criollas de la Costa Atlantica.* Managua.

Mohawk, J. and S. Davis. 1982. "Miskitos and Sandinistas in Nicaragua," *Akwesasne Notes,* late spring, 7–12.

Moore, Barrington, Jr. 1966. *Social Origins of Dictatorship and Democracy.* Boston: Beacon Press.

Muravchik, J. 1984. "Manipulating the Miskitos." *The New Republic,* 6 August 1984, 21–25.

Nietschmann, B. 1973. *Between Land and Water: The Subsistence Ecology of the Miskito Indians, Eastern Nicaragua.* New York: Seminar Press.

Ohland, Klaudine and Robin Schneider, eds. 1983. *National Revolution and Indigenous Identity: The Conflict between Sandinistas and Miskito Indians on Nicaragua's Atlantic Coast.* IWGIA Document 47. Copenhagen: IWGIA.

Olien, M. D. 1983. "The Miskito Kings and the Line of Succession." *Journal of Anthropological Research* 39, no. 2 : 198–241.

_____ n.d. "E. G. Squien and the Miskito: Anthropological Scholarship and Political Propaganda." Manuscript.

Parsons, J. J. 1955. "Gold Mining in the Nicaraguan Rain Forest." *Yearbook of the Association of Pacific Coast Geographers,* 49–55.

Radell, D. R. 1976. "The Indian Slave Trade and Population in Nicaragua during the Sixteenth Century." In *The Native Population of the Americas in 1492*, edited by William M. Denevan, 67–76. Madison: University of Wisconsin Press.

Ramirez, W. 1981. "The Imperialist Threat and the Indigenous Problem in Nicaragua." Paper presented at the United Nations Seminar on Recourse Procedures and other Forms of Protection Available to Victims of Racial Discrimination and Activities to be Undertaken at the National and Regional Level. 14–22 December.

_____ Brooklyn Rivera, and Jorge Jenkins. 1981. "Agreement on Norms for Lumber-Felling." In *National Revolution and Indigenous Identity: The Conflict between Sandinistas and Miskito Indians on Nicaragua's Atlantic Coast*, edited by Klaudine Ohland and Robin Schneider, 95–98. IWGIA Document 47. Copenhagen: IWGIA, 1983.

Rivera, Brooklyn. 1985. Letter to Clem Chartier, President, World Council of Indigenous Peoples. San Jose, Costa Rica. December.

_____ 1986. Letter to Hon. George P. Shultz, United States Secretary of State. 7 March.

Rodinson, M. 1980. "Preface." In *People Without a Country*, edited by Gerard Chaliand, 1–7. London: Zed Press.

Schneider, Robin. 1983. "British Indirect Rule: Miskito Kings and the Repression of Autochthonous Peoples." In *National Revolution and Indigenous Identity: The Conflict between Sandinistas and Miskito Indians on Nicaragua's Atlantic Coast*, edited by Klaudine Ohland and Robin Schneider, 28–35. IWGIA Document 47. Copenhagen. IWGIA.

Scott, J. C. 1976. *The Moral Economy of the Present*. New Haven: Yale University Press.

Sharkey, J. 1985. "Disturbing the Peace." *Common Cause* 11, no. 5 : 21–32.

Stephens, B. and M. Popkin. 1984. "Amnesty Hinders Contra Recruiting." *In These Times*, 11–17 January.

Torres Rivas, E. 1971. *Interpretacion del Desarrollo Social Centroamericano*. Centroamerica: EDUCA.

Vanegas, Luis, Charles Hale, Galio Gurdian, Edmundo Gordon and Marcelo Zuniga. 1981. "Historical and Structural Causes of Racial Discrimination in Latin America and Possible Solutions." Background paper: United Nations Seminar on Recourse Procedures and other Forms of Protection Available to Victims of Racial Discrimination and Activities to be Undertaken at the National and Regional Level. 14–22 December. Managua. Manuscript.

West, R. C. and J. P. Augelli. 1976. *Middle America: Its Lands and Peoples*. Englewood Cliffs, Prentice Hall, Inc.

Wallerstein, I. 1980. *The Modern World System: II*. New York: Academic Press.

Wheelock Ramon, J. 1974. *Raices Indigenas de la Lucha Anticolonialista en Nicaragua*. Mexico: Siglo Veintiuno.

_____ 1981. "Introduction." In *CIERA, La Mosquitia en la Revolucion*, 9–13. Managua: Coleccion Blas Real Espinales.

To Seek Refuge: Nation
and Ethnicity in Exile

FRANCESCO PELLIZZI

> *Man dwells in the world as if he had come to it from a*
> *private domain, a home, into which he might always return*
> *for refuge. He does not come to the world from an inter-*
> *stellar space where he was already in command of himself*
> *and from which he would thereafter have to attempt a*
> *perilous landing.*
>
> —Emmanuel Levinas

From Greco-Roman and Semitic antiquity, exile has been the classic image of individual misfortune and tragedy. China and Japan have a similar tradition. To be excluded from one's native land—"fatherland" or "motherland"—is as cruel as to be rejected by the loved one: the latter is often used as a metaphor for the former.[1] Ithaca longed for by Ulysses from the Western seas, Rome by Ovid from the Black Sea, were reflected in one another through the centuries, till the mythical theme—originally a *figura* of initiation and "conversion" (*return* and divine intercession)—became a bitter, anguished cry of personal self-pity, the extreme expression of the helplessness of one and every man in the face of the Prince (the State) as the agent of fate. Naturally, by that time, the official history of Rome had transformed that archetype into a new ideological *topos*, although still in a poetical form: the exile of Aeneas is *collective* and he *carries* his destiny on his shoulders—as he carries his father. It is a sign of his calling to plant new roots for his people, to found a new center from which memory might unravel. Later in History, refuge was both the solace and curse of exile. As Dante wrote, for an exile, accepting the condition of beggar and the bitterness it brings is the price of safety.

What happens, then, when an entire people is sent into exile, is forced to seek refuge or "willingly" accepts and even seeks that condition? The *individual* exile cannot forget his "country," much less the ties that link him to his people, to those he has left behind, whether dead or alive. The point of reference for a *people* in exile, on the other hand, is the Land, or Place of origin.

Exile creates "ethnicities." No people truly is, *chez soi*, an ethnic group, because that which defines ethnicity is Difference. Difference, historically has always been the work of Conquest; Difference without conquest is the more or less sporadic and superficial experiencing of the alien, or of the exotic. Conquest brings Distance home and establishes Difference.

In the Americas, five hundred years ago as well as now, Difference and exile have always been determined by Conquest. But unlike the eras of the Aztec empire and of the Hispanic colony, modern time (in both the new and the old world) recognizes frontiers without which "true" exile and refuge would be impossible.[2] In the Americas, the Conquest carried a kind of cultural Distance across the Atlantic ocean that could not be bridged and introduced Difference where formerly only *diversity* had existed. What had been "flowery" Indian Wars (*Guerras Floridas*, mainly destined for the taking of captives and the ennoblement of valiant commoners) became mercenary, manipulated civil wars: for the first time, during the Conquest, Indians not only took freedom away from other Indians, but in the process also deprived themselves of it. In this sense, today's Latin American wars still adhere to the model set in motion by the European invasion: they are civil wars manipulated from a distance. This Distance is not just the geographical and economic one of the Great Powers: it is the seed of Difference deeply implanted by the Colony and resown by the nineteenth-century postcolonial nation-states. It is still to be found in the ideologies of whatever color that legitimize Europeanlike central power in these states, or even most of the imported ideologies that aim to subvert it in the name of a new social utopia. This is not to imply that these "discourses" are all equivalent: they are shaped by different forces and interests, but they do share the idiom of "nationalism." Yet this theme has been adopted by neighboring entities whose cultural and historical difference lie *within* their borders, not outside them: they are mostly states that include "nations" within and across their borders, not states made up of one nation—as often their ideologies would have it. They are not, therefore, nation-states.

ETHNICITY AND EXILE

In exile, nations become ethnicities (the Poles, the Italians, the Irish, the Mexicans . . .) and in some cases, cultural and historical groups take on a new standing as nations (the Miskito, the Palestinians, the Jews, etc.). Hence, what seems to define "ethnicity" is a condition of demographic or social *minority*. This is so particularly when this minority, though conscious of its distinct nature, has yet to acquire the confidence to regard itself as a "nation among nations." In many cases, then, nations are ethnicities that have come to aspire to the condition of states (that might be fully independent or not, but are in any case *autonomous*), exerting at least some of the control in the management of their affairs which a state might today exert.

It is striking to note that, in the present, "majority" and "ethnicity" are by and large opposed, as if they were mutually exclusive notions and realities. Essentially, ethnic entities can only exist as minorities, i.e., as *distinct* in an otherwise homogeneous, Westernized, and *urbanized* cultural environment—in other words in the world of modernity. Despite some exceptions and misleading contrary appearances, it is senseless to talk of ethnic minorities in a truly traditional rural environment. One might, in some instances, refer to caste or to feudal relations, but these are *nonquantitative* notions in which the minority / majority variable plays a markedly insignificant role. The striking exceptions in "Latin" America are provided by countries such as Guatemala, Peru, and Bolivia (and there are also several cases in Africa and elsewhere), where socially "inferior" ethnic groups constitute the majority of the population in postcolonial states. These are not minorities (as others have observed) in the usual sense of the word; they are *social* "minorities" because, in spite of their relative numbers, they are excluded from partaking of the Authority that ultimately governs their lives; they are, in a sense, "exiled" in a land that is their own, not only for historical reasons but even by the tenets of modern "democratic" criteria. What genocide did not, and does not accomplish is obtained through other means: the transformation of the status of the vanquished from that of "peoples" to that of cultural "minorities." If their status as nations is not recognized, it is precisely because, *as autochthonous nations*, their claim for an autonomous state of their own might be so strong as to tip the equilibrium on which the *present* postcolonial system of state authority rests. Thus, in one way or another, ethnicity seems to be incompatible with the modern state except as a *minority*. This age-old reality underlies present policies and outbursts of "racial" intolerance, in North America as well as in Latin American countries, that could not be easily justified by the rationale of economic exploitation alone.

REFUGE, PLACE, AND MEMORY

There are two basic configurations of space with regard to exile and refuge: one is eminently *static*—the place *of* refuge; the other is dynamic—the context *through* which escape is effected. In the first, the place becomes a sort of attractive nest, a niche of survival; the second, on the other hand, appears to preclude all hope of permanent asylum and leads instead to a perpetual wandering, beyond the diaspora.

Return is the common reference both alternatives share, though with different connotations. In the former, a link is established between the place of origin and that of refuge; an unbroken thread which implies a tension whereby the refuge becomes a reflected, hence inverted, image of home—seen from a great distance. Conversely, home, which is represented by those who are left behind, becomes truly aware of this new extension of itself only when the link must be severed.

The second configuration of exile and refuge, with its proliferation of departures and, in some cases, with its adoption of Departure as the very mode of "dwelling"—or of drawing the trajectory of life—makes Escape itself the only source of possible safety. In so doing, it exorcises the trauma of the original separation again and again, as it reenacts it. Thus the wanderers of this world, those who live *through*, "in transit," the true homeless / rootless, are created.

For them, the link to a place of origin is necessarily different from that of static refugees. Ever more removed from any *organic* tie with the Land and with those who, for better or for worse, have continued inhabiting it, the prospect of return takes on "messianic" connotations whose phantasmic character has not prevented bellicose missions of "reconquest." Since by necessity or vocation the place of refuge is never truly accepted as the Place-of-Belonging, the land once inhabited as one's *own* becomes, in memory, the Promised Land, a blinding light to which the wanderer is drawn in an increasingly catastrophic vortex. This memory becomes a mythic Memory, and nostalgia, which reverses the process of remembrance, becomes either an obsession with Return or the guilty conscience of *renunciation*, with its imaginary compensations.

On the other hand, for those exiles who have settled in some place of refuge "permanently," making it to some extent *their* land, or for those that are confined to forced settlements, places of *concentration* (labeled "refugee camps"), the other place, the land of origin, must often appear as a source of imminent danger, and therefore as a place from which to flee. Memory is still fresh and real (one might still recall a particular bend in the trail, a sow left behind at the village). For these exiles, it is as if they had never really left. A strange specular relation is then established between the familiar domestic place and the refugee *camp*: the second tends to model itself on the first, even imitating its organizational principles. This is not just out of "conservatism," but rather out of the need to recreate in exile an image of the sacred place of dwelling: the mirror of the Place becomes the unspoken symbol of Hope where hope no longer exists. The camp (whether it is surrounded by barbed wire or not) is reminiscent in its fixity of the slow and steady rhythm of home. So it is both a haven and a place of grief and horror— a haven for the relative safety it provides and for the echo of home given by the presence of all those sharing a common destiny. It is a place of anguish, because it is in fact a grotesque, tragic parody of home and of the self-contained freedom of home: what was no longer truly possessed there—life itself—is relatively secure here; but nothing can be truly owned.

Hence, when the original Place is no longer the *theatrum vitae*, or a support for social play and *continuity*, it becomes increasingly abstract. Social identity feeds on its ghost, or rather, on an *idea* of social identity. The cycle of its traditional mechanism, of the giving to and taking from the Land, becomes a "punctual" time of "before" and "after." In a way, it is also *suspended* time, because no authentic or consequential action is possible there: there can be no action that preserves and builds, which might of itself be either productive or nourishing. The only activity that remains possible, that eludes the snare of charity, is that of maintaining the alienated self. This does not even provide the meager subsistence of former life in the motherland—but merely a means of *survival*.

When scarcity of natural and technological resources and the dynamics of power between groups do not allow for an economy of accumulation and over-consumption, *subsistence* becomes the prevalent mode of existence. It is always directly related to the natural environment in a kind of socio-ecological context. It almost invariably implies an ideal investment that is transcendent, or metaphysical, of the physiognomy of the land—of its surface as well as of its core. It also often constitutes the substantive nucleus of what we call "traditional" religion.

The political economy and spiritual realm of *survival*, often the lot of the refugee and the exile, is something else altogether. It resembles the condition of the shipwrecked, wandering aimlessly, with no control over the elements that hold him in their grasp, of a Tantalus that cannot quench his undefinable thirst nor satisfy his primary hunger. It is not the effect of a temporary or prolonged imbalance with the resources of the land as in the condition of subsistence, but rather the effect of being severed from the root of those resources, scarce as they always were; it is like being orphaned.

A condition today, reminiscent of the refugee, is that of so much of the urban sub-proletariat (lumpen proletariat) made up of foreign and national "immigrants" in the world's larger cities. The lumpen, like the refugees, have also severed their ties with the Place of giving and taking, with the Land; in their extreme circumstances they have also almost entirely lost contact with cultural memory, which for the refugees is still fundamental. Refugees are only potentially lumpen, because they still remember, still cast their minds backwards. Time for the refugee is a time of *waiting*.[3] The alienation of the large urban *bidonvilles* (shantytowns) is different from that of the refugee: it might be defined as intrinsic and *definitive*. Nonetheless, the mode of *survival*—a condition in which expediency and resourcefulness are constantly diverted in nonconstructive circular patterns of action and reaction—is common to both. The cyclical time of the peasant, bound to the demands of the land, of time and the elements, is replaced by the vicious cycle of urban parasitism and exploitation. In that sense, the lumpen proletariat embodies an extreme form of exile, one that has pushed alienation from the place of refuge so far that identity itself is shattered. The "ethnic" refugee still knows *who* he is, what he would like to continue to be, and clings to that belief. The only identity the lumpen can have is that of wanting to be what they cannot be, hence a hollowed identity, *en creux*; but how can one want something so alien that one has no real knowledge of it? Like a child with a new toy, in those circumstances destruction can become a necessary and inevitable outlet.

REFUGE AND THE INDIAN PEASANTRY

On the southern and northern borders of Mexico, semiclandestine emigration prompted by economic reasons has been the practice for many decades. Guatemalans emigrate to Mexico, Mexicans emigrate to the United States: the "industrial" (agribusiness) exerts an irresistible attraction. Numbers vary greatly, of course, but so do the populations and resources relative to the three countries. The benefits to the host nations are well known: it is not out of charity that migrants are tolerated, nor is it out of any deep regard for the law that their flow is controlled. In Chiapas, where migrants served the interests of large coffee plantations, their status was *impermanent* (coffee requires considerable manpower over a short period of time). They were Indians, largely of the Mam Maya language group, but their infiltration did not cause undue alarm because they invariably returned with their meager profits to their Guatemalan villages. Thousands more have arrived since then, from that and other groups across the border, who have no prospect of ever returning.

What must be stressed is the "Indianness" of these refugees who have settled in about seventy refugee camps in Mexico, as well as the

million or so who are living in Guatemala in a state of "internal refuge."
They belong to that "race" which does not conform to the "national"
character either on the far or near side of that border. Despite regional
and historic diversities, this common identity of exiles and "hosts," of
Indian refugees and Indian protectors, is quite specific to the Mexican-
Guatemalan situation (though, once again, similar cases might be found
elsewhere in the world) and it affects the specific *conditions* of refuge
both *within* and *across* the national borders.

It has often been stated, though seldom fully understood, that
Indians in Latin America, particularly in Guatemala, despite the 450
years that have gone by since their colonialization, are culturally quite
distinct from the "white" populations such as mestizos (known as ladinos
in Chiapas) and creoles. The distinction is not merely one of language,
but rather rests in how they perceive themselves and are perceived by
others. That is their native *identity*. Yet Indians are also fundamentally
peasants. This is relevant because it affects the manner in which they
are treated by both "friends" and foes, and in part explains their
persecution. They are nonurban *country* people. That also accounts for
their specific characteristics: they are refugees *from* the land, who have
lost the Land, but also refugees *of* the land, and, for that very reason,
refugees who *seek* the Land. This is not by way of reviving the presumed
Marxist perspective (now fortunately waning) that sees Indians as *mere*
peasants, that is, proletarians cut off from a sense of their status by their
own archaic customs, later reinforced by colonial structures. They are
rather Indian *peasants*, and as such their relationship to the place of
origin—and hence also to that of refuge—is subject not just to their
particular ancestral cultures, fraught with their density of beliefs and
practices, but, perhaps even more radically, by the peasant's particular
way of inhabiting the land.

Thousands of Indians are marching (1983) to orders of present
and past (urban) military dictators.   They march in full garb
(Chichicastenango), their *capitanes* in the lead, obeying the orders of
the Metropolis so as not to lose their land, the Place which is *theirs*.
Who are they? Why do they do it? Just as thirty years ago, at the time
of the U.S.-engineered removal of Arbenz's democratic government
(the only such regime in the history of Central America), the wisdom
accumulated through centuries of having their identity manipulated
drove a majority of Indians into a state of sullen acceptance and of
waiting with regard to the City's decisions. Ultimately, what is essential
to them is that the the land to which they are tied by the strongest link,
the land nourished by their dead and nourishing the living, in a word
the Place of subsistence, be guaranteed.

The primacy of this immemorial need explains many a "surprising" alignment of Indian communities in times of crises, a diffidence of political movements professing to have their "best interest" at heart. It also implies something more specific and profound than a supposed rural "simple-mindedness" before the sophistication of the City: it means that the Indian, *as peasant*, occupies and uses the land in a Time that is obviously *neither quantitative nor uniform*. Consequently, he must be available to the land *when* necessary: unlike the factory worker, he is master of his own time, but he has to help this time flow, in its irregularity and fundamental discontinuity, *on his behalf.* He is not taken over by his work all the time, like urban man, but neither is he free to manipulate and reorganize his tasks within an amorphous time ("leisure" time in the city man being the mirror image of "working" time). To the Indian peasant the land is the place of life and death, of cyclical discontinuity and of continuous regeneration, the place of *Being*, because it is the *only* place of cultural survival, of ethnic identity. This close bond constitutes the strength and the fragility, the *intrinsic* limit of campesino power, as the aftermath of the October Revolution has amply demonstrated.[4]

TOWN, COUNTRY, AND CULTURAL APPROPRIATION

The entire history of autochthonous groups on the American continent following the European invasion is marked by the effort to appropriate first the secret of the *spiritual* power of the invaders (for as long as it was considered to be spiritual), and later, of their techno-material success. But the Indian peasant, as Indian *and* as peasant, was excluded from the Town—where this power resides—and was (and is) in precarious exile when *in* Town.[5]

The fact is that "to appropriate" means "to make one's own," to translate and transfer something into a usable entity of discourse *and* of life, into something that can be experienced. Urban life cannot then be *assimilated* ("made similar") by the Indian peasantry: hence it inspires awe.

The Metropolis is also the Market, a place of exchange, and as such it is necessary to the campo. But the city inhabits the site in a radically different manner. This historical dimension of the problem underlies the urban dissidence and resistance of Indian peasants in Central America. The combination of this irreparable break beneath the symbiosis/dependence of the City and the Land, together with the colonial, asymmetrical play of castelike relations, creates the rift and incomprehension that obstructs organized dissent in these regions.[6] The shift of insurrection from the city to the countryside in the late seventies brought new content and meaning to the old rift: in justifying the military occupation of the countryside, the new strategy gave the central power the means to crack down on all sorts of organizations that were beginning to boost the Indian peasantry. One can safely say, at least in relation to the Indians in the campo, that repression *preceded* insurrection.

LIBERTY AND INSURRECTION

Collective "liberty" is an elusive and problematic notion, yet no matter how one chooses to define it, it can only apply to communities having an autonomous organization. Repression, in the Guatemalan countryside, did not follow insurrection, but rather the gradual constitution of semiautonomous cooperatives and other *local* progressive and noninsurrectional organizations. Throughout the history of the Americas, the tendency of colonial and postcolonial governments has been to impose greater and greater central control on local entities, both Indian and non-Indian.[7]

The response of the Indian communities both increased their marginality and helped them to resist more effectively this growing encroachment on their autonomy, as they developed and maintained a distinct, if "syncretic" identity that would in turn generate a "history" *parallel* to that of the ruling powers. Such an identity invariably uses *cultural elements* in order to substantiate itself. These are not only the "salvageable" remains of precolonial times; they are, in fact, primarily *appropriations* from the ruling culture. The Indian "liberation" movements of today might also be seen as one more such appropriation. The way in which recent Catholic and Protestant "theologies of liberation" are *taken on* by Indian movements is similar to the way "traditional" saint-cult organizations (confraternities, *cofradías*, *mayordomías*) were adopted by Indian communities in the Colony. They were forms of autochthonous organization, hence of self-defense and ultimate spiritual (*and* "economic") autonomy, within the new "Catholicism" itself and despite the manipulation of these forms of worship by the religious authorities who had initially imposed them.

It is my contention, therefore, that *both* the Guatemalan Indians' giving in to the military imposition of civil-militia enrollment and action *and* the Indian support of (or participation in) guerrilla insurrectional activity (in Guatemala, in Nicaragua, in Peru and elsewhere) constitute not so much "revolutionary" movements as strategies for the preservation of Indian identity and existence: *strategies for survival*, whose precedents can be found in colonial times. Those Indian cultures of Latin America that have been colonially linked to Europe for 450 years can be seen as waters on which the colonial raft has been sailing: they *reflect* the invaders, but not clearly, since their depths remain unknowable and even on their surface, which is obtrusively "closed," unfamiliar creatures keep reappearing. "Tradition," then, constantly regenerates itself from these depths and these mirror effects, so that existence-in-connection-with-the-Place (seen above as a preideological root of ethnic identity) can be preserved in the face of protracted occupation by external forces.

Hence, the struggle for freedom of these communities has always expressed itself in their way of belonging-to-themselves. Once again, it has characterized them for half a millennium, not just despite but *through* the process of acculturation; even in times of subjection it has always been a function not so much of "owning" as of *belonging* to the Place. If this is so, we may well wonder what freedom might be, finally, and what "freedom" may in fact mean for these groups, *as* groups, once they are exiled from their lands and forced to seek refuge in other people's lands (the "Country" here is not truly relevant), or, worse still, if near or distant Towns scatter them forever, making of a tight-knit group a nebula of unrelated families at first, and a dispersed and isolated diaspora of individuals later. Examples of the second instance exist today in many urban areas from Florida to California. As for the first, an analogous situation is currently developing in the Mexican state of Chiapas. Over the last few decades, large numbers of Indians there have left their original communities, in a colonizing diaspora that has attempted to reclaim lands long left uninhabited (particularly in the tropical forests). More recently, smaller but still considerable groups have been *forced* out of their villages due to religious dissidence (they have converted to some form of Protestantism or, in fewer cases, have adopted new, post-Vatican Council II, "activist" Catholic attitudes not in keeping with "traditional" practices). Some of them have created relatively large "suburban" communities, that in their initial phase (and at first glance) look somewhat like a cross between an Indian village and a *bidonville*. The comparison between these "internal" Indian exiles and the "external" ones would reveal some very interesting common features and differences.

To sum up my previous observations, I would like to offer these two following points:

a) *Tradition and insurrection*. Because insurrection—the seeking of a *new* kind of freedom—ruptures the traditional relation to the Land, it is already, for the ethnic group members who decide to take part in it actively, a form of exile, a departure from the old ways, a breaking of that univocal (*sacrificial*) bond with the soil that made the preservation of Difference an act both spiritual and concrete. Like the exiled refugee, the guerrilla develops a *new* sense of ethnicity: it is the beginning, for both, of ethnicity *as ideology*. Ultimately, this mode of ethnic identity can make ethnicity and nation coincide by transforming the sense of belonging from the face-to-face mode of the old hunter-peasant communities into the ideological "principles" of common origins, "roots," and generic (*mediated*) "brotherhood."

b) *The refugee as prisoner.* He has lost *all* freedom just when, by crossing the border, he might have thought he had found it again. The "freedom" acquired within his newfound safety is fictitious, even when he is not confined to a camp from which he cannot (or is not expected to) move. This is not only because his condition prevents him from *going home* (which is what defines it): his freedom is an illusion because it doesn't *belong* to him, but rather is given (or lent) him by his host: "Come, here you are free (but only if you 'behave')." It is as striking as it is sad to see how many (particularly "petit bourgeois") refugees end up "more papist than the Pope" in their adoption and championing of the most ingrained and least commendable political prejudices of their host country's dominant groups.

EXILE, REFUGE, AND THE NATIONAL STATE BORDERS

No one would have thought of confining to "camps" the thousands and thousands of exiles produced by "bourgeois" urban dissidence in the 1970s from Guatemala, El Salvador, Argentina, Chile, and the rest of Latin America, where many are currently living and working in jobs of public responsibility. Nor were these exiles threatened with being sent back indiscriminately to face their old persecutors. But for the close to one hundred thousand Indian peasants from Guatemala who have crossed the border into Chiapas (as well as for the Palestinians, the Cambodian peasants, and so many others), it is a different story: it is an attenuated version of that "racism" which makes a peasant temporarily acceptable (even in the underpopulated south of Mexico), only if he might be useful as an underpaid, *seasonal*, hired hand.

The reception of refugees by local Indians across the border, on the other hand, has generally been very good. Leaving aside individual cases of self-sacrifice and even heroism, it would be naive to attribute this generosity solely to some sort of pan-Indian (pan-Maya) solidarity, and to the distant linguistic kinship (their languages are roughly as close as Spanish and Italian).[8] Yet, for whatever reasons, in a certain number of cases these Guatemalan Indians secretly hosted by, and often working for, Chiapas Indians were apparently able to learn the language of their benefactors, and changed costume (when necessary), camouflaging themselves totally to avoid being detected by the Mexican border authorities. The latter are weary of these human "transfusions," not only because of the pressures from entrepreneurial groups (fearing the loss of their control over transient labor), which are real and even sometimes openly expressed, but for what appear to be deeper and more elusive reasons: Guatemalan *Indians* who become, or threaten to become, *Mexican* Indians without going through the filter or the mediation of Mexican identity, of what in Mexico is called the Raza, the *métissage*, constitute a threat to national identity. It is another instance in which "ethnic identity" and "nationality" are apparent. There is, however, another scandal in this situation: control of the borders and of people involves fears that are deeper and broader than the outward fear of an epidemic spread of insurgency (in line with the so-called "domino theory"). These questions are not easily formulated in *overt* political discourse. If "concentrated" and controlled refugees constitute, here as in other troubled parts of the world, an entity which can be gauged and quantified, a trump to be used in international political bargaining, this is not so in the case of the "wild" camps in the Chiapas forest and of those Indians who escape detection by being assimilated with their Chiapas brothers. These refugees *negate, by their very existence, the validity and the inviolability of the Border*, which is one of the fundamental principles of the nation-state. They reintroduce the continuity of traditional territory into the rigid demarcations of the modern state.

In Chiapas the ecological and political problems of refugee camps have all the characteristics and dilemmas of similar situations elsewhere. There is the environmental and cultural continuum artificially split by the frontier, which can lead to pendular reinfiltration, on one side, and to punitive excursions on the other; both neighboring states tend to want to create a sort of "free" zone, a no-man's-land aimed at *isolating* the refugees from those left behind, and to eliminate the scandalous violation of the borders by the back and forth flow of a people substantially identical on both sides, yet quite distinct from those who, on either side, control the central and peripheral bureaucracies of the state.[9]

The state, in turn, tends to exploit the already tragic destiny of the refugees as an argument in the rhetoric of control over its borders; it serves only the interests of groups favored by economic "protectionism" (both national and transnational) and of the managerial-bureaucratic "class." In Central America, the process (also well-known elsewhere) by which refugees become the pawns and pretexts for schemes and counter-schemes of hegemony and expansion, is only just beginning. In the boisterous and threatening declarations of past and present Guatemalan generals, however, as well as in the positions openly endorsed by important leaders of the Mexican business sector and by some of the border administrators, one can already discern the beginning of a manipulation and exploitation of the ethnic element in exile that is certainly not without precedent in recent and less recent history (e.g., in both the Middle East and in Africa).

As we have seen, refugees negate the frontier. But the terrible paradox of their predicament is that it is precisely on this very frontier which they have transgressed, on its solidity, one might almost say on its "inviolability," that their safety depends. In Chiapas, they would like to see the river, across which they look back apprehensively, rise into a sort of Chinese Wall which might cut them off forever from their oppressors. This ambivalent relation with the border is an image of the contradiction, of the ambiguity of the condition of the refugee and of the modern state's way of occupying and controlling the territory. The "sacred" borders, whatever their historical or geographic rationality, tend to cut through socio-cultural realities— now called ethnic groups—that have been there much longer, their territorial organization being the result of quite different historical and sociological factors. The very "abstractness" of these dissections negating ethnic continuity becomes the main motive for the militant armed Power that must serve to "defend" them. The protection of conventional borders, because it justifies a strong military presence, becomes the cover for an even more arbitrary, though masked, control over the internal population. "Protection" of the frontier and frontier areas from infiltration thus becomes the highly charged symbol of a "sovereignty" whose embodiment, whose locus, ultimately, is nothing more than a rhetorical and ideological formula covering the preservation of certain clusters of local and central interests. Not having much choice, the Guatemalan refugees fall into the trap of seeking protection within the national borders. Thus they accept and reinstate, in principle, the very separation from their Maya Indian brothers of Chiapas which (as we have seen) the symbiosis and solidarity of the refuge situation had seemingly obliterated, perhaps for the first time in almost two centuries.

EXILE AND REFUGE:

a) *Cultural premises.* The condition of refuge, as we have mentioned, often contributes to the creation of an "ethnic" identity. But because all exile necessarily implies refuge, it is more accurate to say that ethnicity develops *within* refuge. This is also true when "refuge," paradoxically, is found within the ancestral lands of a people. In this case, it is a forced confinement and relocation which alters immeasurably the value of the traditional site, and literally turns a homeland into an ultimate hideaway. In many instances, the conquered now does not *inhabit* his land, he *hides* within it: *as* one who dwells in *that* Place that represents the ultimate shield of his existence and of his "belonging." Ethnicity comes about as a result of this process. It matters little that creating these areas of internal refuge may sometimes also be in the best interests of the Conqueror, as some have cogently argued: a sort of antagonistic symbiosis is established whereby each side determines its existence in relation to the other. There is the Indian and there is the non-Indian: this is the essence of 450 years of "Latin"-American history (or rather, "Indian-Latin metahistory"). This relation, though, implies a double exile, not only of the Conquered, but also of the Conqueror—for as long as there are connotations of dominion and hence of "strangeness," the Conqueror continues to be a *colonizer*, foreign to the land that hosts him even after his forebears have inhabited it for many generations.

We have seen that the internal exile of the Conquered is a function of their loss of liberty. To this must be added the condition of *cultural dependency* to which the vanquished invariably succumbs. Out of constriction and the hypnotic lure of Power, the Conqueror takes on the role of a model who is, by definition, *unattainable*. This impossibility of truly becoming the model, due to the dynamics of domination and rejection, adds another impulse of defense to the one originally provoked by the violent impact of the conquest itself. This is the one that is translated into "cultural refuge." The makeup of cultural refuge is in turn twofold: it entails both the appropriation of certain alien *forms*, and the secret (hence *indelible*) nurturing of that root of "belonging"—that *hidden spirit*—which is also revealed in the coolness and reserve that is thought to be such a "typical" Indian trait throughout the Americas.

Now, what actually defines the boundaries of this collective "self-possession" are the very limits of what can be appropriated. The culturally *owned* is not merely that which survives, by inertia, the attack of the invading cultural forces. As with any attack, resistance and "evasive" strategies are of course generated, but this is neither the only mechanism nor the most essential for preserving that which is properly "owned," identity, nor, in the end, for drawing ethnicity out from its *seed*. What is at work, rather, is a sort of *vacuum*—or again a "limit"—of assimilation that gives the real push to this sort of subliminal group identity. The Emptiness of deculturation generates a Longing that spreads as a subtle mist over any adopted (but *unassimilated*) cultural element. Only thus can one explain and reconcile the two opposite visions of the intercultural relations of the Colony and some of the present dynamics deriving from it: cultural survival and resistance, versus the "complete" adoption of the Conqueror's religion, etc. If the first is still imbued with a certain anthropological romanticism—a function of our nostalgia for the archaic (or the organic rapport with "nature" we lost in the Industrial Revolution)—the second is no less prompted by our obsessions. The second vision is so mesmerized by the image of the Conqueror that it fails to explain how distinct cultural entities, by the thousands, still exist *despite* a power to destroy them, whose full capacity millions belonging to these entities haven't yet come to understand.

In this case, as in others where actual genocide has not (yet) taken place, there is a *dual*—if not strictly symmetrical—reaction: that of the conqueror, who in many situations may consider it to be in his best interest to preserve an insurmountable castelike difference, and then also that of the one who is conquered, who in the "caste" discovers a domain *of his own*, an unalterable *specificity*, an invisible wall that in some way protects him even when it exploits him. It is a destiny that assigns to him the humblest role in the world and at the same time *guarantees* not only his subsistence in that Place, but also his *legitimate* belonging to that same world, hence a distinct and unerasable cultural identity.

It is in this universe of relation, in this symbiotic *and* antagonistic knot, that what I have called—if I may be forgiven the image—the vacuum of assimilation, is created. It is the cultural undertow, that, even in the most brutal process of acculturation, redeems ancestral values, either as elements of identification—like collective emblems— or as a force behind those very cultural elements which are adopted and extrapolated from their contextual meaning and their original functions. This "pneumatic" nature, so to speak, of the autochthonous contents of ethnicity helps us to see one of its least understood paradoxes—one which occurs when the conditions of exile and refuge (both internal and external) are created: that the most Westernized cultural forms—the very ones that may seem to negate most radically any specific and residual ethnic identity—are precisely those that, acting as an imperceptible but ever-present veil, simultaneously hide and reveal the enduring effects of Difference. Refuge is not only, then, flight and resistance vis-à-vis the Other, it is also Emulation, and the nurturing of an Alternative that is made necessary by the Other and is centered on the Other, but that needs for this very reason to *also* reaffirm itself as autonomous and as *preceding* the advent of the Other. [10]

b) *Universal exile?* Today most of us are not only in varying degrees of exile, removed from our roots, but the *direction* in which our (and the world's) circulation is going, that of the omnipresent media and that of the computer, makes exile, and hence refuge, inevitable even for those who live and suffer this culture without questioning it: 1984 is near. "Exile" has become the condition that perhaps best characterizes us as modern, and like the artist, we all perhaps "need" exile. This at a time when the concept of a millenary "exile in this world" (which has been at the heart of many an extraordinary vision of the last thirty centuries at least) appears forgotten. The loss of Place, in the bureaucratic, managerial state, is not just the destiny of some individuals or groups, it is the result of the new ways of using the world and of the "interiorized" and "separated" forms of consciousness they imply. We could not hope to do more here than evoke glimpses of their complex phenomenology. Let us note again the fact, however, that today we are all, inevitably, "*from* somewhere"—in the sense of a *nonbelonging*—even when this somewhere is the place where we live. This condition is common to all modern and industrial societies, however their "mode of production" may be set up, and to the countryside as well as to the city (there isn't any *real* countryside any more: it has all been swallowed up by the media). As the world, very painfully, shrinks into some form of forced togetherness today, it develops forms of consciousness that make exile and refuge impossible, as they eliminate Difference. Exile itself, though, will not truly disappear: it will acquire a new, all-pervasive meaning, becoming, for the first time in history, an exile *without* refuge. In other words, an unavoidable rift has occurred in the modern spirit; it is the sense of a distance, which cannot be bridged, from any *localized* origin (which is why *ideal* and ideological Root become necessary). As one is always *from* a place, one can never be *of* (or belong to) any one place. On the other hand, if one is to be a true exile one must *come* from a radically *different* place: this today is less and less possible. Where it still exists, this distance from the *group as place* does not imply a loss of the sense of ethnic belonging.

I would like to underline, finally, the *ideological*, that is, at the same time, rhetorical, emotional, and "programmatic" strength of this ethnic sense of belonging that, significantly enough, does not need the support of any single specific cultural element: neither language, nor customs, nor even religion. Its only concrete references are the Place and / or the Race (the Blood), and the importance of these tend to be inversely proportional to their actual *experience*: be it the "Promised Land" or the actual continuity of a "Race." We are, here again, in the order of *mediated*, "reflected" and secondary projections, that is, not in belonging per se but in an "*image-of-belonging*" corroborated by fiction and narrative. The difference between a Discourse that nourishes them and one that is nourished *by* them is the difference between old Myth and that adjunct of Practical Reason that afflicts us: ideology. Increasingly, with the passing of time, we see the development of a *generic*, disembodied memory—the source and justification of *clichés* that are eerily reminiscent of the stereotypes once indulged in by the casual, hard-nosed visitor to the *Heimat* or, when in exile, by the diffident and defensive host.

Nor is refuge really possible today either, except where Difference endures. One of the aims of these general notes was to call attention to the fact that our refugees are already refugees without refuge, because they are unwilling victims and actors, once again, of a *double* exile, one that forces them into a strange land and one that leads them to a different view of their condition and of living in general. This view *tends* toward the obliteration of *all* difference, hence, ultimately, of any collective memory and identity. Even if asylum were still possible in the new land through Memory of the old one, there can be no escape for the exile from the inner destruction visited on him by the full awareness of his condition.

New York, September 1983

NOTES

1. I wrote the following as a general reflection on the theme of collective exile to be read at the colloquium *Ethnicities and Nations*, in Houston, Texas, although it refers mainly to the Central American situation, my area of field research. I had previously dealt with the present condition of Maya Indian communities in the Southern Mexican Highlands in "Misioneros y Cargos: notas sobre identidad y aculturación en los Altos de Chiapas," Introduction to a special issue of *América Indígena* which I guest-edited in 1982 (vol. 42, no. 1). Recently, an even more general (and more personal) treatment of the question of exile has appeared as "Dyptich," in *Normal* 3 (Winter 1987): 41-45. I would like to thank Gini Alhadeff and Rose Hauer for their help in editing this paper.

2. Ovid was exiled at the edge of the Empire but *within* its confines; anything beyond those boundaries would have been unthinkable.

3. As Samuel Beckett has shown, the lumpen are always waiting for an event, a "happening," but at the heart of their waiting there is an emptiness of being, a deep passivity, that dissolves the very object (and Subject) of their waiting.

4. One is reminded of Zapata, who refused to sit in the Presidential Chair, perhaps in reverence for the throne, certainly conscious that it represented a power radically other than that of the campo, and hence, as he put it, "corrupting"; and of so many cases, through the centuries, of victorious Indian-peasant armies stopping, hesitating, sometimes even retreating in the face of the Town (as in Chiapas in 1869; but it could very well have occurred also in 1712 and around 1910).

5. Until quite recently, Indians were not even allowed to spend the night in town, except under Ladino "custody," and still today one cannot see any Indian *identifiable as such* in the streets of Chiapas cities after dark: the temporary refuge in this case was, and often still is, the dwelling of the colonial and postcolonial patron, now on occasion substituted by the anthropologist.

6. To the Indians, since pre-Columbian times, their own town is also a market but first and foremost it is the Center, the Place from which one can

worship and hope to "control" the forces that govern the eternal agricultural cycles; but the "white" town, the City, although it is also often the central market, is never the Center in this sense. One should also remember, in this perspective, the miscalculation resulting in horrendous slaughter of the group of Indian peasants that occupied the Spanish embassy of Guatemala City a few years back.

7. The tendency toward decentralization apparent in some areas of "developed" countries today seems related to the development, through technology and the media, of much more subtle means of control and coercion: under such conditions, one "can afford" to decentralize, since it implies very little change in the *status quo* and no threat to the central authority. The worldwide connection between global media control and regionalist movements would be worth exploring.

8. Often, a kind of symbiotic relationship occurs with the immigrants, due to the lack of local manpower for agricultural activities requiring a concentrated effort for brief periods of time, like coffee picking. The Indian peasants from Chiapas in this area—themselves internal emigrants from the Highlands—- in some instances own small properties (forty acres) with diversified cultures geared to the production of *various* small surpluses rather than of one large one. This small-scale local economy, aimed at achieving a relatively prosperous (and hence *autonomous)* subsistence, does not interest the authorities because it cannot figure in government export statistics and six-year plans. It has also been shown to be unpopular with the private entrepreneurial sector because it drains manpower resources needed by large agribusiness monoculture plantations of neighboring regions, both in Mexico and in Guatemala. (I would like to thank Dr. Duncan Earl for some very useful clarifications on these aspects of inter-Indian and refugee-plantation dynamics in the border areas of Chiapas.)

9. As the general considerations herein advanced have led us to predict, the Mexican government, not very long after these pages were written, forcefully removed most refugees from the border area with Guatemala to remote camps in the wilderness of the states of Campeche and Quintana Roo. In these new areas of refuge, all contact with fellow Indians at home has been effectively severed.

10. *Graecia capta, victorem coepit,* even in Antiquity only actually happened at certain levels. Yet, in Mexico, as several authors have remarked, there certainly are deep "Indian" traits permeating the "national" ethos.

Two Millenaristic Responses

in Oceania

REMO GUIDIERI

> *And now I stand here on trial for hope in the promise*
> *made by God to our fathers, to which our twelve tribes hope*
> *to attain, as they earnestly worship night and day. And for*
> *this hope I am accused by Jews, O King! Why is it thought*
> *incredible by any of you that God raises the dead?*
>
> Acts 26.6–8

I

The adherence and submission to an intransigent belief—what we call initiation—is, programatically, an acquisition, the acquisition of an identity and of membership in the group that confers it.

In this century the idea of identity has become so heterogeneous and so falsely permissive that people think it can be based on beliefs disinterred after centuries of renunciation, beliefs that remain unkown in spite of this. But even more than faith, for which amalgams of *beliefs* have been substituted, it is art that bears witness most seriously to this spiritual babelization.

Peculiar "syntheses," or perhaps we should say *combines*—to adopt an expression that has become popular in contemporary art— have developed because of this. They display a syncretism that is "spontaneous," unaware of itself, proliferating, and intrinsically nondialectical. Compared to present-day syncretism, the appeal to tolerance in Simone Weil's *Lettre à un religieux*, for example, characterized by its author as polytheist and intellectualist, still belongs to a period in which paganism, in the process of being integrated, includes the demiurge of Timaeus, the sacrifice of Odin in the first Edda, and the harmony of the Pythagorean numbers.

This is still a "native" paganism—Aryan, Greek, Semite—even if its unwieldiness is already stifling its grace, even if faith is already taking the form of regret for the lost plenitude of which Virgil spoke when he evoked the ancient philosophers in Purgatory (*Purg.* III : 40–42):

> E disiar vedeste sanza frutto
> Tai che sarebbe lor disio quetato,
> Ch' etternalmente è dato lor per lutto. [1]

This original paganism is only apparently babelic, and quite rightly claims a common matrix. Already the Italian Catholicism of the Renaissance could have adopted the final appeal of the *Lettre*, which today seems outrageously sensible: "Since all secular life comes directly from 'pagan' civilizations, as long as the illusion persists of a rupture between so-called paganism and Christianity, the latter will not be incorporated, it will not permeate all of secular life as it should, it will remain separated from it and as a consequence inactive." [2]

But the paganism of the end of this millenium, that defies our understanding, that we thought we could bring into subjection by assimilating it—whereas it has only been contaminated by our own anguish—really does not belong to anyone anymore: not to the Christians in search of a universal Church through reforms and interposed encyclicals, even less to the agnostics who have become curious about beliefs (but ignorant of their own), [3] and finally, not to pagans exhausted by dead-end biblical compromises. But it also hovers, as an attitude, as an *eidos*, over everyone. "The true idolatry is covetousness" [4]—to have what one does not have, to be what one is not. On the one hand, we see it in the mute gleam of fetishes heaped up like nuggets of gold in the museums: they are cut off from all connection with any sort of piety and yet we expect to incite them to speech by domesticating them; on the other hand we see it in another kind of fetishization: merchandise. To be Christian, in this century, more and more often means to covet something concrete, something endless and formless, and this is perhaps the paradoxical expression of what remains to us of spirituality.

II

This is why, without our really knowing it, for us paganism still has the intensity of an "exotic Immensity" through which the man without the Grail wanders: ". . . an inconceivable mystery of a soul that knew no restraint, no faith, no fear, yet struggling blindly with itself . . . "

(Conrad, *The Heart of Darkness*). A twilight flame, large enough to light the universe. The former pagan kneeling before the white man's idols, not yet molded by humiliation and textbooks, putting Good and Evil, still joined together, side by side, defies ecumenical enthusiasm. His faith is no longer that faith "with glints of silver in which the truth is golden," as Saint John of the Cross says, that faith, which S. Weil, adopting this idea for her own purposes, defends by saying that "The diverse authentic religious traditions are different reflections of the same truth."[5] More than anything else, it is a discourse in which the Christian polarity has become embroiled; in which the negative (evil and idolatry) does not threaten the positive *but helps it*, like an underlying reservoir, to spread, and then immediately subsides into nothingness. In this discourse, ecstasy and knowledge constantly metamorphose into one another. To share this universe is to allow for a disorder and an excess in which existence has hardly any permanence if it does not lie in disequilibrium and metamorphosis, and also has hardly any prospect of redemption or of repose. In this context, man is certainly a miracle, but also a mirage: a precarious presence.

Isn't this perpetual precariousness headed for the same fate as the Western will, which consumes its own freedom in irrationality, which enlarges the void created by its own strength? The knowledge Kurtz has acquired, as that of which Cavalcanti's father speaks, leads to this "unearthy earth" in which all roads meet and end. Water becomes mud. The *selva* triumphs like an overcoat that protects but also stifles.

> In this last of meeting places
> We grope together
> And avoid speech
> Gathered on this beach of the tumid river
>
> Sightless, unless
> The eyes reappear
> As the perpetual star
> Multifoliate rose
> Of death's twilight kingdom
> The hope only
> Of empty men.[6]

III

And so the landscape is becoming the same everywhere. But the human voices we hear are hardly in harmony anymore. On one side, we have a brutal intrusion that continues to make the jungle echo to the sound of a speech that is more and more empty. On the other, we hear magical litanies from masses of people frozen in the expectation of events which do not come to pass. It would be a mistake to think that these two worlds complement one another. The quest for identity among the Melanesian examples that I will mention are dramatic evidence of this.

Sociological appraisals (sociological in the sense of nontheological) of the so-called messianic processes of crisis—in which the secular and the religious, haunted by a "waiting," are telescoped—generally develop two widely held ideas in relation to the theme of identity.

The first views these processes as phenomena of *change* linked to spatial and temporal factors—ethnographic and historical factors. It is always other people, therefore, who are involved; we ourselves seem to be exempt from any messianic change, any millenarian waiting. The second views these processes as a form of cultural and spiritual aberration produced by "cultural stress"; a *weakening* following a situation involving "contact" in which one culture imposes itself on another in a brutal confrontation. *Change, weakening*, and *contamination* are three expressions that modulate most interpretations of non-Western forms of millenarianism. These nosological arguments applied to cultural phenomena are, significantly, *value judgments* based on a perception of cultural change in terms of decadence.[7]

These findings certainly hold true in part, with the limitations that I have just mentioned. But they also foster the diffusion of certain unfounded interpretations—such as, for example, the interpretation according to which the messianic wait hinges on a sort of cultural hybridization. However, we know that such phenomena, in the history of the West (until relatively recently) as well as in the history of the non-Western traditional cultures, may arise independently of any acculturative context—think of the Hassidism of Central Europe in the eighteenth and nineteenth centuries and of the messianic migrations of the Guayaki toward the Land without Evil in Latin America before contact.[8]

The term messianism currently includes a considerable variety of phenomena and implicitly combines a "deviant religiosity"—which does not necessarily imply a syncretism of beliefs—with unusual and spectacular collective behaviors in which dominate the themes of the fall and the redemption, of decline and rebirth. Yet what is generally in evidence is the deviant characteristics of all these manifestations. It is significant that most socio-anthropological approaches to forms of messianism resort more or less openly to psycho-pathological thematics.[9]

As we know, "deviant" should be understood to mean "what is or has been *badly* assimilated," and consequently the inadequacy of the interpretive resources called upon by a culture in order to understand an unfamiliar culture and to adapt to it. The corollary of this deviant behavior is a state in which the poles of reality and illusion, of truth and falsehood, appear *deliberately* confused. In messianism, what is unassimilable is treated with a false remedy—assimilation-expulsion. In the Melanesian examples I will be describing, it will be apparent that there are at least two types of response to the unprecedented. The first is "ritualistic"; the second is "political." These represent the two poles of the so-called (forced) assimilation process, neither of which can be given a definitive evaluation at the moment, one according to which, for example, the first response would be considered a premature response, that is, a "naive" one, and the other an "elaborate" response, that is, one more aware of the stakes inherent in a situation of acculturation.

What I can say, however, is that the "political" version—and this holds true up to the recent period of the gaining of independence—encourages the resumption of nationalist demands in which we recognize openly ritualized forms, beginning, in Melanesia as elsewhere, with all the ritualized aspects of the political game (assemblies, organized struggles, competing government, etc.). [10]

IV

Vailala begins with the taro cult (or cult of the taro): 1911, Mount Victory district (Gulf Division, Papua New Guinea). The myth of origin speaks of a serpent, a reincarnation of the dead man, *baigona*, who, like Moses, descends from the mountain to bring good news. [11] He has some assistants, the *baigona-men*, who practice "healing" to the point of inducing trances. The movement dies down after about ten years. But it starts up again near the Mambare river and spreads along the coast among the Orokaiva. [12] A man is possessed by the spirit of the taro (the dead man); in fact, what we have here are "ancestors who control birth", [13] which is understood to mean growth in general and most importantly the growth of the basic food, which is taro. He goes into a trance during ceremonies (*kasanga*) [14] in which hymns (exhortations) are sung to the taro, until all the participants become possessed. The trance, called *jipari*, [15] of the possessed, *ba-embo*, is conditioned by the respect for certain prohibitions, like that against washing oneself so as not to lose the *mana*. [16] The *jipari*—which is neither the traditional possession dating from before contact (*gishivi*), nor madness (*yauyauri*), nor murderous madness (*bibi* [17])—is triggered by a leader, the *buninia*,

who has been taught the new cult by "the spirit of the father."[18]
The rituals involve a liturgy miming the present-day appearance of
the white man's mealtime: tables, table settings, dishes, pans, etc.[19]
The dances, *hohora*, which Williams translates as "roosters," require
the dancers to imitate the activities of cooking.[20]

Taro, food, cooking, the art of cooking: the sequence is not
surprising. The fact that of all the other plant species (which in other
regions can replace it in the cult) the taro, "fountainhead of the cult,"[21]
should be the one given priority is not at all surprising either, seeing the
place it occupies in the local diet. But never before was it believed that
the ancestors were incarnated in the taro; rather, they were incarnated
in certain animals,[22] especially the reptile, which was still present at the
beginning of the cult in 1911. Now, not only does the taro become an
"incarnation," but other ceremonies attached to the same cult consist
of trampling on the harvests "in view to impart vigour."[23] In the same
context we observe the increased use of plants to attempt to induce the
trance. One must "make oneself sick"—"be heavy," as the adepts of
the cult put it, *"in order to fertilize."*

The sickness has become an apprenticiship. And whereas formerly
the cure, *bari*, was practiced through suction, etc., now it requires
hysteria, trance, helped along by rhythm (drum-beating).[24]

The source of this sickness-that-fertilizes, is the conjunction of the
basic foodstuff, the taro, and the spirit of the dead man (*hae*). Williams
notes that "food supply is governed or at least influenced by the spirit of
the dead."[25] Later he observes: "In the course of its extension the taro
cult has undergone one very profound change, viz., from a worship of
the taro spirit to a worship of the dead."[26] About what defines a dead
man, a spirit, an ancestor, Williams's information remains vague: *binei*,
sovai, *hae*, are translated as "ghost," "spirit."[27] But the same author
observes that in the cult one speaks only of *atiti*, "shadow," "reflection,"
"mere appearance of anything, be it dead or alive."[28] We should also
note, in relation to the choice of the taro, which is a root vegetable, that
before contact the body was buried and later only its skull was removed
to become a relic. The dead man therefore became a chthonic element,
which, as we know, is not always the rule in Melanesia.

For the moment, then, I will hold to the following proposition: that
the choice of the taro is connected with the cult of ancestors; in the
first phase, however, it is merely the attribute of presence, *atiti*, that is
preserved.

Possession, "head had gone round," as one of the adepts said to
Murray, allows "the sky to open" and "J. C. to go through the head."
It appears that this dies out when recourse to imitating the white man's
communal meal takes over (several months after). The first phase

is aggressive toward the white men, and this aggressivity disappears "around the table," one might say, But the presence of the ancestors is spoken of constantly: "The most important and regular duty of this movement," Williams says,[29] "is to carry out the mortuary festivities." And these festivities involve the new communal meal: tables, benches, bottles of beer, etc. The Christian basis of the movement is never denied; on the contrary, the adepts call themselves "Jesus Christ Men"; in their trances they see God; they say that the *hae* "leaves the body to go to Paradise"—*Ihove Kerere*, "land of Jehova." What struck observers is the "violence" of the trances, which was, in fact, penalized by the interdiction. There followed a period of calm lasting several years, which in some sense helped the movement to return to the traditional form of the cult of ancestors. The latter having been suppressed in turn, the effort toward syncretism failed for a time and afterwards Christianity no longer seemed at all inclined toward syncretism.[30] Tables and benches were burned.

V

Through the cult of the dead among the Christianized communities, the other eschatology is reinstated, the other way—dating from before the time of doubt and the threat of oblivion (the loss of identity)— of conceiving of the death-resurrection, death-transfiguration cycle, condensed into the inevitable principle of incarnation (metaculturally, procreation *is* the experienced expression of incarnation).

Which means that the question of continuity between human and nonhuman remains crucial, especially in an acculturative situation. But this situation involved *two* eschatological cycles—two representations of death (which is the annulment, or the risk of annulment, of continuity). One, which remains abstract since the initial sacrifice is not repeated, is exogenous;[31] it describes a sacrifice which is a self-sacrifice legitimized by a need for incarnating within a dualism that up to this point had divided man from divinity; onto this is grafted the theme of atonement through evil (treason, death) against evil. The other, concrete and autochthonous, experienced as inevitable, presents itself as being just as necessary as the repetitive cycle of reproduction. We should point out that conversion to Christianity implies for the convert acceptance of the idea upon which evangelism is based, namely that the autochthonous cycle, in which death and life not only engage in a dialogue but also resemble each other, is henceforth the cycle of Evil. The "synthesis" is conversion insofar as it consists of introjecting-assimilating-suppressing the earlier identity.

The lesson (provisional) of the quest pursued by the *vailala* Melanesians remains entirely theological, in the sense that the endangered identity is measured by the yardstick of the *eschaton*. Cultural identity *is* religious identity, in the same way that the conferring of a new identity goes by way of adopting the values—and therefore the *aims*—imposed by evangelization.

VI

A serpent who teaches—he teaches men what they have to do to enter into the new era—and who, like Moses, descends from a mountain to bring the commandments to mankind.[32] The cult of *baigona*, the name given to this reptilian being (in Raviau, Northern Division of Papua[33]) combines a traditional figure—the deadman-ancestor-serpent—with the biblical theme of the "rules" brought by the prophet.[34]

But this revelation leads to a deviant sort of behavior, that of the "madness"—*jipari*. The trance "teaches" without words, brings with it the knowledge that until then was unavailable to men bewildered when confronting the white men with their mystery, their "*behindtrue*" (pidgin expression meaning the invisible). This knowledge is in part unformulable: it is an experience, and not an apprenticeship like that which the mission had already imposed. At the same time, the effect of it seems to be communication with an undetermined *familiar*. The trance is known in the tradition. In the tradition it is not called by the same name, not only because its "content" is not the same—at least we must suppose it is not—but because henceforth it can, it must (this is the very principle of proselytism) reach the greatest number of people. The kinesthetic paroxysm is a negation of speech, and the *collective* charm is a negation of the ecstatic, clairvoyant, individual way (the *gishivi*); here, possession is simply the ideal form of interpretation of conversion itself. Conversion was a break; now freed of disguises and doubts, one can penetrate the mystery, the mystery that matters. And it is necessary to penetrate it *together*; it is no longer possible, as it once was, for one single man to be possessed for everyone, since from now on belonging and identity themselves are in question.

But the progress of the ecstasy, announced by the prophets who heard the lesson of the serpent (which, moreover, receives at the very moment of Christianization, the stigmata of the Devil, one more reason to translate "ancestor" as *devolo* . . .), here again leads to knowledge: the collective paroxysms are spiritual exercises that affect the body, a gymnastics that prepares the body to listen. The spread of *jipari*, with its numerous recurrences, is reminiscent, according to the observers, of the spread of epidemics—of witchcraft, or of sicknesses caused by witchcraft. "*Vailala madness.*" We should point out that the proselytism and the spread are to all intents and purposes beyond the control of the prophets. And what is more, the ideas advanced to justify this rapid spread, the uneasiness that it causes, and the reprobation that surrounds it on the part of administrators and missionaries, are all characteristic of epidemics. What is interesting about this process is the form in which the unprecedented—experienced as the path to salvation—is approached: as a cure *through* the disorder. This dialectic between (spiritual) salvation, health and abundance, sickness and cure, is entirely based on empty imitative forms—at once *fake* and *bluff*—or in other words, employing what is false *as a means of understanding.* [35]

But the process is also experienced as a real distress, a disorder that must not only be cured (through the sickness, that is to say, through an approach to death) but also displayed in a spectacular manner. What meaning should we attribute to the existence of these signs of a psycho-physical distress if not primarily that of inoculation with a Faith that is already sick itself, and that no longer offers more than forms that are considerably impoverished? Henceforth, redemption demands a temporary departure from life through a slow suicide, or a controlled death agony, which was what the initiation already was; a programmed sickness, which made one pass from the neutral state of ignorance to knowledge, has become the evil necessary in order to do away with the absolute evil—the anti-Christian state of idolatry: the cure, through sickness, of a fatal sickness.

The non-Western forms of messianism, and primarily those known as "cargo cults," literally, "cults of merchandise" (we too often forget the materialist connotation given to these cults and also, as a result, their implicit devaluation, all the more surprising coming from the lips of those very people who profess to be unbelievers), are profoundly and seriously Christian, in the sense that their nature is essentially eschatological. It is not surprising that the West should be astonished. The fact is that the West no longer has any tradition, nor any *eschaton*, even if for the sake of convenience we in the West still speak of a beginning which remains, like all true beginnings, nonhuman. The West, then, denounces as an aberration what others still have and what it no longer has.

Eschatology is a representation of the end—and therefore also of the beginning. We could call it a Dream, as Blake does in his prophetic books; and to an alert ethnological ear the dream understood in this sense is the equivalent of what we call, with excessive nonchalance, "myth." Unfortunately, in History there is never any end. No recourse. The savages know it, and they resort to eschatology. They seek it out and lose it, like a treasure, buried and unburied. Mirage and truth.

VII

"God, the divine, as *attribute* of nationality." "The people are the body of God"—and the people "stubbornly push away all the other gods" (Nietzsche). Question: is a god *equivalent* to an ancestor? *Is* he an ancestor? And is a "clan" *equivalent* to a people? If to impose a God on oneself is a way of affirming one's identity, the "authentic" ones and the "converted" ones must share the same identity. But *what* identity?

For centuries, "Christian" has been superimposed on "People" and on "Nation" in the immense, absurd ecumenical desire to proclaim the universal idea of "people-of-God." It is because of this desire that the "ancient measure" de Tocqueville spoke of has been lost: "The pagan religions of Antiquity, which were all more or less connected to the political constitution or the social state of each people . . . were generally enclosed within the limits of a territory that one rarely saw them emerge from. They sometimes gave rise to intolerance and persecution; but proselytizism was almost entirely unknown to them. Thus there were no great religious revolutions in our West before the arrival of Christianity."[36]

Nevertheless, if this excess, which can only be seen as a worldwide project extended to humanity *in toto*, has almost been brought to pass temporally, it has not, for all that, accomplished its ecumenical project. The aim of the movement of any people, Nietzsche also said, at every phase of its existence, is the search for God, a God of its own, in whom it believes as the only true God. To be itself through its own God. We must also suppose that this theological-anthropological "in-itself" is inherent in the ancient *eidos* and that ecumenism attacks it in order to open it up and abolish it. One exchanges idols, one does not convert them, nor does one convert oneself to idolatry. Idols and idolatry must be understood in the sense of non-Christian, and non-Christianity is what *also* designates the ancient ever since the triumph of Christianity. Here the ancient inextricably takes on two meanings: that of a genealogical and mnesic past in which Divinity and Ancestrality were equivalent, and that of the time before the conversion. If the search for one's own God must be understood as the preservation of the link to the arche, the problem arises here from the conflict between two archai. For the past two centuries this search has taken the form of a "generalization of cults" without, however, as Nietzsche believed, bringing with it "the destruction of nationalities." Ecumenism, nationalism, and colonialism are contemporary everywhere. It is therefore imperative to examine them together.

The metaphysical stamp of the project of conquest that has been carried out in this century at the price of a degeneration of ecumenism itself, which has turned into a crossbred form of monotheism, is to have produced, in the guise of religious conversion, uniformization, at least on the level of aspirations, *not of modes of belief,* but of modes of life. It is the force of a culture, *and not of a people,* that has succeeded, through the *domination* of nonmonotheist cults, in bringing about a unity not of cults but of cultures. One can only wonder if this unity is not a mirage. What is more, Christianity as a disguised expression of a will to dominate has undergone transformations that have profoundly changed its nature: on the one hand, it has been paradoxically diluted, in the course of the process of conquest, into ecumenism and "tolerance," which is a way of inclining toward its own negation. On the other hand, it has always given its own psycho-moral color to the ancient conceptions it was trying to replace.

I maintain, in effect, that prohibition and transgression, like everything that arises from the concept of taboo, must be conceived of, in spite of the existence of penalties that can be carried to the point of death, quite independently of psycho-moral notions such as "Good" and "Evil." In the same way, the Forbidden is not necessarily the Sacred. I agree that all this is unthinkable within the framework of Christianity, and this is precisely why paganism was immediately denounced as "immoral." That a religion may exist without *moralitas* makes it at least as impious as its potential polytheism. It is significant that it was in the historical period in which the Faith permanently ceased to be separate from the Power, that it began to impose the interiorization of Good and Evil. This, I believe, is what could be called the beginning of Christian "syncretism," in which sin becomes legality. And yet for Christ, as Nietzsche again notes, "sin has no importance"— a principle which has been definitively forgotten.

VIII

Entrance into History, mediatized by the missionary Christianity of the nineteenth century, is a traumatic submersion: in effect, unlike any other form of conversion—for example that acquired through traditional initiation—it expects to cancel out the Time that preceded the conversion. History acquired willy-nilly abolishes the time of the tradition since the latter is denounced not only as insufficient but also as erroneous. Time of aberration, in the grip of evil. The new History is universal—"shared"—and as such it condemns what precedes it to exist no longer, cancelling the very idea of identity. From this point of view, we must assert that adherence to Christianity must necessarily pass by way of this paradoxical conversion in which temporality is at once enlarged and rescinded.

It nevertheless remains true that at the very moment when it is exported into the pagan universe, this Temporality really *is no longer* the Christian temporality. Missionary history—especially in the nineteenth century—is the history of exploitation. Its principle is the enslavement of man to man. This principle is difficult to understand—and therefore also to assimilate—because it does not correspond to any relation known in these cultures. And it remains all the more opaque since it is not expressed, and because it goes in opposition to the pretty speeches of the missionaries. Thus is created a typical double-bind situation. On the one hand the convert hears the universalist declaration: "You *are* like the others." He understands: "We are equal," which leads him to this paradox: "We are like the (white) man who exploits us." What missionary Christianity hides under the cloak of egalitarianism is the *de facto* inequality of the relation between colonizers and colonized. In the same way, it hides the rude fact that true entrance into universal history goes precisely by way of exploitation. This concealment resorts to *biblical* history, the history Christianity talks about, which is neither that of exploitation nor, we must add, that of progress. However, exploitation is the motivating force of progress.

The missions proclaim: "Become what you are not and you will be like us"—strong, free, etc. The pernicious (*and non-Christian*) idea conveyed by the missions is that Christianity and progress go hand in hand. This is colonialism's nihilist alibi: faith and progress, that is to say submission and exploitation. This alibi does not win out; rather, it contaminates, poisons, gives rise to cultural sicknesses whose remedy is the syncretic solution. In the beginning, when this solution does not yet exist, disorder sets in. What syncretism means is a way out discovered in the mixture—a dosage which must be fixed—of the old and the new.

IX

In the encounter between Christianity and Paganism described here, in the quest for identity that it involves—accompanied by great distress—we are witnessing the conflict between two cyclical temporalities that lie outside of history understood in the immanent factual sense.

One temporality is eschatological, the other is not. A temporality that is cyclical *and* noneschatological, non-Christian, is the hardest to imagine. A cyclicity that is not also eschatological, in which beginning and end do not coincide, is, in fact, paradoxical. This temporality finds its proper emblem in the movement in which identity is expressed *in* otherness: the particular form of "reabsorption" of the being which is totemism. One might think that this "reabsorption" is comparable to what we find articulated in the eschatological cycle: alpha *is* omega. "Pagan" cyclicity—here I am referring in particular to Melanesian concepts—describes a sequential time; I mean that the *coincidentia oppositorum* is certainly similar for each human being, since each must be totemized (just as each human presence, in turn, derives from a generative totemism), but it is similar one by one, so to speak, individual by individual. This is why I prefer to speak, in the case of the non-Christian, of a temporality that is *short*, existential (provided, however, that we attribute to the latter expression a meaning in which life and death mingle but are not identified, otherwise the principle of totemic identification would lose its meaning); and therefore also speak of a repetitive cyclicity, one bound to each individual according to the principle whereby the human metamorphoses at his death (and initially arises from a being different from him).

In this cycle, the other-life, what is beyond death, does not involve any return. To give a famous example, the Trobriandesian *milamala*, which since Malinowski has been designated as a ritual devoted "to the return of the dead," is in fact an agrarian rite and probably also, at the same time and because of this, a funerary rite.[37] Likewise, even though there is certainly a beginning—*altichera*: "time of the Dream"; arrival of the Argonauts; divinities that descend from the sky to fecundate non-human beings in order to give birth to human, etc.—*there is no end*.[38]

To restate it as a formula: in opposition to the principle of *eschaton*, we have, in Oceanian terms, the principle of *physis*, called "growth": *tupu*. Unlike what *physis* is for us, *tupu* is "impregnable," in the sense that its necessity evades every grasp of transcendence—the latter is powerless to embody nature in a movement in which its end would be inscribed.[39]

The idea of the after-death as a *topos* ("go somewhere," "island," "chthonian world," "place of the dead") has almost no meaning for the non-Christian representation of the cycle that I am referring to. The dead-being certainly must go where the other dead-beings already are. He must be helped by them—and the dead man becomes that "lock-keeper," that mediator, between the dead and the living—but in every case it is a matter of "becoming other," of changing substance rather than changing place. The dialectic here is a dialectic of time and substance rather than space.

What Christianity conveys that is unprecedented is this idea of an unimaginable cycle, and not only unimaginable for the Melanesian caught in the throes of conversion, but also for us, the people of progress, who announce our secular predestination at the same time as we declare that we are anti-eschatological (out temporality is linear, progressive, but without any aim unless it is to grow); it is a matter of breaking with the fixedness characteristic of the *tupu*, with the visible and tangible metamorphosis of totemism, with the ancestralization which attempts, somewhere, to rejoin the *physis* but not necessarily that which is emblematized by the totem.[40] The acceptance of the biblical idea of destiny involves an understanding of the *eschaton*. The *vailala* is a skewed response to that need.

X

The problem of Evil is necessarily involved in this serious quest, in which one could say that the identity is fed by alienation. It is displayed in the process of conversion as in that of acquisition. But if Christianity designates Evil as the threatening-negative, the Melanesian convert displays what is henceforth said to be the Evil in him. He is a "worshipper of Evil": he ritualizes it. In the phase during which conversion is said to be accomplished, one can even witness an excessive display: through rhythm, ecstasy, disguise, *sacra* and basic referents (the sepent-ancestor), the aim is clearly to go beyond the boundaries of the human: to take leave of the human. Now, in the Christian argument, this departure "by the lower path," the animal being "infra-human," is the departure which leads to Evil. Think of the possessed whom Christ *frees*. The possessed convert of the *vailala* declares openly that the being that is possessing him is hardly Christian—it is a serpent, or some other animal of the other neo-Christian forms everywhere in Melanesia. And his submission to this animal consists precisely in incarnating it. The Christian figure of Evil is animality in man. Now we know that throughout the semitic religious tradition up to and including Islam, the animalization of man results from the transgression of taboos concerning the body, and the denaturation of the principal organic functions—feeding, sexuality.[41] In Christianity as in the other abrahamic religions, the struggle against evil consists of tabooing the body even while knowing that this solution remains precarious and that evil will always encroach on the space defended against it.

In the *vailala*, Christianity as "anti-evil" stands side by side with Evil, which is evoked—if only at the moment conversion takes place—but is not fought. It is as though the legislating speech that imposed the new faith and that proclaimed the abolition of everything anterior to it as henceforth negative, has been fully accepted only to be immedistely turned away in favor of a "liberalism" which openly gives access to what is "anti-Christian" in the new faith. Thus the new and ambiguous position both of Christianity itself (the adepts of the *vailala* are Christians) and of paganism (the Christians of the *vailala* are pagans). And thus the dual nature of the movement: dangerous and beneficial, agressive and protective, that is to say, endowed with the contradictory and complementary attributes of the old transcendence. All this is emblematized by the "maleficent act" that brings good: the sacrifice (destruction of food crops, putting-to-death of animal victims, etc.). What is also new, and independent of the sanctions the missionaries may impose on the adepts in order to stay the course of this "madness," is that most of the demonstrations that punctuate the movement are tainted with a terror connected with the excess that the evil leads them into. From this point of view, the discourse of the *vailala* is a modification of the discourse of Sin, but this Sin is experienced as necessary. A passage of Georges Bataille seems relevant here:

Precisely because waking is the sense of dualism, the inevitable sleep that follows it reintroduces the more prominent position of evil. The dullness to which a dualism without transcendence is limited opens the spirit to the sovereignty of evil, which is the unleasing of violence. The sovereignty of good implied by waking and ended by the sleep of the dualist position is also a reduction to the order of things which leaves no opening except toward a return to violence. The ponderous dualism returns to the position of before the waking: from then on the ill-fated world reassumes a value that is perceptibly equal to the value it had in the earlier position. Its importance is less than in the sovereignty of a pure violence, which did not have the sense of evil, but the forces of evil have never lost their divine value except within the limits of a developed reflection, and their apparently inferior position cannot prevent simple humanity from continuing to live within their power. Several forms are possible: a cult of execration of a violence held to be irreducible may captivate the interest of a blind conscience; and interest is openly declared if the execration involves an entire opening to evil, with a view to later purification; and lastly evil, evil as such, can reveal to the confused conscience that it is dearer than good. But the different forms of the dualist attitude never offer more than one slippery possibility to the spirit (which must always respond in the same instant to two irreconcilable demands: to remove and to preserve the order of things).[42]

XI

The other response to the intrusion of the West which I would now like to mention emerged about one generation after the preceding one, farther east of New Guinea (in Malaita and the archipelago of the Solomon Islands) at a moment when the worldwide colonial situation was at a turning point. World War II caused the cards to be redistributed among the Western powers. The colonial "unity" disintegrated and necessitated a new strategy of exploitation. The Pacific emerged as a crucial strategic area, both for strengthening the old positions—though on new foundations—and for forcing the new claimants, especially Japan, to submit to the new world order.

In these circumstances, colonial needs changed temporarily into military needs: in the Pacific, and especially in Melanesia, commercial interests declined, to the profit of the military-strategic interests. Twenty years later, the former would be revived. But the new situation created during the forties gave birth to an unprecedented instrumentalization of the local people and their territories. In order to deal with the urgent tasks imposed by the war, large numbers of the local workers, who up to then had been put to work in the plantations, were diverted into different work for the Army. Similarly, territories that had been cultivated before were abandoned in favor of new spaces—military bases, roads, airports.

This temporary "requisitioning" of the cultivated lands did not affect either the missionary establishments and their dependencies or the routine work of the populations engaged in their subsistence activities; on the contrary, it was accompanied by a *de facto* defection of the colonial administrative authority, which resulted in a strengthening of the authority exercised by the missions. These conditions had to encourage a sudden awareness of what we must call a cultural identity, but resulting from a desire for autonomy made possible by the isolation in which these populations had found themselves for several years. The key word here is autonomy.

Thus it was that in 1946 the movement began in Malaita called the *maasina ruuruu*, "the murmur of brotherhood."[43] Compared to the aspirations of the *vailala*, the claims of the *maasina* were openly pragmatic: reconquest, reappropriation of lands—of the holdings occupied by the whites as well as the others; mobilization of groups for the labor necessary for building roads, stores, schools; the creation of autochthonous commercial networks (*bisinisi, tastom bisinisi*); a political and economic break with the colonial administration and the missions ("refusal to cooperate"); the protection of local languages.[44]

Inaugural gestures mark the beginning of the movement. Openly political, in the sense that their "panache" reflects a strategy, these gestures concretize the claims. Frequent and sometimes even obligatory meetings, where the number of participants must emphasize the "communalist" intention of the leaders who are trying to go beyond the traditional cleavages between lineages, villages, clans, tribes, ranks, etc.; spectacular donations of land announced during the assemblies by high-ranking leaders, as in the south of Malaita at the very beginning of the movement (in the official history which I myself had a chance to record in 1969, these donations of land represent the inaugural act of the *maasina*). In all these encounters, however, the traditional aspects remain important: the strict formalism of the speakers and participants in the assemblies; the maintenance of the tension within the movement (for instance, the people cannot stop attending the meetings, even if they have to neglect their daily activities).

The pragmatic nature of the movement poses the problem of what may be called the "secularization" of the autochthonous movements of reaction against Western culture, in the Pacific as elsewhere. When we compare the *maasina* of 1946 to the *vailala* of 1911, the former does not seem to bear any traces of messianism or syncretism, nor of symbolic assimilation of exogenous factors. The circumstances, and especially the historic juncture at which the regions involved find themselves (the area of the Solomon Islands was the military stake in the Japanese-American war) have certainly encouraged this tendency. The forced abandonment of the Protectorates, the administrative chaos that followed it, and, especially, the insane dynamism of Westerners at war emphasized the separation between a peaceful colonial administration and the economic-military organization that could build an airport in a few weeks. Similarly, the image of the white man was changing. Now he was a soldier, with immense resources at his disposal (this was true, we must add, not only for the Melanesian but also for the European who at that same period, stupefied and passive, watched the war take place). The autochthons discovered the figure, emblematic for them, of the "white-black," the black American, who had the power of the white man but who also had black skin. What was more, in several Melanesian movements after 1945, this composite figure played the role of revealer, of prophet; I was able to observe this myself in some of the ephemeral movements that followed one another chaotically after the failure of the *maasina* and until independence.

One thing clearly differentiating the *maasina* from the *vailala* are the explicitly layic themes and key words: mobilization, and, especially, organization. The idea of trans-ethnicism quickly went beyond the idea of trans-tribalism, at the level of the archipelago. And here we are certainly touching on something essential: from this point on, imitation of the white man will no longer make one into a man of the new faith, preaching a common destiny and a redemptive temporality, but, in a more positive way, into the master of the organization. The idea of autochthony was united with the idea of autonomy, and the latter gave birth to an open process of rejection. For the first time, violent, political conflict between colonized and colonizer became inevitable. The chronicle of the *maasina* that ended in the violent supression of the movement around 1948 was marked by deaths, by military expeditions on the part of the colonial administration, by bloody suppressions and prison.

XII

Now I would like to examine certain official aims of the *maasina* program which were deliberately radical and broke away from the neo-Christian aspirations of the beginning of the century as well as the forced submission to the colonials and the missionaries.[45] These aims were: an autochthonous program of education and the commercialization of local products—mostly copra—outside of the circuits organized by the colonial mediators, growers and Chinese merchants.

In the educational program (the expression "program" should be understood in the same broad and loose sense that it has in any other political program, in Oceania as in the West) what was emphasized was the legitimacy of the autonomy of local languages. The vehicular languages introduced by colonization—English and pidgin—were to be rejected; the "protection" of the local languages would be achieved by teaching them. In this demand, which had only ephemeral applications during the course of the movement's history (and not only because of the repression), there is something paradoxical in which the utopian nature of the open pragmatism of the *maasina* is revealed.

At the time of the *maasina*—Christianization was only about forty years old—the local languages were hardly threatened. English was very rarely spoken by the local people, and pidgin, which they learned spontaneously for business purposes, hardly took the place of vernacular speech. The missions themselves were grappling with the biblical translations necessary for the evangelization. What was more, the missionary school was, and would remain for a very long time, *the* educational model: students were taught the catechism in the vernacular, and, in addition, the best students were taught things that went beyond the basic educational framework of the catechumen. We should bear in mind that the task of the missionary, especially the Catholic missionary, from the beginning of evangelization and throughout Oceania, also consisted of creating local cadres.

Then what was the meaning of the educational demands of the *maasina*? It was the native's aspiration to take the place of the foreigner, the administrator, the colonist, or the missionary. To do what the other teaches us to do and requires us to do; but to do it ourselves. This borrowing left an indelible mark: victory or failure, progress or regress, remained determined by the newcomer, in the sense that they were part of the *mimesis* through which there was "meaning": future, possibilities, *redemption*—even if redemption is understood in an openly immanent sense, as is the case here. What is really new about the *maasina* is this desire to assume control of the secular destiny that results from this irreversible and inevitable *mimesis*, which is certainly the most powerful indication of what we call modernity. Imitation is not only a factor of change in the sense that it flattens differences; it is one of the *strong* modalities that brings about, if not actual change, at least the desire for change (in the same way that, basically, it is through imitation, in this century of technological innovations and cultural mutations, that *borrowing* takes place).

But in this case, imitation ran up against contradictions. They were inherent in the very nature of what was to be adopted. The apprenticeship of a language is the apprenticeship of a culture—or of a tradition, which is the same thing. The Melanesian communities of the *maasina* were very well aware, if only because of the still large presence of non-Christians in these regions (representing, at that time, almost half the population of the principal island, Malaita, where the movement started) that this apprenticeship had precise rules and a precise goal: it was a question of. leading the individual, through initiation, to the point of acquiring the status of member of the community. In the pre-Christian context, but also in the context of Christianization, language was a means—belief was the end. Now, within the borrowed and exoteric framework of the apprenticeship which was the *skul* ("school"), in which initiation consisted of adhering, even if by way of a vernacular language, to nonautochthonous values, what could one learn other than what the missionaries themselves introduced? It is hard to know, now, how far the adepts of the *maasina* wanted to involve themselves in the dilemma. But in any case we must emphasize the ambiguity that inhabited the "pragmatic" aspiration to an autonomous cultural identity as opposed to the borrowed and imposed identity that alienated the Melanesian Christian. In its desire for cultural autonomy, the *maasina* could just as well have taken another path. The "classical" alternative to the pragmatic path is the path of revivalism: to abandon the imitative remedy—"to do what the others do, but to do it ourselves"—in order to gain autonomy. An open restoration, even if it relied on syncretic intermediaries (and thus, on another form of ambiguity) which grew weaker and weaker until they became completely pagan (in the exact sense of non-Christian), would undoubtedly be the most radically anti-Western response to the inauthentic state of the colonized convert. Taking into account contemporary history in the time since these preliminary independence movements, one could perhaps say that this kind of reversal reaction is only possible under certain conditions which deserve careful consideration in themselves. Suffice it to say, at this point, that this backward path is only taken if the revivalist option is somehow fundamentally based on Christian metaphysical foundations. It is certainly no accident that these days Islam incarnates this possibility.

We have only to remember the vicissitudes of the *vailala* to be convinced that in Melanesian revivalism, restoration can only be a return (a hypothetical one, moreover) to the in-oneself, that is to say, to a certain manner of rejecting innovation and, thereby, modernity itself. It can only be a return to a *Weltanschauung* which, through the reappropriation of autochthonous beliefs, denies to the future—that time riddled with the unprecedented—all possibility of redemption, secular or not. It can only be the abandonment of every imitative path except the one that allows for the preservation of Tradition. For this reason it seems significant to me that throughout its short history the *maasina* has remained very indecisive about the language question.

XIII

We now come to the commercial programs which the *maasina* drew up and began to carry out before the British repression. Sketchy though our knowledge of these cultures is, it seems significant that the two principle demands of the movement were the educational program and the activity of trading (or *bisinisi*, to use the accepted pidgin term). As has been consistently observed, the Melanesians are "exchangers."

The following were excluded from the *maasina* plan for reforms, or only very vaguely outlined: the sector of production, which on the whole, except when the movement was just beginning, and, for propaganda reasons, the "gift" of lands involved an ephemeral collectivization of labor,[46] reproduced the traditional divisions of labor (on the basis of lineage and, even more, place of residence and sex— one need only think of the preponderance of women in almost all agricultural activities); the political and military sector—the "police" that was created at that time was merely the institutionalization, and a temporary one, at that, of what could be called a "law and order service" attached as bodyguard to the leaders and supplemented, in a fairly disorderly way, by the most enthusiastic of the neophytes. It is significant that the traditional forms of authority and the titles that embodied them, especially wherever the social structure considered them to be hereditary, were maintained.

The choice of *bisinisi* no doubt corresponded to cultural imperatives which date from before contact and are known as "exchangist necessities" in Oceanian ethnology. Transactions involving goods, whether useful or luxury items, are certainly paradigmatic expressions of the need for confrontation which eminent authors have studied under the name of "the law of reciprocity."[47] Without entering into a debate that is longstanding and probably still unresolved—since it involves a representation that is almost canonical in anthropology of what is to be understood by the term "primitive *socius*"—I will nevertheless remark that the recourse to *bisinisi* as a form of demand for autonomy is probably an option that brings together tradition and innovation in a wonderful way. In it we have several elements: confrontation between groups through the exchange of goods; the political valorization, in the widest sense of the term, of the group that accepts and wins the confrontation; and finally, the adoption, through imitation, of something the whites also, in a massive and exemplary way, engage in—commerce.

Should the leaders of the *maasina* be blamed for having oriented their plans toward a cultural defense which was useless in the end, given the path they took, and toward an acquisition that was bound to fail, in essence since the sought-for autonomy was entirely dependent upon the balance of forces between the colonizers and the colonized? The failure of the movement—in this respect, the chronicle of events between 1946 and 1948 is eloquent—was in large part due, as with many other demands and uprisings of oppressed peoples, to the inequality of existing forces: on the one hand, there was an organized repressive force; on the other, an embryonic and chaotic defensive force. The *maasina*, however political it may have been, was not a revolutionary movement, nor, therefore, a true independence movement. It was more reminiscent of the uprisings that fill the annals of the colonies of the New World and that were primarily motivated by an impulse to *reject*.

But the dominant and, at least potentially, dynamic pragmatic option of *bisinisi* could not have been more consistent with what is, objectively, more than a facile image of white power. The choice of trading implies an adequate understanding of what is one of the principle motivations of the capitalist process. The *maasina* achieved what was an essential part of the Western economic system during its first great expansionist phase. The "wealth of nations" depends on the capacities of the system to stimulate the (Western) sphere of needs to the point where they are clearly multiplying; to dynamize, in this way, the rise in production, which would not be possible without a frantic intensification of exploitation, in the West as in the rest of the world. What the West exhibited as it expanded at the turn of the century, especially in regions like Oceania which are poor in natural resources compared to other colonized continents, was truly its commercial greed, symbolized by boats whose holds overflowed with goods in transit that had been stolen from all parts of the world. Now it seems to me that this accord with the commercial soul of white power, even if unconscious, may constitute the underlying continuity between the "cult of merchandise" of the *vailala*, in which wealth, transfigured by biblical aspirations, takes on the appearance of a miraculous spiritual redemption, and the radical demands for autonomy of the *maasina*, in which it is believed that happiness is a material thing.

As the West itself declines, Economy is substituted for Religion: a *mechane* replaces the *moira*, the illusion of truth takes over from a great illusion that was also a truth. The *maasina* understood what was sensed in the experience of the *vailala*, though it only figured as background: that the circulation of merchandise serves, tautologically, to promote the accumulation of merchandise. It was in this understanding, in profound conformance with the historical stake that henceforth determined the fate of human societies, that the *maasina* was "progressing" in relation to the *vailala*, and that the imperative to organize advanced, even though only in an imitative sense.

But if manual work henceforth replaced ritual work, if *bisinisi* (trading) replaced *jipari* (madness), and if pragmatism constituted in some sense a "qualitative leap" in the quest for identity, what was not achieved, what was still not understood, and therefore also not assimilated, was the true foundation of the Western system, in which the organizing principle that causes goods and men to circulate depends on the organization of exploitation. The advent of the Reign of Quantity is expressed in the Tropics by Christianity and warehouses. The cause of the failure, at least during this period, of the imitative quest—in which Tradition fades away before the New—lay in the relationship to this truth, banal and terrible as it is, the truth of exploitation, which the *vailala* had also not sensed when it confused the new Faith with Kapital.

Vailala and *maasina* are indisputably two "quests for identity." They begin as "quests," which is to say—in the traditional meaning of the word—as "odysseys": the course they follow is an obligatory one, consisting of conquering what they do not have (yet) and recovering what they risk losing. From this point of view, one could say that the two Melanesian examples are evidence of the price that traditional cultures have to pay to enter (world) History—and that price is to be condemned to wander.

(For A.S.) Beirut, June 1983   Translation by Lydia Davis

NOTES

1. Singleton's English translation: "And you have seen desiring fruitlessly men such that their desire would have been satisfied[,] which is given them for eternal grief." (Purgatorio, 1. Italian text and translation, Bollingen Series 80, [Princeton, 1973]).
2. Simone Weil, *Lettre à un religieux* (first French edition; Paris, 1946), 82.
3. The ethnologists' alleged *epoke*, with a few exceptions (which may, moreover, be even more regrettable in the case of the missionary-ethnologists for whom the task of proselytizing is primary) is, from this point of view, an anti-religiosity—paraded, what is more, as a positive attitude—which is transformed into a "religiophilia" that is naive where the beliefs of others are concerned. The mixture of bewilderment and fascination aroused not by pre-Christian paganism but by anti-Christian paganism is certainly a crucial anchoring point for ethnology.
4. Weil, *Lettre*, 15.
5. Ibid., 35.
6. T. S. Eliot, "The Hollow Men" (IV : 57–67).
7. In principle, there is nothing against this kind of Spenglerian representation of cultural changes. As long as one measures the entire historical extent of their implications. Which is to say that other, similar kinds of change in which Christianity is seen as the "contaminator" should be viewed in the same way. In this case, it would be the West itself that would have to be cross-examined. Spengler, and Nietzsche before him, did this. But the sociologists of exotic forms of millenarianism should also take it into account, which they do not seem to be doing.

Furthermore, these presuppositions—which in themselves merit a much longer critical commentary along lines already suggested several years ago by two great historians, Mazzino Montinari (*La fine del mondo antico* [Milan, 1956], about the notion of "decadence" as Fall and Decay in Western culture; see also E. de Martino, *La fine del mondo. Contributo all'analisi delle Apocalissi culturali* [Turin, 1977]) and Irenée Marrou (*Décadence romaine ou antiquité tardive?* [posthumous selected essays; Paris, 1979])—imply a distinction that is hardly self-evident, between "healthy cultures" and "sick cultures" (according to which our culture, "already formed" for a long time, as well as those cultures that have not yet been "contaminated," would belong to the first group). This discrimination, anthropological in the sense of metahistorical, is in fact, a general evaluation of culture which, on the basis of summarily purist principles, attributes "health" to cultures beyond change ("cold societies," as they are called) and "sickness" to cultures that have been the victims of change ("hot societies"). One result, and a paradoxical one, being the notion that history, that is to say change, brings with it sickness and that, conversely, immobile cultures remain safe from any contamination, and thus from any disorder. The champions of these arguments also seem to be ignoring their racist implications, which are well-known and widely practiced in this century.

8. Although in the case of the Guayaki the available documents and commentaries (by Leo Cadogan, *Aywa Rapyta: Fundamentos de la humano lanjage en Guarani* [Asuncion, 1958]; P. Clastres, *Le Grand Parler* [Paris, 1974]; H. Clastres, *La terre sans mal* [Paris, 1975]) confirm what I have just said, the phenomenon of the Hassids merits a more subtle discussion for the simple and basic reason that this messianism is in keeping with a traditional eschatological point of view inherent to the Jewish traditon.

In all the misguided convictions about messianism there is no trace of the following question, which seems to me crucial in every respect: if the "conditions" required for this type of movement to develop no longer exist in the West, isn't this because the latter has become the most secularized cultural universe we have ever known? This would explain why the contact imposed by the West over the last two centuries has produced so-called messianic reactions almost everywhere in the world. The question posed by the "forms of messianism of other people" is therefore one which, through the intermediary of ecumenical Christianity, actually refers to a confrontation between a culture that conquers *because* it is secular and a culture that is threatened *because* it is religious.

9. The work done by R. Bastide is, from this point of view, the best known and the most articulate (e.g., his *Les Amériques noires* [Paris: Payot, 1967]). We might also cite the propositions advanced by G. Bateson in regard to processes of "schismogenesis," presented in *Naven* (Cambridge: Cambridge University Press, 1936) and *Steps to an Ecology of Mind* (San Francisco: Chandler, 1972).

10. In almost every case, independence was granted by the colonial power. Until the seventies, there were properly speaking no independence movements in Oceania. Those which are still going on today, even in violent forms, in certain French territories (New Caledonia, Tahiti), are the results of political decisions a few years earlier that made possible the emergence of new nations on the Continent. On this subject, see, in this same collection, Alain Babadzan's comments on the pivotal role played by Australia in the resumption of the strategy characteristic of the Commonwealth in the region of the Pacific. See also: *Livre blanc sur la Nouvelle Calédonie* (Paris: Publications de l'Antenne, 1985).

11. F. E. Williams, "The Vailala Madness and the Destruction of Native Ceremonies in the Gulf Division of Papua–New Guinea," *Anthropological Report* (Port Moresby) 4 (1923):7. (For more ethnographical details, by the same author, see "The Taro Cult," in *Orokaiva Magic* [London, 1928], 3–104.)

12. Ibid., 9.

13. Ibid., 9.

14. Ibid., 10.

15. Ibid., 44–45.

16. Ibid., 32–33.

17. Ibid., 49. Unfortunately, Williams's sources give us no information, either etymological or symbolic, about this term. Is it a neologism, and if so, what root does it derive from?

18. Since the instructing spirit presents itself as the ancestor incarnated in the tuber, we have here a startling merging of ancestrality (ancestor-worship) and cannibalism, which I will come back to later.

19. "A tall flag-pole, painted red with native paint, and several tables and seats were erected in the village, and I was told that there were still several natives keeping watch for the large ship which is to bring back their ancestors in the form of the white men. A number of men sitting or strolling about in clean new 'ramis,' as, according to the new belief, it is beneath their dignity to work unless it be at the erection of tables in the village, at which they sit once a day" (Murray quoted by Williams, 69).

20. Ibid., 40.

21. Ibid., 24.

22. Ibid., 25–26.

23. Ibid., 43.

24. Ibid., 59.

25. Ibid., 27.

26. Ibid., 66.

27. Ibid., 27.

28. Ibid.

29. Ibid., 345.

30. Ibid., 389.

31. For a Christian, the sacrifice performed during the Mass is not a symbol, as it necessarily is in the eyes of a culture that practices real sacrifices.

32. Readers unfamiliar with the ethnological literature of Melanesia should be reminded that the serpent is the most widespread "incarnation" of the ancestor.

33. Cf. Williams, op. cit., 17 ff.

34. Francesco Pellizzi, with whom I discussed this theme while drafting my article, suggested that the term *baigona* (which is not the usual term for designating the serpent) could be a syncretic version of the expression "bygone." I do not have enough information to verify this hypothesis. I mention it, nevertheless, because other syncretic expressions conspicuous in the literature of Oceania, starting with *devolo* (from "devil"), designating the ancestor in a Christianized milieu, show how frequent this sort of borrowing is.

35. These forms include, among others, greetings (handshakes and movements of the head) repeated for hours at a time, and all the sign language of the white man's meals, without any food actually being consumed.

36. Alexis de Tocqueville, *L'Ancien Régime et la revolution* (1856), 18.

37. In order to understand better that the premises which legitimize a funerary ritual, that is, the ancestralization of a dead man, do not in any way imply the idea that the dead must "come back," it suffices to remember that in these cultures the dead-ancestors are *presences* constantly at work in daily life. To devote a cult to the dead means, precisely, admitting their existence in a

permanent way. (In regard to the *milamala* ritual, see B. Malinowski, *Argonauts of the Western Pacific* [London, 1926]).

38. Whence this other paradox with which we Westerners are henceforth confronted, we who are obliged to admit of a beginning—"God," "Big Bang," etc.—but who can no longer admit, except in terms of decadence and *real* apocalypse, that it will be the end. I will return to this paradox in my conclusion.

39. For a development of this theme, I refer the reader to my essay "Tupu" in Remo Guidieri, *L'Abondance des Pauvres* (Paris: Éditions du Seuil, 1984), chap. 3.

40. In an essay devoted to one form of Melanesian thanatology, ("Shadows," *Res* 2 [1982]), F. Pellizzi and I raise this problem, which is in every respect crucial, by posing a question we do not go on to answer: "Up to what point does the ancestor remain human and from what point on is he no longer human?"— which is to say, is he suppressed as an ex-human in the nonhuman universe of the *physis*?

41. But mysticism resorts to the same methods . . .

42. Georges Bataille, *Théorie de la religion*, 1948: III: La médiation; l: Faiblesse générale de la divinité morale et force du mal, in *Oeuvres Complètes*, vol. VII (Paris, 1976), 330.

43. On this movement, despite its spread and the ideological impact that it had later on in the contemporary political history of the ensemble of the Melanesian archipelagos, one only has at one's disposal a documentation astonishingly sporadic, fragmentary, and rather biased. Of such a viewpoint, see Colin H. Allan, "The Marching Rule Movement in the British Solomon Islands Protectorate" (Master's thesis, Cambridge University, 1950). More recently the analysis of the *maasina* has widened, impelled by local political events (independences, rebellions). Cf. R. Keesing, "Politico-Religious Movement and Anticolonialism in Malaita Rule" *Historical Perspective, Oceania*, (1978) 48:243–61; 49:46–73; and the excellent number of *Mankind* 13, no. 4 (August 1982): "Reinventing Traditional Culture: The Politics of Kastom in Island Melanesia."

44. This is certainly a minor theme and, as we will see later, a demagogic one. Moreover, it was to be the only one that would really be taken up again and expanded by the advocates of independence in the seventies, in the Solomon Islands as well as elsewhere in Melanesia.

45. As far as I know, there has been no record of any movement of the *vailala* type in the archipelago of the Solomon Islands since the beginning of colonization and missionary activity dating approximately from the end of the last century. During the first two decades of this century, we know of only very sporadic movements in Malaita that from all appearances (the information available is rather vague) revolve around an autochthonous "educational program" (*skul*), an imitation of the one in the missionary schools, inspired by a spirit significantly known as *Bulu*, a generic term for stars in the languages of Malaita. These facts are mentioned by C. H. Allan, "Some Marching Rule Stories," in *Journal of Pacific History* 9 (1974): 182–86. Yet it is important to point out that the emphasis lies on "book" rather than on goods and abundance.

46. This was the case especially in the southern regions of Malaita, where Polynesian-type divisions between ranks largely determined land holdings. In central and northern regions of Malaita, as well as on other islands that belonged to the movement (mainly the northwestern group of the archipelago) this sort of "real-estate reform" was not known, land holdings being generally the lineal unit in the patri-uxorilocal or bilateral forms of the "branching" type.

As for the female role in the sexual division of labor, as well as its status of dependence in relation to the male role, the *maasina* did not take it into consideration. There is no reason, however, to say that where this was concerned, at least, the movement was purely and simply conservative: it is still too early to form an opinion about how its attitude toward the sexual division, so important in Melanesia, might have changed. What was involved here was a process witnessed in its earliest stages and still in progress; furthermore the impetus of the movement was in itself at once progressive and conservative, seeking to attain a cultural and economic autonomy in relation to the colonizers and to reestablish the conditions of autonomy that existed before colonization. And that that necessarily had to restore the old roles and functions, though they would now be "revalued."

47. For more about this, I refer the reader to various texts in which I disagree with this representation. In chronological order, they are: "*Kula*, ovvero della truffa," *Rassegna Italiana di Sociologia* 9 (1975); "Enclos et clôtures. Remarques sur la discontinuité et la segmentation en Océanie," *Revue des Études Océaniennes* 39, no. 2 (1976); "Essai sur le prêt," in *L'Abondance des Pauvres*.

Kastom and Nation-Building in the South Pacific

ALAIN BABADZAN

La société porteuse du spectacle ne domine pas seulement par son hégémonie économique les régions sous-développées. Elle les domine en tant que société du spectacle. Là où la base matérielle est encore absente, la société moderne a déjà envahi spectaculairement la surface sociale de chaque continent. Elle définit le programme d'une classe dirigeante et préside à sa constitution. De même qu'elle présente les pseudo-biens à convoiter, de même elle offre aux révolutionnaires locaux les faux modèles de révolution.

—Guy Debord, *La Société du Spectacle*

DEPENDENT INDEPENDENCES

Oceania is a mosaic of cultures, languages, and ethnic groups. Scattered here and there between Asia and America, on either side of an immense liquid continent, or loosely joined together to form one territory, the pieces of such a puzzle seem doomed to isolation and seclusion. This is an inevitable situation, typical of insularity, and reinforced by a cultural division unique in the world, especially in Melanesia: 110 languages are spoken in Vanuatu by a population of 120,000; and there are 700 different languages in Papua New Guinea. For the anthropologist or the linguist, in spite of their differences these cultures are very closely related. Even the usual distinction between Melanesia, to the west, and Polynesia, to the east, cannot be considered as definitive: the fragments of this mosaic also carry, each in its own way, particular variations on a series of common themes. Born out of a progressive cultural and linguistic differentiation, the cultures of the Pacific do not consider recovering their lost unity. The situation is hardly favorable to the success of any "pan-Oceanism" conceived in the image of European pan-Germanism or pan-Slavism. For the time being, each culture so holds fast to its own specific ethnicity or "nationality" that the ruling elites' empty declarations about a "Pacific way" and a hypothetical transnational Oceanian identity does not seem likely to diminish that hold for some time. The peoples of Oceania are too much preoccupied with their independence to be concerned with "Oceania."

Colonized rather recently and in extremely different ways, the Pacific is also the last region in the world which has progressively, archipelago after archipelago, obtained political independence. Independence has been granted much more in a paternalistic manner by the Western powers (namely Great Britain, France, New Zealand, and Australia) rather than wrested by force in wars of liberation. Western Samoa was the first independent state in the Pacific, then Nauru became independent in 1968, Tonga and Fiji in 1970, Papua New Guinea in 1975, Tuvalu and the Solomon Islands in 1978, Kiribati in 1979, and finally Vanuatu (New Hebrides) in 1980. Besides the three French Pacific "Overseas Territories" (French Polynesia, New Caledonia, Wallis and Futuna), the tiny Pitcairn (Great Britain) and Easter Island (Chile), only the territories of Micronesia under U.S. administration, U.S. Samoa and the western part of New Guinea (Irian Jaya) have not gained independence yet. In Irian Jaya, formerly under Dutch control, and annexed in 1963 by Indonesia, a bloody guerrilla war is taking place to the indifference of world opinion.[1]

Although independent, the majority of these new states are still members of the Commonwealth. The Cook Islands, Niue and Tokelau remain linked to New Zealand as "states in free association" or "dependency" (as is the case for Tokelau). The three French Territories of the Pacific themselves benefit from a relative autonomy internally, and are moving in the direction of complete autonomy, if not toward full independence, accompanied by a likely increase of the already considerable financial transfers from France to these Territories. At least such is the (hardly) secret wish of the local bourgeoisie, who are concerned with defending, along with their economic and political power, a standard of living which cannot be matched by the actual resources of these countries, whose totally artificial prosperity is based solely on the public expenditures (civil and military) of the French government.[2]

What holds true for the French possessions is also true for the other young nations of the Pacific, namely that political independence always parallels increasing economic dependence on the former metropolitan countries, on transnational corporations, and on international monetary institutions. Commercial deficits, foreign indebtedness, an economy based on the monoculture of colonial products, and dependence upon international aid: such are the plagues of modern Oceania, just as in the rest of the Third World. Only one does not die of hunger in Oceania.

The progressive shifting of world economy from the Atlantic to the Pacific[3] is accompanied by a renewed interest in Oceania for the Western world, and for the transnational corporations whose control over these fragile, insular economies is encouraged by the official policy of "aid" to the Pacific countries. When such policy is not directly linked to the selling of Western goods, it is meant to make "attractive" for foreign investment the economic areas of interest to transnational corporations, such as mineral resources, fishing, forestry, tourism, and agriculture.[4] Most nations in the Pacific are becoming dependent on such foreign investment and on the development of such resources. The distribution network, the banks, and the air and sea communications in the area are in the hands of international companies which draw considerable profits from them.[5] A new market of several millions of underequipped consumers is opening up. However small, it is rapidly expanding thanks to the assistance that Australia, New Zealand, the United States, France, and Japan continuously offer despite the economic crisis that affects them. The economic interests represented by the Pacific have grown steadily since the discovery in the ocean floor of rich polymetallic nodule deposits (containing cobalt, manganese, nickel, molybdenum, etc.) which are particularly sought after by the space and aeronautics industry. The value of the most recoverable nodule deposits is estimated at more than U.S. $ 3 trillion, and the transnational corporations have already invested hundreds of millions of dollars in technological research concerning deep seabed mining.[6]

While they certainly are economic, the new stakes in the region are also, and perhaps above all, of a political and strategic value. The Pacific islands have powerful neighbors (U.S.S.R., Japan, China, Australia, the U.S.A.) who represent the greatest part of the world's military and economic potential. It is clear that the geographic position of these islands has a strategic value of prime importance, as was evidenced for the first time during World War II (i.e., control of commercial and military maritime routes in the area, military bases such as Guam situated close to Southeast Asia and China, etc.). Since the fall of the Indochinese "dominoes," the Pacific represents for the U.S.A. a second line of defense behind Thailand, Malaysia, Indonesia, and the Philippines.[7] The huge increase of Australian aid to the South pacific since the end of the Vietnam war is no mere coincidence. It was raised from A$ 5 million for the period 1971-73, to A$ 120 million for

1980–82 and to A\$ 300 million for 1983–87.[8] Tied to the United States by the ANZUS treaties (Australia, New Zealand, United States), and thus involved in the Indochinese conflict, Australia now acts as "policeman of the Pacific." In increasing its aid to the South Pacific, the chief beneficiary being its former colony, Papua New Guinea, Australia's concern is to obstruct any tendency on the part of the new Oceanian states to slide in the direction of Communism, or even of "Melanesian Socialism." In 1975, rumors regarding an offer of Soviet aid to Tonga and Western Samoa resulted in a strong warning of the nations of the Pacific on the part of Australia. The following year, the Australian Minister of Foreign Affairs announced a tripling of the aid to the South Pacific (from A\$ 19 million to A\$ 60 million), and it has since increased considerably, even though Australia itself has plunged into an economic crisis.

Economic assistance does not have as its sole objective the countering of "Soviet influence" in the area, as the Australian Prime Minister Malcolm Fraser declared after the invasion of Afghanistan. It also provides the United States with the effective support of several Oceanian delegations to the United Nations. Thus, the Solomon Islands, after being fleetingly tempted by socialism, were among the Third World countries most closely aligned with the U.S. policy when voting on the issues of Lebanon and El Salvador in 1982. Fiji, whose foreign debt amounted to 264 million Fijian dollars in 1981, accepted U.S. miliary aid and cooperates in the multinational peacekeeping force in Sinai and Lebanon. One could cite repeated examples of the political consequences of such dependency.

It is within this briefly outlined context that the time has come of independence and of the construction of unlikely national unities. And this occurs when Oceania finds itself brutally faced with a social and cultural change unprecedented since that which was engendered by its discovery by the West. Colonial society and its three symbolic pillars (the missionary, the planter, and the official) is now replaced, at times without any transition, by modernity and artificial economic development.

International aid, foreign debt, and the investments of transnational companies favor the rise of an overabundant stratum of native civil servants, the development of new businesses and of a small national capitalism (small processing factories, building industries, etc.). The sudden appearance of a wage system allows in turn the development of internal consumption, the creation of jobs related to commerce, and the emergence (or increase) of a bourgeois merchant class. The results are mass rural exodus, then proletarianization and urbanization. At a second stage, because of the scarcity of housing, work, or sufficient salaries, islanders sometimes "choose" to emigrate to the former mother country. This is the case for the islanders of Samoa, Niue, Tokelau, and the Cook Islands, who are emigrating in large numbers to New Zealand.

Under these conditions, money quickly becomes a necessity, the mediator of all kinds of exchange in a way that it never was in the economy of the colonial period. Then, cash crops often represented only a complement (sought after, imposed, but rarely indispensable) of the traditional subsistence economy. Today, everything is becoming, or is liable to become, a commodity: garden produce, for city people no longer have access to gardens; estates, for housing migrants; but also culture itself has entered into the realm of commodities.

In rural areas, social change deals a terrible blow to traditional social organization. The few ethnic groups of Melanesia which had been spared from the contact with the West, as well as the societies already evangelized and integrated into the colonial economy, discover now the modern world of wage-earning and commodities. The shock is undoubtedly as great for the one as for the other. The latter had endeavored more or less successfully to *adapt* their institutions and their cultures through a variety of syncretistic compromises, wherein some of the principles constituting their cultural identity were maintained and brought into play in the reinterpretation of the world. In Melanesia, the "cargo cults" were the most remarkable form of such native efforts to account for the unknown. The current upheavals represent for these societies a new form of acculturation. The practical urgencies with which these traditional (or neotraditional) societies are today confronted, such as overcoming decomposition and ensuring social reproduction, survival in short, also present them with a cognitive and intellectual challenge: they have, once again, to conceive modernity, that is, to think about the place to assign to fundamental traditional values in relation to *modern* Western values. This becomes a task all the more delicate as the appearance of modernity has changed. Not only have Westerners been replaced by native administrators, but neocolonial values no longer seem to allow any space for God and religion. In doing so, they turn their back on syncretistic interpretations of the colonial universe.

The world of commodities is a world without God. It is only a world of commodities, where commodities represent nothing but themselves and their universal equivalent: money. There is no longer any need for some transcendent figure perceived as the original source of wealth and abundance. Hence the anachronism and the obsolescence of Oceanian syncretisms, not only when they try to penetrate the mystery of the supernatural *origin* of the "cargo," but when they seek to interpret in eschatological terms the *access* to commodities as a promise of messianic expectations or the result of a "liturgical technology" suited to the appropriation of those mysterious objects.

The question of access to commodities has sustained considerable secularization. The inequality of access becomes more and more clearly a question of social inequality. It ceases to be thought of, for example, as the result of a fraudulent misappropriation by the whites of riches produced by the ancestors in the world of the dead. And this new social inequality that now cuts across native society has generally nothing to do with the disparities of status or even the social cleavages that constituted colonial and precolonial Oceanian social structures.

Within this context of rapid social change, new forms of political expression appear in the small urban centers of the Pacific, together with new stakes. Throughout Oceania, with local variations, a new discourse is aimed at celebrating and defending Tradition, whose values are also reputed to be at the base of the modern nation-state policy. This discourse requires the greatest attention for at least three reasons. First, because it is today the most prominent and general expression of the relationship that certain Oceanians have established with modernity, social and cultural change, and their traditions. Second, because while conveying a quasi-systematic valuation of the past, this discourse also carries, in practice, a modernistic "development" project. Finally, because this discourse is equally a nationalistic ideology *and* a state ideology, whose primary purpose is the cementing of a national unity and the legitimation of the state's power over the multiple ethnic groups which make up the nation. It seems particularly significant—and intriguing—that these objectives should be pursued through recourse to philo-customary or philo-archaic representations. It is from these three remarks that I shall endeavor to examine the new nationalistic discourse in the Pacific, with a particular emphasis on its paradoxical relationship to Tradition and to the West.

KASTOM

I shall begin by saying what these modern nationalisms are not. They are not ideological instruments created for a national liberation struggle, or for making a specific ethnic claim, or for a contest to obtain power or bringing pressure to bear on the ruling powers.

The first of these determinations leads us to observe that the peoples of the Pacific did not have to struggle for their independence,[9] and in some cases no liberation movement or independence party appeared beforehand, prepared to seize and keep power. The absence of a precise ethnic claim can be explained by the extreme ethnic divisions that characterize most nations of Oceania: no native ethnic group has overshadowed others. Colonialism had already put all the ethnic groups on an equal footing, one might say, by keeping them all without exception away from any possible position of power in the economic and political colonial apparatus. The fact that in most Oceanian archipelagos there was no policy of massive European settlement, or no displacement of populations of Asian origin, also contributes to the absence of an "ethnic minorities" problem in Oceania. The nationalist claim in Oceania is not to be mistaken as the claim of a native *minority* oppressed by a majority of foreign origin. This is true with two exceptions: New Caledonia, where in 1976 Melanesians only represented 42 percent of the population (and Europeans 38 percent), and Fiji, where two "ethnic majorities" are face to face and in balance (in 1977, Fiji's population was composed of 44.2 percent Melanesians and 49.8 percent Indians).[10] Finally, bearing in mind the particular situation in Oceania, these nationalisms do not represent a political manipulation of the nation-state at the ethnic level, in the same way as do, for example, the Western ethnic lobbies or certain European regionalist movements, which are careful not to question the legitimacy of the state. With the exception of New Caledonia,[11] Oceanian nationalisms do not seek to negotiate with the state or to seize power: they *themselves* represent a state ideology. Their emergence is indissociable from the decline of colonialism and the birth of independent states in the area. In Oceania, they are the dominant ideology of their time, dominant as the ideology inspiring official policies of the state, and as the ideology of the social groups which gained *political* power with the independence (such groups may not necessarily hold economic power). These considerations will be taken up again later on.

The time has now come to define, and as much as possible to analyze, the main themes of what may be termed (with all the many minor local variations) Oceanian nationalistic discourse. We shall begin with exploring its "mythology" and the way in which reference to "Tradition" and "Custom" functions within it.

The equivalent to the pidgin English concept of *kastom* in Caledonian-French is *la coutume*. In Samoa, it will be referred to as *fa'a Samoa*; in Tahiti as *la culture* or *peu ma'ohi*. The concept is central to this discourse and the contradictions which run across it. Its essential feature is an opacity which can never be questioned, lest the notion should lose its ideological properties.

Kastom refers loosely to customs, values, beliefs, and traditional institutions, whether long abolished or still alive (whatever their state of preservation). It is generally difficult to determine, unless the context clearly specifies which traditions peculiar to a given ethnic group at a particular moment in its history are referred to as *kastom*. Proposing to

Melanesians that it is necessary to return to *kastom* leaves them puzzled, and requires a subtle exegesis in which all interpretations of *kastom* are possible.[12]

Yet, in its most modern ideological sense, the notion of *kastom* has a firm meaning. The values of *kastom* form a contradictory pair with those of modernity. The world of *kastom* and the Western world are in opposition within a new Manicheism that reverses the postulates inherited from the missionaries—the struggle of the Light of the Word vs. the Darkness of Paganism—but prolongs them in an unexpected way. *Kastom* people now have as their historical task the preservation of their ancestral values. They are urged to keep away from Westernization, represented as temptation and cultural sin.[13] The ideology of *kastom* defines itself as anti-Western and philo-traditionalist. However, these two stands, loudly proclaimed throughout the Pacific, appear all the more paradoxical as they emanate from the most Westernized social classes, those most removed from traditional lifestyle and values and most involved in modernity. This paradox, striking for an outside observer, is even more so from the perspective of traditional populations, who have not yet relinquished their culture, and who are referred to by the philo-archaic discourse. No one has forgotten that the relationship maintained only ten or twenty years ago by the bourgeoisie and urban elites with native cultures and with the rural milieu in general, was marked with the interiorization—in varying degree—of Western racist discourse. Those who used to mock the backwardness of "savages" in the name of Progress and Civilization are now (verbally) the fiercest defenders of primitivity and archaic values.[14]

Opposing the values of *kastom* to those of the West may appear paradoxical on another level: as *a Western criticism of Westernization*. Not only does this criticism borrow from the West a certain number of its patterns, such as missionary Manicheism (the terms of which are inverted), ruralist and ecologist ideology, and the modern Western ideology of ethnicity; it also constructs and describes the antagonism between the two poles of *kastom* and Western modernity in a typically Western way.

Everything begins with the very definition of each of these two poles, which, in order to be thus opposed, undergo what I would call a twofold "fetishist reification," which makes the criticism of Westernization and the apology of primitivity nothing but false criticism and false apology. The first type of reification concerns the process of Westernization (or acculturation), which is never defined as a historical relationship between two social structures but is mistaken for its result: the accumulation of imported goods. The consumption of these goods is assigned a negative moral value and symbolizes in a way modern cultural perdition and alienation.[15] Conversely, nonurban tribal or village communities, which are clearly less involved in modern economy, are perceived as a sort of repository for ethnic values and "authenticity" because merchandise still has little or no hold on them. Consumption thus becomes in itself the very symbol of acculturation. The presence or absence of Western goods becomes the acceptable criteria for measuring the progress of the disease. Such "spontaneous sociology" does not make much of the fact that Western objects have been present in the Pacific ever since the voyages of Captain Cook, and that the peoples of Oceania have since then displayed a fund of energy and inventiveness to capture these fabulous (and so convenient) objects without giving up their traditions. Today in Oceania, the fetishism of merchandise (in the Marxist sense of the term) finds new followers, who go so far as to credit the simple presence of commodities with the power to change the world.

At the other pole, *kastom* also functions as a symbol reified in Western terms. Nationalist discourse never explicitly refers to the relationship that customary society maintains with the urban society and the West. The realm of *kastom* is opposed in such an absolute way to the Western world that both worlds seem to have nothing in common. In this ideological representation (not to be mistaken with the popular representations) *kastom* is defined as an accumulation of disjointed cultural signs, as a list of unconnected cultural traits which, moreover, one would not seek to connect. *Kastom* is not represented as a *system* (social and cultural) but as an assemblage of discontinuous, observable and thus reproducible material elements (that they should allow reproduction is of particular importance for the policies of "culture revival"). These signs of primitivity are principally objects ("art" objects, handicrafts, or implements), public singing and dancing, music, recitations of myths, or, less frequently, ceremonies (e.g., ceremonial exchanges, slaughter of pigs, initiation rites), provided that these objects or ceremonies exhibit the dramatic characteristics of the "exotic" or the "picturesque," in the average Western meaning of these terms.

It is important to note that this implicit definition of "culture" directly expresses an internalization of the Western attitude toward alterity, and most especially the internalization of the system of categories that constitute what Remo Guidieri calls the "inventory knowledge" with the help of which positivist ethnography has been attempting to master Difference for a century, representing it as a sort of rather picturesque, heterogeneous catalogue of exotic manifestations. This enterprise is a deliberate negation of difference, reducing it to phenomena that the West already recognizes, or to mere lexical variations on a universal cultural syntax.[16]

The ideology of *kastom* does not have the same purpose. It does not seek to "understand" change, or to master a different reality. On the contrary, it strives to make differences absolute, and to reinforce the gap which seems to be diminishing. Nevertheless, the ideology of *kastom* remains trapped in a Western pattern of thought in that it searches for differences where they do not exist, and where they are not likely to be found, while confusing the "ready-made" objects of Western understanding about these cultures with difference and cultural identity themselves.

Therefore, these disparate cultural items ("singing," "dancing," "handicrafts," etc.) are reified as symbols of identity after being abstracted in thought from the ceremonial and liturgical context where they are (or were) inscribed, after being separated both from their traditional conditions of transmission and from their symbolic and institutional background. Some official policies inspired by a desire for "cultural revitalization" even endeavor to encourage the massive reproduction of these identity symbols, which are deemed proof of the vigor of indigenous cultures and of their resistance to Westernization. To the commodities symbolic of Westernization, a set of reified and folklorized cultural items is thus opposed as an ideal merchandise contrasting with other types of merchandise. The Western fetishism of merchandise and the folkloristic reification of traditional cultures are the two inseparable elements of the modern ideological celebration of *kastom*.

The relation that this ideology maintains with the past and with history is also very revealing. The valorization of the cultural past that it orchestrates is absolute and distinguishes very rarely or not at all among cultural traits belonging to different historical periods. And, especially, it does not take into consideration the fundamental break separating the colonial from the precolonial periods in this history of these cultures. Thus *kastom* ideology celebrates as authentically *kastom* practices marked by decades of acculturation as well as practices rooted in tradition. Pagan songs and church hymns are put on the same plane in French Polynesia; in New Caledonia, "art festivals" where *la coutume*, gagged by a century of colonialism, is supposed to thrive freely, begin with masses and religious hymns; in Vanuatu, since independence, *bislama* (a local variant of pidgin English) is referred to as a *kastom* language: a very serious conference on the return to the "original purity" of *bislama* was even organized, which condemned its current decay (that is, the growing anglicization of its lexicon).

More than a negation of history or a sudden and incomprehensible (because total) cultural amnesia, it is a refusal to grasp the historical dimension of the relationship native societies have sustained with the West since cultural contact. The "Westernization" so decried by Pacific politicians can only be understood as the effect of an uninterrupted, multistage historical process that is nothing but a process of adaptation of traditional thought and institutions to changing acculturative situations.

Oceanian nationalisms do not turn to the past for analysis. They do not even draw lessons from former anticolonial movements, syncretistic cults, or popular attempts at social and political reorganization that endeavored in their own way to counter the threat of deculturation by reformulating the transcendent values of tradition, that is to say, by stressing their permanence. The past is only taken into account as the subject of an ideological representation: the past—the whole past—is good. And since the different "pasts" are interwoven within the same valorization, the "Christian" past as well as the "pagan" past are considered as carriers of cultural authenticity and of the values of *kastom*. Cultural sin (The Fall) can thus only be inherent to the present; it cannot be rooted in the history of acculturation. Within the context of this ideology, the responsibility for the perversion of *kastom* lies not with the ethnic community itself but with external Western agents. Erasing history in this way also allows the bourgeoisie (particularly the *demis* of Tahiti) or certain dominant groups to avoid questioning the true historic origins of their ruling position, as well as their responsibility in accelerating the process of Westernization, or even the nature of their identification with the values of *kastom*.

While the nationalist ideology repudiates history in the celebration of a reified *kastom*, it takes care not to explicitly equate *kastom* and the past. If *kastom* comes from the most remote past, it is also considered as *living in the present*. It is also likely to be the foundation of modern practices, and indeed to inspire original, typically *kastom* solutions for the future. As such, *kastom* cannot be represented as a "survival," even less as a "resurgence." *Kastom* lives in the present, *but not as an anachronism*, even though the present itself is far from being purely *kastom*.

Nevertheless, some cultural traits, practices, even institutions are found in the present which are indeed derived from the native cultural past and which are *not* represented as *kastom*. Rather, they are seen as pretenses of authenticity, as false-*kastom*, or as the alienation of *kastom*. For the anthropologist, these familiar elements of the Oceanian cultural landscape hardly seem less authentic than those which are precisely referred to as properly "traditional" in the nationalist discourse. One can wonder on what arguments Oceanian ideologists found their claims that such elements are unworthy of being *kastom*, for example certain messianic cults (such as the Jon Frum cult on the island of Tanna,

Vanuatu), or certain current configurations expressing popular beliefs inherited from the abolished pagan religion and related to the powers of the spirts of the dead (as in French Polynesia). One could mention, in a different perspective, the criticism generally incurred by the changes Pacific artisans bring to their work if they reflect *too* overtly Western techniques or ornamental motifs, even though these activities (reputed to be *kastom*) are *already* outside the context of tradition, and subject to the determinations of the artistic or touristic market.

Although specific limitations in the sphere of this reverse side of *kastom* may vary according to local context, those productions judged as worthless "hybrids" have something in common: they belie the above-mentioned negation of history which attempts to mask the syncretistic reality of most social and cultural traits in contemporary Oceania, and must therefore be excluded from what is given as representative of tradition.

The recent (1982) demonstrations of the Tahitian independentist pseudo-prophet Tetua Mai were soon repressed and were considered as shameful by the Tahitians, including the most ardent promoters of the "revival of Polynesian culture." His methods, such as imitating the external signs of national sovereignty (flag, *ma'ohi* identity cards), keeping civil status registers, organizating militias on motorcycles (whose uniform imitated exactly that of the French police), and his messianic-biblical, apocalyptic-antinuclear, and independentist-xenophobic rhetoric, as much as the rapid increase of his movement (despite their earlier skepticism, twelve thousand Polynesian were entered into his *ma'ohi* civil registers), clearly mark the Prophet-President and his party as direct descendants of a subversive prophetic tradition originating in Tahiti in the 1820s with the Tutae Auri and Mamaia syncretistic movements. The repugnance and awe which, according to Mary Douglas, invade the human mind when faced with unclassifiable hybrid phenomena may partly account for the fact that Tetua Mai got no support from the local advocates of the "return to traditions." [17] This type of "resurgence" appears indeed as *too* syncretistic and *too* hybrid to pass as tradition. There should be no mistake: a "provisional *ma'ohi* government," identity cards and police on motorcycles are not attributes of *kastom*, unlike other distinctively Polynesian symbols such as the Christian religion, Sunday Hymns, the production of copra and patchwork quilts.

Such rejection, indeed such struggle against what one could call "survivals as false tradition" must be related to what Remo Guidieri wrote regarding the West's attitude to its own survivals: "We can speak of survivals only because the idea of 'Progress' has become an established idea for us. Survivals are all the behaviors, the aspirations, the values that remain where they should have disappeared, swept away by the course of progress. Survivals are of the present, but they do not belong to modernity." Under such conditions, the elimination of these cultural residues ignored by progress, appears as a *rational* operation. The Oceanian ideologies of *kastom* themselves subscribe to the idea of Progress, and, accordingly, to the notion of "survivals." But they do not ascribe to *kastom* the status of a cultural residue. They establish a division between "real traditions" and "false traditions," as between "good progress" ("development") and a hateful Westernization. The good traditions (*kastom*) must be considered as "pure" elements (not hybridized from Western contact), as much as guides for development. Conversely, hybrid residues are to be rejected, precisely because of their obviously composite nature. One cannot help but consider this as another aspect of the West's attitude toward other people's traditions. Here a philo-archaic ideology is developed that stems from the earlier notion of the Noble Savage: "This impassioned defense of primitivity rules out its modern derivatives as impure hybrid forms, as survivals contaminated by modernity, as fringes of the present which embrace Third World nations and the ghettos of industrialized societies. It excludes those millions who develop unprecedented spiritual despair by turning to their archaic heritage, combining it with, in an efficient though marginal appeal to, the consumist spirit."[18] It is significant in Oceania today that the fight against survivals, against syncretistic resurgences or cultural deviations of all kinds should be led in the name of Progress, in the name of the Purity of the Origins.

Oceanian nationalist ideology recognizes the ever-present and always unpredictable threat of a sudden claim for ethnic or cultural specificity. In the temporary absence of social claims among the exploited classes now emerging in urban centers, the rise of ethnicity is the only truly serious threat to centralist policies and to the power of the new states, and this threat is recognized as such. It then follows that the state's customary ideology has an urgent need to provide the collection of ethnic groups and social classes one representation of *kastom* suitable for collective identification. In other words, it is urgent for them to reduce the various ethnic identities to one national identity by appealing to some hypothetical common tradition.

Therefore, in its representation of *kastom* this ideology takes care not to give preeminence to one ethnic group by exclusively valorizing cultural traits specific to it only. All of *kastom* will be valorized, but no one specific *kastom* in particular. Again, vagueness is a necessity here. So that everyone may recognize himself in this group portrait, it is also necessary that nothing in it be recognized too precisely as the image of the Other. The main advantage in this process is clearly the erasure, in thought, of Difference, that is, the abolition of the distinctive cultural features such as customary land rights, political institutions, and ceremonies, which had enabled these cultures to maintain their specificity against Westernization and neighboring cultures for more than a century.

In this respect, state *kastom*, at least wherever its content will be represented in ceremonial, political, or folk celebrations, will appear in a striking and sometimes picturesque manner as a sort of gigantic neocustomary or neotraditional "bricolage," a medley of disparate cultural traits from different cultures, broken up, extracted from their context, and juxtaposed with elements directly inspired from Western or Westernized practices, especially religious practices.

Throughout the Pacific the spread of this representation is considered as a primordial ideological stake, liable to condition the success of independence itself. In order to spread this national myth, the intelligentsias of the Pacific have devised a particular form of rite: "Art Festivals." Such performances, which are the modern ritual *par excellence* of new Oceanian nationalisms, deserve detailed examination.

FESTIVALS

> *Tout ce qui était directement vécu s'est éloigné dans une représentation.*
>
> —Guy Debord, *La Société du Spectacle*

In the mid-1970s, independences, and with them nationalist ideologies, take hold in Oceania, and the intelligentsias of the area suggest organizing, at regular intervals, festivals aimed at promoting popular artistic traditions. They are supported in this by international cultural institutions, themselves concerned with the problem of the "preservation of Pacific cultures" (UNESCO, South Pacific Commission).

In New Caledonia, Catholic women's groups of the "Women's Association for a Cheerful Melanesian Village" (*sic*) devoted their energy to promoting the quality of housing and gardening among Melanesians, and to fighting "alcoholism and idleness." In 1973, they decided to organize the "First Melanesian Art Fesival." One of the principal protagonists of the venture, Jean-Marie Tjibaou, explains: "The idea gained ground. . . . After the elaboration of the 7th Plan, 100 Melanesians of influence were consulted, and [there was] created, with a few Europeans, the 'Committee for Development'. Together with the Melanesian Cultural Association, they made the Festival a proof of the vitality and dignity of Melanesian life and a new awareness."[19] The first of its kind in New Caledonia and called "Melanesia 2000," all the ethnic groups ("*tribus*") of the Mainland and the Loyalty Islands had the opportunity of meeting each other in various folk shows, which included songs, dances, demonstration of artistic or agricultural techniques, and games ("throwing the assagai and the sling, peeling and grating coconut, braiding mats and wreaths"). That Festival had considerable, almost unexpected success: fifty thousand people came in four days, that is, a third of New Caledonia's population (composed at the time of 58 percent non-Melanesians) and was the forerunner of other similar manifestations.

Jean-Marie Tjibaou made a statement of intentions in the report on "Melanesia 2000" presented to the French national and territorial authorities. It deserves careful reading. At the time, Tjibaou was the Melanesian leader of the Caledonian Union (the main independentist party of New Caledonia); he is today (1983) the vice-president of the Government Council, i.e., the head of the executive of the Territory of New Caledonia.

As a vast cultural inventory, this Festival will allow us to take stock. Furthermore, as a reflection, it will help us to specify what the autochthonous way of life really means in 1975. This Festival must allow the *Canaque* to project his own image in order to rediscover and redefine his present-day identity. The Festival must help him regain confidence, regain more dignity and pride by relating to a cultural heritage recognized today as a living element in the culture of mankind. . . . To exist fully, this culture, just as the *Canaque* world, essentially and vitally needs to be recognized by the surrounding world. Non-recognition, which leads to indifference and lack of dialogue, can only end in suicide or rebellion.[20]

Jean-Marie Tjibaou's text is a model in that it provides a resume of the objectives pursued in this type of mass manifestation, and of the virtues it is supposed to have. Eight years later, some ideologists in Noumea go even further, and claim that, from its own impulse, the Festival favors collective awareness and rehabilitation of a cultural identity, as well as national liberation. The Fourth Pacific Arts Festival, to take place in Noumea in September 1984, coincides with the date of independence, showing the importance of the politico-cultural stakes in this enterprise.

One could say that too much significance is thus ascribed to mere folk demonstrations, which are not unlike the religious schools' annual fairs. Yet it is in this mirror that "*le Canaque*" will have to project his own image in order to "rediscover and redefine his present-day identity," i.e., a *national* identity common to all Melanesians of New Caledonia and based upon a common archaic cultural substrate, *la coutume*, which transcends ethnic and linguistic divisions in the Melanesian world. The "vast cultural inventory" of which Tjibaou speaks will be the inventory of *la coutume* as the central notion of "*Canaque* identity," as well as the inventory of the Melanesian cultural mosaic itself. This cataloguing task means that diversity must be shown, only to be immediately reduced into one sole identity, *one although plural*. *"La coutume* has to be shown," say Melanesian intellectuals. Showing *la coutume* (a step judged necessary and even sufficient for the awakening of national consciousness), means assessing differences, but differences *already abolished* in thought.

Cultural reification materializes in the production itself of the Festivals, which appear as a twofold "collage" and a twofold inventory dealing with two sets of cultural objects. The first set is composed of disjointed items which, when gathered in the folkloristic inventory, are supposed to represent *la coutume* of each ethnic group: dances ‡ songs ‡ sculpture ‡ handicrafts ‡ architecture ‡ costume, etc. The second inventory will gather a set of ethnic groups in the artificial arena of the ceremony, each group presenting the greatest possible number of cultural items corresponding to the categories of the first inventory. *La coutume* will appear as the intertwining of these two sets, as the ideal representation of the ideal of national unity (or international unity in the case of international festivals, where each Pacific nation shows the others its own *"kastom"*).

One might wonder whether one ethnic group could express its own *specific* traits in a context where each culture can display nothing but variations on a single theme. In some cases it is only from consulting the program of events, the placards, or the announcements over a loudspeaker that a spectator could impute one ethnic origin or particular significance to performances in which specificity no longer can express itself except as a "stylistic" variation. One cannot help drawing a parallel between these ceremonies (the tropical replicas of Western folk festivals) and sports competitions, particularly the Olympic Games—except that no ranking or medal rewards the "best" performances of the participating ethnic groups. But if a competitive dimension is not (as yet) attached to Oceanian Folk Festivals, unlike their counterparts in Eastern Europe,[21] the national (and nationalist) dimension with which they are invested, as much as their unifying function, makes them very similar to Western sporting events, which were formerly (and still remain) a privileged occasion for a particular sort of national, chauvinistic assertion, and thus promoted ethnic integration into the nation-state. It is no accident if international folk festivals in Oceania appear at about the same time as the "Olympic Games of the South Pacific," and if during the last "Pacific Art Festival" held in Papua New Guinea in 1980, the uniformed "national teams" (themselves representing a national selection of the "best" groups of dancers, the "best" artisans, etc.) were seen to march behind their flags while the national anthems were played.[22]

The few critics who protest against this vast enterprise of folkorization are hardly heard. In New Caledonia, this is the case of the Palika, the "Kanak Liberation Party," a radical group of independentists founded by the most politicized fringe of Melanesian intelligentsia, which is composed of former students returning from France after May 1968. They call this type of thing a "prostitution of *kanak* culture," intended for strangers (the whites of Noumea and the tourists), and turning into a show ritual ceremonies which have no meaning outside the village and the ethnic group, outside their proper time and place. The organizers of the Festivals grudgingly admit that such events at times do violence to native culture, and are worried by the strong reluctance which appears in rural areas ("we want roads, not Festivals"), even within the ranks of independentist parties. But such a snag seems to them minor compared to the likely benefits, such as the hastening of independence through "collective awareness of *Canaque* identity." The need to organize at all costs the 1984 Fourth Festival reflects the need to "show *la coutume*" to the *Canaques*, but also to others, particularly in the Pacific, but especially to the whites. For "cultural assertion" is both an assertion of the *value* of native culture as well as its existence *as culture* in the common French sense of the term, viz., an ensemble of intellectual and artistic products. The local intelligentsia thus tries to show that "there is *culture* in Melanesian culture," and to prove with a great "exhibition" that Melanesians also have their own artists and their Fine Arts.

Such an approach, unable to free itself from Western categories (common-sense categories as well as anthropological positivism), leads to cultural folklorization, hence to abolishing the specificity of native culture as opposed to Western culture (since they both are put on the same level and precisely compared), and to abolishing local cultural specificities, this last point being of course part and parcel of the will to forge a national identity. The need to "show *la coutume*" appears here again, if we consider that this display has much the same attributes as traditional initiatory revelations: it publicly discloses secrets during a ritual. But outside any appropriate initiatory context, this disclosure addressed to strangers (whites as well as Melanesians belonging to other ethnic groups) is also a deliberate profanation. It is opposed by the Westernized radical left as well as those in the bush who perceive the threat, or the imposture. Elsewhere, in Vanuatu for example, some ethnic groups agree to participate in the "Art Festivals" on the condition that only the parts of their rituals which can be seen by women (and thus by everyone) will be produced. They obstinately refuse to publicize any of the crucial sequences of these ceremonies, which are under a strict taboo. Displaying those to everyone would mean destroying them. It is no accident if modern Oceanian nationalists attach so much importance to the public display of all that was previously concealed, and to the transformation of the traditional stakes of native cults and ceremonies into cultural entertainment or cultural merchandise. It is no accident either that they should expect from this "revelation," which eventually implies the irremediable destruction of the last traditional ceremonies, the emergence of a national identity.

CULTURAL REVIVAL

The different philo-customary nationalisms of the Pacific have this in common: they are not *ethnic*, in the strict sense of the term. Their referent is not one distinct ethnic group, but a compound of cultural traits deemed capable of expressing national identity and unity. As state ideology, the discourse on *kastom* attempts to give credence to a fictive construction: that of an *imaginary mono-ethnism*. And it does so despite the varying multiethnic and multicultural characters of the Oceanian nations. These characters are either combated when they attempt to assert themselves (particularly against the state: cf. the events of 1980 in Vanuatu), or, since they cannot be concealed, invoked verbally as evidence of the richness of *kastom*, but suppressed in practice in the process of folklorization. This imaginary mono-ethnism refers to some ideal people, itself imaginary: the people-of-*kastom*, defined by its national identity,[23] which itself derives from the physical presence of this people inside the state's borders and from its belonging to a supposed common culture.

Paradoxically, the state's discourse on *kastom* is accompanied by the valorization of *kastom* at the local level and by official policies of cultural revival. It even seems to contradict the objectives of national unification: is the emphasis on *kastom* not liable to increase particularisms and to revive centrifugal tendencies?

It does not seem to be the case, although, at the dawn of independence, it is too early to say. The "cultural revitalization" that the state's ideologists have in mind is a delusion. They do not intend to revitalize *as a whole* the cultural traits, practices, and institutions locally recognized as *kastom*, by helping them to survive and to be passed on. They are only interested in "revitalizing" (and it will be shown in what way) a very specific sector: local "artistic production." For "Art" is seen today as endowed with the strange power to accomplish the redemption of a culture. The planned reproduction of "works of art" is thus mistaken for the reproduction of culture.

We find here again the underlying purpose of the Art Festivals. But artistic revival policy does not aim only to equip the villages with the necessary structures for the preparation of the Festivals (in which case, the villages would function somewhat like local teams as opposed to the national championship team in sports). Promoting traditional arts and crafts in the villages concerns daily life, even though it is ostensibly related to the new cultural rituals of the state: it is above all a matter of production, which has become clear in spite of the original wave of ideological pronouncements. Art, the most remarkable achievement of Oceanian societies according to both Western and Oceanian philo-customary discourse, is now becoming a purely *economic* activity, which is intended to provide the rural populations with an extra monetary income, indeed to become their principal source of income.[24] The aim is to stop rural exodus and to reduce the number of unemployed people and delinquents in urban centers. Thus, rather than providing the rural populations through land reform with the means to be self-supporting, living off their own agricultural production on their own land, a new sector of activity has been developed, which is narrowly dependent on tourism, or what amounts to the same thing, on the development of a domestic market for "native handicrafts," which is the case in Tahiti. And here, beneath the ideological, moral, and purely economic motivations of this new kind of ergotherapy, one again finds cultural folklorization and its devasting effects. From this point of view, the example of the Gogodala is particularly illuminating.

The Gogodala live in the Western Province of Papua New Guinea, in a marshy region between the Aramis and the Fly rivers. Like other Oceanian cultures, the Gogodala underwent massive acculturation, which has contributed to the disappearance of the traditional religious cults and of male initiation rites. These elaborate rituals involved the production of many painted and carved objects, such as ancestor effigies, totemic animals, masks, ceremonial dugout canoes, etc. The influence of the missionaries (beginning in the 1930s) was decisive in suppressing such activities. By order of the missionaries, huge auto-da-fés took place, in which the Gogodala burned all the cult objects that had remained in their possession after the passage of the administrators and anthropologists at the beginning of the century.

In the early 1970s, after the Christianization of the Gogodala, when their children were attending missionary schools, and rugby, soccer, and speedboats made their appearance, the Gogodala were subjected to a far-reaching attempt at "cultural revival." James Baldwin's description deserves quoting.[25] Commentary is not needed: I have confined myself to emphasizing (italics) certain passages that are particularly significant with regard to what has just been discussed.

[At that time] the Federal government of Australia was studying a proposal to create a National Museum of Art in Canberra. An Australian research worker, Anthony L. Crawford, who had taken part in the project, came to New Guinea in early 1972 with the aim of gathering documents about the Gogodalan art objects that already were in Australia. He also wanted to determine if other works of art could be collected in the region for the proposed museum. Crawford's investigations came to nothing but the discovery of one traditional object: a big drum that had somehow remained hidden and been kept safe by the men of the village of Kala, who of course refused to part with it. During his trip, Crawford carried an album of photographs of traditional Gogodalan objects, which he showed to the *sakema* (the professional sculptors of the village). To thus rediscover their lost works aroused keen emotion and nostalgia among many of them. When Crawford asked them if they would like to recreate such works, they [said] that it would be a sin, an alliance with evil spirits, a denial of Christianity. Crawford tried to convince them by showing them Christian art from Europe, Australia and other regions of the Pacific, that one could be an artist without abandoning Christianity, that the art of a people simply expressed their pride and identity, and that the art of the Gogodala was the only evidence of their history. . . .His arguments roused a passionate debate among the gogodala about the possibility of rehabilitating the old artistic traditions.

With the support of the Commonwealth Art Advisory Board in Australia, Crawford decided to live among the Gogodala for a period of time with his wife in the village of Balimo. During the first few months of 1973, several old men from Balimo and from other surrounding villages, who had learned their craft three or four decades earlier, were convinced by Crawford's arguments and began to work, mixing their paints, sculpting "totemic" characters, and making dance masks. At first, their efforts produced nothing but crude results, but, through practice, they recovered the style and forms of the old pieces preserved in foreign museums. In addition, younger men imitated their elders and soon the designs, *gawa tao*, were taught to the younger generation. Crawford understood rapidly that to better realize his project a place was needed, an art center that would be not only a workshop but also a place to exhibit the objects as living symbols of the Gogodalan heritage. With the cooperation of the men of Balimo and of other villages, Crawford decided to build, or rather rebuild, a traditional communal house at Balimo. . . . [It] was finished in June, 1974, and on August 29, 1974, *the "Gogodalan Cultural Center" was officially opened by Michael Somare, then "Chief Minister."* The house reconstructed at Balimo was 36 meters long, which is small compared to the houses originally built by the Gogodala. Furthermore, *it differs from the ancient constructions in its function*; they were places of habitation, whereas the new house is used as a cultural center, including a working space for artists. [The new house] is also a place where local *primary school children learn traditional dances, songs, sculpture, and painting.* It also contains *a space for exhibiting the sculptures and masks*: more than a thousand objects are exhibited there.

With the same view in mind of conserving the techniques of Gogodalan sculpture and painting, the Gogodalan Cultural Center decided to *revive the Aida Maiyata ceremonies* ["a rite celebrating the cult of an ancestral hero," according to the author], which were performed for the first time in decades. Then, in September 1975, *during the regional festivals of independence, the initiation rites, which had been abandoned in the late 1930s, were presented,* using ceremonial dugout canoes. . . .

The success of the Gogodalan Renaissance is beginning to have an impact outside the region. Dances and an exhibition of Gogodalan art were particularly noted during the fourth Festival of New Guinean Art held at Port Moresby in September 1974. When Queen Elizabeth visited Papua New Guinea in 1977 for her Jubilee, she watched a performance of Gogodala dance. Also in 1977, a famous American actor, who is an amateur of primitive art, was photographed in Los Angeles standing next to a recently sculpted anthropomorphic Gogodalan piece he had acquired. The government of Papua New Guinea recently issued two *stamps* featuring the Gogodalan art that has been revived in the Aramia region. Finally, and what is perhaps the most important, *the Gogodalan Cultural Center now serves as a model for the creation of other cultural centers* that the government is trying to found in other regions.

Although the sale of traditional objects was never the principal aim of the project, it appears that *the revenue from it is beginning to make itself felt,* particularly from *the sale of objects to merchants* in the urban centers of Papua New Guinea and whatever rare *tourists* manage to reach Balimo. However, to avoid the kind of mass-produced art that is sold in the airports of tourist centers in the South Pacific, where unfortunately there exist so many examples, the project's directors and the *sakema* themselves have endeavored to maintain artistic quality and *true authenticity.*

All of this has not occurred without the foreign missionaries' opposition (*two missionaries left the region after the debate about the Cultural Center*), and that of several Gogodalans also who opposed the project since the construction of the communal house in Balimo. People threatened to burn down the center, and the Gogodalans who were actively involved in the project were *condemned by their pastors.* During religious services prayers were said to save their souls.

Far from being an exception, the case of the Gogodala is indicative of a trend. It is also a prototype of its kind. Oceania has now become covered with small "cultural centers," which are half folklore museums and half workshops. Exhibitions of popular art are held periodically in urban centers, and the creation of handicraft cooperatives is being encouraged. A concerted effort is also being made to train native Oceanian anthropologists and archaeologists, with the aim of "recording traditions" (legends, songs, and dances) and passing them on as widely as possible, particularly in the schools where young Oceanian teachers teach, not without reluctance, the rudiments of *kastom.* "Culture" clearly has become a political stake. Whites are no longer preeminent in the foreground, and the presence in the Pacific Islands of foreign anthropologists, linguists, and archaeologists is only tolerated provided they contribute to the "technical" training of their future Oceanian colleagues (teaching them how to use tape recorders, video cameras, and how to carry out excavations); true professional training is often considered as superfluous, or is even dismissed with mistrust. No "scientific" discourse is considered as acceptable any longer because it originates from whites, who cannot possibly "understand" (through empathy) the inexpressible dimension of *kastom*. However, it is a sometimes hasty reading of the early twentieth-century ethnographers' classic monographs that now serves as the reference for the attempts at folkloric reconstruction of *kastom*; it even functions as a collective memory for the local intellgentsia and as the (hidden) foundation of a knowledge of *kastom* upon which its claim to cultural power, or power itself, is grounded.

Attempts at cultural revival are not oversubtle. The spreading of this new Gospel, which is always presented in moral terms (the financial arguments come later), is undertaken with the zeal of recent converts. Populations which have long been Christianized, and which are already involved in the market economy, are induced to worship what they had endeavored to suppress. They are urged to return to their traditions, to reintroduce the past, or certain aspects of it, into their daily lives.

Initially, the reactions are almost always negative: if the rehabilitation of a past that has been condemned, according to the missionaries' Manicheism, as purely negative (*taem blong Devil*: Time of the Devil) is not to be considered, neither is the repudiation (in the name of what ?) of the material advantages of modernity such as kerosene lamps, metal utensils, and outboard motors, which the ideologists of cultural authenticity naively fight. Some of the people nevertheless agree to play the game, to ape themselves, to produce an image of their culture that others in town have conceived as being relevant to their true identity and therefore as being the right way to Salvation.

But those who accept playing the game are not necessarily taken in. Indeed, how could they trust in the sincerity of the promoters of such enterprises, obviously members of the most acculturated social groups? Their social origins, and even in some cases (in French Polynesia, for example) their sudden change of attitude regarding the values of the traditional world, escape no one's attention and immediately rouse suspicion. The generous ideological aims that they profess to have no longer deceive anyone either. Those who accept to participate in the ideologues' cultural fantasies do so generally because they hope that their compliance will provide them with a new source of income. The more acculturated a society becomes, the more likely it is to lend itself to policies of cultural revival. The success of those policies is conditioned by the concerned populations' wish to get even more deeply involved in modern consumption. The promotion of *kastom* at the local level indeed leads to "development," i.e., to a greater dependence on the market economy.

This is undoubtedly one of the reasons why the ideology of *kastom* can temporarily ward off centrifugal forces threatening to break up national unity: far from accomplishing an impossible comeback of primitivity, the policies of cultural and artistic revival actually contribute to hastening the Oceanian societies' swing toward Westernization, that is, toward cultural uniformity.

DEVELOPMENT

The sudden (and, in certain cases, unexpected) rehabilitation of *kastom* raises delicate problems of adjustment to the state's injunctions, calling for an interpretation of what this term refers to in the official discourse. The official notion is sufficiently vague for *everyone* to hope to profit from this new context favorable to *kastom*, and eventually even draw material or political benefits. As Roger M. Keesing[26] has noted, the concept of *kastom* has already long been used at the ethnic or village level for the most diverse ends, in line with local political and cultural stakes themselves variable: "*Kastom* as political symbol can be used to justify anticolonial and anti-Christian conservatism or to rationalize partial abandonment of ancestral ways. It can be used to legitimize customary law in opposition to colonial (or neocolonial) law. It can be used to establish the authority of local leaders parallel to those of the government, by depicting the traditional order as prior and endogenous and the colonial order as introduced and alien. It can be used to validate land claims. And it can be used to defend the values of kinship, community and continuity with the past which are being visibly eroded by the development process."[27] But this notion can also be invoked in other contexts to legitimize local plans for capitalist development: "An ideology of *kastom* can serve to deny the contradictions between *bisnis* / material prosperity and ancestral ways by making *bisnis* a collective venture of the community, by emphasizing the communalist aspects of custom, the communalist possibilities of *bisnis*, and the obligations of the successful entrepreneur to share his rewards."[28]

Despite the elasticity of the meanings the state gives to the concept of *kastom*, despite the ever-present possibility of putting the official celebration of *kastom* to the strategic use of local groups, conflicts between local *kastom* and state *kastom* nevertheless do arise. This confrontation will then be presented (by each camp) as the struggle of authenticity against deviation, of truth versus falsehood, indeed (in Tanna, Vanuatu) of *kastom* against "politics." These conflicts are not generally new, even if the state's official concern with *kastom* seems to have revived them. Beyond police or military repression, the "customary state" has in this case a weighty ideological argument: those who are opposed to it are opposed not only to independence and national unity, but to *development*. And that is the other main dimension of the question.

Oceanian nationalist discourse is *a discourse about Progress, indissociable from a discourse about the necessity of Regression*. One of its objectives is to mask the contradiction between change and preservation, tradition and modernity. It is the discourse which claims that *kastom* and development are not only not contradictory, but can go hand in hand. In other words, the state does not only count solely on the invocation of archaism, which could eventually present political risks when local traditions cannot be transformed into merchandise or reified into folkloric representations: it also manipulates the values of development.

If it is a fact, as Claude Karnoouh shows with respect to the Roumanian case, that the state's constant reference to the distant past is "an axiom of its own theory of legitimacy and not a series of verbal concessions destined to conciliate the rural populations,"[29] it is equally true that the manipulation of such reference, although necessary, is not sufficient for the legitimation of a state whose objectives are not, and could not be those of Tradition:

. . . the political bureaucracies of Eastern countries sense the perils which archaic peasant ideology contains; they know, by their own experience and social origin, the irreconcilable opposition between the social contract principles on which the peasant community is based and the Hegelian-Leninist principles on which they establish both the materiality and messianism of their own power. Also, the Communist parties, besides the rigid organization of folklore, must, concomitantly, reinforce the images and social values attached to the model of which they are the "vanguard": the worker. But this is not an ideological instrument capable of affirming the autonomous and original power of the nation-state; on the contrary, it underscores both the internationalism of a world process of industrial development and its technological dependence on Western capitalist countries. Only the peasantry can give the state the framework within which the plan of national independence can be carried out, since, despite its past submission to various foreign sovereignties, the peasantry has preserved the ethnic and linguistic identity desired by this same state.[30]

In the particular case of Oceania, it is the reference to *development* (and certainly not to the working class) which acts to counterbalance the invocation of the past. This notion is at least as mythical as that of *kastom*. It is synonymous with "a modernization respectful of customary values," that is, a *modernization without Westernization*. In this model, the contradiction between *kastom* and development ceases to apply, since *kastom* itself is represented as a tradition living in the present and not as an obsolete, moribund survival. Although the state is verbally based on *kastom*, the "defense of tradition" is not a sufficient argument to justify its existence: it must also promote new values, and promote them as *not* contradictory with *kastom*. This is as much for defusing the political risks tied to a "*kastom*-criticism" of the Westernization of the state's practices, as for legitimizing the latter's pursuit of non-*kastom* political, economical, or socio-cultural objectives, such as the creation of cooperatives, the development of a small capitalism, the appeal for foreign investment, the development of tourism, sexual equality, contraception, and the mass media.

The mono-ethnic fiction which underlies the discourse about *kastom* goes with the fiction of a national consensus about development: both back the state by mandating it to promote in the nation's name both *kastom* and the modernization-without-Westernization. The proliferation of new state rituals such as folklore festivals, Independence Day ceremonies and the like also functions, even better than voting, as the repeated expression of this popular consensus. With the state's independence, it is the (Western) notion of the irreducibility of the nation to the ethnic group, of public interest to private interest which takes hold. And with it, if need be, the justification of any repression of "local particularisms."

As an ideology, the nationalist discourse is also intended to simultaneously conceal and legitimize a political domination, which, in the Oceanian context, is twofold—domestic and international. In the domestic sphere, the erasure of history mentioned earlier allows the conditions under which the socially and/or economically dominant groups have emerged to be concealed. It does so by establishing their domination as something natural. In an even more general way, the denial of *kastom*'s obsolescence, of its inability to adapt to the modern objectives of the state, leads to masking the domination of archaic or neotraditional social and political structures by those of the modern society. The substitution of an hyperbolic valorization of *kastom* for any serious sociological or political analysis about the nature of the rifts between ethnic and social groups allows setting up a representation of national unity which acknowledges only *folkloric* differences between ethnic groups. Once the colonizer is expelled, the independent nation is composed of only one single group: the people-of-*kastom*. "*Wan pipol, wan neson*" (one people, one nation), as they say in Vanuatu.

At the international level, nationalist ideology seeks to conceal the nation's domination by and dependence on the former colonial power, on international aid, and on the world economy in general. It does so by attempting, as we have seen, to abolish in thought the contradiction between *kastom* and development. And it is only because modernism, whose agents are the bourgeoisie and the dominant groups, assumes the mask of *kastom*, that *it can plainly appear as modernism*, but a modernism of a new kind, since it is inspired and guided by tradition itself. In this framework, this improbable "customary modernism" functions as the denial of dependence on the West, since it seeks to accredit the notion that it is possible to master, or even to control it. The miraculous solutions based on ethnic genius and authenticity (the "Pacific Way") which it offers are thus presented as bound to succeed, and sufficient to guarantee independence as much as the nation's enduring cultural specificity. Here the myth of "good development" appears as the obverse of the symbolical rejection of the superficial effects of Westernization: both attitudes proceed from the same illusion, that is, from the same pseudo-criticism.

Translated by Michele Blum

Acknowledgments. I would like to thank the Rothko Chapel for having generously financed a period of research in the Pacific (from September 1982 to February 1983), without which this essay would never have been realized. My thanks go most especially to Dominique de Menil and Francesco Pellizzi, who lent all their support to this project, to Remo Guidieri, whose work, as well as our conversations over a period of years, was instrumental to the orientation of this essay, and to Martine Karnoouh-Vertalier who reread a first draft of the translation of the text.

NOTES

1. For more information on this poorly understood conflict reminiscent of ethnocide, see the chapter recently devoted to Irian Jaya in: *Politics in Melanesia*, a collected work published in 1982 by the University of South Pacific, Suva, Fiji. The Australian government's lack of strength in the Irian Jaya affair can only be explained by its desire to maintain good relations with Indonesia for reasons at once strategic and economic. One will note that Australian aid to the Pacific countries (in the greater sense of the term) benefits especially the ASEAN countries: for the year 1981–82 they have received A$ 308 million in the name of "bilateral project assistance," whereas the South Pacific countries received A$ 73 million (source: "Why Australia is No. 1," *Island Business* 1 [January 1983] : 39).

2. This "prosperity" is especially perceptible in French Polynesia: the Territory's exports in 1980 amounted to 719 million Pacific francs, while imports reached 42,030 million, that is 58 times more (which was approximately equivalent, in 1980, to 400 million U.S. dollars).

3. "In 1980, for the first time in modern history, the value of the trade carried across the Pacific exceeded that of the Atlantic" (James E. Winkler, *Losing Control: Towards an Understanding of Transnational Corporations in the Pacific Islands Context* [Suva, Fiji: Pacific Conferences of Churches, 1982]).

4. "The extraction of mineral resources is the largest source of export earnings from the Pacific Islands, totalling A$ 751 million in 1979, or 42 percent of all export earnings. The economies of four nations—Kiribati, Nauru, New Caledonia and Papua New Guinea—are heavily dependent on mining, and gold mining has long been significant in Fiji. . . . Fishing is a major industry in the South Pacific. Fish and seafood exports from the Pacific Islands totalled A$ 179 million in 1979, making it the third largest export industry in the region. More than half of the total A$ 108 million came from American Samoa, where canneries are operated by two U.S. transnational corporations, Ralston Purina and H. J. Heinz. Fishing in the South Pacific is important to the U.S. and Japan. Fishing is the major U.S. economic interest in the region, being a multi-thousand million dollar industry. Japanese fishing interests have increased and altered their involvement in South Pacific fishing in crucial ways since the oil price rise of 1973 and the introduction of the 200 mile Exclusive Economic Zones (EEZ) in 1977. . . . In 1979, the export of wood and by-products from the Pacific Islands amounted to A$ 67 million, almost all of this being generated by Papua New Guinea and the Solomon Islands, where transnational forestry operations have been greatest. Japan is the major market for Pacific Islands timber exports. . . . Most processing takes place in metropolitan countries. Between half and two-thirds of PNG's exports are unprocessed logs, as are nearly all of Solomon Islands' exports. At the same time that Japan's traditional suppliers, like Indonesia and Malaysia, are demanding that Japan accept processed wood from them, Japan is turning to new suppliers, such as the South Pacific. . . . Villagers in the Solomon Islands who protested to the Government about the careless destruction of their forests by Levers Pacific Timbers Ltd., a subsidiary of the giant Unilever, were told that to oppose Levers was the same as to oppose the Government. . . . The export earnings of fruits and vegetables, coffee, tea, cocoa, copra, coconut oil, sugar, palm oil and other crops from the region amounted to A$ 587 million in 1979. For the most part these crops were introduced to the region through European colonization and the use of forced or indentured labour. . . . As more land in Pacific Islands nations is being set aside for the production of cash crops (much of the best land is already used for this purpose), the production of food is stagnant or dropping in relation to population growth and food imports are rising." (Winkler, *Losing Control*, 44, 47, 50–51, 55, 56.

5. The Burns Philp Australian trust, which operates on all Pacific Islands in the most diverse sectors (retail commerce, hotels, plantations, insurance companies, shipping, travel agencies, etc.) has seen its profits double between

1974 and 1980 (from 9.2 to 17.6 A$ million), while Burns Philp South Seas, its subsidiary which operates solely on Fiji, Tonga, Samoa, and Niue tripled its profits during the same period. In 1977–78, 63.3 percent of the turnover of B. P. came from domestic operations in Australia, but only 39.9 percent of its profits issued from Australia itself (Source: Winkler, *Losing Control*, 27–28.)

6. Winkler, *Losing Control*, 57–62.

7. "The region not only surrounds the access routes to Guam, but also those to the Near East, and our sources of raw materials can be controlled from Micronesia. Moreover, a north-south line of communication, of greater and greater importance, passes through the region, linking our Northern allies, Japan and Korea, to our allies and friends in the South, Australia and New Zealand, the Philippines and Indonesia. In the strong sense of the term, the U.S. must remain a Pacific power," declared the U.S. Secretary of Defense, James Schlesinger, in 1973 (quoted in Winkler, *Losing Control*, 23–24).

8. *Island Business*, 1 op. cit.

9. There must be no mistake about the rising of the Nagriamel movement on some of the New Hebrides Islands, culminating in 1980 with the spectacular secession of the island of Santo, put down without difficulty by the Papuan New Guinean army: it was an *anti*-independentist movement opposed to all forms of centralization under state control.

10. New Caledonia is the only Pacific country (with the obvious exception of Australia and New Zealand, which I do not take into account here), that was massively settled by whites. The Europeans of New Caledonia, some of whom have families living on the island for four generations, consider themselves as "native," as much as the Melanesians. The situation of these Caledonians ("Caldoches") may compare to that of the *pieds-noirs* of French North Africa. In Fiji, the presence of Indians results from their immigration to the island, around 1879, when they were recruited as indentured laborers on sugar cane plantations. A subtle political equilibrium was instituted by the Constitution and the Fijian electoral system between the two communities, which exist side by side, jealous of their prerogatives and suspicious of any infringement on their rights. The political bipolarization around two main parties reflects the dominant ethnic division. The rise of an extremist Melanesian party, nationalist and racist, seemed to threaten the status quo during the 1970s, and contributed even further to heightening the tensions between the two communities. It did not win any seat in the elections of July 1982 although the polarization of the vote according to ethnicity had never been so evident.

11. The different Melanesian political movements of New Caledonia, united within the Independentist Front, *are now in power* in the colonial political apparatus. They are engaged in delicate negotiations with Paris toward obtaining independence.

12. Consult on this point the important collection of articles published in a special edition of the journal *Mankind* (13, no. 4 [August 1982]) edited by Roger M. Keesing and Robert Tonkinson entitled: "Reinventing Traditional Culture: The Politics of Kastom in Island Melanesia."

13. It is important to note that the members of the intellgentsias, who

produce this discourse, were strongly marked by a religious education, and sometimes even belong to the native priesthood.

14. As Remo Guidieri has shown, the archaic "is not only ante-Western, it is also anti-Western." The emphasis placed on the contemporary valorization of the archaic stems from a myth specific to our time that modern anthropology has largely contributed to creating and disseminating (see Remo Guidieri, *L'Abondance des Pauvres* [Paris: Le Seuil, 1984]).

15. Cf. the *extra* fetishism of merchandise within the pseudo-criticism of the "consumer society" emerging in the West in the 1960s, a criticism condemned to become (*via* the "consumerism") the auxiliary of merchant economy, which clearly could not be ruined by economic abstinence or marginalization.

16. This criticism of the "anthropological knowledge" is the subject of the concluding chapter in *Le Route des Morts*, by Remo Guidieri (Paris, Le Seuil, 1980).

17. However, Tetua Mai had the financial and political support of the Vanuatu government, which two years previously had crushed the Nagriamel rebellion, led by a prophet who also printed passports, coined money, and organized militias in the name of the defense of *kastom*. No man is a prophet in his own country. . .

18. The quotations from Remo Guidieri are taken from *L'Abondance des Pauvres*, op. cit., 13–14 and 26–27.

19. Jean-Marie Tjibaou, *Kanake* (Editions du Pacifique, 1976), 31.

20. Tjibaou, op. cit., 32.

21. On the functions of folklore and "peasanist" ideology in relation to the strategies of the nation-state in Eastern Europe, the reader is referred to Claude Karnoouh's article: "National Unity in Central Europe: the State, Peasant Folklore and Mono-ethnism," in *Telos* 53 (Fall 1982): 95–105. Claude Karnoouh's analyses concerning the cultural folklorization in Eastern Europe are valid in totally different cultural and political contexts, and I shall return to this later: "The already ancient organization of folklore presentations removes the peasantry from its own local identity to the extent that it is led to contemplate some performances resulting from a synthesis between different regions that are strangers to one another. The folklore is detached from the times and places which condition it: the village, the region, the ethnic group, the religious and natural cycle of the seasons—which are replaced by the cycle of administrative life. Finally, by scheduling a calendar of radio and television competitions similar to the one that regulates sport championships, the state transforms folklore into a vast enterprise of national and international leisure" (op. cit., 103).

22. By pursuing the sports metaphor, one could say that in the framework of national Art Festivals the ethnic groups in attendance are to their state what football players are to their team: parts of a whole, which itself is something other than the simple addition of its parts. The difference among ethnic groups can no longer be anything other than functional. Like the players of a football team, ethnic groups have *specialties*: one is famous for its beautiful masks, another for its basketry. But these specialties, which only have sense in regard

to the idea of the "game," are at once necessary and interchangeable: it is *necessary* that *la coutume*, in order to be a "true culture," should produce songs, dances, houses, matrimonial rituals, culinary arts, etc. From the point of view of the final result it does not matter which ethnic group will carve out the canoes or weave the mats. "What matters," precisely, "is to participate."

23. In Vanuatu, one speaks of the *"ni-Vanuatu"* ("men of our land"); in New Caledonia (renamed Kaledonia by some independentists), of the *"kanak* people" (Melanesians were named *Canaques* by the colonizers); in Tahiti, of the *"ma'ohi* people" (meaning "Polynesian," as opposed to Chinese, or Europeans). This new "identity" allows dispensing with reflection on multiethnicity, and on what ethnic status should be conferred on "half caste" people.

24. Some states, such as Papua New Guinea, even envisage orienting the production of art and crafts toward exportation and making it one of the principal short-term sources of foreign currency for the country (cf. *Broad Framework of Accelerated Development Plan for Artifacts and Handicrafts in Papua New Guinea* [Port Moresby: Department of Commerce and Industry, 1978]).

25. James Baldwin, "Renaissance artistique chez les Gogodala," *Journal de la Société des Océanistes*, Paris, Musée de l'Homme, no. 63 (June 1979).

26. Roger M. Keesing, "Kastom and Anticolonialism on Malaita: 'Culture as Political Symbol,'" in *Mankind* (13, no. 4 [August 1982]), 357–73.

27. Ibid., 371–72

28. Ibid., 371

29. Karnoouh, op. cit., 103.

30. Ibid., 104–5.

Remodeling Broken Images: Manipulation of Identities Towards and Beyond the Nation, an Asian Perspective

SERGE THION

THE "I" OF THE KINH

To be Vietnamese is to be *kinh*. Designating the Court, the town, the center of power, this term has neither ethnic nor geographical connotation. *Civis* rather than *homo*, it is an acknowledgment of political subjection; or rather, since more than in other places, here the political includes all of life, of cultural subjection. In a world whose center is China, Vietnam is the part which is situated in the south— *Nan* in Chinese, *nam* in Vietnamese. To shed light on the formation of Vietnamese unity, one must look at this characteristic of Chinese culture, which perhaps sums up its lasting significance—its "civilizing" project of expansion.

As far back as one can see into the past of this continental mass, China (before present-day China) appears as a mosaic of peoples, tribes, and clans, fragmented and heterogeneous in terms of language and customs. These differences, traces of which can still be seen, are, however, scarcely visible in the material and technical life of these groups, and there is no evidence that China was built on an advanced material foundation. Moreover, increasingly one sees that the periphery of China—or what its "culturocentrism" leads us to perceive as being its periphery—has undergone an evolution of its own. The most ancient potteries known to date are Japanese. Pottery, agriculture, and metallurgy all appear in Southeastern Asia at the same time and no doubt much earlier than in the Chinese world. A cultural flow moves toward the North, from *Nanyang* or the South seas, carrying with it, in particular, rice. That is why the concept of the barbarian, *man*, invented very early by a China in formation, must be understood in a very narrow sense: that is, of people not within the trajectory of the kingdom, and later the Empire—an Empire which called itself the "Land of the Middle," *zhung guo*, center of the square in which the earth itself was entered. It is this trajectory which is implied by *kinh*, when it was attributed to the throne of the Emperor of the South. But this regime had the highest conception of itself: it considered itself to be a civilizing agent, or in more conventional terms, to be humanizing. The nature/culture dialectic did not have to wait until the Enlightenment: it occurred well before the unification of the second century B.C.E., even before Confucius, who imparted his literary luster to it. No one is quite as human as the Chinese, this particular synthesis of cultures of the alluvial plains of the North, rich with their harvests of millet. Attitudes, dress, prayers, aesthetic forms, language, writing, administration, the tilling of the soil, and classification of men: these are what define the Chinese, and they were acquired through territorial advance, or by wanderers who came as mercenaries or invaders. This is also what later will define the Vietnamese, by their own reckoning. There is thus a long and profound work of acculturation and assimilation, in the most etymological sense, which China must devote itself to in its vast south or, as one might be tempted to say, its "far-south." In a sense, military conquest is only the first step; it loses its rationale in proportion to the sinicization of the indigenous peoples. We know that, toward the Christian era, this venture had spread to Southern China and crossed over onto the plain of Tonkin. It should be remembered here that China first developed on the plains. The mountains, which could not be subjected to the regularity required by the rice fields, were outside ordinary methods or administration. They were the refuge of hermits, outlaws, and savages with whom one traded in order to receive the forest products which were essential to civilized living. The sinicizing advance passed by and hence included the moving frontiers, through interior marches that established the pattern of relations in the ever-shifting frontiers pushing toward the South. Moreover, it stopped at the bottleneck created by the narrowing of the Tonkin, between the sea and the Annamite Cordillera. The mountain passes were held by the formidable Chams, Hinduized Malay seafarers, who were nationalistic and believers in Vedism. Over the centuries an indecisive struggle for control followed.

It was here, in this scaled-down Tonkin area, that Vietnamese identity was slowly formed. When soldiers, administrators, and Chinese colonists installed themselves there, at the dawn of the Christian era, these scanty, shifting plains, fissured by rivers, and penetrated by sharp, serrated rocks from the massive mountains, had already had a long history of human contact that has been represented poorly to us. In fact, one of the most brilliant bronze techniques flourished there, as did the famous drums of Dong Son which are found throughout Southeast Asia. Rice cultivation, fortified towns, and maritime commerce are evidence that the Chinese had not come to the land of "savages," but rather, using their annals as testimony, to the land of "barbarians." Precisely because of these preconceptions of the Chinese chronicler, the cultural aspect is not very clear.

The Chinese had to subdue the local chiefs, who were probably descendants of clans which had ruled over the "tribes," and whose revolts were numerous. Matrimonial alliances and the politics of assimilation created, little by little, a layer of what Edward Schafer rightly calls *creoles*, Sino-barbarian métis by blood, but culturally more and more sinicized. The old common cultural bases of the ancient peoples of Indochina and Southern China, often Mon-Khmer or Thai-Kadai speaking, were becoming submerged. The barbarians, "naked and tattooed," chewers of betel, learned good manners and in turn imposed them on their rustic country serfs. It is from this creole elite that, later, the partisans of secession and independence broke away. Invested with traditional power through their local kinship ties, they felt they were as legitimately Chinese as the administrators who continued to urge the throne to control their distant provinces. The violent tremors and the weakness of the Tang culminated in the secession of the tenth century and independence.

From that time, and until the end of the nineteenth century, Vietnamese identity revolved around one axis: conformity to the Chinese model, standard of perfect humanity, and distrust, if not hostility, toward a China always suspected (not without good reason) of refusing to admit that such a perfect emulation of her civilization could remain outside of her direct control. Tribute—both symbolic and commercial—was sent by the Vietnamese court to a suzerain who was recognized as such only to the extent to which he graciously refrained from exercising any trace of hegemony. The earth has but one center and the sky but one axis: it is to this that the Vietnamese emperor paid homage, he who resided in the south, in the warm seas and pestilential climates which could make no claim to centrality. He therefore had to show his independence in relation to the Chinese, but the best way to do this must also be the most Chinese. In order to survive, the old Austroasiatic bases of beliefs, tastes, and gastronomical or aesthetic preferences had to be adapted and camouflaged. As in all of China, moreover, cultural resistance to Confucian imperiality continously reappears and imparts to local history the appearance of a balancing act, with its vigorous contrasting calls for the return to the orthodoxy of the royal and Mandarin milieu. The memory of non-Chinese origins is lost, but not the feeling of uniqueness, until the legitimate appearance of the Annamite court in the middle of the seventeenth century, when the Manchus overthrew the Ming dynasty.

The Vietnamese, among other peoples in Asia, thus appeared as a sort of nation, even before the period of nationalism. This is not to say, however, that what binds the edifice together is a nationalism ahead of its time; up to the colonial period the state ideology that kept it centered around a son of Heaven was Confucianism. It is Confucianism which held in check all the temptations to return to formulas of the feudal type, which assured economic integration by means of enormous public works, and which, by codifying and making uniform the rites, the language, the literary canon, and so on, achieved cultural homogenization. Here we see processes and directions, not stable established institutions.

Of all the states within the Sino-Confucian movement, Korea was perhaps the most unified linguistically and culturally. China still has not completed its development even today, and bulwarks of the "barbarian" world are still to be found. The preliminary results of a recent census in China show sixty million "minorities" out of a total of almost one billion people, with territories encompassing an enormous part of the present Chinese state. This number includes the pastoral and nomadic peoples of the north and west, who speak Turkish, Mongolian, and related languages. Since prehistoric times, this "empire of the steppes" has continously sent waves of people who have blended into the Chinese melting pot.

In the great South and Southwest, there was a different historical situation. Faced with the military-administrative advance of the Imperium, areas ruled by clan and tribal chiefs had to choose between surrendering and thus becoming acculturated, pulling back into the less easily controlled mountain and desert zones, or retreating, and migrating in stages toward ever more distant regions. On occasion, some groups have simultaneously adopted all three attitudes.

Some authors believe that the origin of the Burmese should be looked for at Kansu, in northwestern China. For reasons which are unknown, a group linguistically akin to those which were going to, or were in the process of, inhabiting Tibet, set out toward the south, changing its environment and material culture, and becoming, especially in the Thai milieu, horsemen and horsebreeders like the Thai. New upheavals put them on the move again, this time toward Ta-li, in the west, whence, they emerged around the year 1000 through a classic corridor into Upper Burma. It is here that they encountered

Buddhism, which would provide them both with the resources of the State and the means of resisting the pressure of the Chinese who followed close on their heels. Innumerable peoples were to migrate in this way, spasmodically, in order to escape integration into the Chinese imperium. Thus, a tenacious tradition brought to Tonkin, long before the Chinese armies, one of the basic groups in Vietnam. Originating in Fou-kien, opposite Formosa, these people bore the name of Yueh, or Viet, meaning approximately "those who have crossed over, who have deserted," doubtless referring to refugees from the expansion of the Tchou or Tsin state.

The largest migration was that of the Thai-speaking people. Coming perhaps from the center of China, today these Thai-speakers still form, under the name of Chuang, the largest "minority" of the southwestern corner—Kouang-si, Kouei-tchou, and Yunnan. But their migrations have gone on throughout the centuries. The Mon-Khmer element has doubtless been submerged in this Tonkinese prehistory, given the hypothesis that it is they who are responsible for the tonalization of the Vietnamese language. The history of Indochina is in large measure the history of the infiltration of the Thai and their rise to power when they too encountered Buddhism and its political philosophy, practiced by the Mon and the Khmers. Even today, but this time more within the framework of a search for "roots" inspired by modern nationalism, the Thais are fascinated by this district which points to the south of Yunnan, just to the north of Laos—the Sip Song Panna, where an easily recognizable Thai is spoken but where the old culture has had less of a hold than in Thailand or Laos, having been reshaped by Buddhism and Western influences. Needless to say, the Chinese authorities have attempted in numerous ways to exploit this recent nostalgia for "roots."

Clearly, no geographical barrier has been able to stop the expansion of the Chinese state in her mission, as she understands it, to civilize and humanize, except the vast stretches of desert in which ecology imposes an essentially nomadic way of life. It was only in the seventeenth century that Formosa became completely integrated into the Chinese world. Today, before our eyes, the process continues—on the one hand by colonizing the Mongolian steppes, Dzungours, Ouighours, and the vast mountain spurs of Tibet, and on the other by efforts to sinicize the nomadic Muslim minorities of the north, the Lamaist Tibetans, and other minorities of the southwest. The so-called respect for the customs of national minorities, for their language in particular, is on a par with a political, economic, and administrative integration which transforms culture into folklore, and local autonomy into an instrument for the penetration by the central State.

It is hard to explain why these *man* peoples, "barbarians," throughout every stage of their history, have refused, at least some of them, integration into the State. Perhaps the essence of this phenomenon can be grasped if one examines the most recent of these refractory peoples, the Hmong (often called Méo). More than any other group in the region, the Hmong, without a doubt, foster the feeling of the perfection of their own humanity, to which one belongs both by ancestry and by adherence to their customs and unique culture. This gives rise to an easily offended, quasi-absolute traditionalism, and a knowledge of the "other" Hmong that decreases rapidly with distance. Itinerant agriculturalists, caught up in the flow of a centuries-old migration, the Hmong live in very small dispersed units, on the crests of mountains, the sides and the valleys having been populated through much older migrations. An anarchic society, uncontrolled and uncontrollable, it is limited in the scope of its sense of self and little troubled by its past; knowing no territorial bounds, it has at best established only an armed peace with its neighbors. By their sense of themselves, the Hmong remind us irresistibly of those American Indians who have successfully resisted extermination by sheer moral force, that is to say, by the unshakeable conviction, in the face of the most overwhelming circumstances, of their identity and of its worth.

With considerable variation in the content of their cultural identities, one finds the same pattern among nearly all the peoples of the region—Yao, Karen, Akha, Kachin, Lolo, Yi, etc., not counting the small groups of Mon-Khmer speakers, isolated areas bearing testimony to a long-ago era when Austroasiatic cultures had dominated the region. In reality, it is primarily the linguist or ethnologist who puts these scattered fragments of people together into their imagined original forms. The members of these dispersed entities manifest no desire to re-form themselves, or to form larger units, even in the midst of the worst political upheavals. During the Indochinese War the Hmong found themselves serving on both sides, *nulla vergogna*. If one speaks, therefore, of the Hmong "people" in this context, it can only be a purely theoretical sense: the reality—the extent of their cultural and political identity—is the village and those neighboring it (sometimes quite far away) which are connected with it through kinship and exchange. Consciousness of identity stops there, a few days' walk away.

These groups which refuse to become integrated also reject any possibility of integrating and assimilating a foreign Other, although obviously their cultural endogamy cannot be absolute. I remember having read, in an old *Burmese Gazetteer*, the somewhat astonished comments of a British administrator in northwest Burma; he had interrogated a group of "Kachin," and the latter had explained that they came from another valley where they had lived for twenty years *in the proximity* of a Kachin village, that they had taken on its language and customs, but that earlier they had lived elsewhere and they were *not* Kachin. But nobody could tell him what their prior "identity" had been, and the eldest among them seemed not to remember the language they had previosly spoken. This group, apparently consisting of a few related families, had thus "borrowed" by osmosis an identity, unbeknownst perhaps even to the involuntary lenders. They held on to it until the group migrated perhaps a valley or two further on, when a new opportunity might give rise to still another change in identity.

This type of situation must be quite common. History certainly shows how languages maintain themselves in the face of all opposition, but also the disconcerting ease with which some groups, sometimes very numerous, have at the mercy of circumstance changed their language and donned a new culture, as if from a second-hand clothing store. That the fragmented Levant—Hellenized, Byzantinized, Christianized, Persianized—became so quickly Arabized with the advent of Islam, is truly astonishing. But that at the same time there continued to exist up to our century so many minorities, all more or less schismatic, and as far away as villages in Syria and Iraq, where Aramaic is still spoken, is hardly less surprising. Thus, from one locality to another, one passes from the malleable to the infrangible. Is there any historical sociology that can account for the existence of this handful of villages in the middle of Thailand, where, as the French linguist Diffloth has recently shown, the old Mon language survives though surrounded on all sides by the Thai tongue for a thousand years? The people are evidently unaware that they speak Mon: they have been cut off by the centuries and by hundreds of kilometers from those populations in Burma who are the heirs of the language and of the brilliant Mon past.

But let us return to our Annamite (Annamese) cordillera. While the creole elite of the Chinese colony of Tonkin succeeded in gaining its emancipation, it had no choice to but take the problem of relations with the *man*, those who are called, in Vietnamese, the *moï*, the savages.

The mountain masses of the west and northwest were held by tribes that historians find it difficult to identify. These tribes even succeeded at one point in banding together into a powerful state, the *Nang Chao*, which defied China. In the south, the Chams kept watch. With the mountain people, a pact was necessary: the Vietnamese system could only function on the plain, where the large rice-producing market towns could be equipped with a complex and costly hydraulic system. The march toward the south, begun two thousand years before in the Hoang Ho basin, had to be followed by the conquest of the plains. These, on the coast of what was to become the future center of

Vietnam, were pitted with rocky ridges plunging down into the Sea of China.

War and military colonization, Roman style, with the *don điên*, villages of veterans demobilized on the spot, were to be the means for a step-by-step advance, which for three or four centuries went quite slowly. At this stage, it was total war: the defeated population was dispersed, even space was reorganized: the colonists went so far as to redesign the local hydraulic system. But in the fifteenth century, with the definitive fall of the last Cham kingdom, the political situation changed. While nothing remained of the political and religious institutions of the Cham kingdom, their monuments are still there (occasionally to be reinterpreted by Vietnamese popular religion) and the people are also there.

One part of the Cham people was exiled in Cambodia (where they had fought fiercely); the other part, however, remained in place, even conserving the Islamic religion which had for so long permeated the popular classes of this Hinduized state. As in southern China, the wave which brought the state apparatus and its civilizing process turned the rest of the Hindu-Malaysian-Javanese world toward thalassocratic tendencies and isolated it. The Chams were locked in and fell into oblivion: they reestablished a chiefdom, hid their treasures and the sacred objects of their royal cult with their mountain allies, and fell back on a religion that they understood poorly, its significance eluding them.

Much like those Japanese Christians who, after the proscription, continued to perform the rituals and pronounce the magic words in secret, in the process distorting a Latin that they did not understand, so the Chams, in the era of their defeat, mimicked an Islamic tongue whose meaning was quickly obscured as maritime contact ended. Thus they lost the meaning of this "Latin," which for them was Arabic. And when, later, contact was reestablished, primarily with the Muslim world, part of the Chams refused to undergo a second Islamization, to return to an orthodoxy which seemed to them to be a renunciation of the religion of their fathers.

While they lost contact with the exterior, and even with their brothers in Cambodia, the Chams did not lose touch with their mountain allies. The latter have often used Cham, both as the language of culture and in ordinary speech right up to the beginning of this century. The past was no longer supressed, and the re-Islamization favored endogamy. Arrogantly neglected by a Vietnamese society totally preoccupied with clearing and occupying the vast horizons of the great South, the Chams, bitter and impotent, fell back on themselves. They remained mistrustful of a modern nationalism, because it did not seem possible that they could fight a Vietnam armed by the state.

After conquering and assimilating the territory in which the isolated pockets of Cham lived, the Vietnamese embarked on a new world, the vast plains, tropical and swampy, of the Mekong delta. There, for as far as the eye could see, was more flat land than in all of Vietnam at the time. Standing at the edge of the Mekong delta in the seventeenth century, the Vietnamese undoubtedly felt much the same distress as some of their remote ancestors had when the Son of Heaven ordered them to set out for the South, to serve there as administrators and soldiers. The South has a torrid, pestilential climate; nature there is savage, defying domination and regulation. It is a place full of dangerous animals, beasts, and poisonous plants; of naked and unpredictable savages, lewd women and sorceresses; and of unknown demons. The complaints of some of the Tang mandarins oscillate between those of Ovid exiled at Tomes, writing the *Tragedies*, and those of Bardamu, employee of the Pordurière Company of Little Togo (see Schafer).

This humid, wild brush was barely developed. Under the loose suzerainty of a Cambodian monarchy in complete decline, the country was dotted with Khmer hamlets; in the north it was overrun by the formidable hunters known as the Stieng. The memory of a time some fifteen centuries before, when these infertile areas had harbored great trading ports—agencies of exchange between an expanding India and China—had totally disappeared. They were sunk in mud, as at Oc-Eo, where archaeologists later would rediscover the remnants of a large emporium containing Hindu and Buddhist statues, even pieces of Roman money. "Founan" was perhaps an Indian agency when the Han had arrived in Tonkin.

But here too, soon enough, at this Cochin-Chinese point, a creole world was being born. It is here, in an era of which we know almost nothing, that we have to look for the mystery of the formation of the Khmer people. For everything seems Indian—the statuary, the first inscriptions, even the names of kings and places transmitted to us through the Chinese Annals. Their reconstruction from Chinese phonetics (itself reconstructed for the era) unquestionably has a Sanskrit aspect. There is not even categorical evidence that the inhabitants of Founan spoke Khmer (although Founan has been traced to *bhnam*, modern Khmer *phnom*, mountain), but their political ancestry clearly is from Founan, arriving at Angkor via Chenla. By successive climbs toward the interior, they arrived in historical Cambodia, the center of a vast empire whose visible institutions owed almost everything to India. This borrowing by a ruling elite of a system so alien to local customs (no matter what the proportion was between notable immigrants and local chieftains at its center) inevitably created problems in acculturation for the mass of producers, who were not only agriculturalists, but also hunters and gatherers. Undeniably the birth and growth of Cambodia was a "civilizing" phenomenon in the sense that it integrated, transformed, and standardized the various groups. But this influence was neither as profound nor as lasting—all things considered—as that of the Chinese. Perhaps the reason for this will become clearer if we examine the history of India itself.

The unifying power of Indian civilization seems to lose its force in proportion to its descent downward on the social pyramid that it itself has set up. Purity, relationship to the divine, are a function of the individual's place on this pyramid. It is held together, one might say, by the top; it is the summit which guarantees a base that, by itself, has almost no value. And under the base itself, inaccessible to the grace given off by the Brahman high priest a kind of inhumanity with a human visage swarms—untouchables, outcasts, aboriginal tribes, etc., which Karmic law drags out from the lowest spheres of the reincarnation cycle, an indescribable mixture of human and animal nature. At the same time that Hinduism unified and brought together, it divided society definitively by erecting impassable barriers between castes. It is this Hinduism of warrior-kings and priests, of *kshatriya* and Brahmans, that was exported to Indochina and the Indian Archipelago, apparently affecting only the ruling classes. Only in Bali, where Hinduism has held its own, do we find vestiges of a caste system. They are not detectable elsewhere, probably because the system never really worked, except for the priests and kings.

The documents reveal a steady expansion of the Khmer empire up to its heyday in the twelfth and thirteenth centuries, but they say little about the social reality thus encompassed. This was also the time when Theravada Buddhism was substituted for Hinduism, and today one can grasp the Khmer existence only within the Buddhist setting: the two are co-existent and indivisible. In this part of the world as in India itself, Buddhism came after Hinduism, which had provided the ideological underpinning for the first large states. Buddhism even extended the goals of the State because, in providing for the redemption of humanity *in toto*, it transcended inequality and the caste system. In this, it was revolutionary. The Buddhist king, replacing birth by the virtue of *dharma*, had more inclination toward universal sovereignty than the *kshatriya* king, *primus inter pares*. But whereas in India Hinduism had never stopped being the religion of the majority, so that it succeeded in diminishing and extinguishing Buddhism, in Southeast Asia Buddhism gave much greater vigor to the political structures it inherited, and thus assured their lasting permanence up to our own era. Only the Buddhists knew how to unite against the Chinese and halt their descent.

Khmer identity was thus carried on a wave of Buddhist thoughts and images which projected it toward the universal, coming together with the flow of the world and the transmigration of matter itself. However, the true state of things, the reality of power, the affairs of the kingdom—in brief the ordinary human condition—is always far from complete, from the realization of *dharma*, from the definitive accomplishment of the cardinal virtues. This distance, this lack of achievement, even when infinitesimal, represents fracture, a huge void. This failure in the political realm can become a battlefield and incite those forces which seek to replace one legitimacy by another. Religion relates to politics as a tourniquet, putting into power only that which has been tested, never taking power for itself, and bringing it not support so much as a request for its own protection.

It will be readily understood that the adherence of the faithful could not be converted without risk into loyalty toward a sovereign; candidates to the throne could be so numerous that more than one Buddhist king had to resort to massacring part of his own family in order to reign peacefully.

The great fission in these political systems is reflected in the way in which the subjects offer their membership and loyalty: to the kingdom rather than to the king. This abstraction does have a concrete form: the territory in which one lives and moves about, marked out by pagodas, carved out along the borders of the forest—another world. The Khmer use one and the same word to designate both the kingdom and the territory (a part of the province): *srok*. Nothing precisely defines the *srok*: it is neither a network of villages, nor an ecclesiastical unity, and barely an administrative unit; it is above all a range of multiple activities that one can cover by foot. But the framework is not very strong. Houses are often dispersed, religious activities are voluntary, the administration is present only to levy taxes, the king is far away. The society provides hardly any institution which might serve as intermediary between the immediate family and the kingdom, one which would enable the individual to hold on to and expand his identity.

Over the cultivated territory that it recognizes is superimposed another which is at least as important: it is the supernatural, which overlaps into the natural and determines it. The Buddhist framework can remain; it is flexible enough to adjust to an enormous population of diverse ghosts and spirits whose requirements, although matter-of-fact, are no less determining. This invisible world has been studied, with more or less analytical success, by E. Porée-Maspero among the Khmers, S. J. Tambiah among the Thai of the North, by Melford Spiro among the Burmese, etc. Clearly, these are neolithic religions, fresh and lively before the birth, almost simultaneous, of Confucius and Gautama. The Shamanist component, in particular, is very revealing of a great prehistoric pan-Asiatic cultural base, which rises up from underneath the "historical" elaborations at the first opportunity. These components, I believe, are the essential ones in the identities of these groups. No doubt some ambitious anthropologists could show, in the manner of the *Mythologies* of Lévi-Strauss, that the ancient and preliterate cultures of the Asiatic world (and the Oceanic and the Amerindian), still alive and perceptible, are the shreds and fragmentary variations of a whole which no people has ever held in its totality, but out of which each has selected and adapted some elements which were compatible with it.

The very name Indochina, which the Europeans invented, describes the setting: the place where the civilizations of India and China met face to face and joined together. But there is a contrast to which very little attention has been paid. For two thousand years, China has considered that she had outposts in the area, has kept abreast of what happens there, and does not hesitate to intervene directly—the last time was in 1979. India, on the other hand, appears never to have been interested in this region. The archives are silent: one finds in them no trace of any desire on India's part to intervene. Indians learned of the existence of an Indian cultural influence in Southeast Asia only at the beginning of the twentieth century, when European scholars discovered, identified, and analyzed monuments, inscriptions, and institutional evidence. They found undeniable Indian influence, going back at least to the early Christian era. These discoveries played a role in the birth of nationalism in India; a Greater India Society was soon started to glorify the historical role of overseas India. Despite certain excesses, many Indian scholars contributed much that was valuable to Indochinese studies. Today, as we know, Indochina occupies a privileged place in the foreign affairs of independent India.

Everything happened, it would seem, as if India had never been aware of what she did overseas, and I believe this is how it must be understood. Merchants, missionaries, and adventurers trafficked in this area, undoubtedly for their own profit. When later the maritime routes were confiscated by the Moslems, then by the Portuguese, the earlier memory was erased—all the more since Hinduized Southeast Asia became either Buddhist or Muslim. But there is another reason: it is that this Indian influence, particularly spectacular since it produced such sublime masterworks as Angkor and Borubudur, as well as the music, dances, and shadow plays of this entire region, seems to me to be superficial. It in no way *produced* Indians, in the sense in which China had *produced* Chinese—and by the millions.

There is one exceptionally clear border: the line of mountain tops which separates the basins of the Brahmapoutre from those of the Chadwin, and which serves, *grosso modo*, as a frontier between India (Assam, Manipur) and Burma. There one finds the Naga, the Mizo, the Kachin, and other indomitable peoples. To the west is Assam, Bengal, India. In the east is a world without a name, and with a radius of about two thousand kilometers from east to west and five or six thousand from north to south, extending from the Mongolian steppes to the outskirts of Saigon, its sides furrowed by the rice-growing, state-controlled plains. This is the world of those people—between thirty and forty million—who have rejected both India and China, turning down their writings and their great religions, and who have kept their shamans, their digging sticks, and their slash-and-burn agriculture. They are not a people; they do not even form tribes. I do not know what to call them since they have no collective identity. Sometimes they are related culturally, sometimes linguistically. I would like to use the term *neolithic*, setting aside the question of their tools, in order to indicate that they belong to one of the longest epochs in the life of modern man (*sapiens sapiens*). This they show by their *esprit*. They have sustained for two or three thousand years the pressures and assaults of a modernity—that is, of societies that have overstepped the human scale, and which impose themselves on the individual like a *fatum* hypostasized by kings and other bearers of charisma—of which we are only the last, blind avatars.

To recapitulate our contemporary data on the Indochinese checkerboard: four population bodies, four cultural traditions which seem to oppose and fight one another. First, the Vietnamese stream, which has recently reached the southern tip of the peninsula. The physical contribution of China is far from negligible here, but essentially it developed through mutation *in loco*. Next, the Thai stream, which flowed into the Menam and Mekong valleys and ended by creating Buddhist principalities there. As George Condominas says, they developed, by a process of interlocking, into powerful States, the principal one being Thailand. Then the Khmer or Mon-Khmer world, the oldest population of the region, and indeed the most important substratum underlying the Vietnamese and Thai populations. Over a vast zone, it has held on and is now coming into view. The Khmer empire was brought together and homogenized, one part of it quite profoundly, as the E hemoglobin distribution map shows. Even within its borders the state was not always in a position to "khmerize" its cousins of the forests and the mountains. One of the surest and most often used means of "civilizing" the "savages" (*phnong*) was by launching military raids to capture slaves, or deporting populations to the plains. Even in the heart of the Khmer world there is thus also played out this dialectic of refusal to recognize the State, the maintenance of a "neolithic" identity. (It will be easier to understand what I mean by neolithic if I say that I include the Kuy of Cambodia, who inhabit [or inhabited] the forests of the northeast, and who were traditionally the most skilful blacksmiths in this region. Several of these refractory groups, moreover, are noted metallurgists.) Finally, the fourth group—all those peoples without a state, sometimes referred to as "montagnards," who are present in all the States of the region, but who are poorly or not at all integrated into them. They belong to various linguistic groups (to name the most numerous, Mon-Khmer or Austroasiatic, Malayo-Polynesians or Austronesian, Thai, Tibetan-Burmese, and Vietnamese itself—if one thinks of those ancient Vietnamese who in some way seceded several centuries ago and who are known by the name Muong [see J. Cuisinier]). Physically, they represent only a small fraction of the total population, but geographically they cover and exploit enormous areas, several of which have become strategically important.

For the above reasons, the sense of identity which the subjects in these States have of themselves is, in part, determined by relations with their neolithic periphery. Vietnamese, Thais, and Khmers absolutely refuse to see their own origins there. It is perceived as an insurmountable gulf. Those who have received "civilization," when they are not mistrustful, set themselves up as protectors and project onto the Other "savage" the kind of relations that they themselves have with their masters, the owners of the State. The Thai, in the north, make an effort to establish relations of dependence and of patronage with the *tribespeople*, sending Buddhist priests to the villages to spread the good word. The Khmers, who have forgotten that most of their ancestors were slaves to kings or noblemen, have not forgotten servile passivity in the face of the more powerful. And, in the Pol Pot reversal, this is what they expected from the *khmer-loeu*, when the "Khmers from on high" became the masters, in possession of the Party's truth by the very fact of their being "savages." The best disposed among the Vietnamese always think that they must reform the minorities for their own good, teach them the flooded-rice system and the alphabet, and believe that it is up to them to decide what is important to conserve in the tradition, or, because a particular custom would run counter to "progress," eliminate.

In the past, certainly relations were quite well-regulated, implying considerable economic exchange. The forest provided goods of great value to the economy of the plains, especially for the luxury of the Court. The latter wanted, moreover, the "tribute" which the montagnards paid to its grandeur. The colonial period upset this always precarious equilibrium by furnishing to those in the lowlands the means, medical among others, to penetrate and install themselves in the highlands. Apparently, the plains people who followed in the wake of the first European colonizers were not the cream of the crop. An era of violence, of plunder, exploitation, and of deportations and mass murders followed, in which thousands of villages disappeared. The professional denouncers of "genocide" were conspicuous by their absence.

Here is a quotation from Paul Mus:

To become aware of the contact between two cultures, it is good to leave them both; and it is the reaction of a *moi*, a man of the forest in the hinterlands of Phan-Thiêt, which has best clarified for me this matter of Franco-Vietnamese relations. The Churu, who was at ease with me because we spoke together in his Cham dialect, told me of his admiration for the material power of the Vietnamese, for their scientific and industrial superiority; he tossed around this idea, apparently lacking words of this kind. He paid numerous compliments to the Vietnamese for their photography, for the automobile, for the railroad, and for the telegraph. I felt I could suggest that the French had something to do with all this, but my rough-hewn comrade roared with laughter: "The French have brought the automobile, photography! When you have operated your camera, who has the secret for bringing out a picture? Aren't you going to find the Vietnamese in Phan-Thiêt? And your autos, is it you or your chauffeurs who know how to drive and repair them?" Mus then asked him just what he thought the French had done here and he replied: "You are very great, very strong, nobody knows how to become as angry as you, so the Vietnamese take you for soldiers and police agents. They are shrewd customers, they know everything and they help themelves to everything." (Mus and Mac Alister, 86–87)

WHEN ARE YOU LEAVING?

Around 1900, a missionary who traveled in western Cochin China met up with a local Vietnamese leader on a sampan (flat-bottomed boat) which took them both away. After some time had passed, the Vietnamese leader posed a question, which he seemed to have spent a good deal of reflection upon: "I know that I can trust you and that you won't repeat to the administrator what I am going to ask you, but I beg you, tell me candidly how long the French are going to remain in the country?" And as the Father was astonished, the Vietnamese leader went on: "You don't want to say it, but you must know it. Come, is it in one or two years that the French are going away?" ("La Revue Indochinese," 1902, in Mus and Mac Alister 1972, 122).

This story reveals what thousands of other anecdotes have illustrated in every part of the world; that the behavior of the Europeans was so strange, so incomprehensible to the eyes of the indigenous peoples, that the logical explanation must be concealed. There had to be a secret that explained the colonial presence. The appearance of the Europeans on the coast touched off an ethical and philosophical debate different in each locale. Mus, for example, noted that the Vietnamese, located as they were south of the Center, experienced a sort of discreet satisfaction at seeing the appearance of a power to the West; it lightened the weight of the Center on them. One also recalls the truly ethnographic descriptions of the *Black Ship Scroll*, the report embellished with encyclopedic illustrations, which was written down by Japanese mandarins who were sent by the Court to observe Perry's fleet during his first journey into Japanese waters.

This incomprehension, at the moment of contact, is itself readily understandable. The seamen displayed only a microcosm, partial and distorted, of their societies of origin. But above all, contrary to the idea prevalent today, the Europeans did not seem very dangerous at first. By the time the local populations knew more about the strength of the Europeans and the effects of their brutality, they could think of little more than to make use of the Europeans in local conflicts. Taking on the functions of intermediaries and advisors, the mercenaries, tradesmen, Westerners of all kinds—rough Portuguese soldiers, Spanish priests, French cadets, Dutch merchants—who plowed through Asia from the sixteenth to the eighteenth centuries played only a minor role. The Churu's reflections in the conversation with Paul Mus would have been entirely relevant at the very end of the eighteenth century, when Nguyên Anh used the services of the bishop of Adran, Pigneau de Béhaine—his boats, artillerymen, and the soldiers of fortune recruited in France *ad majorem Dei gloriam*—in order to overthrow the Tay Son "usurpers" and reunify Vietnam under a new crown. But this era, when the local potentates could utilize European power and knowledge to their advantage, often also at their own risk and peril, was destined to end with the beginning of the massive industralization, first of England, then of Western Europe.

In a Confucian world, in which mercantilism certainly had a place, but a subordinate one, European expansion was clearly menacing. First Japan, then China, Korea, and Vietnam, would shut themselves off from the West. That these barbarians were agents of disorder and of moral decadence was hardly surprising, since their place of origin was eccentric (off-center). To them, the animality of the human soul was proportional to the distance between place of birth and the Middle of the World, which is, opportunely, occupied by the son and representative of Heaven, the paragon of actualized humanity. They had nothing to lose by rejecting the invasion of this corruptive disorder.

Nguyên Ahn, who became the Emperor Jia-Long, had clearly

perceived the risks. He demanded that his successors do without the aid of foreigners on whom he himself had greatly depended. The new dynasty would strengthen itself through an orthodoxy renewed at the classical Chinese fount. Faced with these rising perils, which were strongly evident even in the forbidden towns of Huê, of Yeda, and Peking, it was necessary to have recourse to the supreme weapon of virtue, of harmony with the decrees from Heaven and the will of the ancestors. The subversive elements left behind after the missionaries were finally expelled were like abscesses in which the virus of treason pullulated, and they must rid the country of them.

The concern with moral perfection did not interfere with concern for material efficacy. The image of an Orient snugly wrapped up in itself, ignoring the movement of the world, is of course only one of the wretched myths justifying all the piracy committed there. There were anguished calls for reform among the modernist mandarins, who were also touched by the philosophy of the Enlightenment (which they obtained in Chinese translation). Political struggles based on different viewpoints toward reform have now been well documented. Furthermore, internal crises, like that of the Tai Ping, were pointing to the urgency of the need for reform.

What was also lacking was a thorough analysis of the Western "phenomenon." Asia did send information missions to Europe and America in the nineteenth century, but the information circulated slowly and not very widely. One recalls, for example, the decision of the Court of Huê to purchase at Manila one of those steamships whose maneuverability had posed insurmountable problems to the Vietnamese fleet during the war. This precious acquisition was entrusted to the most competent metallurgists in the country, artisans whose talent still compels the admiration of modern technologists. Piece by piece, they copied the components of the machine, but, evidently because they lacked the theoretical knowledge, they could never make their imitation work. Fifty years later, the French were to rediscover it, quite rusted, at the arsenal of Huê.

This anecdote can be seen as a kind of exemplary tale: Asia (let us say the Third World) had understood that there was a secret to the power suddenly manifested by Europe, a secret she could understand only after having been destroyed by it.

The colonizers were not squeamish: if there were obstacles, they had to be removed; if there was opposition, it had to be erased. This esoteric trick had to be imposed on the local culture by kicks in the rear. The moment soon came when what was essential seemed, in the eyes of a part of the traditional elite, to be menaced with complete destruction. This was manifested in both Cambodia and Annam, in 1885–86, by legitimist revolts which marked the last convulsive movements of an agonizing political body. Whereas in Burma the subjects of Her Gracious Britannic Majesty abolished the monarchy with a stroke of the pen, the French republicans resurrected the Vietnamese, Khmer, and Laotian thrones in the hope of capturing the loyalties attached to them. The logic was not totally absurd. At three or four generations' distance, one can well see why ex-king Sihanouk was obliged to hold back for so long before he could enter the political arena. Yet there wasn't a politician in Saigon before 1975 who had not thought, from time to time, of resorting to Bao Dai, one of whose rare glories would have been to agree at the moment chosen by destiny, to become the special advisor, Vinh Thuy, of the republic of Ho Chi Minh.

The Vietnamese led an orphanlike existence after the revolt of the literati failed, just before the triumph of Paul Doumer at the turn of the century. A nagging doubt could no longer be avoided. Why was virtue defeated? What model should be followed? The Chinese republican movement? The *meiji* reform? Was it necessary to try to master Western knowledge? So many questions, and even more paths to explore.

We know the rest: the almost simultaneous emergence, in the period following World War I, of one nationalist current that can be called bourgeois, and of another that was nationalist-communist. I use this unusual name in order to show that the history of the Indochinese Communist movement, strongly orthodox in other respects, has always centered around the national question. The chronology of events since 1930 is well known (see Marr, Rousset, Turner, and many others), but what is important to grasp here is the veritable intellectual mutation which made them possible. The concept of the nation, with all the passions it entailed, underwent a radical transformation. It is not heir to but rather the abandoning of the concept elaborated in Europe in the nineteenth century. It is the reinterpretation of a past over and done with, with which continuity had been broken, more through the failure of the resistance to colonization itself than by the colonial intrusion per se. And if we refer back to the superb and prophetic manifesto of Go-Cong, which proclaimed a fight to the death, we see that our reading of it can easily explain this failure. Not only did resistance stop at a given moment, the people letting go of the sticks which should have driven the invader out, but the colonization profoundly altered both the landscape and, especially in the South, the society. This "liberation of productive forces" broke the traditional model, rendered it inoperative, and, selectively idealized, set it in the past. This rupture—occurring during the first three decades of the present century, which, we might note, were also the decades in which the apotheosis of the colonial system was marching with great strides toward its Tarpeian Rock—

broke the image that the Vietnamese had developed of themselves. And while their image had to be rebuilt out of this debris, it would be done according to a new, imported logic, that of the modern nation. Like any "Poland," it would never stop subjecting itself to foreign invasions in order to free itself of them, but would constantly submit to others and reject them anew, as if a trans-historical and immutable identity, "Vietnamity," had remained hermetically sealed within itself, under the sign of the phoenix, always to return to its true being. Modern nationalisms are adept at creating these immutable histories. At the same time that this mythical core arose, becoming the common ground for intense trajectories, the remainder of the ancient tableau had to be repressed. Under these conditions, is it surprising to see among these hardy peasants-turned-revolutionaries—fighting cadres, technicians of agitation—the resurfacing of this Confucian conservatism which permeated village culture and which, after being ignored and repressed, has reemerged in the spirit and methods of the Communist cadres of today?

It is impossible here, in a few pages, to describe Vietnamese culture in a way that would allow us to discern the identity which is at its core. Once again, we return to the writings of Paul Mus, to the thesis of Dinh, and, especially, to the still unedited text of Neil Jamieson. The latter provides an interpretive framework, beginning with a subtle discussion of the concepts of *yang* and of *yin* which is extremely stimulating. He also very accurately pinpoints the cultural break, at least where it can most easily be seen, that is, in the literary movement.

On March 10, 1932, there appeared in Saigon, in a weekly publication, a poem entitled *Tinh Giâ* ("Ancient Love"), written by a most esteemed poet and essayist, Phan Khoi. Breaking with the thousand-year-old forms of classical poetry, he created a new mode of expression in which new sentiments could be expressed. To be brief, we can label this individualism. This point of departure for a "new poetry" in Vietnamese marks the tilting toward a new world, one which had asserted itself for a long time, but which only now, after a half-century of tension, succeeded in bringing to light the ancient principle of identity.

The movement gathered strength, several months later, with the transformation of a review, *Phong hoa* (Customs), under the direction of Nguyên Tuong Tam. Here is Jamieson's description: "From the first issue published under his direction, Tam launched a powerful attack against the very fundamentals of Vietnamese society. . . . Tam tried to demonstrate that the traditional culture was so narrow, rigid, and outmoded that it had to be abandoned. He believed that national independence, prosperity, and the happiness of the individual had been rendered impossible by an overly sentimental attachment to outdated traditional values. According to him, this cultural conservatism was the greatest weakness of the Vietnamese people. He wanted to use his review to destroy the lure of the tradition and to create a new system of values, a new literature, a new society, a new way of life" (Jamieson 1981, 13).

"Each side," wrote Tam in October 1932, "has its good and bad aspects, and one still doesn't know where morality is to be found. But when we take the ancient civilization and put it into practice before our very eyes, the result does not satisfy us. We can only continue to pin our hopes on Western civilization. Where it is leading us, we don't know. But it is our destiny to journey into the unknown, to continue to change and to progress" (cited in Jamieson 1981, 14). To the indignant protests which everywhere arose, Tam responded abruptly: "The conservatives don't understand that one must destroy if one wishes to build. And these people, even if they had lived in the great era of the Yao or the Sung, would still have ended up lamenting the 'decline of customs,' and wanting to return to an even earlier era, to the time of caves and of raw meat" (ibid., 15).

Phenomena of this kind, with every conceivable variation and difference in point of view, occurred throughout all the states of this region. We are not speaking here of nationalisms which affected regions such as Malaysia or Indonesia where there had never been any political unity before colonization. The two most interesting cases to observe are Thailand, which was able to protect itself from direct colonization, but not from the impact of the West; and Cambodia, where the development was both slower and later.

Rupture was inevitable. The "anciens regimes"—to use the conventional term—are not what we call today, also by convention, *nations*. The term itself underwent a change, recovering its Latin and medieval origins (sometimes "tribe," sometimes "civilization"; of the *nations* which amalgamated the students of the Sorbonne in the Middle Ages were France, Normandy, Picardy, and Germany). This rupture between the Old (regime) and the New (the "national" order born in the West) can take on the most varied forms. In Thailand, as in Japan though in a different way, the rupture was progressive, and developed principally at the instigation of a part of the small ruling class. The name most often associated with the emergence of the modern state is King Chulangkorn (1868–1910), because of the reforms which he introduced in the role and functioning of the administration. Ground had been broken by his predecessor, King Mongkut, who had initiated an important religious reform. The social ramifications of these alterations in the role of the state were to make themselves felt in

1932—an interesting coincidence—with a coup d'état which relegated the monarchy, henceforth constitutional, to the background, a symbolic token of the political administration. This "revolution" marked the arrival on the scene of the power of a new generation—a new social class, with a new political and cultural attitude. For the first time the sounds of a new language were heard, that, precisely, of national identity; for the first time a new principle outstripped in the hierarchy of values the two cardinal orders of monarchy and Buddhism. This is the concept of the Nation, to which henceforth these two principles were to *be subordinated*. The rupture had occurred. The content of this new idea which was being promulgated could remain vague and diffuse, and it was still limited to restricted circles. The significant fact was that the political goal had changed. It was no longer a question of striving for universal sovereignty, of the realization of *dharma*. The monarchy, its rituals and its charisma, were now to constitute one instrument, among others, for proceeding toward the new goal of national integration.

The process was still underway. National integration worked poorly in the north, where it was up against the montagnards, or in the south, where accommodation with Islam remained rather ticklish. But it operated well in the Khmer-speaking provinces of the southeast where assimilation to Thai identity had recently begun and was progressing very rapidly. There, as elsewhere, national feeling, linked in its origin to the interests of a small commercial and administrative class that succeeded in bridling the aristocracy, spread out from the top toward the bottom of society, through indoctrination and recruitment among the younger age groups, who had nothing to gain from the older totalitarianisms. During these same years there emerged in Burma the Thakin group, which forged a comprehensive conception of the Burmese nation, a reform movement and a struggle for national independence, as well as a socialist ideology which incorporated the essential elements of Buddhist thought. It was certainly the most ambitious of the movements of synthesis and renewal of the traditional framework—perhaps made easier by the abolition of the monarchy in the nineteenth century—but the fascinating originality of the Burmese experience remains little known on the outside. Perhaps better adapted than others to its local context, it did not spread beyond its natural environment.

The thirties also brought nationalist seething to Cambodia, centering around Son Ngoc Thanh, his journal "Our City," and the Buddhist priests and other satellites of the Buddhist Institute of Phnom Penh. But, essentially because of Cambodia's peripheral character in relation to the great economic channels and hence with the central currents of colonization, things moved more slowly in Cambodia and for a long time nationalism remained weak, fragmented, and poorly articulated. Only very slowly did nationalism penetrate an urban elite—in large part Chinese and Vietnamese—who could not make themselves understood in the rural countryside until the decade of the sixties, with the development of public education. (Elsewhere I have touched on the problem of the evolution of certain concepts, in particular that of revolution, where the environment is not very favorable to their growth.)

Briefly, one can say that what occurred in 1932 in Siam and Cochin China happened again in the old *srok khmer* in 1970. The overthrow of the monarchy was accompanied by an explosion of speeches— republican, Jacobin, nationalistic, and xenophobic—which tried to project the image of a strong and united state, the victorious expression of a nation rudely awakened, standing upright and facing the future. It was a comedy which was played out in Phnom Penh by the bourgeoisie, the minor civil servants, and school youths; it caught on very well in the cities, but fell flat throughout most of the countryside. The peasantry, hardly troubled by a modernization which as yet had scarcely touched them, chose to follow Sihanouk, whose rhetoric was at least as nationalistic, but was, in essence, royalist. Being counts more than saying in a village world where it is being that gives authority to saying and where saying is not the cause of being, as it is in modern politics.

We know that the huts where such simple calculations were weighed were soon to ignite under the explosion of iron and of fire, launched from the sky via that extraordinary modernizing agent, the USAF (United States Air Force). We also know that the struggle ended for lack of combatants, and that a handful of ultranationalist ideologues, extreme Stalinists, became the masters of the countryside. They were bearers of an interesting ambiguity: they proclaimed that the fixed aim for all was the (re)construction of the nation, that it was necessary to ensure its grandeur and its power. At the same time, in practice they believed that they need not abide by the forms which were customary in their ordinary political and social life, since they were treating the entire population as if, in varying degrees, it was part of the Communist Party. The population must comply with its ethics and its demands and be punished in case of failure, as if it had already joined the Communist avant-garde. The nation was, therefore, no longer the "classical" nation with its ecoomic diversity, its classes, its regions, and its cultural components. All marks of heterogeneity had to be abolished, and millions of people were relocated in an attempt to create a homogeneous mixture. The effect was atrocious and the penalty rapid: a profound and overwhelming discomfiture was to lead the Khmer Rouge to become what they had been before 1970—small unsubdued bands roaming in a hostile forest.

Today Cambodia poses an extremely interesting case for specialists in political pathology, but one which they seem reluctant to examine closely. Here is an ancient country, heir to the oldest traditions in the area and possessor of Angkor, one of the wonders of the world, which finds itself doubly orphaned from what the modern world has everywhere imposed: a state and a nation. The state set up by the Vietnamese in 1979 has little substance, few resources, and its principles scarcely accord with reality. It is as if suspended above a country which it controls only from afar. In the villages, and on the outskirts of ancient urban centers, peasant society has reestablished itself unaided, retrieving its land and customs. Trade is conducted more or less freely across the Thai border, flooding the country under the passive eye of an impotent administration, which hardly commands the resources which would enable it to intervene. As for the nation, whose modern image had not yet reached the remote areas, it seems to be a theme and a form of discourse which are remarkably ineffective as an appeal to be invoked by all the political factions in the struggle. In 1979, when Vietnamese troops seized the country, the overwhelming majority of the populace accepted the foreigner with ease; a large number of those who then left belonged precisely to those strata of society which inclined toward the dominant bourgeoisie, and who did not feel they were in a position to regain their power. Their nationalism led them straight to the refugee camps, and from there to the great cities of the West, where they could at least attain their dream of rising in the social scale, at the price of abandoning their political ambitions.

It is not the natural exercise of good sense that was at work here. It is the fact that nationalism, when it is the ideology of the propertied or ruling class, is used only to justify their own ambitions. This is quite different from the situation prevailing among Cambodian farmers, who are more preoccupied with local conditions, and for whom Khmer identity is not an object of grievous concern, as it is for the intelligentsia and the petty urban bourgeoisie, who are always ready to protest the disappearance of the Khmer *race*. The concept of nation has not been developed to the point where it can be disengaged from the traditional images and concepts which center around the *strok* and the *sang* of the Khmers. For the peasant, these things, which signify membership are self-evident, and since they are lived there is no need to turn them into words. There is, moreover, a more general statement to be made here: the appearance of Tradition, of identity, of culture in a discourse which questions their foundations or their future, can only take place among people for whom such things are dead. Negritude can only be the concern of "white" blacks. It is more than a little paradoxical to hear the complaints—precisely on the part of those who have chosen Westernization above all else—about the dangers weighing on the future of Cambodia and on the Khmer civilization or "race." The villagers whom I have seen are more concerned about the coming of the rains. Myself included.

When, in the 1930s, the dam broke in the small Indochinese colonial world, the breach grew rapidly. The war, the placing of the French administration under Japanese guardianship, the Vichyist policy of mobilizing local youth, in a word, the acceleration of history, would widen the gap even further. The formidable intellectual resources of a people nourished in the space of a generation—to a remarkable mastery of Western culture. By the tens of thousands, young Vietnamese would integrate themselves into a world which, compared with that of their fathers, must not have seemed particularly complicated, certainly without refinement. In the lycée in France, in the 1950s, we all encountered Vietnamese among our fellow-students; they were cheerful young men, invariably brilliant.

Throughout the country, conservatism quickly surrendered. Westernization invaded the public world—street, dress, all outward appearances—but it stopped at the threshold of the home. There the Vietnamese family dwelled, like the dragon watchman, and the altar of the ancestors remained its center. The front of the house, facing on the street, was reserved for show, for the master of the house who, in the midst of his traditional furniture, received his visitors. The rear of the house remained the domain of the women, children, and servants—a sort of effervescent gynaeceum, full of comings and goings, of murmurings, of small conspiracies. It is here that the real affairs of the family are transacted—the family finances, the marriages, the economic and political arrangements. In appearance the men do everything, but in reality the women have decided everything. It is a world where a man is nothing and has nothing if he does not have a wife or a mother who will obtain everything for him from the wife or from the mother of some influential person, and who owes his own influence to the activity of the women in his household. Westernization stopped there. Sometimes it penetrated the front of the house: the old furniture was replaced by modern hardware, the wife sometimes appearing there to greet people. But these are insignificant details; the distribution remained the same.

The American war was to shake up the entire edifice and wreak havoc even here: sons, brothers, and sometime fathers, left for war, and were killed or injured; the daughters, working in the peripheral economy of the American bases, earned more than their fathers.

Amidst these crises, these dissolutions, the reaction was to recreate what remained of the family, exactly as it had been before. Ruined, murdered, corrupted, the families at each catastrophe—and what family did not experience them?—tried to reconstitute themselves as if nothing had happened, because the family represented the sole haven, the only security in this insane upheaval.

And then the war ended. It was time. Millions of individuals were stranded, uprooted from the benevolent family hearth. The cessation of combat also meant, from the very first days, the reunion of families. Brothers, cousins, who had not seen each other in thirty years because they had chosen opposing camps (most often with the general agreement of the family, anxious to diversify its loyalties) knew what they had to do—first find each other again.

While the family remained a protective harbor, it was nevertheless immersed, sometimes submerged, in an intensely modern life. After having hesitated during the two generations which followed the conquest, the Vietnamese choice was complete and determined, especially in the great South. Peasant conservatism still existed, but often only as a calculated precaution in the face of innovation. In this delta, recently won over to agriculture, covered by great landed estates, the roots of the peasantry were superficial, compared with the thousand-year-old history of the villages of Tonkin. The center, poorer, confined in its narrow plains, was more conservative; since it was nearer to Huê and the *mana* of royalty, this too was economically rational. It is the South, young like the United States (when compared with Tonkin, which is old like France) which had to lead in modernization, above all the newly rich, who had been direct collaborators in the colonial enterprise. The American war was to furnish new and extraordinary means for gaining entry into a world whose model then was—and quite logically—Japan, example of an Americanized Asia, rather than old Europe. The yearning for this way of life was, quite clearly, great and profound; it touched the masses of people whose economic situation made such a fate most unlikely. The same thing also occurred in Cambodia. A sort of frenzy took hold of the townspeople, who waited for American gold just as some Melanesian peoples had awaited the arrival of *cargo*. I would, moreover, be tempted to extend the parallel somewhat further, because it was not simply a question of waiting: in both cases there was a misreading or misunderstanding regarding the mechanisms of production and the eventual place that these people could obtain in their midst. Western wealth presented itself as something to be captured by whatever means. It is an illusion that still exists, even today, in the China Seas.

The bias in this view of the West and of its potential, merits examination: in this respect Communist politics also appears, in effect, as a type of Westernization. The Communist reverence for "progressive" customs, has never created any illusions. It articulates a program which will cast aside the local bases in an attempt to transform society completely, since its intent is to establish a new economic base from which the rest must, objectively, follow. This productive aspect dominated their perspective, giving it locally a bias which was apparently the exact opposite of that imposed under the umbrella of the American war, which was essentially consumptive. It was in this interspace that a large part of the bourgeoisie chose to set itself up in April 1975, with the fall of Saigon. From a national perspective, on the verge of civil peace the priorities of the day were economic and social reconstruction. As for politics, it was conceded that that would be the prerogative of the conquerors, who had earned it, precisely by their national worth. One waited for them to harness the energies which would inevitably arise in order to heal the wounds and rebuild the country, with or without the money promised by the Americans. The redeployment of productive capacity was quite logical, and many people accustomed to the excessive consumption were ready, without doubt, to rally to this point of view which promised, ultimately, the coming of comfort and modernity, established on much saner foundations. Elsewhere, perhaps, one could chronicle in detail the failure which followed. For many reasons, which must include the politics of the new leaders, they were unable to reestablish an industry which would justify this choice. Once this situation became clear, the exodus began. The people who left, and who are still leaving, belong to varied social groups, and the individuals who are willing to take the risk of leaving the country do not all do it—far from it—to meet up with a fortune awaiting them abroad. But they all carry with them one conviction: the absence of a future. Whether the incompetence of the regime clearly demonstrated this, or because their social background condemned them to remain forever marginal, they were convinced that they would never regain, or acquire, the Westernization that they knew or dreamed about.

But even for those who remained, the demon of this murky modernity has not been exorcised. Once again it ran through the organism of the Communist state and entered sectors which had up until then seemed immune. Years after the departure of the Americans, Saigon continued to pour out a staggering quantity of "consumer goods" and to secrete parallel economies that ensnare a good number of the inflexible civil servants that the North has dispatched there since 1975. The abundance—infinitely fragmented, finely sliced—showed that the present regime was in no position to really bring about full-scale modernity. It is perhaps here that the break between (nationalist) communists and (nationalist) bourgeoisie which had divided Vietnamese society for fifty years, was reactivated.

The political stakes were clearly drawn: there were those who wanted abundance against those who wanted order. These are two versions, two sides of Westernization, stemming from the relation between people who cannot communicate, have nothing more to say to each other, because their horizons do not converge.

*

"The Falkland Islands," wrote Jorge Luis Borgés (*Le Monde*, 28 January 1983), "was a war between two bald men who fought over a comb." This brilliant summary aptly points up the stake which nationalist manipulation has in our world. Up to a point, it achieves a lasting change in feelings of identity and cultural and social adherence, which is indeed a matter of particular cases and circumstances. The real threat, which risks the almost complete erosion of these feelings and their reduction to a few folklore notations with no practical relevance, does not stem from this. One can always assume that at any given moment a certain number of people will be ready to fight for their country, but not all of the people all of the time. No, the prodigious capital of feelings, tastes, passions, and of awareness of choices, which have been accumulated over hundreds of generations by groups of humans who were separate and unique, but also who were changing and exchanging, is today in the hands of a strange involuntary coalition. I cannot examine it in detail here but it can be called *cultural industry*. Nor does it help to harp on the old theme of the inevitably poor quality of these products. Does one really believe that traditional cultures created products of good quality only? Read the *Rayamana*—it is a typical potboiler of the *Fantomas* genre.

What sets in is consumption. It will be easier to understand what I mean if one bears in mind that the world of industrialized consumption, which has only been established for about a generation at the mass level in Western societies, has created, practically speaking, no needs. Before, as after, this eruption, the individual had to be sheltered, to eat, to make "pipi-caca," to move about, and so on. It is in the manner of doing these things, in the ways and means of gratifying these needs and of access to them, that everything has altered. The idea that this new society creates new needs does not bear up under examination: all it does is to manipulate desires issuing from a common origin, to arrange them according to what is momentarily available in the marketplace. In the past, people were nourished on numerous vegetables, each available in its season. Today we derive nourishment from a few vegetables which are available in all seasons. The nutritive result is undeniably the same and has the advantage in terms of absolute quantity. The same holds true for the nutritive needs of the soul—culture, emotions, everything that an atrocious psychology labels as affects. My comparison with vegetables remains pertinent: before society was based on consumption it would seem that there were fewer choices, and therefore less freedom. In reality, however, there was more, since there was a greater diversity of seasonal products on the market with a great variety of natural flavors. There was also regional diversity; from one district to another, the configuration was different. We might add that the mode of production also provided a thousand ways of acquiring these products, either at no cost or at prices based on personal human relationships. In the world of consumption, these singularities have disappeared—flavors are constant and predictable, regional disparities have been eliminated. The use of money as a medium, made ever more generic and universal by banking practice, reduces the possibilities for personal access to goods to practices of theft and misappropriation. It seems to me entirely legitimate to transpose these data, which are concerned with the satisfaction of the stomach, to those of the spirit, since the processes of manufacture obey the same principles of organization, distribution, profitability, and therefore consumption.

Gradually, through the worldwide expansion of markets (observable and observed for a century and a half), in a process which still is very far from having reached its limits, the masses of humanity have, little by little, become incorporated into it. There is, however, a time lag of roughly one or two generations between their induction into the circuit of industrialized production and their capacity to consume the goods they manufacture. This has been seen in the West, but nowhere more strikingly than in Japan today. Economists will tell you that, contrary to widespread opinion, Japan exports no more than any European country, indeed, less than many, because of the great increase in its internal market. But it is imperative to add, as one observes with amazement the truly frenzied consumerism of the Japanese, that this is a recent development, of little more than a decade. In this short time it has transformed Japanese society from top to bottom, not so much because it has changed the material structure, but because it has suppressed their traditional identity and experience. Time, time to be, no longer exists; it has been worn away by work, ground down by the thousand demands of consumption. All that made Japan, Japan, is still there, within reach, but no longer is there contact with it, because the drift toward the separate life, forced by new constraints rather than by new needs, renders it inaccessible.

The Japanese are obviously still Japanese, but they no longer have the time to be so. The real novelty is the young generation, whose first steps took place in this new atmosphere and who are not yet twenty years old. This generation has never known Japan—it has had none of the experiences that go into making up the Japanese identity. On the contrary, it has been built around those elements of the industrialized culture which are available on a market which is no longer Japanese, but worldwide; which seems—I say seems—American. The mecca of the young Japanese is now New York. Japan, like Auvergne, is finished. What remains is folklore, fit for wedding-breakfasts, and very importantly, the language. It is language, I am convinced, which will be the last element of the traditional substance to drift away.

The capacity of modern capitalism to penetrate the entire planet—its mountains and its beaches, its men and its women—can, of course, be questioned. There are so many marginal areas which have nothing that warrants serious exploitation, that one can doubt that there ever will be any interest in them. That is another debate. But if already we must think that the richness and variety of humanity is destined to survive only in these interstitial niches, then we can indeed pass judgment on our present world, which for the price of one sanitized and disposable way of thinking, suppresses thousands that burst forth spontaneously out of a past which created us too, but which no longer does.

Translation by Karen Turnbull

REFERENCES

Barkus, J. 1981. *The Nang Chao Kingdom*. Cambridge: At the University Press.

Condominas, Georges. 1980. *L'Espace social à propos de l'Asia du Sud-Est*. Paris: Flammarion.

Cuisinier, Jeanne. 1948. *Les Mu'o'ng*. Paris: Inst. d'Ethnologie.

Dinh Van Trung. 1974. "La Psychologie du paysan du Delta." Thesis, Paris.

Fynn, Henry Francis. 1950. *The Diary of Henry Francis Fynn*. Pietermaritzburg.

Jamieson, Neil L. 1981. "Vietnam: A Study of Continuity and Change in a Socio-Cultural System." Ph.D. diss., University of Hawaii.

Marr, David. 1971. *Vietnamese Anti-colonialism, 1885–1925*. Berkeley: University of California Press.

_____ 1981. *Vietnamese Tradition on Trial, 1930–1945*. Berkeley: University of California Press.

Mus, Paul. 1971. *Ho Chi Minh, Le Viêt-Nam, l'Asie*. Paris: Seuil.

_____ and John Mc Alister. 1972. *Les Vietnamiens et leur révolution*. Paris: Seuil.

Ngugi Wa Thiongo. *Petals of Blood*. London: Heineman.

Porée-Maspero, Evelyne. *Étude sur les rites agraires des Cambodgiens*. 3 vols. Paris: Mouton.

Prescott, William H. 1847. *The Conquest of Peru*. Harpers and Bros.

Rousset, Pierre. 1978. *Communisme et nationalism vietnamien*. Paris: Galilée.

Schafer, Edward. 1967. *The Vermilion Bird, T'ang Images of the South*. Berkeley: University of California Press.

Spiro, Melford E. 1967. *Burmese Supernationalism*. Philadelphia: ISHI.

Tambiah, Stanley J. 1970. *Buddhism and the Spirit Cults in Northeast Thailand*. London: Cambridge University Press.

Thion, Serge. 1983. "The Cambodian Idea of Revolution." In *Revolution and Its Aftermath in Kampuchea*, edited by D. P. Chandler and B. Kiernan. Yale University Southeast Asia Monograph, 25. New Haven: Yale University Press.

Todorov, Tzvetan. 1982. *La Découverte du Nouveau Monde*. Paris: Seuil.

Turner, R. F. 1975. *Vietnamese Communism*. Stanford: Hoover Inst. Press.

Territorial Imperatives:
Akha Ethnic Identity and
Thailand's National Integration

CORNELIA ANN KAMMERER

Cultural identity implies, and fundamentally presupposes, a sense of territoriality.
—Remo Guidieri, Francesco Pellizzi (1980)

In the modern conception, state sovereignty is fully, flatly, and evenly operative over each square centimetre of legally demarcated territory.
—Benedict Anderson (1983)

With the emergence of modern nation-states in peninsular Southeast Asia in the post-colonial era, the structure of the hill / valley conjuncture altered fundamentally. The territorially bounded states in the Western mode that emerged through the colonial encounter replaced the center-oriented "galactic polities" of traditional Indianized principalities whose "borders were porous and indistinct" (Tambiah 1976; Anderson 1983, 26). Today, these new nations challenge the legitimacy of highlanders'cultural *cum* territorial existence in a way unknown under the older order.

Anthropological research among both hill-dwellers and valley-dwellers in Burma and, to a greater extent, Thailand has focused on processes of ethnic differentiation and identification since the publication of Leach's iconoclastic-turned-classic monograph, *Political Systems of Highland Burma*. Drawing mainly upon this now substantial literature, I attempt to formulate an analytical approach toward ethnic identity that I hope will illuminate the current confrontation of mountain minorities and the consolidating nation-states of continental

Southeast Asia.[1] Ethnic identity here designates explicit self-definition which is cultural but not coterminous with culture. Applying this approach to the case of Tibeto-Burman-speaking Akha in the hills of northern Thailand, I argue that Akha identity is based upon common clanship and shared "customs," and presupposes a duplex concept of territory not shared by the lowland Thai majority. In the concluding section, prospects for Akha and other highlanders are considered in the light of efforts by the central government of Thailand to integrate "hill tribes" into a territorially bounded nation.[2]

ETHNIC IDENTITY IN THE MAINLAND SOUTHEAST ASIAN CONTEXT

Ethnographic fieldwork, by its very nature, impels questions of ethnic likeness and difference to the fore (Moerman 1968, 165–66); not only does each observer seek a monograph-sized sociocultural entity, but observer and observed encounter one another as strangers. Yet the emphasis on ethnicity in anthropological accounts of mainland Southeast Asia cannot be written off as a true reflection of the anthropologist's interests and methods and a distorted image of the anthropological object. In the Southeast Asian context, concerns of anthropologists and natives coincide. Most, if not all, researchers who have worked in upland Southeast Asia would, I believe, echo Moerman (1968, 165) in claiming that "ethnic identifications . . . have high priority to the people I studied." Stories and myths often include characters from other ethnic groups and frequently explain social and cultural differences between groups. For example, Akha, Chin, Karen, and Lahu all relate tales that account for their lack of writing and its presence among neighboring cultures in the valley.[3]

To students of Southeast Asian sociocultural systems, Leach bequeathed a structural model of group definition through opposition, which demands that social groups be viewed relationally rather than as stable isolates. By demonstrating that Kachin speak mutually unintelligible languages and display significant cultural differences, by documenting that individual hill-dwelling Kachin become valley-dwelling Shan and vice versa, and by establishing the interdependence of Shan and Kachin political systems, Leach (1954, 281) challenged "conventions as to what constitutes *a* culture or *a* tribe" shared by colonial administrators and social scientists alike. In *Political Systems of Highland Burma*, Leach (1954, 43) simultaneously undermined the evolutionist / biological view that "race" is "a synonym for language" and that the inhabitants of British Burma are representatives of successive waves of migrations of diverse races, as well as the structural-functionalist conception of a tribe as a discrete, homogeneous social unit in Radcliffe-Brownian equilibrium.

Beginning with Lehman's (1963) study of Chin as a "subnuclear" tribal people adapted to Burman civilization, students of the hill / valley conjuncture have built upon Leach's lead. Whereas Leach's aim is to show *that* valley neighbors influence hill sociocultural systems, Lehman's aim is to show *in what ways* they do so. Two recent works expand and refine Lehman's focus on the molding of highlander cultures through opposition to dominant lowlanders: Alting von Geusau (1983) examines dialectical oppositions such as upslope versus downslope developed in Akha oral tradition in response to the presence of stronger valley-dwellers, and Radley (1986) investigates Mong (Hmong) tiger myths as embodiments of attitudes toward the powerful Chinese. In a complex dialectical process, patterns of social interaction and adaptation shape cultural traditions and definitions of identity among hill and valley neighbors, which in turn influence patterns of social interaction and adaptation.[4]

Uplanders are well aware of both the material advantages and the greater political power of lowlanders, but they also demonstrate deep respect for the traditions handed down by their ancestors. Commentators since Lehman (1963) have drawn attention to the double ambivalence displayed by mountain people. Attitudes toward valley civilization combine admiration with distrust; attitudes toward their own customs combine pride with feelings of inferiority.[5] Distrust toward valley-dwellers can be interpreted, following Hinton (1979, 85–86), as a consequence of long-standing oppression, and feelings of inferiority can be viewed not simply as reactions to obvious inequality in material resources between hill and valley, but also as the internalization of opinions of those politically and economically dominant.

It should be pointed out that hill / valley is always a significant axis for self-definition among highlanders, but it is not the only one, and, furthermore, that self-definitions may recognize similarity as well as contrast with others. For example, Karen, whose perceived place within the sphere of the valley state is an essential ingredient in their self-identification, consider Lua' to be different but nonetheless akin on the basis of their common residence between plains and mountain tops and their similar positions vis-à-vis traditional valley principalities, at the same time that they feel no affinity with hillmen of the higher slopes (Kunstadter 1967b, 1969, 1979; Marlowe 1969, 1979). Karen and by analogy Lua' represent the " 'hills' as an extension of the 'sown'," whereas the true highlanders such as the Akha, Hmong, and Lisu represent the " 'hills', qua 'hills' " (Marlowe 1979, 196). These hill-dwellers distinguish themselves one from the other, yet recognize more affinity among themselves than with inhabitants of the valley below: Akha acknowledge a basic likeness among "mountain people," and the Mien creation myth recounts the emergence of "hill people" and "plains people" (Kandre 1967, 621). Content and consequences of ambivalence as well as axes of contrast and affinity must be established through research and cannot be assumed to be stable through time.[6]

Ever since Moerman (1965) posed the question "Who Are the Lue?,"[7] anthropological attention has focused on native definitions of group affiliation.[8] As an ideological formulation, ethnic identity is cultural, but it is not coterminous with culture. To my knowledge, no ethnographic case has yet been reported in which the set of attributes included within a culture's definition of ethnic identity is coincident with the total culture of people claiming that identity, nor should such a case be expected. I would argue that isomorphism between ethnic identity and culture is impossible because ethnic identity is explicit and self-conscious whereas much of culture is implicit and unconscious (in Bourdieu's [1977] sense).[9] Accordingly, in the perspective adopted here not all sociocultural change entails change in ethnic identity. Ethnic change is here understood as either a claim to membership in a different group (e.g., Lua' become Karen or Northern Thai [Kunstadter 1983a, 151]) or as an alteration in self-definitional criteria for membership in a particular group (e.g., Lua' remains Lua' but differently defined [Kunstadter 1983a, 151]).[10] Since criteria for group self-identification are not uniform or universal,[11] "it therefore becomes the ethnographer's task to discover, in each instance, which features are locally significant for purposes of assigning ethnic labels" (Moerman 1965, 1220).

To understand the degree of resilience or vulnerability of ethnic identity in the context of shifting patterns of intergroup relations, it is necessary not only to determine the content of ethnic self-identification but also its configuration. Besides differing in content, ethnic identities exhibit greater or lesser degrees of systematicity and complexity. For instance, the cultural features Thai Lue consider markers of their identity include the female sarong, a recessed fireplace, a village spirit house, and a style of folk songs (Moerman 1968, 156–58). On the other hand, Mien define themselves as Mien on the basis of adherence to a named "socio-economic-ritual system" (Kandre 1967, 584–85).

The ethnospecific cultural subsystem is called by native informants "The Custom" (*lei nyei*), which corresponds to the Chinese concept of *Li* [good customs, rites and ceremonies. . . .] (Kandre 1976, 172, brackets in the original)

Some self-definitions, like that of Mien, take the form of interlocking networks of cultural attributes. Others, like that of Thai Lue, are loose sets of traits akin to anthropological trait lists of a bygone era. Definitional sets may also be implicational or hierarchical, with traits logically ranked one with respect to another. For example, there appears to be an implicational relationship among the criteria of Karen-ness cited by Kunstadter (1979, 125) in that knowledge of the Karen language is a prerequisite for knowledge of Karen folk tales. Indeed, Kunstadter isolates language as the most important criterion. In the case of loose sets, it is possible that one element might be dropped or replaced without threatening the viability of the definition. In the case of implicational or hierarchical sets, perhaps an element of lesser rank might be abandoned without the definition collapsing. Self-definitions, like that of Mien, which isolate a specific cultural subsystem rather than an inventory of traits as distinctive of group membership, appear to be more fragile by virtue of greater internal coherence; however, the presumption of fragility rests upon the questionable assumption that ideas and practices belonging within a named cultural domain, for instance "The Custom" of Mien, are themselves immutable. A label may be retained while that to which it is applied alters considerably. The amount and kind of change a specific cultural subsystem can absorb is a subject for research in each particular ethnographic case.

Beyond looking at the content and configuration of self-conscious definitions of group membership, it is also important to explore connections between identity and other explicit and implicit aspects of culture. If a self-definition does not incorporate all the conditions necessary to meet standards of group membership, identity can be threatened by change affecting those conditions that are presupposed by the self-definition but not directly included within it. To give one illustration, although the Mien language is not included in definitions of Mien-ness, one cannot follow "The Custom" without knowing the Mien language (Kandre 1976, 173). For Mien, then, a loss of language would entail a loss of identity (as presently defined), despite the fact that language is not an explicit element in self-identification. Thus self-conscious bases of identity need not coincide with the effective bases of identity. Self-referential behavioral indices vary in the number and intricacy of what might be termed felicity conditions, that is, nondefinitional prerequisites for behavioral realization. Thus dress appears to be unencumbered relative to ritual, which presupposes conventional spatial and temporal frames, properly prepared practitioners, etc. The same cultural criterion might be differentially encumbered in two cases: both groups might specify knowledge of folk songs as an essential mark of membership, but in one it might be possible to sing them anywhere anytime, while in the other singing them might be restricted to specific ritual contexts.

The first epigraph at the beginning of this paper proclaims that "cultural identity . . . presupposes a sense of territoriality." Although "a sense of territoriality" is often an explicit element in ethnic identification, either tangibly as a particular parcel in possession (an occupied homeland) or intangibly as a memory (a former or mythic homeland), it need not always be self-consciously incorporated into ethnic identity. If not explicit, a conception of territory is in many, and perhaps all cases, implicit. What is at issue here is not territory as tract but territory as idea. I hasten to add that this does not mean that territory as tract is of no consequence to the fate of ethnic minorities. Territory as idea cannot be tilled. Since nation-states in the modern mode themselves presuppose a single conception of territorial legitimacy that, as the second epigraph indicates, admits no alternatives, I believe that it is important to unravel the explicit or implicit "sense of territoriality" in highlander identities in order to understand the current minority-majority conjuncture in the nations of peninsular Southeast Asia.

An argument made in connection with language can, I believe, be applied to ethnic identity to help account for differential kinds and rates of ethnic change. Hymes (1971, 116) contends that "the role of language may differ from community to community." Transposing his argument to the question of ethnic identity, I contend that the role of ethnic identity may differ from community to community. Whereas one community may show little tendency toward ethnic change, whether from one label to another or in the content ascribed to a continuing label, another community may change readily either by adopting a new label and all that it entails or by altering the definitional criteria of the label retained.

Since Leach (1954) first drew anthropological attention to the phenomenon, shifts in claims to group membership have concerned students of mainland Southeast Asia. As Dentan (1976, 78) observes,

multi-culturation in Southeast Asia provides many people with a series of identities which they can don and doff as particular interactions dictate. Goffmanesque models of self-presentation and interaction ritual are adequate to describe this behavior, often with only tangential reference to notions of ethnicity.

In keeping with Dentan's own emphasis on the potential dangers of scholarly research and writing on ethnicity in Southeast Asia given the existence of real ethnic tensions, I would like to draw attention to a potential danger of the recurrent stress in the anthropological literature on the "donning" and "doffing" of identities. It is one thing for a person to alter her / his behavior to suit the situation (as perceived by that actor), and it is an entirely different thing for alteration to be demanded by another person (or government) to suit the situation (as defined by that other person [or government]). Willingness to adapt one's behavior to a particular context should not be interpreted as absence of attachment to an identity not then in play.

Andrianoff (1979, 77), Hinton (1969, 4–5), and Kunstadter (1983b, 38) observe that not all ethnic groups in Thailand are assimilators to the same degree. As Hinton (1969, 4) notes,

it is probably significant that researchers who have been preoccupied with changing cultural identity have been students of the Thai, Karen, Lua', Thai Lue and Shan peoples. The identity of some other groups seems to be rather more rigidly defined.

The other groups to which he refers are Hmong and Mien, speakers of related Austro-Thai languages (Matisoff 1983, 65), and the three Tibeto-Burman-speaking groups, Lahu, Lisu, and Akha. Andrianoff (1979) and Geddes (1967, 568) support his view concerning Hmong, Kandre's (1967, 1976) work echoes him on Mien, and my ethnographic experience certainly corroborates him on Akha. It seems that among the first set of peoples loyalty to ethnic identity is not as strong a cultural value as among the second. I hasten to add that it is not my intention to indicate that the cultural evaluation of ethnic identity is the sole variable in determining the speed and direction of sociocultural change, nor to convey the impression that this evaluation is independent of historical circumstances. The cultural weighting ascribed to group identity is but one factor among many to be considered in the study of ethnic change, but it is a factor that should not be ignored.

The content, configuration, and evaluation of ethnic identity are products of history, which in turn pattern perceptions of change and channel change itself. Hmong, Mien, Lahu, Lisu, and Akha are all groups to which Alting von Geusau's (1983) characterization "perennial minority" applies; all are marginalized people who have historically withdrawn from and / or resisted pressure posed by dominant valley-dwellers (Radley 1986). Though their ethnic identities differ as do the cultures of which they are part, members of these groups appear to share a positive evaluation of allegiance to ethnic identity. All live in highland villages interspersed with those of other ethnic groups, and none has a tradition of stable, patterned political connections with powerful lowlanders. They define themselves in relation to valley neighbors, but, unlike more ready assimilators such as Karen and Lua', (former) dependence upon a (former) valley-principality is not internalized into self-identification.

The mountain minorities have for centuries, even millennia, been in contact with more powerful valley-dwellers. Consciousness of their relative weakness is not new; it is part of tradition itself. It may well be that self-definition through opposition is a feature of all cultural systems and that autonomous cultural systems are a myth of the tribe of anthropologists.

Membership in a group, incorporation within it, is dependent upon a category of the excluded, a sense of otherness. . . . The Outside, then, is necessary to the Inside. (Murphy 1964, 848)

For highlanders in mainland Southeast Asia, the dominant other is an age-old counterpart. Yet during this century a fundamental transformation is evident: traditional ethnic self-consciousness has in some cases metamorphosed into political ethnic self-consciousness. Assertive, politicized ethnic self-consciousness seems to incorporate aspects of the Western notion of the bounded territorial nation-state. While Weber (1978) and Keyes (1976, 1981) suggest that ethnic self-consciousness can be considered a form of "descent," I suggest that politicized ethnic self-consciousness can be considered a form of dissent. Whereas the first claims to differ, the second differs to claim.[12]

The general approach to ethnic identity presented here demands that in each ethnographic case the content as well as the configuration of the self-definition of group membership be investigated. Unraveling links between the self-conscious bases of identity and other explicit as well as implicit aspects of culture, exposes sources of resilience and vulnerability, and of flexibility and rigidity, in the face of changing intergroup relations and politico-economic circumstances. Of particular importance in the context of today's world of nation-states is the "sense of territoriality," either explicit or implicit within definitions of ethnic identity. Finally, a culture's evaluation of allegiance to group membership provides a clue to differential rates and kinds of ethnic change. Applying this approach to a particular ethnographic case, the bases of ethnic identity among Akha in northern Thailand are examined, and the confrontation between Akha as well as other highlanders and the national government is explored.

AKHA ETHNIC IDENTITY

Akha as an ethnic group are here distinguished not on the basis of any objective criteria, but rather as the people who identify themselves as Akha. Population statistics for mountain minorities in Southwest China and Southeast Asia are notoriously unreliable. Suffice to say that there are between three and five hundred thousand Akha residing in Yunnan and in the highlands of Southeast Asia stretching from Burma's eastern Shan States through northern Thailand and western Laos, apparently into the northwest corner of Vietnam.[13] The first Akha settlement in northern Thailand was founded just after the turn of the century (Alting von Geusau 1983, 246). Through both natural growth and immigration from Thailand's politically troubled neighboring states, the population of Akha and other highlanders has increased substantially since the 1960s. In 1964 there were under seven thousand Akha (L. Hanks, J. Hanks, and Sharp 1964, facing p. 5); in 1986 there were more than thirty-three thousand (McKinnon and Vienne 1988, Appendix I). Most reside in Chiang Rai, the northernmost province; the remainder reside in Chiang Mai, Kamphaeng Phet, Lampang, Phrae, and Tak, other northern provinces (McKinnon and Vienne 1988, Appendix I).

In the ethnic mosaic of the highlands, autonomous Akha villages are scattered among those of other ethnic groups. Like other hill-dwellers, Akha cultivate swiddens in a belt of land surrounding their community. Dry rice is the main subsistence crop and the focus of required calendrical rituals. Every traditional settlement must have a village founder-leader (*dzoema*), who is responsible for leading community-based ceremonies.[14] The position is restricted to men and is often hereditary, but the village founder-leader is in no sense a ruler. Disputes are settled through discussions among male household heads, and fines are paid at the village founder-leader's house. Descent is patrilineal and residence patrivirilocal. The effective unit in the regulation of marriage is the exogamous, unnamed sublineage, rather than the named patrilineage. A woman joins the household and lineage of her husband at marriage. Although there is no indigenous supralocal political organization, Akha in geographically dispersed communities are bound by ramifying ties of consanguinity and affinity.

The ethnographic research (1979–81) from which data are drawn was conducted in Chiang Rai Province among self-designated *Jeug'oe* Akha traditionalists. With Alting von Geusau (1983, 246) and Lewis (1968, viii) and contra Feingold (1976, 91–92), I consider *Jeug'oe* to be a native classification corresponding to a dialect group. Based upon the comparability of Lewis's findings in Burma and both Alting von Geusau's (1983) and my own findings in Thailand, I believe it likely that the ethnographic information presented here is of general applicability to those *Jeug'oe* speakers who have not abandoned their inherited "customs" in favor of Christianity. They recognize that members of other subgroups are also Akha, and they can detail variations in practices between subgroups. My suspicion is that comparative work among other subgroups will reveal that various sorts of Akha define themselves as Akha in a similar manner.[15] After all, the mode of self-identification described below acknowledges likeness and allows for differences among Akha.

Ethnic group as clan. From the Akha point of view, their ethnic group is what is called a clan in anthropological parlance. Akha believe themselves to be lineal descendants of a single apical ancestor, "Main Sky, Middle Sky" (*Mmamg'ah*), below whom there were nine generations of spirits before the first man, *Smmio*, appeared. The various named, unranked patrilineages to which all Akha belong segment below *Smmio*. The Akha genealogical system is described as "universalistic" by Feingold (1976, 88) because a person can add his name below that of a specified ancestor and thereby become an Akha. Although it is true that non-Akha may become Akha in this way, the genealogical system is not universal in the sense of embracing all people. As descendants of *Smmio*, Akha are set apart from non-Akha. The system is universal in that it encompasses all Akha; "it pronounces that all Akha are brothers" (J. Hanks 1974, 126). [16]

A child becomes a member of its father's patrilineage not at birth but shortly thereafter at the naming ceremony. The genealogical name given at this ceremony follows the Tibeto-Burman pattern of patronymic linkage in which the last one or two syllables of a father's name become the first one or two syllables of his child's name (Lo Ch'ang-p'ei 1945). Thus, for example, Liba's child might be named Bado. Through her / his genealogical name a person is linked to the chain of patrilineal ancestors stretching back sixty or more generations to the apical ancestor. Every Akha has both an everyday name and a genealogical name. Use of the latter is restricted to contexts that are included within the domain of "customs." During curing rituals the patient is addressed by that name and thereby identified to ancestors whose aid is sought. The recitation of the deceased's genealogy is central to the funeral ceremony (J. Hanks 1974; Hansson 1983, 280–81). A woman who dies before marriage is buried following the recitation of her father's lineage; a woman who dies after marriage is buried following the recitation of her husband's lineage. Akha say that every man should be able to recite his genealogy. Some men have neither the gift nor the inclination to commit the sixty plus names to memory, but at least one older man in each sublineage must know it. Reciters (*phima*), ritual specialists whose grasp of the branching genealogical system is particularly extensive, as well as other knowledgeable elders can readily identify the critical point of segmentation not only of their own lineage but also of others.

Ethnic identity as customs. In addition to defining themselves as descendants of a single apical ancestor, Akha also define themselves on the basis of their adherence to a specific set of "customs" (*zah*). To be an Akha is to uphold the prescriptions and proscriptions for action which constitute Akha customs (Lewis 1969–70, 24). [17] According to Akha traditions, long ago the various peoples were differentiated at the bestowal of customs. In Bradley's (1983, 52) phraseology, "the source of ethnic distinctions is cosmologized" in the myth which relates that Northern Thai, Chinese, Lahu, Akha, etc. were called together and given customs. The Northern Thai, Chinese, and Lahu all went carrying loosely woven baskets. In some tellings, not only were these baskets woven with wide spaces between the bamboo strips, they were also broken and torn. Unlike the others, the Akha went to fetch customs carrying a tightly woven sack, the kind in which rice is brought back from the fields so that not one precious grain is lost. The Northern Thai, Chinese, and Lahu put customs into their baskets and returned home. On the way customs fell through the holes and were lost. The Akha, on the other hand, placed customs inside the sack and on the way home not one piece fell out. This is the reason that the customs of others are few while those of Akha are many.[18] The story permits the addition or deletion of other groups depending on both current and past intergroup relations, and on the inclinations of the teller. Akha in northern Thailand do not live near Shan, but many older Akha who used to live near them in Burma include Shan when recounting this story.

Not only do Northern Thai, Chinese, Lahu, Akha, etc. all have their own customs, so too do different sorts of Akha. A particular ritual may be performed differently by members of one named lineage than by members of another. For example, all Akha coffins are made from hollowed tree trunks, but deceased members of the *Anyi* lineage are placed with their feet toward the base of the trunk, whereas deceased members of other lineages are placed with their heads toward the base. A common expression is "Everyone has their own customs," which may be said with reference to groups such as Northern Thai and Lahu or with reference to individual Akha belonging to different lineages. Akha accept and are tolerant of variations in customs at either the ethnic or the intra-ethnic level, since Akha assume that customs at all levels are legitimated in the same manner, that is, by being handed down from the ancestors.

Akha customs include the plethora of rituals crowding Akha life: calendrical ceremonies, life-cycle rites, curing ceremonies, rituals concerning rice cultivation, and corrective rites of numerous sorts. In addition, customs encompass much that anthropologists generally label kinship, such as rules concerning lineage segmentation, permissible marriages, and affinal responsiblities. Also included in customs is patterned behavior not part of ritual performances or kinship relations, for instance, activities permitted and not permitted on various days of the Akha week. Many customary injunctions concerning everyday behavior are the obverse of ritual injunctions. To give one example, hanging wash out to dry on the porch as sunset approaches is normally prohibited because during a funeral a blanket belonging to the deceased must be hung out to dry there late in the afternoon following burial. An action permitted, indeed required, in its appropriate ritual frame is prohibited on any other day. As a system of rules, customs stipulate not only actions, actors, recitations, and ritual paraphernalia for all ceremonies, but also proper and improper behavior in many nonritual contexts.

The well-known highlander self-reflexive ambivalence is evident in two oft quoted sayings: "Akha customs are many" and "Akha customs are difficult." These two are pronounced with self-deprecation, with pride, or with both. On one occasion, an Akha man was prompted by his long description of the proper procedures for a short segment of the elaborate funeral ceremony to recount the story of receiving customs. He concluded by declaring that the Akha who fetched customs in a sack was stupid. Another time, after an old man finished the tale, a young woman turned to me and only half-jokingly said,"Go ahead and tell him that the Akha was stupid." However, Akha also proclaim their customs to be many and difficult when their importance is being stressed. The old which has been handed down from the ancestors must not be allowed to disappear. As a fragment of ceremonial song emphasizes, "in father's footsteps on the earth, a son should walk; in mother's footsteps on the earth, a daughter should walk."

The many customs are difficult in being both complex and costly. Minutely specified procedures must be followed precisely; an offering incorrectly performed must be repeated. To enact annual rituals, curing rites, and ceremonies of the life cycle each household must sacrifice a great number of animals. In Thailand today customs are becoming more difficult because many Akha are increasingly hard pressed to raise or to acquire the necessary sacrificial animals. Highlanders are numerous and hill land is scarce; lowlanders, themselves impoverished, cut swiddens on mountains slopes; and government reforestation programs reduce upland farmland by planting trees while, at the same time, licensed and illegal logging removes trees. Akha who convert to Christianity often do so because they can no longer afford to make the sacrifices demanded by the many and difficult customs of their forebears.

The legitimacy of customs rests, as noted above, on the authority of the ancestors. Since customs were originally received they have been passed down from one generation to the next; however, it would be a mistake to assume that they are static. Customs can and do change. The following example is chosen because it is relevant to the dicussion in the next section of the "sense of territoriality" implicit within Akha ethnic identity. Besides the village founder-leader who is responsible for internal village affairs, there is a second official who is responsible for matters concerning hill-valley relations. This man is the village headman (called *phuujajbaan* in Thailand), who is appointed or confirmed by valley political authorities. According to customs, men who have held this position are the only Akha eligible to receive a horse at their funerals. Not so many years ago, in order to offer a horse, more than one buffalo also had to be sacrificed. Buffalo are expensive and it is now difficult for a family to provide even a single buffalo for a funeral; therefore, the procedure for a horse funeral was recently changed by male elders after discussions among themselves. Now the sacrifice of one buffalo suffices to permit the offering of a horse at a village headman's funeral. Customs, then, can be altered in response to changing circumstances, including the deteriorating economic situation of mountain minorities. Newer practices share with older practices the same stamp of legitimacy. By virtue of being labeled customs, inherited traditions and innovations are invested with the authority of the ancestors. The adaptability of customs has been and continues to be crucial to the survival of Akha as an ethnic group; yet, the limits of adaptability of customs as a coherent, cosmologically-grounded cultural subsystem could well be reached in the not so distant future.

Implicit duplex "sense of territoriality." Each Akha community is identically structured according to the dictates of customs. The boundary between a community and the surrounding forest is demarcated by two village gateways renewed annually at a ceremony presided over by the village founder-leader. No fence encloses the community, but the dividing line separating the domain of people within the settlement from the domain of spirits in the encircling forest is no less real for being intangible. Portions of many rituals, especially curing rites, must be enacted at a village gate; it is not necessary, however, to go to one or the other gateway. Although there are only two gates with wooden uprights and crossbeams, a certain point on every path leading away from the residential compounds is labeled by the same term applied to these two gates. From any such point, the wandering soul of a sick person may be called back from the forest, the domain of spirits. In the ordered Akha universe, people, ancestors, rice, and domesticated animals belong to the village realm, while spirits and wild animals belong to the forest realm.

One of the many segments of ritual text recited during three nights of chanting at an elaborate funeral as well as during various other rites is called "Descent of the Dwelling Places." This text recounts the Akha journey southwards over lands and rivers from China to Thailand. Akha deem their past and present dwelling places to be tokens of a single type, replicas of a single cosmologically grounded model. Villages are united through their shared structure despite being geographically separated. Not only are living Akha, wherever they reside, linked by common community order, so too are the living and the dead. Ancestors reside in a village structured like villages of the living. Just as the first house to be built in a new settlement is that of the village founder-leader, so the first grave to be dug in a community burial ground is that of the village founder-leader of the ancestor's village. The apparent emphasis in the Akha conceptualization of the historical branching of villages in the descent from China is not on a social genealogy, with one village the parent of the next, but upon the structural identity of each village as a microcosm.

Akha villages are identical islands surrounded not only by forest, but also by hills, valleys, and rivers as well as by villages inhabited by members of other ethnic groups. Among *Jeug'oe* Akha in Burma and Thailand, the "Offering to Lords of Land and Water" follows the renewal of the village gateways in the annual ritual cycle. Lewis (1969–70, 256–57) reports that Akha in Burma acknowledge that this rite was borrowed from Shan some two generations ago. The recitation is done in Shan, in a combination of Shan and Akha, or in Akha alone.[19] Features of the ceremony are similar to two Shan rituals described by Durrenberger (1980, 51–54): the rite for spirits of valleys and hill fields and the rite for the ruler of the country. Elements of the Offering to Lords of Land and Water such as popped rice, burning candles, and white umbrellas are clearly Shan (-Buddhist) and do not appear in other ceremonies belonging to Akha customs.

At the required time each year, a procession of men headed by the village founder-leader goes to an altar in the woods beyond the confines of the community. There two chickens and a pig are sacrificed while the village founder-leader or another knowledgeable male elder begs the "owners" (*yawsah*) of nearby mountains and rivers and the "Lords of Land and Water" (*misahchusah*) for abundant harvests and for healthy people and domesticated animals. The term *mi* means "soil" or "earth" (from *mitsa*) as well as "country" or "territory" (for example, in *Thaimitsa*, the Akha name for "Thailand"). The English gloss "land" captures both aspects of the meaning of this word. Although the term *sah* comes from *yawsah* meaning "owner," I prefer to follow both Alting von Geusau (1983, 251, 268) and Lewis (1968, 203) in rendering it as "lord." I do so because when asked to whom the ceremony is addressed Akha answer either "Owner of Land" (*mitsayawsah*) or "Lord of Land" (*mitsasahpha*). The latter term apparently derives from the Shan word *saohpa* meaning "prince" or "feudal lord" and is applied by Akha to leaders of political domains. According to Alting von Geusau (1983, 251), the dominant valley-dwellers' control over the land is acknowledged in the performance of the Offering to Lords of Land and Water. I would argue that it is not the political order of the dominant valley-dwellers which is acknowledged so much as it is the special relationship between the dominant group and the spirits of the land in the region.

Customs then presuppose a duplex conception of territory: every village as an identical movable microcosm and each village as situated within a specific geographical sphere that includes more powerful ethnic groups. Correspondingly, the Akha polity has a dual nature: within a community the village founder-leader represents the ordinating principle of the village as microcosm, while the village headman links the village to the dominant political authorities in the region. These orientations of polity, like both conceptions of territoriality, are implicit within customs. The village founder-leader, who is indispensable to the enactment of customs, is mentioned frequently in the ancient ritual texts of the oral tradition. Although the village headman is not mentioned in these texts, customs decree that he alone is entitled to a horse offering at his funeral. Since both the practice of Offering to Lords of Land and Water and the position of village headman are fairly recent innovations, it may well be that Akha conceptions of territory and of polity were each simplex rather than duplex a few generations ago. But the duplex "sense of territoriality" and the duplex orientation of polity are important implicit aspects of the ethnic identity of Akha in Thailand today.

MOUNTAIN MINORITY IDENTITY AND
THAILAND'S NATIONAL INTEGRATION

The ethnic identity of Akha in northern Thailand is based upon shared lineal descent from an apical ancestor and adherence to common customs inherited from the ancestors. The Akha ethnic group as clan has persisted for generations and appears likely to continue for generations to come.[20] The shared "socio-economic-ritual system," here glossed as customs, is a strikingly intricate and complex cultural subsystem. Structured relations between living and dead, between humans and spirits, and between wife-givers and wife-takers encoded in customs generate and maintain order within the Akha world. Though adaptable, customs are not infinitely flexible. A central axis of customs is rice, which is the focus of special calendrical ceremonies and annual ancestor offerings. Having reached the end of the mountain ranges extending southwards from China, Akha are well aware that, given their present technology, expanding highland population, and increasing competition from valley farmers and loggers for scarce hill land, their economic situation will continue to deteriorate. They are eager to adopt agricultural innovations provided these do not jeopardize their subsistence base. Any development schemes which ignore rice cultivation in favor of cash crops will not only endanger the subsistence base, but will also threaten the core of Akha customs and thereby threaten Akha ethnic identity. Akha in the mountains of northern Thailand see their southward journey at an end and consider Thailand to be their home. Their duplex conceptions of territoriality and polity permit them to respect their inherited traditions at the same time that they participate in the Thai nation-state.

Of all the nations in mainland Southeast Asia, Thailand may well have entered the post-colonial era with the brightest prospects for successful national integration. Whereas in Burma the Burman majority resides in a minority of the land and in Laos the Lao majority is the numerical minority, in Thailand the highland region is a bare one-fifth of the national territory, and the highland population is perhaps 1 percent of the national total. Unlike Burma and other neighboring countries, Thailand has no legacy of direct colonial rule that accentuated divisions between hill-dwellers and valley-dwellers (Kyaw Thet 1956, 161). Thailand also has no legacy of politicized ethnic self-consciousness like that which has fractured the Union of Burma. Furthermore, Thailand's kings skillfully withstood colonial pressure, and the traditional monarchy has remained in constitutionalized form to serve as a symbolico-political center for majority and minorities alike. I would, however, argue that the sources of Thailand's potential success may prove instead to be the seeds of its failure in fostering the integration of lowlanders and highlanders.

Akha are one of the so-called "six tribes" of Thailand, that is, one of the six major mountain minorities. Five of these, including Akha, have already been characterized as reluctant assimilators. These five—Hmong, Mien, Lahu, Lisu, and Akha—are relatively recent immigrants into the territory now constituting Thailand. Only members of the sixth and by far the largest highland minority, the Karen, were in the area prior to the colonial era. Traditional relations between Karen and northern prinicpalities, like those between Lua' and these principalities, were severed early this century with the commencement of the bureaucratic and symbolico-religious integration of the northern region into the emerging Thai nation-state (Keyes 1971; Tambiah 1976).[21] As the periphery was consolidated into the centralized Thai kingdom, in large measure in response to jockeying by colonial powers, "the gulf between the hill people and the representatives of lowland authority" widened (Walker 1979–80, 428; see also Keyes 1979b, 53). Not until the 1950s did the central government begin to fill the vacuum which resulted from its very creation.

Present and prospective relations between the national government and highlanders in Thailand can be approached with the aid of an analysis concerning the transformation of the Burmans' relations with peripheral peoples in the post-colonial era. According to Lehman (1967, 103),

Throughout the pre-colonial period of history the Burmans had a reasonably correct tacit understanding of the nature of their relations with bordering peoples, tribal and non-tribal. That Burma seems to have lost this understanding today is almost certainly directly attributable to the importation of very explicit European ideas about nations, societies, and cultures, and the kinds of phenomena that they are taken to be.

Hinton (1983, 167), who has done field research among Karen, contends that in Thailand an appropriate "tacit understanding" remains. That I take exception to his conclusion is, I believe, directly attributable to the fact that I worked among Akha, one of the more recently arrived groups.

Among officials in Thailand, Karen (and Lua') society is apparently taken to be significantly different from the societies of the remaining five "hill tribes." According to a publication of the Tribal Research Centre (now Institute) (1967, 6) of the Department of Public Welfare,

The Yao [Mien], Meo [Hmong], Lisu, Akha and Lahu are all shifting cultivators who farm land above 3,000 feet. Rice and corn are their main subsistence crops, with opium poppy, miscellaneous vegetables and jungle products being chief sources of cash income. Because shifting agriculture dictates periodic change of residence, all . . . tend to be widely distributed through the hills. The numerous Karen, and similar groups such as Lawa [Lua'] . . . and [Thai] Lue have more or less sedentary agricultural economies, cultivating terrace or lowland rice fields. Consequently, they tend to be concentrated in particular regions.

The first five groups mentioned are lumped together not only as residents of higher elevations, but also as the "opium-growing tribes" (Patya Saihoo 1963, 37) even though many among them live below 3,000 feet and many cultivate no opium.

As recent arrivals, Hmong, Mien, Lisu, Lahu, and Akha are considered immigrants with no historical or legal claim to the land. All the land upon which highlanders reside is government property (McKinnon and Wanat Bhruksasri 1983, xii). The Land Code, which prohibits damaging land in the hills by fire, essentially outlaws their traditional slash-and-burn agriculture (Sophon Ratanakhon 1978, 48–49). Although their illegal method of cultivation is generally tolerated by officials, it is widely regarded by Thai both within and outside government as destructive to forests and watersheds, and floods in the lowlands are attibuted to swidden practices in the highlands (*Bangkok*

World 1970, 3). Swiddening practiced properly with sufficiently long fallow periods is, in fact, the most productive system of cultivation in upland forested areas and is not destructive to the land (Race 1974, 89, n. 6). The problem in the mountains of northern Thailand is not slash-and-burn agriculture itself, but the limited size of land relative to the population to be supported by this mode of agriculture. Many farmers in the hills swidden improperly not through ignorance or preference, but because they must eat. In contrast to the five recently arrived mountain minorities, Karen are taken to be more benign: their agricultural methods are familiar, their settlements reassuringly stable, and their crops comfortingly legal. Furthermore, recognition of the historical depth of their presence in Thailand provides them with a legitimacy denied the other "hill tribes."

Mountain minorities of the higher slopes are alien and intrusive in the eyes of government representatives, while the Karen, though "hill tribe," are nonetheless akin and indigenous. Not all Karen are descendants of residents; some are recent immigrants from turbulent Burma. Nevertheless, the history of some bestows an aura of legitimacy on others. Thai authorities have consistently underestimated the length of residence of members of the five remaining major mountain minorities. Akha, for example, had been in Thailand almost seventy years when it was declared that they had arrived "no longer than 30–50 years" ago (Tribal Research Centre 1967, 6). Such underestimates are not surprising given the vacuum that existed between the turn of the century and the reestablishment of official contact in the 1950s. These underestimates are, however, unfortunate because they inhibit the extension of the type of "tacit understanding" which continues to be operative in Karen-Thai relations to relations between the so-called "opium-growing tribes" and the Thai. Instead, understandings derived from "very explicit European ideas about nations" determined the nature of initial contacts with these highlanders in the 1950s and have profoundly influenced government policies and programs concerning hill-dwellers since then.

Reestablishment of official contact with peripheral peoples in the north was the consequence of efforts by the newly founded Border Patrol Police (BPP) to secure and safeguard the national frontiers.[22] Not long thereafter, the BPP program expanded to include social welfare projects in highland villages, notably Thai-language schools.[23] Since 1959 the National Tribal Welfare Committee, headed by the Minister of the Interior and composed of representatives from the Department of Public Welfare and the Ministries of Agriculture, Education, and Public Health, or its 1974 successor, the National Tribal Committee, have been responsible for overseeing the many government agencies and programs concerned with the approximately five hundred thousand hill people in the nation's north. The objectives of the central government in its relations with highlanders were summarized at a 1967 symposium at the recently established Tribal Research Centre (Suwan Ruenyote 1969, 13):

1. To prevent the destruction of forest and sources of natural streams by encouraging stabilised agriculture to replace the destructive shifting cultivation . . .
2. to end poppy growing, by promoting other means of livelihood;
3. to develop the economic and social conditions of hill tribes . . .
4. to induce the hill tribes to accept the important role of helping to maintain the security of national frontiers, by instilling in them a sense of belonging and national loyalty.

Each year Thailand's government, with aid from numerous international agencies and foreign governments (especially the U.S.), has spent ever-increasing sums on ever-mushrooming programs to realize these objectives.[24] The so-called "hill tribe problem" was originally defined, as numerous commentators have noted, in terms of national interests and needs rather than in terms of the interests and needs of highlanders.[25] Despite humanistic attitudes toward highlanders on the part of the present monarch King Phumiphon, and other members of the royal family as well as of some representatives of the national government, this original emphasis continues to predominate.[26] Indeed, the four objectives listed above were tellingly reduced to three with the deletion of the third by one high official interviewed in the mid-1970s (Bo Gua 1975, 76). This same official equated the maintenance of the security of the national frontiers (objective 4 above) with "combating communist terrorism among the hill tribes" (Bo Gua 1975, 76).

I believe the image of the highlander as insurgent that is pervasive among government officials, rather than the small number of highlanders who have resisted or might resist government pressure by force, is the most dangerous element in the present hill / valley conjuncture. This dangerous image of largely imaginary danger results from the application of the "Red Meo" model to highlanders generally. A brief look at the origins of this model is revealing. The first armed clashes between highlanders and the government in 1967 did not involve the few Hmong (Meo) communist ("Red") cadres. Rather, they arose "in response to extortion by Thai officials for so-called 'illegal' agricultural activities [i.e., slash-and-burn cultivation]" of Hmong villagers (Turton 1974, 339; see also Bo Gua 1975, 71; Cooper 1979, 326; Race 1974, 98–99). Now any highlander who so much as questions government corruption or policies is liable to be labeled a communist. Many government officials are so preoccupied with suppressing communism that they ignore economic and social conditions. Rather than asking whether highland villagers have enough rice, they ask whether there are any communists in the area.

Although Geddes (1967, 556), an Australian anthropologist who served as the initial foreign advisor to the Tribal Research Centre, advocated a policy of "open-ended integration" to the Royal Thai Government, the thrust of numerous programs is obviously asssimilationist. For example, schools established in the highlands are taught exclusively in the Thai language, and the Public Welfare Department supports an extensive program under which missionary monks propagate Buddhism among highlanders (Keyes 1971; Tambiah 1976, 434–54). The philosophy underlying the resettlement program initiated in the late 1960s was "accelerated integration," and the aim was to transform "former hilltribe villages" into a "normal Thai village" (Krachang Bhanthumnavin 1972, 23, 31). This program was operated by the Communist Suppression Operations Command (CSOC), which has since been renamed the Internal Security Operations Command (ISOC). It was initiated in response to the massive refugee population created by the Royal Thai Army's bombing and napalming of suspected insurgent strongholds, particularly in Nan Province, and developed into an evacuation program aimed at removing highlanders from areas of suspected communist influence (Thomson 1968).[27]

Not all Thai supported this resettlement policy. For example, in an article entitled "The Hilltribes: Who Should Do the Moving?" which appeared in the English-language newspaper *The Bangkok Post*, Suthichai Yoon (1970) urged that "instead of moving them to the officials, the latter should move closer to the hilltribesmen both physically and psychologically." Yet the policy of evacuating highlanders to the lowlands was abandoned not because their right to remain in the hills was recognized, but because it was feared that additional highlanders from neighboring Laos and Burma would simply move in and fill the void. The wisdom of the position advocated by Suthichai Yoon has been recognized by the Department of Public Welfare, which now concentrates on delivering agricultural, educational, and medical aid to hill people through a system of selected core and satellite villages rather than by continuing to follow its original program of creating " 'settlement areas' (*nikhom*)" in the highlands and "encouraging tribes to migrate to these settlement areas" (Manndorff 1967, 531–32).

It is both ironic and significant that the resettlement program was touted as "the first time officials have faithfully carried out government policy in treating the tribesmen as full Thai citizens" (Krachang

Bhanthumnavin 1972, 23). The irony is that most highlanders today remain noncitizens. The government, it is argued, "cannot ease regulations [concerning conditions for registering as a citizen] too much or quicken registration, for fear that this would serve to further encourage already substantial immigration" (McKinnon and Wanat Bhruksasri 1983, xii). The significance is that a full citizen is envisaged as indistinguishable from an ethnic Thai. Some officials see national integration not as the incorporation of distinctive parts into a united whole but as the homogenization of disparate parts into a uniform whole. What such officials seek is not the identification of mountain minorities with the nation but their identity with the national majority.

This monolithic notion of national identity held by some Thai officials as well as by some Thai not in government seems to represent the coupling of a European conception of a bounded territorial state with an older conception of Thai identity. Not only is just one "sense of territoriality" considered legitimate, so too just one sense of identity is considered legitimate. Both should be "fully, flatly, and evenly operative" over the entire nation (Anderson 1983, 26). The pre-colonial "tacit understanding" of hill / valley relations permitted peripheral peoples to retain an identity different from those at the center. Now many Thai do not recognize the possiblity of dual identities or loyalties; the extreme position is that "To be Thai is to speak only Thai, to be Buddhist" (Keyes 1979a, 19). As the overwhelming majority and as the residents of most of the land, Thai are not forced to realize that "bilaterality of integration" is required (Maran La Raw 1967, 143). Not only must minorities adapt to the nation, the majority must accord them an equal place within it. Lacking assertive, politicized ethnic identity, mountain minorities have not persuaded the Thai government to redefine its objectives so that the highlanders' problems replace the highlanders themselves as the "hill-tribe problem."

The highlanders' problems are likely to become more severe. Continued economic marginalization appears inevitable given an expanding population in a limited area dependent upon an agricultural technology predicated upon the availablity of either sufficient land for swidden rotation or new land for settlement. Government programs have paid little attention to stabilizing the subsistence rice economy, and few of the many cash crops such as coffee and decorative flowers initially introduced to replace opium poppies has had widespread success. More recently, crops like cabbages and tomatoes have been highly lucrative but have exacted a heavy toll from the land, in the form of increased erosion, and from the people, in the form of side-effects from pesticides and fungicides. The subsistence economy is collapsing at the same time that its long-term companion, the cash-crop economy, is not expanding rapidly enough to fill the gap. Highlanders are increasingly forced to join the wage-economy of the northern hills. A small but growing number of Akha, for example, live in leaderless hamlets on the outskirts of market towns. Hanks and Hanks (1975, 75) found that in these abject, amorphous aggregates "collective life within the Akha tradition had shrunk near a minimum while hungry householders struggled to find something to eat."

Although all mountain minorities will face increasing economic hardship, Karen overall will probably experience less cultural disruption than others provided that Thai continue to grant them a legitimate place within the nation by virtue of their history and do not further assimilate them to the "hill tribe" model (Keyes 1979a, 1979b; Kunstadter 1979). Unlike Karen, members of the remaining five major highland groups—Hmong, Mien, Lahu, Lisu, and Akha—are not permitted to retain their traditional identity and to be Thai simultaneously. If members of these groups who are strongly attached to their respective ethnic identities are allowed to slip into Thai identity only by default, through gradually abandoning their inherited identities because poverty prevents them from fulfilling the demands of those identities, they will never gain the "sense of belonging and national loyalty" the government claims to desire for them. I do not share Bradley's (1983, 54) confidence that "positive group identity" alone is sufficient in the context of modern nation-states for preserving ethnic identity, either as traditionally defined or as consciously refashioned by the people themselves to meet changing circumstances. As the economic situation continues to deteriorate, the role of those in government who recognize that dual identity and dual "sense of territoriality" are possible, and who believe that it is imperative that national integration be forged within diversity, will become increasingly crucial.

*

Since this paper was originally written (1983–84), it has become increasingly likely that the sources of Thailand's potential success in fostering the integration of lowlanders and highlanders will instead prove to be the seeds of its failure. There is growing evidence that rather than moving "closer to the hilltribesmen . . . psychologically," as Suthichai Yoon (1970) urged nearly twenty years ago, officials have moved away. In Thailand today the territorial imperative of the nation-state is clearly dominant. Now that the uplands are riddled with roads connecting them to the lowlands and all villages have been pulled into the orbit of the centralized bureaucracy, concern with incorporating the highlands and highlanders administratively has been eclipsed by concern with controlling the utilization of mountain land in what is perceived to be the national interest. And the highlanders themselves are seen to have no share in that national interest and indeed are doomed to be inimical to it.

It is not the image of highlander as insurgent that now pervades official thinking. Largely because of the collapse of the Communist Party of Thailand in part due to the government's amnesty program initiated in the late 1970s, this image is no longer at the fore. In its stead is the image of highlander as destroyer of the nation's forests and watersheds through slash-and-burn agriculture and log poaching and as destroyer of the nation's international reputation through cultivating opium poppies and trafficking in illegal drugs. Recent statements by the deputy secretary-general of the National Security Council and by the commander and the chief-of-staff of the Third Army Region (covering the North) confirm the prevalence of these unjust stereotypes (*The Bangkok Post* 1987; Sinfah Tunsarawuth 1987; *The Nation* 1987a, 1987b).

A two-pronged policy has begun to be implemented to remove highlanders from mountain land. Involuntary resettlement is designed to relocate uplanders into low-lying areas, and involuntary "repatriation" is aimed at driving so-called illegal immigrants into either Burma or Laos. Given that resettlement was abandoned as policy some two decades ago after being effectively challenged by Thai within and outside the government on both humanitarian and pragmatic grounds, its recent resurrection is particularly disheartening. Like resettlement, "repatriation" must be questioned on similar grounds.[28] In late September of this year (1987), Akha and other highlanders expelled from thirteen villages in Chiang Rai Province were left at the Burma border with neither food nor shelter. Since many highlanders, even those born inside Thailand to parents who were themselves born inside Thailand, do not have citizenship papers, it is difficult to distinguish between legal residents and illegal immigrants. It is also hard to determine from official statements the basis upon which legal residence is determined. In fact, "repatriation" is a misnomer because many highlanders are stateless persons who are not accorded citizenship either by Thailand or by its neighbors. Moreover, no provision is made for due process to allow those scheduled for expulsion to argue against the claim that Thailand is not in actuality the country of their birth or is not the country in which they have a right to citizenship. From a political perspective, forced expulsions of the type carried out in September can only serve to create fear and antagonism toward the government on the part of those highlanders who can legitimately claim membership in the Thai nation.

While forest conservation and watershed preservation are important for all Thailand's people, highlanders and lowlanders alike, there is little scientific support for the view that the only way to achieve these aims is to remove highlanders from the hills. Development workers argue that agriculture can be practiced on steep slopes in a manner (for example, strip farming) that prevents erosion and soil depletion. In addition, recent projects in social forestry enlist the support of uplanders and lowlanders in the revitalization of overworked areas for their mutual benefit. In these critical days there is hope that policy-makers will heed those inside and outside government who see the current crisis in the mountains of northern Thailand not as "the hill tribe problem" or even as the problem of the hill tribes but rather as the problem of the entire nation which can only be solved by highlanders and lowlanders in cooperation.

*

Acknowledgments. Field research upon which this article is based was conducted in Chiang Rai Province, Thailand, between 1979 and 1987. Research permission granted by the National Research Council of Thailand and financial support provided by the Fulbright-Hays Doctoral Dissertation Abroad Program and by the International Doctoral Research Fellowship Program of the Social Science Research Council (New York) are gratefully acknowledged. This research was assisted by a grant from the Joint Committee on Southeast Asia of the Social Science Research Council and the American Council of Learned Societies with funds provided by the Ford Foundation and the National Endowment for the Humanities. Preparation of this paper was supported by Mrs. John de Menil, originator and sponsor of the Rothko Chapel colloquium. I am indebted to Leo Alting von Geusau and to Elaine and Paul Lewis who generously shared their knowledge with a newcomer to the field of Akha studies. F. K. Lehman's influence on my thinking about ethnic identity is, I hope, obvious. The call for papers by Remo Guidieri and Francesco Pellizzi provided an important stimulus for this paper. My thanks to F. K. Lehman, Paul Lewis, Howard Radley, and the editors of this volume for their helpful comments as this paper evolved. I am especially grateful to Charles Keyes for his comments concerning contrasting attitudes on the part of Thai officials toward Karen and Hmong which largely inspired the reworking of the final section, and to Richard Parmentier for numerous stylistic and substantive suggestions. John Connell, Yves Conrad, John McKinnon, and Patricia Symonds provided much appreciated advice on the 1987 update. To the many Akha, young and old, who patiently taught me about their world and allowed me to share it, my deepest thanks.

NOTES

1. Since the politically and economically dominant group need not be the numerical majority (as is, in fact, the case in Laos) the majority-minority opposition does not always accurately reflect the demographic situation. Adopting the position of Wagley and Harris, Vincent (1974, 376) argues that a group is a majority, regardless of its numerical strength, by virtue of its economic, political, and social dominance. My usage, which follows Vincent, differs from that of Kunstadter (1967a, 17), who applies the term "tribe" to those people thus far referred to as hill-dwellers and reserves the term "minority" for valley-dwellers whose ethnic affiliation is not with the "dominant national majority." See n. 2 on uses and implications of the term "tribe."

2. Although the term "tribe" is sometimes applied both to groups without permanent supralocal political structures and to groups such as Shan and Burmans with Asiatic state systems in publications of the colonial period (e.g., Temple 1910), in much of that and later literature (e.g., Lehman 1963), it is reserved for populations lacking stable forms of indigenous political organization above the village. Along with many students of mainland Southeast Asia, I avoid the term because it carries incorrect and undesirable connotations (Kunstadter 1969, 70). Complex and rich traditions and institutions of highlanders cannot be placed at a level below those of valley-dwellers, but some who hear or see the term "hill tribe" assume that it implies backwardness or inferiority because "tribe" has often been used to designate a level of progress or evolution. Moreover, in the mosaic of Thailand's northern mountains, exclusive ethnic territories are absent, but according to some usages a tribe by definition inhabits a tribal territory. Despite the unfortunate misunderstandings use of the term "tribe" may engender, the term is unlikely to disappear if only because it has been adopted by Southeast Asians. In Thailand the name of the section of the Department of Public Welfare concerned with mountain minorities is officially translated into English as Hill Tribe Welfare Division.

3. For a published version of the Akha story, see Lewis (1969–70, 787–89). On Chin see Lehman (1963, 33), on Karen see Hinton (1979, 86) and Kunstadter (1979, 153), and on Lahu see Jones (1971, 6) and Kandre (1967, 621). Interestingly, in one Karen rendition the valley neighbors are Europeans (Hinton [1979, 86]).

4. This process is elucidated not only in Alting von Geusau (1983), Lehman (1963), and Radley (1982), but also in Kandre (1967), Keyes (1981), and Marlowe (1969).

5. In addition to Lehman (1963), see Alting von Geusau (1983), Condominas (1951), Dentan (1979), Hinton (1979), Jones (1971), Kandre (1967), Keyes (1979a), Lehman (1979), and Marlowe (1979).

6. Scholars have emphasized that "identification by others is an important

feature in the establishment of self-identification" (Ardener [1975], 348). For this to be true, internal and external criteria of identification need not coincide. As elaborated below, Akha consider themselves to be Akha on the basis of descent from an apical ancestor and shared Customs. Thai, on the other hand, appear to identify Akha primarily on the basis of the women's distinctive hat and short skirt. In addition, the delicacy of internal and external classification is not always comparable: for example, whereas Akha consider themselves to be different from Lahu and Lisu as well as from Northern and Central Thai, many Thai of both sorts view Akha together with Lahu and Lisu as generic "hill tribe."

7. For readers unfamiliar with the ethnography, Thai-speaking Lue are not to be confused with the culturally distinct Mon-Khmer-speaking Lua'.

8. It should be noted that although Leach's (1954) description of the society of the Kachin Hills Area of Burma as including both Shan and Kachin inspired these analyses of native definitions of group affiliation, ethnic identity as explicit self-definition is irrelevant to his own analysis. For example, it is not significant to Leach's project whether Lisu speakers who are incorporated into the Kachin marriage system (*mayu-dama*) and thereby into the Kachin political order consider themselves to be Lisu, Kachin, or, for that matter, both simultaneously or sometimes one and sometimes the other.

9. In an article published after this paper was originally delivered, Bradley (1983) presents an analysis of identity among highlanders in Thailand which, although similar in certain respects, differs significantly from that presented here. Although Bradley mentions "felt identity," he does not distinguish carefully between self-definitional bases of identity and culturally distinctive features apparent to an observer. Furthermore, Bradley identifies some criteria such as language and religion as universal components of identity. I reject this view below.

10. Kunstadter (1983a) provides an interesting recent example of this second type of ethnic change among Lua' in northern Thailand.

11. Although features seized upon as components of ethnic identity are not themselves universal, it is possible that these contents of ethnic self-definitions exhibit universal regularities. Numerous scholars from Weber (1978) to Keyes (1976, 1981) have made cross-cultural generalizations concerning subjective criteria of ethnic identity. For both Weber and Keyes "the diacritics always have about them an aura of descent" having no necessary connection with actual biological relationship (Cohen 1978, 387). While this characterization is applicable to Akha ethnic identity, I do not believe that it covers all ethnographic cases. Hastrup (1982, 155) suggests that the "idea of history" is "the ultimate prerequisite of ethnicity." As with Weber's and Keyes's generalizations, Hastrup's generalization is not universally applicable.

12. See Hickey (1982a, 1982b) for an extended historical analysis of the rise of ethnonationalism among highlanders in Vietnam, and see Keyes (1984) for additional commentary.

13. Akha are called Ekaw / Ikaw / Igor by Thai. In Western accounts they appear under various labels such as Akha, Aka, Kha Ko, and Kaw. In China,

Akha are included within the category Woni or Hani.

14. The gloss adopted here, which was suggested by Leo Alting von Geusau (personal communication), captures the essence of the office. It is not a direct translation of the Akha term.

15. As Feingold (1976, 91) notes, not enough is yet known about Akha dialectology to make firm generalizations about the relationship between dialect communities and lineage groupings.

16. When two Akha strangers meet, they usually identify themselves by naming their lineage. By so doing, they situate themselves not only within the branching system of patrilineal descent, as both Feingold (1976, 87) and J. Hanks (1974, 119) observe, but also within the affinal network.

17. For additional discussion of customs, the reader is directed to Alting von Geusau's (1983) excellent article "The Dialectics of *Akhazan*: The Interiorization of a Perennial Minority Group."

18. Just as variants of the story explaining the absence of writing are common among highlanders, so too are variants of this tale. Kunstadter (1979, 144) reports that Karen and Lua' agree that Lua' have the most spirits because they carried them in a tightly woven and covered basket, Karen have fewer spirits because they carried them in an uncovered basket, and Northern Thai have none because they lost them all from their basket. In the same manner, Thai-ized Lua' in Chiang Mai Province continue to account for their having more spirits than their Northern Thai neighbors (Katherine Bowie, personal communication).

19. According to Paul Lewis (personal communication), in Burma the language(s) used depend upon the length of residence in a given area. He reports that Akha believe that if they entered a particular territory recently, the spirits of the land know the Shan language better than they know Akha.

20. When customary ritual obligations to ancestors are not fulfilled, as is the case for converts to Christianity, the traditional ethnic identity based upon shared patrilineal descent falters. While Akha Christians remain Akha in their own eyes, they are ambiguously Akha in the eyes of traditionalists. A Christian continues to belong to a named Akha patrilineage, but he no longer fulfills the ritual obligations to his patrilineal kin dictated by customs. Moreover, he no longer fulfills customary affinal ritual obligations. If an Akha Christian takes a wife from a non-Christian village, the woman joins her husband and becomes a "Christ person." If a woman from a Christian village marries into a traditional village, she comes under the care of her husband's ancestors. Since her natal patrilineal kin cannot perform the cosmologically crucial ritual obligations of affines, such a woman is not a desirable wife for a traditional Akha. The claim to difference from, as well as the claim to equality with, dominant valley-dwellers entailed by highlanders' conversion to Christianity demands further study, especially in light of the (re)structuring of self-definitions of identity (Keyes 1984, 180; Kunstadter 1983a, 150–52; Lehman 1967, 97–98, 120).

21. Relations between northern princes or their local delegates and some later arrivals such as Lahu were also severed at the same time (Walker 1979–80, 427).

22. While the operative "ideas about nations" can be characterized as European, it is important to remember that the U.S. has provided significant encouragement and financial support for Thailand's efforts to secure its frontiers. Modern nation-states exist not in isolation but in the context of world power politics. See Lobe 1977 for information concerning U.S. government, including CIA, backing for the BPP. Interest in the northern borders was in part a reaction to the 1949 revolution in nearby China, activities by the Burma Communist Party and various ethnic minority armies in the neighboring Shan States, and continuing conflict in adjacent Laos.

23. It is interesting and perhaps signficant in the overall development of modern highlander-goverment relations that the BPP mandate did not extend to the Karen (Moseley 1967, 406).

24. Many of the articles and volumes cited thus far contain information about Thai government policies and programs directed toward mountain minorities and about highlanders' reactions. Sources that contain substantial reviews and / or recommendations concerning government policies and programs include Aran Suwanbubpa 1976, Bo Gua 1975, Cooper 1979, Geddes 1967 and 1983, Hearn 1974, Keen 1973, Manndorff 1967, Patya Saihoo 1963, Suwan Ruenyote 1969, Walker 1979–80, and references cited therein.

25. See Bo Gua 1975, Cooper 1979, Hearn 1974, Jones 1980, Moseley 1967, and Walker 1979–80.

26. The priorites underlying the King of Thailand's Project differ profoundly from the four listed above. These humanistic priorities as listed in Bo Gua 1975, 81, n. 24 from an unpublished royal manuscript ("His Majesty's Assistance to Hill Tribes," unpublished manuscript by Mom Chao Bhistej Rajani) are:

    i. give help to fellow men
    ii. raise the standard of living
    iii. prevent forest destruction and halt the narcotic traffic.

27. See Hearn 1974 for a critical study of the program.

28. In addition, a determination must be made of the legal status, in both Thai and international terms, of the Ministry of the Interior's proclamation and the Council of Ministers' policy which are used to justify expulsions to Burma and Laos respectively. It is possible that these instruments contravene Thai law and / or international law.

REFERENCES

Alting von Geusau, Leo. 1983. "Dialectics of *Akhazan*: The Interiorization of a Perennial Minority Group." In *Highlanders of Thailand*, edited by John McKinnon and Wanat Bhruksasri, 243–77. Kuala Lumpur: Oxford University Press.

Anderson, Benedict. 1983. *Imagined Communities: Reflections on the Origin and Spread of Nationalism.* London: Verso.

Andrianoff, David I. 1979. "The Effect of the Laotian Conflict on Meo Ethnic

Identity." In *Nationalism and the Crises of Ethnic Minorities in Asia*, edited by Tai S. Kang, 77–80. Westport, Conn.: Greenwood Press.

Aran Suwanbubpa. 1976. *Hill Tribe Development and Welfare Programmes in North Thailand*. Singapore: Regional Institute of Higher Education and Development.

Ardener, Edwin. 1975. "Language, Ethnicity, and Population." In *Studies in Social Anthropology: Essays in Memory of E. E. Evans-Pritchard by His Former Oxford Colleagues*, edited by J. H. M. Beattie and R. G. Lienhardt, 343–53. Oxford: Clarendon Press.

The Bangkok Post. 1987. "Tribesmen Forced Back into Burma." September 26, 5.

Bangkok World. 1970. "Ravaged Earth Blamed in Chiang Rai Floods." July 6, 3.

Bo Gua. 1975. "Opium, Bombs and Trees: The Future of the H'mong Tribesmen in Northern Thailand." *Journal of Contemporary Asia* 5, no. 1:70-81.

Bourdieu, Pierre. 1977. *Outline of a Theory of Practice*. Translated by Richard Nice. Cambridge, Eng.: Cambridge University Press. (Original: *Equisse d'une théorie de la pratique, précédé de trois études d'ethnologie kabyle*, Switzerland, 1972.)

Bradley, David. 1983. "Identity: The Persistence of Minority Groups." In *Highlanders of Thailand*, edited by John McKinnon and Wanat Bhruksasri, 46–55. Kuala Lumpur: Oxford Univerity Press.

Cohen, Ronald. 1978. "Ethnicity: Problem and Focus in Anthropology." *Annual Review of Anthropology* 7:379–403.

Condominas, Georges. 1951. "Aspects of a Minority Problem in Indochina." *Pacific Affairs* 24:77–82.

Cooper, R. G. 1979. "The Tribal Minorities of Northern Thailand, Problems and Prospects." *Southeast Asian Affairs* 6:323–32.

Dentan, R. K. 1976. "Ethnics and Ethics in Southeast Asia." In *Changing Identities in Modern Southeast Asia*, edited by David J. Banks, 71–81. The Hague: Mouton.

——— 1979. "Identity and Ethnic Contact: Perak Malaysia, 1963." In *Nationalism and the Crises of Ethnic Minorities in Asia*, edited by Tai S. Kang, 81–88. Westport, Conn.: Greenwood Press.

Durrenberger, E. Paul. 1980. "Annual Non-Buddhist Religious Observances of Mae Hong Son Shan." *Journal of the Siam Society* 68:48–56.

Feingold, David A. 1976. "On Knowing Who You Are: Intraethnic Distinctions among the Akha of Northern Thailand." In *Changing Identities in Modern Southeast Asia*, edited by David J. Banks, 83–94. The Hague: Mouton.

Geddes, W. R. 1967. "The Tribal Research Centre, Thailand: An Account of Plans and Activities." In *Southeast Asian Tribes, Minorities, and Nations*, edited by Peter Kunstadter, vol. II, 553–81. Princeton: Princeton University Press.

——— 1983. "Research and the Tribal Research Centre." In *Highlanders of Thailand*, edited by John McKinnon and Wanat Bhruksasri, 3–12. Kuala Lumpur: Oxford University Press.

Guidieri, Remo, and Francesco Pellizzi. 1980. "Ethnicities and Nations: Contemporary Reinterpretations of the Problematic of Identity (Ten Themes of Reflection for a Colloquium)." Manuscript.

Hanks, Jane R. 1974. "Recitation of Patrilineages among the Akha." In *Social Organization and the Applications of Anthropology: Essays in Honor of Lauriston Sharp*, edited by Robert J. Smith, 114–27. Ithaca: Cornell University Press.

Hanks, Lucien M., and Jane R. Hanks. 1975. "Reflections on Ban Akha Mae Salong." *Journal of the Siam Society* 63, no. 1 : 72–85.

Hanks, Lucien M., Jane R. Hanks, and Lauriston Sharp. 1964. *A Report on Tribal Peoples in Chiengrai Province North of the Mae Kok River*. Bennington-Cornell Anthropological Survey of Hill Tribes in Thailand, Data Paper Number 1. Bangkok: The Siam Society.

Hansson, Inga-Lill. 1983. "Death in an Akha Village." In *Highlanders of Thailand*, edited by John McKinnon and Wanat Bhruksasri, 278–90. Kuala Lumpur: Oxford University Press.

Hastrup, Kirsten. 1982. "Establishing an Ethnicity: The Emergence of the 'Icelanders' in the Middle Ages." In *Semantic Anthropology*, edited by David Parkin, 145–60. New York: Academic Press.

Hearn, Robert. 1974. *Thai Government Programs in Refugee Relocation and Resettlement in Northern Thailand*. Auburn, N.Y.: Thailand Books.

Hickey, Gerald Cannon. 1982a. *Free in the Forest: Ethnohistory of the Vietnamese Central Highlands 1954-1976*. New Haven: Yale University Press.

———. 1982b. *Sons of the Mountains: Ethnohistory of the Vietnamese Central Highlands to 1954*. New Haven: Yale University Press.

Hinton, Peter. 1969. "Introduction." In *Tribesmen and Peasants in North Thailand: Proceedings of the First Symposium of the Tribal Research Centre Chiang Mai, Thailand, 1967*, 1–11.

———. 1979. "The Karen, Millennialism, and the Politics of Accommodation to Lowland States." In *Ethnic Adaptation and Identity: The Karen on the Thai Frontier with Burma*, edited by Charles F. Keyes, 81–94. Philadelphia: Institute for the Study of Human Issues.

———. 1983. "Do the Karen Really Exist?" In *Highlanders of Thailand*, edited by John McKinnon and Wanat Bhruksasri, 155–68. Kuala Lumpur: Oxford University Press.

Hymes, Dell. 1971. "Two Types of Linguistic Relativity (With Examples from AmerIndian Ethnography)." In *Sociolinguistics*, edited by William Bright, 116–67. The Hague: Mouton.

Jones, Delmos J. 1971. "Village Autonomy, Cultural Status and Self Perception." *Anthropological Quarterly* 44, no. 1 : 1–11.

———. 1980. "Report to the National Research Council on Research Carried out among the Black Lahu of Northern Thailand." Manuscript.

Kandre, Peter. 1967. "Autonomy and Integration of Social Systems: The Iu Mien ('Yao' or 'Mien') Mountain Population and Their Thai Neighbors." In *Southeast Asian Tribes, Minorities, and Nations*, edited by Peter Kunstadter, vol. II, 583–638. Princeton: Princeton University Press.

———. 1976. "Yao (Iu Mien) Supernaturalism, Language, and Ethnicity." In

Changing Identities in Modern Southeast Asia, edited by David J. Banks, 171–97. The Hague: Mouton.

Keen, F. G. B. 1973. "Zonal Development: The Basic Proposition." *South-east Asian Spectrum (SEATO)* 2, no. 1:54–57.

Keyes, Charles F. 1971. "Buddhism and National Integration in Thailand." *Journal of Asian Studies* 30:551–67.

_____ 1976. "Towards a New Formulation of the Concept of Ethnic Group." *Ethnicity* 3:202–13.

_____ 1979a. "Introduction." In *Ethnic Adaptation and Identity: The Karen on the Thai Frontier with Burma*, edited by Charles F. Keyes, 1–23. Philadelphia: Institute for the Study of Human Issues.

_____ 1979b. "The Karen in Thai History and the History of Karen in Thailand." In *Ethnic Adaptation and Identity: The Karen on the Thai Frontier with Burma*, edited by Charles F. Keyes, 25–61. Philadelphia: Institute for the Study of Human Issues.

_____ 1981. "The Dialectics of Ethnic Change." In *Ethnic Change*, edited by Charles F. Keyes, 4-30. Publications on Ethnicity and Nationality of the School of International Studies, University of Washington, 2. Seattle: University of Washington Press.

_____ 1984. "Tribal Ethnicity and the State in Vietnam." *American Ethnologist* 11, no. 1:176–82.

Krachang Bhanthumnavin. 1972. "Overcoming the Problems of Resettling Hill Tribes." *South-east Asian Spectrum (SEATO)* 1, no. 1:23–34.

Kunstadter, Peter. 1967a. "Introduction." In *Southeast Asian Tribes, Minorities, and Nations*, edited by Peter Kunstadter, vol. I, 3–72. Princeton: Princeton University Press.

_____ 1967b. "The Lua' and Skaw Karen of Maehongson Province, Northwestern Thailand." In *Southeast Asian Tribes, Minorities, and Nations*, edited by Peter Kunstadter, vol. II, 639–74. Princeton: Princeton University Press.

_____ 1969. "Hill and Valley Populations in Northwestern Thailand." In *Tribesmen and Peasants in North Thailand: Proceedings of the First Symposium of the Tribal Research Centre, Chiang Mai, Thailand, 1967*, 69–85.

_____ 1979. "Ethnic Group, Category, and Identity: Karen in Northern Thailand." In *Ethnic Adaptation and Identity: The Karen on the Thai Frontier with Burma*, edited by Charles F. Keyes, 119–63. Philadelphia: Institute for the Study of Human Issues.

_____ 1983a. "Animism, Buddhism, and Christianity: Religion in the Life of Lua People of Pa Pae, North-Western Thailand." In *Highlanders of Thailand*, edited by John McKinnon and Wanat Bhruksasri, 135–54. Kuala Lumpur: Oxford University Press.

_____ 1983b. "Highland Populations in Northern Thailand." In *Highlanders of Thailand*, edited by John McKinnon and Wanat Bhruksasri, 15–45. Kuala Lumpur: Oxford University Press.

Kyaw Thet. 1956. "Burma: The Political Integration of Linguistic and Religous Minority Groups" In *Nationalism and Progress in Free Asia*, edited by Philip

W. Thayer, 156–68. Baltimore: Johns Hopkins Press.

Leach, E. R. 1954. *Political Systems of Highland Burma: A Study of Kachin Social Structure*. Cambridge, Mass.: Harvard University Press.

Lehman, F. K. 1963. *The Structure of Chin Society: A Tribal People of Burma Adapted to a Non-Western Civilization*. Illinois Studies in Anthropology, 3. Urbana: University of Illinois Press.

_____ 1967. "Ethnic Categories in Burma and the Theory of Social Systems." In *Southeast Asian Tribes, Minorities, and Nations*, edited by Peter Kunstadter, vol. I, 93–124. Princeton: Princeton University Press.

_____ 1979. "Who Are the Karen, and If So, Why? Karen Ethnohistory and a Formal Theory of Ethnicity." In *Ethnic Adaptation and Identity: The Karen on the Thai Frontier with Burma*, edited by Charles F. Keyes, 215–53. Philadelphia: Institute for the Study of Human Issues.

Lewis, Paul. 1968. *Akha-English Dictionary*. Southeast Asia Program, Data Paper Number 70. Ithaca: Cornell University, Department of Asian Studies.

_____ 1969–70. *Ethnographic Notes on the Akhas of Burma*. 4 vols. New Haven: Human Relations Area Files.

Lo Ch'ang-p'ei. 1945. "The Genealogical Patronymic Linkage System of the Tibeto-Burman Speaking Tribes." *Harvard Journal of Asiatic Studies* 8, nos. 3–4 : 349–63.

Lobe, Thomas. 1977. *United States National Security Policy and Aid to the Thailand Police*. Monograph Series in World Affairs, 14. Denver: University of Denver, Graduate School of International Studies.

McKinnon, John, and Bernard Vienne, eds. 1988. *Hill Tribes Today: Problems in Change*. Bangkok: Orstom and White Lotus.

McKinnon, John, and Wanat Bhruksasri. 1983. "Preface." In *Highlanders of Thailand*, edited by John McKinnon and Wanat Bhruksasri, ix-xii. Kuala Lumpur: Oxford University Press.

Manndorff, Hans. 1967. "The Hill Tribe Program of the Public Welfare Department, Ministry of Interior, Thailand: Research and Socio-economic Developement." In *Southeast Asian Tribes, Minorities, and Nations*, edited by Peter Kunstadter, vol. II, 525–52. Princeton: Princeton University Press.

Maran La Raw. 1967. "Towards a Basis for Understanding the Minorities in Burma: The Kachin Example." In *Southeast Asian Tribes, Minorities, and Nations*, edited by Peter Kunstadter, vol. I, 125–46. Princeton: Princeton University Press.

Marlowe, David H. 1969. "Upland-Lowland Relationships: The Case of the S'kaw Karen of Central Upland Western Chiang Mai." In *Tribesmen and Peasants in North Thailand: Proceedings of the First Symposium of the Tribal Research Centre, Chiang Mai, Thailand, 1967*, 53-68.

_____ 1979. "In the Mosaic: The Cognitive and Structural Aspects of Karen-Other Relationships." In *Ethnic Adaptation and Identity: The Karen on the Thai Frontier with Burma*, edited by Charles F. Keyes, 165–214. Philadelphia: Institute for the Study of Human Issues.

Matisoff, James A. 1983. "Linguistic Diversity and Language Contact." In *Highlanders of Thailand*, edited by John McKinnon and Wanat Bhruksasri,

56–86. Kuala Lumpur: Oxford University Press.

Moerman, Michael. 1965. "Ethnic Identification in a Complex Civilization: Who Are the Lue?" *American Anthropologist* 67:1215–30.

———. 1968. "Being Lue: Uses and Abuses of Ethnic Identification." In *Essays on the Problem of the Tribe: Proceedings of the 1967 Annual Spring Meeting of the American Ethnological Society*, edited by June Helm, 153–69. Seattle: University of Washington Press.

Moseley, George. 1967. "Voices in the Minority." *Far Eastern Economic Review* 55, no. 9:405–7.

Murphy, R. F. 1964. "Social Change and Acculturation." *Transactions of the New York Academy of Sciences*, 2d ser., 26, no. 7:845–54.

The Nation. 1987a. "Illegal Border Immigrants Will Have to Go." October 15, 5.

———. 1987b. "Repatriation of Illegal Highlanders: Senior NSC Official Denies Using Violence." October 13, 3.

Patya Saihoo. 1963. "The Hill Tribes of Northern Thailand and the Opium Problem." *Bulletin of Narcotics* 15, no. 2:35–45.

Race, Jeffrey. 1974. "The War in Northern Thailand." *Modern Asian Studies* 8, no. 1:85–112.

Radley, Howard. 1986. "Economic Marginalization and the Ethnic Consciousness of the Green Mong (Moob Ntsuab) of Northwestern Thailand." Ph.D. diss. Institute of Social Anthropology, Oxford University.

Sinfah Tunsarawuth. 1987. "Govt Pushes out Illegal Burmese Immigrants". *The Nation*, September 26, 1–2.

Sophon Ratanakhon. 1978. "Legal Aspects of Land Occupation and Development." In *Farmers in the Forest: Economic Development and Marginal Agriculture in Northern Thailand*, edited by Peter Kunstadter, E. C. Chapman, and Sanga Sabhasri, 45–53. Honolulu: The University Press of Hawaii for the East-West Center.

Suthichai Yoon. 1970. "The Hilltribes: Who Should Do the Moving?" *The Bangkok Post*, September 7, 7.

Suwan Ruenyote. 1969. "Development and Welfare for the Hill Tribes in Thailand." In *Tribesmen and Peasants in North Thailand: Proceedings of the First Symposium for the Tribal Research Centre, Chiang Mai, Thailand, 1967*, 12–14.

Tambiah, S. J. 1976. *World Conqueror and World Renouncer: A Study of Buddhism and Polity in Thailand against a Historical Background.* Cambridge, Eng.: Cambridge University Press.

Temple, Richard C. 1910. "The People of Burma." *Journal of the Royal Society of Arts* 58, no. 3003:695–711.

Thomson, John R. 1968. "The Mountains Are Steeper." *Far Eastern Economic Review* 60, no. 15:139–41.

Tribal Research Centre. 1967. "Introduction." In *Social Scientific Research in Northern Thailand.* Bulletin Number 1 of the Tribal Research Centre, Chiengmai, Thailand (Department of Public Welfare, Ministry of Interior, Government of Thailand), 5–7.

Turton, Andrew. 1974. "National Minority Peoples in Indo-China." *Journal of Contemporary Asia* 4, no. 3:336–43.

Vincent, Joan. 1974. "The Structuring of Ethnicity." *Human Organization* 33, no. 4:375–79.

Walker, Anthony R. 1979–80. "Highlanders and Government in North Thailand." *Folk* 21–22:419–49.

Weber, Max. 1978. "Ethnic Groups." In *Economy and Society: An Outline of Interpretive Sociology*, edited by Guenther Roth and Claus Wittich, vol. I, 385–98. Berkeley: University of California Press.

Ethnic Fratricide in Sri Lanka:

an Update

STANLEY J. TAMBIAH

In the spring of 1986, my book *Sri Lanka, Ethnic Fratricide and the Dismantling of Democracy*, was published.[1] It dealt with the Sinhalese-Tamil conflicts in Sri Lanka up to the early part of 1984. Here, I discuss the major events that have taken place since that time. In addition to documenting the particular Sri Lankan case, I trust the analysis will shed some light on the dynamics of "ethnicities and nations" as they occur in many other parts of the world.

Since 1984, the conflict in Sri Lanka has raged unabated—indeed, it has worsened. It has also become "internationalized," with world powers (primarily India, and to a lesser extent, the United States) attempting to persuade the contending parties to begin deliberations toward a political settlement. In August 1986, when I wrote this essay, the "Political Parties Conference" convened by President Jayawardene was taking place in Colombo to discuss the terms of a settlement—the third such attempt since the 1983 riots.

A SYNOPTIC VIEW OF SRI LANKA

Sri Lanka is a small island with a population of some 15 million people, of whom 70 percent speak the Sinhalese language and 20 percent the Tamil language. In terms of religious affiliation, 67 percent are Buddhists (and Sinhalese); 18 percent are Hindus (and Tamil).[2] The island, famed for its beauty and its "friendly" people, in recent years has been a tourist attraction governed by a pro-Western "rightist" government bent on attracting foreign industrial investment. In late July and early August of 1983, it was rocked by explosive and virulent riots that erupted after Tamil youth terrorists ambushed and killed thirteen Sinhalese soldiers who were travelling in the Northern Tamil territory. The Sinhalese Buddhist majority reacted with violence, killing many hundreds of people, methodically burning the homes and shops of Tamil residents in Colombo and other places, and destroying industrial plants and factories. As a result, the government's economic gains in recent years were seriously compromised, and some one hundred thousand persons, many of whom were Sinhalese, were left jobless.

The conflict between the Sinhalese and Tamils is compounded of linguistic and religious separations, intensified by competition for white-collar and professional employment in an economy that has a narrow industrial and manufacturing base. The confrontation between these two "ethnic," linguistic and religious communities became acute only after the island attained independence in 1948. Since this fateful date there have been at least six bloody riots (the worst of them occurring in 1958, 1977, 1981, and 1983) in which the Sinhalese have been the physical aggressors and the Tamils the victims.

In the riots of 1983, there were critical developments that may signify a radical breach between the two communities—a polarization difficult, if not impossible, to heal. Within the ranks of the Tamil community there emerged in the late seventies a militant youth movement engaging in guerrilla action. And on the side of the Sinhalese, the recent riots evinced a degree of organized violence never before witnessed in this form. (There were, for example, armed gangs carrying voter lists, knowing all of their victims' addresses, systematically destroying Tamil homes, shops, and factories.)

This particular manifestation of violence gives us cause to reflect on a larger issue: the unprecedented use of organized violence today in several parts of the globe, in conflicts between ethnic groups, between nationalities, between minorities and majorities. The current violent eruptions and incidents in Northern Ireland, Nicaragua, El Salvador, Lebanon, Sri Lanka, India, Burma, Laos, and Cambodia—to name a few instances —are signs of a more general malaise.

It is in the postindependence, nationalistic, allegedly "modernizing" epoch of democratic politics that the Sri Lankan ethnic conflicts have worsened. To begin an analysis, clearly the most relevant point is the era of British colonial rule, especially in the nineteenth and twentieth centuries, when the two indigenous ethnic communities, previously separate, were brought together under imperial rule. The British imposed a single administration, educated an English-speaking local elite drawn from Sinhalese and Tamils alike, opened up plantations and imported a new population of South Indian Tamil laborers to work them. Up to a point, they created a single polity and a plural society. In 1948, they transferred power to the local elites, who had already begun to experience the divisiveness of ethnic, linguistic, and religious affiliations in local participation in representative government.

Not only did universal franchise, territorial electorates, and majority politics produce divisions along party lines within Sinhalese society; they also worked against the interests of minorities who would have preferred quotas and special constitutional protection. Thus, in the postindependence era, national languages were espoused to replace elitist English as the media of educational instruction and administration. Unfortunately, instead of equalizing opportunity in the populace at large, this policy resulted in dividing, rather than uniting the body politic, and unleashed ethnic conflict. Additionally, the revival and sponsorship of Buddhism as an integral feature of Sinhalese "national" identity and cultural pride resulted in adding religion to language as an emotionally charged factor in Sri Lankan politics.

It is at this point of increasing tensions between linguistic and religious groups focused on the prizes and spoils of twentieth-century politics that the Sinhalese first, and the Tamils subsequently, have invoked, manipulated, and exploited the mythic histories, and the rhetoric of primordial bonds, which were originally set down in chronicles and texts written in the first centuries A.D. The resurrection of long dormant politico-religious myths—as if they were memories continuously alive, energizing the actions of present day actors—opens up a number of problems for scholars concerning the uses of the past for present purposes, the role of ideology in interested action, and the contemporary functions of historical symbols.

In my book I brought a double identity to the discussion of the ethnic conflicts between Sinhalese and Tamils in contemporary Sri Lanka. On the one hand, as a social scientist I viewed the phenomenon from as much "distance" as was possible in order to achieve a maximally "objective" picture. On the other hand, as a person of Tamil origins I was, despite being an expatriate for over two decades, to some degree an "insider" with personal, even partisan, sentiments. I therefore attempted to probe my own inner tensions and paradoxes by referring to the perspectives and postures of Sri Lanka's two greatest politicians since Independence: D. S. Senanayaka, a secular-minded constitutionalist to whom the British transferred power as the "father of the nation," and S. W. R. D. Bandaranaike, the Buddhist-Sinhala nationalist, who initiated the so-called social revolution of 1956 and simultaneously exacerbated the conflicts in this society of multiple ethnicities.

THE SPIRALING OF VIOLENCE SINCE 1983

In the years following the 1983 ethnic explosion, the scale and pattern of violence have worsened, exhibiting new cancerous features. Both armed contenders—the Tamil rebels organized in increasingly factional separate movements (with acronyms such as LTTE, PLOTE, EROS, and so on), and the Sinhala government relying more and more on its army and police, beefed up by new weaponry and foreign experts in guerrilla warfare (drawn chiefly from Israeli Mossad and British ex-SAS mercenaries)—have become locked in violent attack and counterattack, with possibilities of an amicable political settlement receding into a vague hope.

The Tamil youth militants have intensified their guerrilla activities. Not only have they increased their hit-and-run activities against the security forces, but in 1985 they took a fateful step: In reprisal for the army's burning of a school with the children trapped inside (this was in the northern coastal town of Valvettithurai, probably the most important center of Tamil resistance), the Tamil rebels *for the first time* attacked and killed *Sinhalese* civilians. To compound this action, they carried out this killing in the Buddhist sacred city of Anuradhapura, which is for the Sinhalese a reminder of their ancient glory and a locus of active nationalist revivalism today. The Sinhala army had previously in many instances demolished Hindu temples and killed their priests; now the Tamil rebels did the same, hitting the Sinhalese at their holy of holies, thereby making a statement that they were prepared to indulge in the same kind of violence against civilians, bystanders, and nonmilitary targets as the armed forces did. This act on the part of the Tamil rebels was decisive in at least one way: they lost their "moral advantage" in the contest by imitating the indiscriminate violence of their enemy.

Once launched on this form of counterattack, both the army and the rebels moved to the next phase—the battle for the northeastern buffer zones and boundary regions between Tamil and Sinhalese settlements in Vavuniya, and, more importantly, Trincomalee districts, whose empty spaces and remote settlements became the arena for intimidation, slaughter, and scorched-earth actions. Civilians, both Sinhalese and Tamil, were the victims in this territorial struggle.

Previously the Sinhala government had spoken of settling some 250,000 Sinhalese peasants in the Northern and Eastern regions as a way of "reoccupying" lands that allegedly belonged to the Sinhalese in the remote golden epochs of Anuradhapura and Polonnaruva, thereby—as a geopolitical strategy—changing the *present population balance*. It now took the ominous and unprecedented step of arming Sinhalese civilians in the Vavuniya-Trincomalee regions, encouraging them to engage in violent actions against Tamil settlements. Arms were distributed to Sinhalese Civilian Home Guards (as they were called), supplementing the not-so-successful efforts of a demoralized army which, bottled up in its camps, was unleashed for unrestrained onslaughts on the Tamil enemy, who were treated as all alike—whether they were civilian or guerrilla, farmers peacefully toiling in the fields or gun-wielding rebels dedicated to suicidal missions.[3]

The most recent phase in this spiraling violence was that of the Tamil rebels' bomb attacks in 1986. These were carried out with impunity in the capital city of Colombo itself—at the central telegraph office, the central bus station, even a police station at Wellawatte, killing and injuring Sinhalese civilians. Moreover, these acts also had shock value, making the Sinhalese public realize that the militants were now organized and capable of professionalized violence, that the country's security forces could not achieve a military solution, and that some form of political settlement was urgently needed.

THE REFUGEE PROBLEM

The displacement of people from their homesteads and settlements, which produced the refugee problem, has spread and grown in magnitude. Soon after the 1983 riots, many tens of thousands of Tamils, both Sri Lankan and Indian, were forced into refugee camps. In an effort to deal with this problem, these people were transported to Jaffna, transplanted to new refugee colonies in Vavuniya and Mullaitivu, or transferred to India. However, the continuing violence created even more massive displacements among *both* ethnic communities, and masses of Tamil—who were the most severely victimized—were forced abroad. It has been reported, on the basis of estimates from Government officials and human-rights groups, that from three hundred to five hundred thousand Sri Lankan Tamils have been driven from their homes as refugees.[4]

In 1984, as the guerrillas mounted their attacks up north,[5] the Sri Lankan army and navy enforced their "surveillance policy" on the northern coast from Mannar to Valvettithurai, and on the offshore islands. The Tamil populations of the coastal villages were subject to army shellings, burnings, and killings. Worse still, on account of its long term consequences, was the disruption of the fishing activities from which they earned their livelihood. Boats were burned and fishing crews massacred on unproven charges of ferrying of rebels and engaging in gunrunning and contraband trade. As a result, tens of thousands of Tamil coastal peoples fled to South India, creating a refugee problem on Indian soil (estimates of refugees there range from 135,000 to 150,000). Inevitably, the surveillance policy also penalized some of the Indian fishing crews operating from the South Indian coast. One can imagine how the presence of grief-stricken and desperate Sri Lankan Tamil refugees, along with the deprivations suffered locally, has inflamed public opinion and the sentiments of Tamil Natu's own chauvinists who have urged "intervention" by their own government on behalf of their brethren in Sri Lanka.

The current civil war has spawned a new development, with the Sinhalese civilians themselves under attack in the northeastern border area. According to Crossette, thirty-five thousand Sinhalese have been displaced by the civil war.[6] These displaced persons, carrying their own horror tales, are deposited in camps at the margins of towns such as Anuradhapura and Polonnarura, adding fuel to an already raging fire.[7] In Sri Lanka itself, this unabated violence and displacement has deepened the alienation between the Sinhala and Tamil communities. Thus, while the scale of entrenched and ever-spreading violence forces on the public's consciousness the need to arrive at a political settlement, at the same time there has been a hardening of inimical feelings and attitudes among even the liberal, educated, and politically vocal elements *on both sides*. It seems that the vast majority of the Sinhalese middle class may by now have lost its sympathy for and become immune to the Tamil predicament. And ominously on the Tamil side, as the sense of helplessness and hopelessness on the part of civilians increases, the radical militants are attempting to squeeze out the liberals and moderates, depicting them as ineffective and therefore secondary, if not irrelevant, in the process of reaching a settlement with the Sinhalese government. At the beginning of the Thimpu talks (see below), two Tamil TULF[8] moderates, both members of Parliament, were assassinated by the militants. The message seemed to be that since the militants had done all the hard and dirty work of resistance, they, not the TULF, should direct the negotiations, taking the credit for any settlement and the responsibility for its implementation. Factionalism was equally evident on the Sinhalese side: at the precise time when the negotiations were scheduled to begin, Sinhalese politicians opposed to the ruling UNP started a campaign to undermine them.

INDIAN INTERVENTION AND THE THIMPU CONFERENCE (1985)

Thimpu, the capital of Bhutan, was chosen as the site of the conference presumably because it was both distant and "neutral"— not only to the contending parties in Sri Lanka but also, with some credibility, to India, the giant neighbor and the outside country most concerned with bringing about a political settlement. (Earlier, there had been an abortive attempt in 1984 by President Jayawardene to hold deliberations in Colombo [the so-called All Party Conference] to which opposition political parties including the members of the banned Tamil United Liberation Front (TULF) were invited. But Jayawardene had invited representatives of the Buddhist clergy to attend; their adamant opposition to any concessions to Tamils, on the plea that the

Buddhist island of Sri Lanka cannot ever be dismembered, poisoned the proceedings.)

The Thimpu deliberations marked three significant shifts in the process of peace-making, even if in the end the deliberations failed. One shift was the beginning of an open and *decisive* intervention by the Indian government in the political turmoil in Sri Lanka. The second was the more or less realistic apprehension by the Sri Lanka government that its own armed forces were probably unable to quell an insurrection that had become both entrenched and militarily competent. (Time and again this realization would be clouded over by atavistic attempts to wipe out the rebels by military action, but the lack of results would progressively strengthen the perception of a stalemate.) The third shift, whose significance is not entirely clear since the Tamil militants were not a declared party to it, was the giving up by the TULF leaders of a demand for a separate state of Eelam for Tamils.

These three shifts cumulatively pushed the conflict along the track of peace-making in both 1985 and 1986. But there were other pushes and pulls which would periodically hold it back. On the one side, there was the Sinhala Buddhist backlash of opposition parties including the Sri Lanka Freedom Party (SLFP), which allied itself with sections of the Buddhist *sangha* (order of monks). On the Tamil side, there was a corresponding rebel backlash in the form of the extreme demand for a separate Tamil state (Eelam) and the dismemberment of the island. And, of course, that simultaneously with efforts toward peace-making, the unbridled violence of the army and the rebels toward each other and against civilians caught in the middle continued unabated.

The positive shifts that made the Thimpu negotiations possible have important implications. To begin with, India's intervention was both inevitable and consequential, and 1985 was an appropriate time for an open show of interest. Mrs. Indira Gandhi and Jayawardene had disliked and distrusted each other; now Mrs. Gandhi was dead, and her successor, Rajiv Gandhi, could start anew. He had to solve both the vexed problem of Sikh violence in pursuit of their own separate state in Punjab, and the conflict in Assam. With these ethnic or "communal" conflicts on his hands, he could not afford to have South India involved in the Sri Lankan conflict. A persisting sore problem over many decades had been the plight of the Indian Tamil laborers in the island's central highlands, revolving around their lack of citizenship and their disenfranchisement. The Ceylon Workers Congress (CWC) under the leadership of Thondaman had always depended on the Indian government to push their claims. But now the plight of the Sri Lankan Tamils, subject to Sinhala violence and "genocide," which resulted in the flight of thousands to South India, inflamed Tamil Natu sympathies. Given the Punjab problem and the general uncertainty of his Congress Party's political strength in the north, Rajiv Gandhi could not afford to alienate South India, let alone risk the possibility of South India's direct intervention in Sri Lanka. In any case, from the point of view of the Tamils of Sri Lanka, the participation of India in the making and implementing of a peace settlement is a *sine qua non*. Indeed, Tamils see the threat of India's armed intervention as the most powerful restraint on the Sinhalese. Finally, the strategic importance of Sri Lanka to the world powers, especially its port of Trincomalee, was a consideration that would impel India to monitor the Sri Lankan conflict and keep at bay any active intervention by the United States, the United Kingdom, or the U.S.S.R.

On the Sri Lankan government's side, the decision to negotiate directly with representatives of the rebels together with TULF leaders was an act of enlightened diplomacy. (No doubt the fact that in mid-1985 the consortium of aid-giving countries were to meet to decide on the size and terms of financial aid acted as a spur to holding the meetings.) Aside from disrupting law and order and political stability, the ethnic conflict was taking a tremendous toll on the economy of the country. The bad international press for the island, the reporting of sordid acts of violence by the undisciplined army and the police, the equally bloody murders by the Tamil rebels and the Sinhalese civilian home guards— all these affected the tourist trade, which in 1985–86 had fallen by at least 30 to 40 percent. To compound matters, the high tea prices in 1984, which gave a sense of prosperity, were followed by a fall steep enough to markedly affect export earnings. Though this negative effect was somewhat cushioned by a fall in oil prices (oil being the island's costliest import), exports still cannot be expected to rise fast enough in the near future to reduce the pressure that international debt servicing put on the balance of payments.

In the face of such difficulties, the enormous sums of money—the reported amount in 1985 was some $300 million, a figure that has ballooned since then—spent on purchasing arms from abroad to equip the army, combined with the domestic costs of maintaining the army and fighting a war, seems a suicidal madness from a "rational" economic point of view. Such expenditure on arms means a siphoning off of foreign balances that could be used for more constructive purposes, and it is clear that the pace of economic development will be slowed down as long as civil war continues. By no means an insignificant consideration is the prospect of foreign firms in Sri Lanka's Free Trade Zone pulling out or shying away from future investment. Compounding factors are the economic damage which the army's scorched-earth policy inflicts on many agricultural villages in the north and east, and of course the provision of food and shelter to refugees.

The Thimpu conference produced few clear results. The immediate reasons for its breakdown and disbanding were the cease-fire violations on both sides—the Sinhala army and the Tamil rebels—and the inability of the participants at Thimpu to negotiate in good faith. The army (in August 1985) gave the Tamil rebels their "justification" to walk out: goaded by rebel sniping, the army went on a rampage and killed many civilians in Vaviniya, including some Sarvodaya self-help workers. Of this atrocity Christopher Moore wrote in the *Manchester Guardian* (19 August 1985): "Vavuniya is a town in shock, its shops and bazaars closed, its streets empty and the only visible activity the collection and burial of the dead. More than 200 people may have died there during the last three days according to reliable sources."

During the cease-fire the Tamil rebels had also committed and escalated violent action, which would progressively earn for them the appellation "terrorists." Aside from hit-and-run actions on army patrols, they had killed two Tamil TULF moderate politicians, as well as murdered Sinhala peasants living in the marginal areas of the Vavuniya and Trincomalee districts. The following is a statement by The Committee for Rational Development, which is composed of enlightened Sri Lankans dedicated to seeking a just solution to the ethnic issue: "Cease-fire violations by some of the [rebel] groups, killings of Tamil moderates and increased violence directed at the Sinhala civilian population has displayed an ugly face of the Tamil nationalist movement. It has also provided the government with a justification for increased militarization and political inaction" (*Lanka Guardian* 8, no. 11 [1 Oct. 1985]).

So fraught was the situation in late 1985 in the Trincomalee-Vavuniya districts that President Jayawardene described it as a "state of war." For their part, the ENLF (coalition of militant rebel groups) proposed that the cease-fire violations by the government necessitated the appointment of a third party to maintain the peace. However, fearing that foreign mediation on Sri Lanka's territory (and with India the obvious choice) might diminish its sovereignty, government circles saw this as a menacing prospect and were less than receptive.

Behind the lack of good faith—both sides used lulls in negotiations to strengthen themselves and to continue the violence—is the lack of a clear vision of exactly what the terms of a settlement might be. This despite the fact that both sides had come to recognize that in the long run some form of political agreement had to be negotiated.

The Tamil militant groups put forward four basic requirements as their conditions for a settlement: (1) recognition of the right to self-determination for the Tamils; (2) recognition of the Tamil-speaking people as a distinct nationality; (3) recognition and guarantee of the integrity of Tamil homelands; and (4) the granting of citizenship rights to all Tamils resident in Sri Lanka.

Of these four, the critical issue for a political settlement is that of the "Tamil homelands" and the devolution of powers by the central government. The other demands are ancillary to it, and would be practically realized when a satisfactorily demarcated "homeland" is given political and administrative definition. In fact, some months after the collapse of the Thimpu talks, President Jayawardene came to an agreement with Mr. Thondaman of the CWC, who had threatened widespread strikes in the tea plantations if the question of citizenship was not settled. By the stroke of Jayawardene's pen, some ninety thousand Indian Tamil residents were enfranchised, thus taking some wind out of the sails of the Sri Lankan Tamil cause. With this swift move, Jayawardene managed to keep the Indian labor and the CWC within the government at arm's length from the political demands of the Sri Lankan militants. The point was forcibly made that the wily and practiced "old man" wielded the necessary power and authority to bring about and enforce decisions, even if they were politically unpopular among some Sinhala circles.

I now propose to tackle the issue of Tamil homelands and show why it is so tangled and explosive, telling the story from both sides. First, why the question of devolution and the recognition of a separate Tamil region / province is so difficult for the Sinhalese to contemplate and reconcile themselves to. And second, why the Tamils see the winning of their own homelands as their last stand, the only way they can achieve some peace and security for themselves in the face of a Sinhalese majority increasingly bent on their eradication.

SINHALA RESISTANCE TO A DEMARCATED TAMIL REGION AND TO DEVOLUTION OF POWERS

The Sinhalese resistance to Tamil homelands—that is, the demarcation of a Tamil region in the Northern and Eastern Provinces as a unit of government within a unitary state or a federal union—has many bases.

a) First is the emotive Sinhala-Buddhist-"nationalist" claim enshrined in the *Mahavamsa* chronicle. Reactivated since Independence, particularly after 1956, it is now an unquestioned tenet in the populist ideology. The claim is that the island of Lanka, colonized by the Sinhala people under the banner of Vijaya, was destined to receive the legacy of a pure Buddhism; the protection of this legacy is its historic mission. This mission and the integrity of the island as a Sinhalese-Buddhist complex has always been threatened by invading

Tamil Hindus from South India. This proposition has been inculcated as historical truth with increasing vehemence since the bifurcation of primary and secondary education into two separate streams—Sinhala and Tamil—allowing populist textbook writers to elaborate on the theme and to spice it with "racial" ideology. On a more general scale, Benedict Anderson,[9] has acutely analyzed the linkage between literacy and nationalism: how "print capitalism" can be used to disseminate an explosive "official nationalism" through a vernacular literature that joins tendentious authors with a vulnerable reading public. This is a theme that applies to Sri Lanka as well.

b) There is also quite another basis for the fears of large numbers of Sinhalese people that the granting of regional autonomy and the devolution of significant powers to a province or region would impair the sovereignty and territorial integrity of the country. This fear is based in part on the legacy inherited from the British *raj*: the British rulers, the Governor and his council of officials, wielded a strong centralized power from Colombo. The same pattern, assumptions and preferences were transmitted relatively unchanged, even when the British progressively transferred power to Ceylonese leaders (especially under the Donoughmore Constitution), culminating in the charter of Independence. Thus, following British imperial precedent, Sri Lankan ministers and members of Parliament have been reluctant to "lose" their powers by devolution to local government authorities (municipalities, urban district councils, village communities) and to provincial/district administrations. Although there has been some romanticized talk in the twentieth century of the ancient "village republics" and of the self-governing *gansabhawas* of old, in fact the tradition of local government had not been strong, nor had the existence in Sinhalese society of regional or local interests in opposition to the center been persistent.[10]

The vast country of India—with its provinces and native states, its regional interests, its regional peoples and cultures—was necessarily seen as a mosaic, a multicentric entity in which any centripetal imperial or federal center would have to hold its own against the centrifugal tendencies of the subcontinent. Since Independence, India has had a rich experience of regional secessions and of local government. By comparison, Sri Lanka's small size and its acceptance of a dominant center in Colombo has led to the perception that internal federal divisions and regional interests are a threat to the integrity of the body politic. Neither the Sinhalese politicians nor the Sinhalese public at large has expressed interest in the numerous international examples— such as Canada, Switzerland, Britain, Belgium, and so on—where regional and other forms of devolution have not only worked but have done so without eroding the unity of the polity as a whole.

c) The third basis for Sinhala resistance to Tamil homelands is perhaps the weightiest in terms of immediate demographic and economic realities. In Sri Lanka, the term "Peasant colonization" refers to the settlement of landless and economically deprived peasants from densely populated regions. They are moved to newly opened up or reclaimed lands which have been made cultivable by restored or newly built irrigation systems in the thinly populated jungle lands of the Northern, North Central, Northwestern, and Eastern Provinces. Sri Lanka's most extensive—and expensive—mode of combining agricultural development with relief of rural misery in this century,[11] "Peasant colonization" has recently culminated in the vast Mahaweli Scheme currently being constructed. As it happens, the vast majority of these transplanted peasants are of Sinhalese origin, while most of the peasant colonies opened up are situated in districts (Anuradhapura, Polonnaruva, Amparai, Vavuniya, Mannar, Mullaitiva, and Trincomalee) that are on the margins and border zones that separate the Tamil peoples of the North and East from the Sinhalese people of the interior.

The internal migration and population movements within Sri Lanka in recent decades, primarily as a result of peasant resettlements, have exacerbated ethnic tensions in Sri Lanka.[12] There is no doubt that the movement of persons, mainly Sinhalese, from the densely populated southwestern zone to the northern and eastern zones, in large part under governmental sponsorship and facilitation, has progressively blurred "the porous imaginary boundary that had long separated the predominantly Sinhalese and the predominantly Sri Lanka Tamil regions."[13]

A comparison between census figures of 1911 and 1981 shows quite dramatic changes. While in 1911 Sri Lankan Tamils were a clear majority in all districts of the Northern and Eastern Provinces, by 1981 there had been a notable growth in the proportions of Sinhalese in the Trincomalee and Amparai districts[14]—the increase in the latter being a conspicuous result of the government's development of the Gal Oya river basin. In sum, the Sinhalese composition in the total population of the North and East rose from less than 2 percent in 1911, and 5 percent in 1946, to slightly more than 13 percent in 1981. Conversely the proportion of the Sri Lanka Tamil population in the East has declined steadily.

The influx into and the expansion of Sinhalese people in the North is only the outer edge of an even larger push into those parts of the Dry Zone always considered to be a Sinhalese majority area—namely Anuradhapura and Polonnaruva districts, the sites of the earlier historic and much celebrated Buddhist-Sinhala civilizations whose settlements subsequently declined and reverted to jungle. Thus, between 1946 and 1981, 665,000 Sinhalese were added to the area's total population of slightly more than 850,000, pushing up the Sinhalese proportion from 80 to 91 per cent.

Although the proportion of Tamils living in the North and East has declined accordingly, there has also been a Tamil push, particularly into the Vavuniya and Mallaitivu districts. Thus, in the thirty-five years between 1946 and 1985 their population grew by nearly 650 percent, and it is Sri Lankan Tamils who contributed the largest numbers to this growth (a total of about 53,000 in the decade 1971–1981) supplemented by Indian Tamils (15,500 in this period). It is important to note this because it indicates the *imminent face-to-face collision* between the two colonizing ethnic populations, and it is partly in terms of these trends that the battle for Trincomalee, together with the control of its harbor as the chief prize, must be understood.

THE TAMIL CLAIM OF HOMELANDS—THE LAST STAND

These population movements explain why the Tamils have feared that the infiltration of more and more state-sponsored Sinhalese peasants into Vavuniya, Mullaitivu, and Trincomalee, their own areas of dominance, poses the threat of their becoming a minority in their traditional homelands. Indeed the Federal party under the leadership of S. J. V. Chelvanayagam, at its very founding in 1949 objected vehemently to state-sponsored peasant settlements in the North and East, whose primary beneficiaries would be the Sinhalese: this was the time the Gal Oya scheme was being implemented, and all the desirable allotments with sufficient water were reserved for Sinhalese settlers, while the much less viable backwoods at the tail ends of the channels were relegated to the East Coast Muslims and Tamils. And twenty-five years later the TULF call for a separate state of Eelam was in some ways the climactic expression of fears about the Sinhalese determination to deprive the Tamil areas of their majority.

From the Tamil point of view, as expressed by the TULF elected leaders and the militant rebels, the insistence on a Tamil homeland region—whether as a separate state of Eelam or as a region/province commanding real powers in a federal union—is the last hope that they will not be totally engulfed by the expansionist Sinhalese majority. Since 1956 the Tamils had progressively lost their political battles. First, when the English language was replaced by *swabasha* ("one's own language"), "Sinhala only" had been declared the official language of the country. Then followed the compulsory provision of two separate streams of education: Sinhala for the Sinhalese, Tamil for the Tamils, which initiated "affirmative action" on behalf of the Sinhalese majority.

Since Sri Lankan Tamils had lived in regions with few resources, removed from the developments in commerce and the tea and rubber plantations under the British *raj*, many had concentrated on higher education and on securing white-collar and professional occupations. Greatly exaggerating the alleged unfair advantages the Tamils enjoyed in the administrative services and professions, a succession of Sinhalese governments since 1956 discriminated against the Tamils in their recruitment policies—culminating in the "standardization policy" of the early seventies that introduced a quota system penalizing Tamil-language candidates who sought places in the universities. While the Jayawardene government revised this blatantly discriminatory policy with a new standardization, it still puts demographic claims above merit in university recruitment, reserving 55 percent of university admissions to candidates on the basis of population size in revenue districts, and another 15 percent to candidates from revenue districts deemed educationally underprivileged.

Increasingly, the Sri Lankan Tamils have lost their employment prospects through education and have felt demeaned by consignment to second-class status. Accordingly, the idea—first mooted by the Federal Party in 1948—that the only hope for the Tamils against invasive Sinhala domination was a separate Tamil region under their own administrative control, has gained strength. They see the government's peasant resettlement policy as another attempt by the Sinhalese to realize their claim of the entire island.

One must separate fact from fiction with regard to the Sri Lankan Tamil claim of "traditional homelands" that have belonged to the indigenous Tamils of the north and the east as a homogeneous collectivity. This mytho-historical claim is really a statement of twentieth-century political interests and objectives, rather than an accurate description of the state of affairs in pre-British times. [15] Indeed, the precedents that were set under British rule after the entire island was brought under the control of a single power, and which continued after Independence, have greater relevance for the present conflict. The British carved the island administratively into provinces, and since then the Northern and Eastern Provinces have been regarded as a zone where the Tamil people were preponderant. The various censuses have reiterated this understanding. [16]

The *geographical limits* of the Tamil "homelands" are not uncontroversial. However, the existence of the North and East as Tamil regions, in a general sense, was accepted as a premise in various political deliberations that resulted in short-lived pacts between Sinhalese prime ministers and Tamil leaders. These same deliberations also took for granted that state-sponsored peasant settlement and the alienation of land to colonists was a central issue bound up with the terms of devolution of powers to Tamil regions or provinces.

A survey of the periodic deliberations and ensuing pacts illustrates this point:

a) The *Bandaranaike-Chelvanayagan Pact* of 1956/57 was the most creative (and sadly doomed) blueprint, one that had the chance of solving the ethnic conflict in its infancy. Among other things, it accepted the following: that Tamil would be regarded as a national language and as the language of administrative work in the Northern and Eastern Provinces; that the Northern Province would constitute one regional area, while the Eastern Province would be divided into two or more regional areas; that provision would be made for two or more regions to amalgamate even beyond the provincial limit, and for two or more regions to collaborate for specific purposes of common interest; that regional councillors would be elected to office. Most importantly, Parliament was to delegate powers to regional councils, which would have power over such matters as agriculture, cooperatives, lands and land development, colonization, education, health, industries and fisheries, housing and social services, electricity, water plans and roads. Significantly, the Pact declared that in the matter of colonization schemes the powers of the regional councils should include the selection of land allottees to and the personnel to work in such schemes. Finally, it was agreed that the Central Government would provide block financial grants for regional councils, while the regional councils would have powers of taxation and borrowing money.

b) The *Senanayake-Chelvanayagam Pact* of 1965 was even more explicit on the question of peasant settlement, because Tamil grievances against the state-sponsored schemes were mounting. Charles Abeysekere has reported: [17]

Mr. Senanayake . . . agreed that in granting of land under colonization schemes, the following priorities would be observed in the Northern and Eastern Provinces: (1) first, to landless persons in the district; (2) second, to Tamil-speaking persons resident in the Northern and Eastern Provinces; (3) third, to other citizens of Ceylon, preference being given to Tamil residents in the rest of the island.

c) Most recently, "Annexure C," based on the understanding of 1983 between Indira Gandhi and President Jayawardene, provided for one consolidated Tamil region consisting of Tamil majority areas in the North and East. This was to be one of the accepted planks for a discussion by an "All Party Conference" convened by President Jayawardene. This conference, which met throughout 1984 without resolving the ethnic issues, had the following as one of its main agenda items:

A national policy on land settlement and the basis on which the government will undertake land colonisation will have to be worked out. All settlement schemes shall be based on ethnic proportions so as not to alter the demographic balance [of the area] subject to agreement being reached on major projects. [18]

The Thimpu deliberations of 1985 was the next round at which the militants (and the TULF representatives) made the four Tamil demands—recognition as a distinct nationality, right of self-determination, traditional homelands, and the merger of the Northern and Eastern Provinces as the unit of devolution. I have already discussed the course and outcome of this conference, but here let me take up the question of the merger of the two provinces and their territorial and demographic limits as the Tamil homelands.

The merger of the Northern and Eastern Provinces as they are demarcated now is complicated by the presence in these provinces, especially in the Batticaloa and Amparai districts of the Eastern Province, of a large number of Sri Lanka Muslims. Though Tamil-speaking, they consider themselves to be, by virtue of their Islamic affiliation, a distinct "ethnic" or "communal" collectivity. According to the 1981 census, one-fifth of the entire Muslim community, amounting to 206,000 persons, lived in the two provinces which the Tamil nationalists sought to merge. The ethnic conflict between the Sinhalese and Tamils did inevitably drag in the Muslims: in 1985 there was an outbreak of violence between the Tamils and Muslims, fueled by Sinhalese collusion. However, the Tamils and Muslims in the East have a long history of coexistence, although Muslim politicians have by no means seen their interests and party affiliations as concordant with those of the Tamils. Before the Thimpu conference began, a delegation of Muslim leaders went to South India to meet the Tamil leaders, making it clear that they were opposed to the merger of the two provinces, but would consent to the creation of two separate provincial councils to administer the Northern and Eastern Provinces as presently demarcated.

In the face of Muslim opposition to a complete merger, the next step for the Tamil nationalists is to seek the separation of the areas of Muslim concentration in Batticaloa and Amparai, and the merger only of the Northern Province and that part of the Eastern Province in which the Hindu Tamils are preponderant. Whether the Sinhalese government would be prepared to grant this merger and thereby accept the claim of indivisible Hindu Tamil homelands is one of the critical issues under consideration in the very latest round of the All Parties Conference convened in July 1986. [19] Aside from the sizable Muslim minority in these provinces, there is also a not insignificant Sinhalese presence as a result of the peasant resettlement and recent immigration, especially in the Trincomalee and Amparai districts, where in 1981 they represented 33.6 percent and 38 percent of the population, respectively. It is clear that Amparai cannot be placed within a merged Tamil region; the real battle is now being waged over the control of Trincomalee, where the Sinhalese and Tamils are equally balanced and the Muslims are only marginally smaller (by 4 to 5 percent). Moreover, the dispersion of Muslims in the Eastern Province makes it impossible to carve out a continuous region in that province composed exclusively of Tamils. Thus, for all these reasons it looks as if the Tamils and Muslims of the Eastern Province would much rather have a separate province of their own than seek a merger with the Northern Province.

The latest round of deliberations began on July 1986, when President Jayawardene convened the Political Parties Conference (PPC). On the side of Jayawardene, his United National Party (UNP) and his government, there appeared on this occasion to be a more genuinely positive orientation toward a settlement than in the past. In addition to the increasingly unavoidable realization that the rebels are more than a match for the army and police in the North and East, and that Sri Lanka's economy is sorely affected by the toll of civil war, there has been a near ultimatum from India that a political settlement must be sought in earnest.

In the months immediately preceding the Conference, Sri Lanka–Indian relations had deteriorated seriously. Spokesmen for the Indian government had openly attacked the Sri Lankan government because of its human-rights violations and arbitrary, indiscriminate killings of Tamils, bordering on genocide. The Indian government was also disenchanted with the Sri Lankan government's reneging on its promises whenever extremist Sinhala opposition groups arose to denounce any meaningful concessions to Tamils.

This time, the Indian delegation, led by Mr. P. Chidambaran, had had promising discussions with the Sri Lankan president and his government; with Mrs. Bandaranaike, leader of SLFP, the largest opposition party; with Mr. Thondaman, leader of the Ceylon Workers Congress (CWC), the organization of Indian Tamil labor, and others. But just when the stage for settlement seemed set, a moment arose which the government could not resist in its atavistic fantasy of arriving at a military solution. The two major Tamil rebel groups became locked in a fratricidal massacre in the North and the East. The Liberation Tigers of Tamil Eelam (LTTE)—the largest and perhaps the most disciplined and militarily competent group, led by Velupillai Prabhakaran—attacked the Tamil Eelam Liberation Organization (TELO), killing its leader Sri Sabaratnam and over 150 members.

Thus it became the uncontestable foremost rebel faction.[20] The Sri Lankan army, hoping to exploit this internecine strife among the rebels, began a military push (optimistically dubbed "Operation Shortshrift"), with a movement of troops accompanied by bombings of Jaffna and other northern towns. These army maneuvers were unsuccessful: the rebel LTTE effectively contained the troops, proving their military prowess and establishing themselves as the dominant Tamil group. Hereafter, the LTTE would have to give their assent to, and in some way underwrite, any future political settlement.

Although President Jayawardene invited all political parties to the August 1986 Conference, not all attended. A six-member delegation of Sri Lankan Tamils representing the TULF arrived in Colombo, not to participate in the conference itself, but to engage in discussions and negotiations outside it. Although no member of the Tamil rebel groups was deemed eligible to attend, the TULF has made it known that the participation of these groups is necessary if there is to be an acceptable and viable political settlement. Also excluded were the Buddhist clergy and other interest groups. As evidence of his positive decision and genuine desire to effect a settlement, President Jayawardene placed the government's proposals at the commencement of the conference as the main item on the agenda. In addition, he proclaimed (at a press conference on 26 June) that legislation to carry out the government's proposals would be introduced in the following month, whether the Tamil leaders (and other invited parties) gave their consent or not. The President stated that he would consider any amendments which did not reduce the scope of the government's proposals, predicated as they are on the continuation of the unitary constitution of Sri Lanka. He would not have recourse to a referendum, and, if the Tamil militants agreed to lay down their arms, he would grant them amnesty.

The government's peace proposals did not provide for a merger of portions of the Northern and Eastern Provinces, or a consolidated and unitary Tamil homeland. They did provide for elected provincial councils, with the Northern and Eastern Provinces each having a chief minister and a cabinet or council of ministers, comprised of members of the group (or groups) with a majority in the provincial councils.

The crucial issues for negotiation are (1) the units of demarcation, such as provinces and regions; (2) the powers to be devolved to them; (3) the constitutional procedures for any future modification of such powers; (4) the terms of accountability, and the corresponding institutions, of provincial councils toward the central government; and (5) provision for adequate financing to enable the demarcated areas to function. In substantive terms, the question of devolution will have to arrive at agreements on such matters as peasant colonization and the future allocation of agricultural land; education at all levels; the financial contributions of the central government and the rights of local bodies to raise local revenues. Knotty constitutional issues relate to whether the terms of the political agreement are to be enshrined in the Constitution, and the rules and procedures by which they can be protected against future amendment by unilateral action. Given Sri Lanka's propensity in the past for spectacular swings at elections, winning parties with huge majorities in Parliament might be tempted to alter—in favor of the center—the terms of a settlement to the ethnic conflict so painfully arrived at.

There is no doubt that the most problematic threat to the success of the Political Parties Conference was the determined and conspicuous absence from it of *the major Sinhalese opposition parties.* Thus, the Sri Lanka Freedom Party (SLFP) led by Mrs. Bandaranaike, and the Mahajana Eksath Peramuna (MEP) led by Mr. Dinesh Gunawardene boycotted the peace conference, and aroused feelings against concessions to the Tamils.[21] Simultaneously with the conjunction of trends working toward a political settlement, well-entrenched divisive forces have come into play, working against that goal. Factionalism is pervasive. While TULF has emerged as a single dominant group among the several rebel militant groups on the Tamil side, these groups are not in accord with the TULF parliamentary politicians, and a united Tamil consensus on a political settlement will be hard to achieve. But the discord seems even worse on the Sinhalese side, where the UNP (the ruling party) has been riven by factions, and divided by the issue of a successor to Jayawardene. Any strong faction promoting a political settlement faces the opposition of the other factions, who can easily whip up the feelings of the Sinhalese public against giving too much to the Tamils and thereby dismembering the indivisible island. An even greater danger to peace stems from the opposition parties, such as SLFP and MEP, who see much political advantage from resisting a negotiated settlement, and who would much rather force the country to elections, or even a referendum, thereby seeking to defeat the UNP. For it is very possible that, put to a vote, the Sinhalese electorate might come down against a settlement that the Tamils would find minimally acceptable. In Sri Lankan politics in recent decades, short term calculations of electoral advantage and the strategies of winning power have almost always taken precedence over considerations of statesmanship on behalf of the country as a whole.

It is difficult to find the right words to explain the interaction, or dialectic, between two sociopolitical processes that are at work in Sri Lanka today, as well as in in many other Third World countries like it. One relates to the ubiquitous patron-client networks that operate in commerce (the *mudalali* or the acquisitive entrepreneur with henchmen to protect his enterprises and keep his competitors at bay), and in politics (the elected politician and boss who has patronage to distribute in the form of jobs and funds). Trade wars, election campaigning, and intimidation at the voting booths, manufactured protest meetings and strikes, illegal drug-traffic and felling of state-owned forests, payoffs for development contracts—these are the circumstances where such networks are most salient. In a "post-traditional" country like Sri Lanka, the older loyalties and ties of family and kinship, and at the next remove, of caste, are factors that are still strong and play a part in patron-client networks. But, in its present phase, institutions of democratic politics—such as universal franchise and elections on the basis of parliamentary constituencies—provide new contexts for collective action. Thus, collectivities are being formed around politicians and brokers that are wider in scope than kinship and caste, or are able to encompass and subordinate them without rejecting them. Similarly, when rural villages are pushing out many of their marginal or deprived folk into new peasant colonies, or into other cities and towns, we once again find volatile, mobile, and fairly anonymous persons ready for mobilization on the basis of patronage around brokers, *mudalalis*, members of parliament, and the like. These patron-client networks and groupings are the stuff of entrepreneurial politics and adventure capitalism in a Third World country like Sri Lanka.

At the same time, there is another complex of affectively charged sociopolitical processes and ideological themes, one that can amalgamate the contending, faction-ridden, volatile groups into a larger whole still more volatile, much more short-lived, but capable of tumultuous mass actions like ethnic riots, holy wars, and militant millenarianism. Sinhalese versus Tamils in Sri Lanka, Malays against Chinese in Malaysia, Sikhs against Hindus in Punjab, Christians versus Muslims and Druse in Lebanon: some combination of language and religion in variable mixes, further compounded by more elusive conceptions of distinctive historical origins or race, and the like, seem to be providing the basis for a larger collective identity and action, usually against similarly constituted rival collectivities within the same countries. Words such as "ethnicity," "nationality," or "ethnic nationalism" label these collective identities; their spectacular potency is their ability to "homogenize" a people ridden by other more particularistic loyalties of kinship and caste, and differentiated by wealth and "class" status, into a massive unity which can be led and manipulated by charismatic populist leaders, and by the media, in the service of direct action.

The involution of factional politics and ethnic nationalism—the leaven of populism—are simultaneously in operation in Sri Lanka and elsewhere; at certain phases factionalism may be the more conspicuous, and at others ethnic populism. But they are intertwined and can work in tandem. One might hypothesize that in certain kinds of Third World contexts, the phenomena of ethnic nationalism and conflicts are likely to occur: for example, in those societies where population expansion, insufficient industrial expansion, and uneven economic development are accompanied by the migration to cities of large numbers of rural people who, while forming a labor supply, do not constitute organized labor markets and have not yet formed worker-interested labor unions. Steep differences in income distribution and privileged, wealthy elites do exist, but a self-conscious division of the society into social classes, with recognized differences of class interest organized for class action, are absent. Instead, homogenized collectivities on the basis of a religious revivalism and fundamentalism, or on the basis of language as a road to educational and occupational privilege and a vehicle for claims of cultural and literary heritage, seem to provide a more seductive and attractive basis for collective identity, even in those societies which in gross terms have recently experienced a rise in wealth and economic productivity. Punjab is the clearest example.

"GENOCIDE" AND "TERRORISM": INTERNATIONAL READINGS OF THE SRI LANKAN CONFLICT

I hope the foregoing documentation has successfully shown that the thicker the description of a situation, the more microscopic the viewing, the more "parochial" the account of its "involuted" texture—the more difficult it becomes to see it in simple black-and-white terms. Conversely, when a situation such as the Sri Lankan violence-imbued ethnic conflict is disengaged from its distinctive parochialism and is placed in an international context, its significance changes, as does the judgment the viewer places on it. Thus, "internationalization" of the Sri Lankan conflict has taken two forms.

One is a telescopic view that relates the conflict to universalistic and non-negotiable standards of human rights, civil liberties, due process, justice, fair play—a cosmopolitan, humanistic, enlightened-liberal monitoring, publicizing and evaluating of events. Since this monitoring is West-inspired, the standards also may include the practice of democratic forms of government, including universal franchise, free elections, etc.

In Sri Lanka, this work has been performed by several agencies. One is Amnesty International, which has issued reports on violations of human rights, including torture by the Sri Lankan government and its security forces; another is the International Commission of Jurists, on whose behalf Virginia Leary and Paul Sieghart have written two powerful reports condemning (among other things) the incarceration of persons without due process, the terrible implications of the Prevention of Terrorism Act, and the government's dismantling of democratic processes.[22] Within Sri Lanka itself, the Civil Rights Movement, under the leadership of the late Bishop Lakshman Wickremasinghe and Mr. Desmond Fernando, has courageously documented and protested such violations.

A new organization called International Alert was founded in 1985 "to focus attention on problems of group conflict which violate human rights, inhibit development, and result in mass killings and even genocide."[23] International Alert's concern with Sri Lanka is a continuation of the work of the Standing International Forum on Ethnic Conflict, Development and Human Rights.[24] Founded in 1985, it considered the situation in Sri Lanka to be of "such paramount importance" that the first committee it formed was the International Emergency Committee on Sri Lanka. Maintaining that "development and human rights are both victims of the continuing violence," this committee pointed out that as a result of the ethnic conflict, aid programs are being suspended in certain parts of the island and that nongovernmental development programs are being frustrated. Moreover, the high level of international aid for development allowed the government to use its other resources to fund the internal warfare. Thus economic development and human rights (political development) were both endangered by civil war.

Dame Judith Hart, chairperson of the Emergency Committee, visited India and Sri Lanka in 1986. She reported that she "had advised President Jayawardene and members of his cabinet of the intention of the International Emergency Committee to advocate the cessation of government aid to Sri Lanka pending a political settlement acceptable to the peoples of Sri Lanka" and that she would recommend that "a fund be established to assist in the implementation of a peaceful political solution and the rehabilitation of the economy and the well being of the Sri Lankan Peoples."[25]

The results of her advocacy were disappointing, perhaps showing the difficulty of private agencies attempting to apply sanctions on countries without possessing the power of enforcement. The consortium of aid-giving countries did, in fact, meet in 1986 (it is probable that President Jayawardene convened and timed his Political Parties Conference in order to persuade the consortium of his efforts toward peace); not only did they agree to give aid with no strings attached, but they increased it to an unprecedented level of about 700 million U.S. dollars. At the same time, the annual report of the IMF Board of Directors noted a concern about the "surge in defense expenditures (nearly ten billion rupees by now), the relatively poor export performance, the rising foreign debt, and huge losses incurred by some public enterprises, and the evident lack of strict budgetary control."[26] The frustration of Dame Judith's mission was in large part due to the unwillingness of the Western world powers to let an essentially pro-Western and pro-capitalist Sri Lankan government go further downhill in its economic slide, despite its violation of human rights and of democratic principles. For one thing, Jayawardene could be relied on to keep Trincomalee harbor accessible to the United States and Britain.

A second global concern, one that powerfully colors the foreign policy of the United States and which tends to taint the American vision of the Sri Lankan conflict, is "international terrorism." For while Amnesty International, International Alert, and other nongovernmental guardians of human rights first and foremost see the Sri Lanka government's *oppression of a minority* and the danger of *genocide*, the American and British governments see the actions of Tamil rebels as a local manifestation of an international cancer, namely *terrorism*. In a brief visit to Sri Lanka in early 1986, Margaret Thatcher chose to condemn only the "terrorism" of the militants (somewhat to the embarrassment of many of her countrymen). Similarly, the United States has chosen to follow the most punitive and retaliatory path against terrorism of the Middle Eastern variety, claimed to be sponsored by Libya, Syria, Iran, and the Palestinians.

International terrorism, perpetrating the horrors of kidnappings, killings, hijackings, and bombings, and striking ubiquitously—with the Islamic Middle East being the primary instigator at present—has indeed produced a general atmosphere of fear and helplessness. I do not wish to mitigate its evil or underrate the existence of an international network of conspiracy among diverse terrorist gangs fighting their alleged causes in different countries. My point, however, is to show the processes of "generalization," whereby the Sri Lankan violence of the kind now practised by the Tamil militants (who may indeed have certain tenuous links with terrorist groups elsewhere) is "assimilated" by the United States government to "international terrorism" in general, and thereby given a totally negative evaluation. The complexities of the local situation are diminished and reduced to the label "terrorism." In turn, that tendentious reading dictates a foreign policy of noncondemnation of the even more horrible violence practised by the Sri Lankan government, of noninterference in the alleged "domestic politics" of this friendly country, and the eschewing of sanctions to encourage a political settlement. Wearing glasses similarly tinted by the interests of world dominance, Americans can thus label "contras" in Honduras as "freedom fighters," rather than as terrorists. In this way, the U.S. perception of "international terrorism" affects its engagement, or lack of it, with the Sri Lanka ethnic conflict.

NOTES

1. As I sit down to write this essay in mid-August 1986 I recall that almost three years have passed since the Rothko Chapel Colloquium on Ethnicities and Nations took place in October 1983. There I made a presentation entitled "The Sinhalese-Tamil Conflicts in Sri Lanka (as told by a Tamil Anthropologist)." That presentation, charged and motivated by the horrors of the ethnic riots of 1983, represented the early stage of a compulsion I experienced to put down on paper, as a form of therapy, my own understanding of, and coming to terms with, those events that were simultaneously tearing apart the Sri Lankan body politic as well as the personalities of individuals, Sinhalese and Tamil alike. My therapeutic exercise conducted in my capacities as both Sri Lankan and social scientist resulted in a long essay of some two hundred typescript pages. It was then published as a book in the Spring of 1986, under the title *Sri Lanka, Ethnic Fratricide and the Dismantling of Democracy* (Chicago: Chicago University Press).

2. The two other religious minorities are Muslims (7 percent) who mostly speak Tamil as their home language, but consider themselves a separate ethnic group on religious grounds, and Christians (8 percent) who are drawn from the Sinhalese, Tamil, and other communities. The Tamils divide into two groups, namely the "indigenous" Sri Lankan Tamils who have been resident in the island for many centuries, and therefore have "historical" claims equally valid to those of the Sinhalese to being "natives" of that island, and the Indian Tamils who are descendants of South Indian Tamils brought by the British since the nineteenth century to work in the tea estates in the central highlands.

3. After a massacre of some Sinhalese at Mullaitivu, President Jayawardene was moved to say in Parliament: "If we do not occupy the border, the border will come to us. We intend to act before they [the rebels] succeed."

4. See Barbara Crosette's informative account entitled "Tamils Flee Uncertain Sri Lanka Future" in *The New York Times*, August 24, 1986.

5. Examples are the demolition of a police station at Chavakacheri, and later in the same year, the massacre of seventy-two Sinhalese in Mullaitivu—the government claimed they were colonists, the Tamil side claimed they

were former convicts who with their families were armed and settled on land previously occupied by some Indian Tamil refugees of the 1983 riots.

6. See n. 4.

7. As I wrote this essay, news of a dramatic incident was being flashed in headlines with photographs in the U.S. and Canadian papers, representing a further chapter in the ever-lengthening saga of refugees—at present estimated at about sixty thousand—who attempt to escape from Sri Lanka and India to Europe (West Germany in particular), to Australia, and to North America (Canada in particular).

For several days, in the second week of August 1985, newspapers headlined the spectacular tales of 155 Sri Lankan refugees who were plucked from the water, drifting in two crammed lifeboats, by Canadian fishermen near St. Mary's bay off southeastern Newfoundland. The refugees told a chilling tale of boarding a freighter off the coast of Madras, of being confined in the bowels of the ship until the mystery freighter in which they sailed (whose name they did not know and whose captain's name they did not know either) disgorged them onto lifeboats off the Canadian coast and melted away. It was soon evident that the refugees were lying: they had boarded in West Germany on a German boat, but had indeed been exploited and mistreated by the captain and his accomplices. The Canadian public was enraged by the ruse; the Canadian government neverless decided to provide refuge on humanitarian grounds, and the sheepish Sri Lankans confessed. This is the last adventure in a long trail: of Tamil youth boarding Aeroflot flights from India to East Germany, then crossing into West Germany and seeking asylum there, and in the face of increasing West German toughness, seeking a haven in a more hospitable country. These refugees are acting as many others have done before them, with equal guile, cheating and resourcefulness—Poles, Czechs, Haitians, Cubans, Vietnamese boatpeople, all victims of war, purges, and persecutions by authoritarian governments.

8. The Tamil United Liberation Front is the label of the elected Tamil politicians who have made the claim for a separate Eelam for the Tamils as part of their manifesto. The TULF was banned after the 1983 riots, and virtually all its members have taken refuge in South India (Madras).

9. Benedict Anderson, *Imagined Communities: Reflections on the Origin and Spread of Nationalism* (London: Verso Editions, 1983).

10. There was a time earlier in this century when the Kandyan Sinhalese conceived of themselves as a minority and wanted to ensure their interests against the intrusions of the low-country Sinhalese, but that sentiment has evaporated.

Already in 1926, Mr. S. W. R. D. Bandaranaike proposed to the Donoughmore Commissioners a federal form of government as a solution to Sri Lanka's problems. The three self-governing areas were to be (1) the central Kandyan highlands, (2) the Southern and Western Provinces, (3) the Northern and Eastern Provinces. Even before that, in 1920, a Kandyan delegation consisting of J. A. Halangoda, T. B. L. Moonemalle and G. E. Madawala went to London to urge "communal" (virtually "ethnic" in present-day jargon) electorates for the Kandyans because they were a "minority community." The Donoughmore commissioners, and the Soulbury commissioners after them, consistently opposed "communal" and "minority" affiliations as a basis for parliamentary constituencies; together with this well-meaning opposition went a lack of interest in regional forms of local self-government.

11. Peasant colonization was begun in British times, and was extended and glorified after Independence by D. S. Senanayake, in whose time the landmark multipurpose Gal Oya Scheme was launched (the early 1950s). The policy has continued to the present.

12. Robert N. Kearney and Barbara D. Miller, "The Spiral of Suicide and Social Change in Sri Lanka," *Journal of Asian Studies*, 45, no. 1 (November 1985): 81–101.

13. Ibid.

14. It is relevant to bear in mind that the district of Amparai was newly carved out of the southern and western portions of Batticaloa district, and that in the late 1970s Mullaitivu was created from the northern part of Vavuniya and a small part of eastern Mannar.

15. For example, there is little basis for saying that the Tamil kingdom of Jaffna to the north, say during the fourteenth to the sixteenth centuries, exercised direct political control over the Tamil-speaking inhabitants of the Eastern Province (the Batticaloa region). There is more reason for asserting that the eastern zone was probably a satellite or peripheral region of the Kandyan kingdom, say during the sixteenth to the eighteenth centuries.

16. Thus A. J. Wilson has recently written recently as follows (*Tamil Times*, 4, no. 11 [September 1985]): "The Northern and Eastern Provinces have since British times been demarcated as such. They have been recognized by every Sinhalese government since independence, and even before, as the national homeland of the Tamils. The problem to be resolved, however, is not 'Tamil homelands' but the extent of power that can be devolved to the units concerned."

17. "Settlement of Sinhalese in Tamil areas," *Tamil Times*, 4, no. 10 (August 1985): 10-11.

18. All Party Conference (Sri Lanka), "Annexure C." Statement of His Excellency the President and Chairman of the All Party Conference (Colombo: All Party Conference Secretariat, 14 December 1984).

19. The following population figures are relevant. According to the 1981 census, the Northern and Eastern Provinces *minus* the Amparai district has 1.7 million people, of whom 75 percent are Sri Lankan Tamils, 12.5 percent are Muslims, 8 percent are Sinhalese and 4 percent are Indian Tamils. If Amparai were included, the percentages are 65 for Sri Lankan Tamils, 18 for Muslims, 13 for Sinhalese.

20. Prabhakaran has now been admitted to the gallery of guerrilla leaders of international stature, as evidenced by his photograph and biography being published in international magazines and newspapers.

21. Addressing a meeting in Colombo on 27 June, Mrs. Bandaranaike declared: "We are prepared to help solve the ethnic problems, but we will

not allow the division of the country or let down the Sinhalese people." The most disconcerting feature of Mrs. Bandaranaike's campaign is her alliance with a vociferous section of the Buddhist monks led by Bhikkhu Chanananda, the head of the Asgiriya Chapter of the Siyam Nikaya. Chanananda's invocation of slogans concerning the indivisibility of an island dedicated to Buddhism and owned by the Sinhalese, and his ability to mobilize monks, raises the specter of political monks, who in 1956 helped put S. W. R. D. Bandaranaike in power, and afterwards killed him when he would not bend to their attempts to shape politics on their behalf.

22. I have reported these matters in some detail in my book *Sri Lanka: Ethnic Fratricide and the Dismantling of Democracy*, chaps. 2–4.

23. See *International Alert: Emerging Sri Lanka 1986*. The board members of this organization include Theo van Boven (Netherlands), Bishop Desmond Tutu (South Africa), and Rodolfo Stavenhagen (Mexico), with Martin Ennals as Secretary General. International Alert proposes to work with organizations, institutions and universities "to identify present and potential conflicts where international public opinion and approaches to governments can be effective in bringing about peaceful settlements."

24. This International Forum was founded by the following nongovernmental developmental agencies and human rights groups: The Netherlands Institute for Human Rights (SIM), The International Peace Research Institute Oslo (PRIO), and the United Nations University, Colegio de Mexico.

25. Ibid.

26. See *Lanka Guardian*, 9, no. 8 (August 15, 1986) : 5.

The Ethnic Background of Issues Affecting Bilateral Relations Between Malaysia and Thailand

SURIN PITSUWAN

HISTORICAL BACKGROUND

Within the Association of Southeast Asian Nations (ASEAN), Malaysia and Thailand are probably the only two members that have had no history of open hostility toward each other. The Philippines only recently formally relinquished her claim over the Sabah; Malaysia and Indonesia have had their bitter experiences during the "confrontasi" period; and the troubled relations between Singapore and her fellow colonial country Malaysia, prior to the final separation in 1964, are still fresh in the ASEAN memory.

Thailand and Malaysia, however, have had a very smooth relationship from the very first day of *merdeka*, Malaysia's independence. Prior to that, if there was any bitterness, it was between the British and the Thai authorities, resulting from their dealings both before and after the Anglo-Siamese Agreement of 1909, when the four Northern Malay states of Kelantan, Trangganu, Kedah, Perlis and the adjacent islands were formally ceded to the British. The personal affinity between the leaders of Malaysia after independence and their Thai counterparts has been a decisive factor. Indeed, it accounts for much of the accommodative and supportive characters of the two neighbors' bilateral relations. And it should not be underestimated.

Emerging from the devastation of World War II, during which the Japanese turned over the four Malay states to Thai rule, Malaysia faced a time of grave communist threat known as the "emergency period." Although demarcation of the border, begun in 1909, was still unfinished, there was remarkably no border conflict between Thailand and Malaysia throughout this turbulent era of pre-independence. This is even more remarkable if we consider the fact that in the northeastern border areas with Laos and Cambodia, as it was known then, border clashes were common during the late 1950s and early 1960s. The Khao Phra Viharn issue between Thailand and Cambodia demonstrated clearly how critical were such border conflicts and how threatening to security and stability in the area.

Scholars and historians still have very little appreciation of the trust and confidence, indeed, pride, the Thais have had in the first Malay head of government, Tunku Abdul Rahman. They took pride in the fact that he is "half-Thai" through his mother and was educated in Bangkok during his primary years under the royal patronage of King Vachiravudh (Rama VI). Trust, confidence, and pride have colored much of the Thai perception of Malay politics and development during the past two and a half decades. They still have implications for the Thai attitude toward Malaysia today, but changing circumstances have also affected these sentiments (Boyce 1968, 229).

Thus, during the time of Thailand's own emergency with the communists in the Northeast, the southern border was left relatively unguarded and undefined. The presence of members of the Communist Party of Malaya (CPM) and the brewing problem of the Malay-Muslim separatist movement along their common border caused tremendous anxiety to both. But personal assurances between leaders of the two countries were apparently enough to avoid misunderstanding and the risk of turning the border issue into an international crisis. From the very beginning, the agreement has been that the CPM issue is a common threat and the Muslim separatist problem is Thailand's domestic affair. That general agreement still stands, but, like everything else between the two neighbors, it is in the process of change.

Another aspect of Thai-Malay relations strikes observers as being unique, defying simple explanation: this being that in spite of their differences in culture, language, religion, and historical experiences, the two have been getting along better than Thailand and her mainland neighbors of Indochina, with all the cultural and historical ties between them. For some yet unclear reason, the bitterness and hard feelings the Thais harbor against the French over Indochina, in relation to the loss of territories, have been more severe and deeper than their feelings against the British over the southern territories (Jones 1948, 4–5). It is very possible that the French were perceived as taking away territories that were much more closely connected to the Thais, and for a longer time, than those in the South which the British took. The sense of being wronged and forced to cede what was *theirs* for a long time makes the Thais feel their loss in the Northeast much more. The smooth relations of the Thais with the Malaysians since independence appear to support this contention, especially when compared with their troubled relations with the former colonies of the French.

As Thailand and Malaysia move further and faster along their respective roads of national development, they can no longer depend on the personal sentiments of the leaders and the peoples' feelings which have given shape and form to the relationship. Circumstances have changed and new situations require new explanations and solutions to the ever more complicated relations.

There are a myriad of issues that are potentially disruptive to Thai-Malay relations. Here we will limit ourselves to three major areas in many ways intertwined. All three have deep roots in the differences between various ethnic groups both within and along their common border. They are the issues of (1) members of the Communist Party of Malaya operating along the Thai-Malaysian border, (2) the difference in the perceptions of the threat to peace and stability in the region and of the role of the People's Republic of China within it, and (3) the problem of the Malay-Muslim separatist movement in southern Thailand. These issues can be examined in a way that will reveal some answers to the following questions: how bilateral relations between two nations are affected by the presence of ethnic minorities; how the peace and stability of a region are endangered by ethnic ties that outside powers have with domestic groups; and how the process of national development aggravates or influences the sense of ethnic identity and the political consciousness of minority groups in some—artifically defined—modern states.

THE COMMUNIST PARTY OF MALAYA (CPM)

The communist threat in Southeast Asia is identified with a specific ethnic group—the Chinese. Although both Malaysia and Thailand profess their absolute opposition to communism as an ideology, the experiences of the two countries in their struggle against that ideology have been different. Malaysia emerged from her colonial background with a life-and-death question of putting an end to the threat from the CPM. As Tunku Abdul Rahman put it to Chin Peng, the Secretary General of the CPM, when they met to discuss amnesty terms: "Malaya and communism can never coexist." Chin Peng and his followers were, and still are, mostly of Chinese stock.

That was back in 1955 when Thailand was just beginning to feel the menace of communism, particularly in her northeastern region. For Thailand, the surrogates of the communist ideology have been the Chinese, the hill-tribe peoples, and the Laotian ethnic group of the Northeast. The campaign against communism did not begin in earnest until after Marshal Sarit Thanarat took over the helm from Marshal

Philbul Songkram in October 1957. From then on the fight against communist ideology meant suppressive operations and psychological warfare among the ethnic groups in the North and Northeast. Little attention was given to the South, where the CPM and its armed elements operated. As Miller puts it, there was a "tacit agreement" for coexistence between the Thai authorities and the CPM leadership. He writes:

They never considered the CPM a serious threat; they were prepared to leave Chin Peng and his men alone as long as they behaved themselves (which they did) and as long as their "take-over" ambitions did not include any slice of south Thailand. Indeed it was reported recently that "a tacit agreement"—those were the words used—had existed between the CPM "and Bangkok" under which the communists "guaranteed" to direct its [sic] activities at West Malaysia only and not to attack Thai officials or stir up or back the Muslim dissidents in Patani. (Miller 1972, 206)

Whether or not it was an official policy of Bangkok to leave the CPM alone cannot be easily verified. But local officials who have to deal with the problem of law and order and the containment of the Malay-Muslim separatists' activities apparently prefer to deal with the CPM for both tactical and economical reasons. (Officials in the Center for Administrative Coordination for the Border Provinces in Yala confirmed that at least this was true among the military and police officers of these provinces [Yala, Patani, Narathivat, and Stul, where over 75 percent of the population are Malay Muslims].) They explain that by cultivating good relations with the CPM, the local Thai officials can contain the Muslim dissident activities and can also keep the pressure on the conservative Malay-Muslim elements in the northern states of Malaysia who have been lending support to the Malay separatists of southern Thailand.

Since 1952 (when its headquarters was moved from Pahang to Betong, a district in Yala province in south Thailand) the CPM has built up its network of rubber plantations, its timber industry, and its tin-mining operations, and developed an assortment of other activities such as the smuggling of goods and narcotics. In early 1981, for example, at the height of violence in Betong between the CPM members and the Malay-Muslim separatists, it was revealed in Bangkok that a senior police officer of the district had a close working and personal relationship with a Chinese sympathizer of the CPM (a son-in-law) who had a vast empire of interests in the border area. Local corruption and payoffs in the area also involved merchants whose interests span across the border. "Most [law and order] problems in Su-ngai Padi [of Narathivat], for example, involve the CPM and its interests in the timber industry," which is supervised by Thai officials (Reungyot 1980, 222).

Because of such entrenched interests, interlaced with the local officialdom and complicated by ethnic ties, efforts to eradicate the CPM elements have not yielded satisfactory results from the very beginning. Mutual suspicion seems to be the main obstacle to effective joint border operations. The Malaysian authorities regard the ethnic Chinese inside Thailand as potential and active sympathizers of the CPM. Thai officials, on the other hand, favor them as economic partners who contribute handsomely to the nation's economic well being. This difference in perceptions of the CPM, in the words of Datuk Seri Mahathir, the Prime Minister of Malaysia, "would continue to . . . sour currently good bilateral relations" between Malaysia and Thailand (*Far Eastern Economic Review* [Hong Kong], 9 October 1981, 23).

The fact is that relations between the two countries, at least at the local level, have been sour for quite some time. Each side has expected cooperation from the other on issues whose urgency is not regarded equally by the parties. Indeed, in the case of Malaysia, the issue of rendering assistance to suppress the irrendentist Malay Muslims of southern Thailand is considered off limits or even sacrilegious. This is because the question of the Muslim minority has been such an emotional issue for the conservative Malay politicians of the northern states of Malaysia; any sign of cooperation on supression efforts by the federal government would most certainly invite a chain of events that could threaten the stability of this racially fragile society.

But the Thai authorities along the border have been less than willing to cooperate with their Malaysian counterparts on another highly sensitive problem which is supposed to be of mutual interest: the suppression of the CPM, whose members are predominantly Chinese. Early this year an internal memorandum circulated within the Department of Local Administration, Ministry of Interior, noted that "the supression efforts succeeded inside Malaysia but failed miserably in the Thai territory." And the author suggested that serious reconsideration of the present tactics and attitude of Thai officials along the border is needed. He obviously questioned the wisdom of the policy of "benign neglect" maintained by the provincial officers along the border (Hiranyato 1983, 23).

Since 1952, the year the CPM retreated into the jungle along the Thai border, there have been small-scale joint border operations. At the beginning the main task was given to the provincial police force of Zone 9 in Songkhla, with sporadic support of the military units and the special branch police. When Field Marshal Sarit came to power, the border patrol police branch was created and was charged with the security of the border. Malaysian forces were not physically involved during this first stage. Some field intelligence had been exchanged.

The second stage came in 1959, when a high-level border committee was established to replace the respective security units on both sides of the border. On the Thai side the Communist Suppression Command for the southern region, headquartered in the Sena Narong Military Camp in Had Yai, was given full authority to eradicate communist insurgency. It was also charged with establishing contacts and cooperation with the Malaysian authorities in the effort to suppress the CPM. In the early 1960s, the Malaysian forces for the first time crossed the border into Thailand officially and openly in pursuit of the communist guerrillas.

THE QUESTION OF SOVEREIGNTY AND ETHNIC OVERTONES

As soon as the Malaysian forces were permitted to cross into Thailand, the sensitive question of "sovereignty" arose. The agreement of 13 March 1965, came under political attack in the Thai Parliament, forcing the government of Field Marshal Thanom Kitikachorn to renegotiate the border agreement. Thanom sent his deputy, Air Chief Marshal Dhawee Chulasap, to Kuala Lumpur to request some changes in the document. He won a small concession from his Malaysian counterpart when the word "soldiers" (who would have the right to cross the border in their pursuit of the communist terrorists) was changed to the term "police field forces." Apparently the new agreement which was initialed on 6 March 1970 was enough to keep the Thais satisfied for a while.

While the pressure on the Thai government increased during the early 1970s (an elected parliament came into being after almost two decades of military dictatorship), the Malaysian authorities also became very concerned with the threat emanating from the Thai jungles, especially after the infamous race riot of May 1969. Thus when Thai authorities were forced to be sensitive about the issue of joint border operations by fear of opposing popular nationalistic sentiment, Kuala Lumpur felt the renewed urgency to wipe out the CPM insurgents who tended to exploit the race issue to their advantage. Both Bangkok and Kuala Lumpur sought some support from each other in a way that could not be adequately satisfied. The seed of suspicion took root.

What is of interest to observers is the shrewdness the CPM members showed in exploiting the rising sense of nationalism in the Thai polity for their own advantage. Throughout the early part of the 1970s, the Thai authorities had to work harder at explaining to the people the necessity for the joint border operations with Malaysia. As the threat of communism increased with the deteriorating situations in the Indochina states, culminating in the fall of all three regimes in 1975, the Thais' fear of communism grew.

One would have expected that the perception of threat spilling across the Mekong would result in a bolder drive against the communists along the southern border. But the changed circumstances resulted in more antagonism to the Malaysian forces already stationed on Thai soil and an increasing skepticism toward any future joint border operations. But if communism is supposed to be a real threat to Thailand's own national security, why not cooperate with the Malaysians in suppressing the communists?

The explanation for this rather peculiar turn of events lies in the ever-rising nationalism among the Thais. The conservative elements and the aristocrat-turned-businessman sector of Thai society reached down into the wellspring of national pride. Once the threat was identified and the remedy was agreed upon, there was no stopping and no discrimination between different kinds of foreign "intrusion." The antagonism promoted against an "alien ideology" swallowing up the peoples of Indochina was also directed against "foreign troops" operating on Thai soil along the southern border. Despite the fact that both were combating a "common enemy," the presence of Malaysian soldiers was considered an infringement upon Thailand's sovereignty. Fear was also expressed about the negative impact of the Malaysian forces upon the Malay-Muslim minority along the Thai southern border (Chaweewan et al. 1982).

While in October 1973 students were still elated with their unexpected victory over ironclad authoritarianism, they focused primarily on the abuse of power by government officials and the protection of the nation's sovereignty. Thus they moved to pressure the interim government of Professor Sanya Thammasak to get rid of the American bases and, once again, encourage the Malaysian authorities to wind up their operations and withdraw into their own territory.

Sociopolitical developments in Thailand during the early and mid 1970s did not square well with the "new emergency" brewing in Malaysia. As Thanin Kraivixian wrote in 1973: "Prime Minister Abdul Razak said recently that when the emergency was declared over in 1970, most Malaysians thought that the menace of the communists was already wiped out from Malaysia. . . . But, as it turned out, it was only a temporary thing. Right now the communist threat is back and they are committed to take over Malaysia by violent means." Accordingly, the request for troop withdrawal by Bangkok could not easily be responded to by the Malaysian leadership because of the CPM's increasingly violent and overt operations in both rural and urban areas throughout the country. The situation deteriorated, and the difficult relationship spanned four Thai administrations from 1973 to 1977 (in the latter year Thanin's regime was overthrown on 20 October).

Throughout this period, the CPM leadership did not let an opportunity pass without exploiting it. The "anti-Malaysian" movement was brought to a boiling point during the Seni Pramoj government of 1976. Careful analysis would show that the movement was organized and spearheaded by ethnic Chinese who were sympathizers of the CPM (*The Bangkok Post*, 5, 7 May 1976). In opposition to the presence of Malaysian security forces along the border, particularly in Betong, the CPM stronghold, a dubious group was formed with the self-appointed mission of "protecting Thai sovereignty." It called itself, appropriately enough, "Thailand's Sovereignty Protection Group" (Thomas 1977b, 380) and presented the following demands: first, it wanted the goverment, as of midday 2 May 1976, to order the 410 Malaysian security men out of Betong within forty-eight hours; second, there should be no more "violation" of Thailand's territorial integrity by her southern neighbor; third, the Kuala Lumpur government must pay compensation to Thais whose relatives had been killed or wounded due to the Malaysians' actions; and last, they demanded that the Ministers of the Interior and Foreign Affairs come to Betong, where over ten thousand people demonstrated (Pairatchakarn 1979, 62–98).

The Malaysian authorities both at the border and in Kuala Lumpur viewed these developments with both skepticism and alarm. The CPM seized the occasion and skillfully played on the sensitivity of the Thais about the issue. The fact that the wounded and killed were Chinese members of the Communist Party of Thailand (CPT) was ignored. Both the Thai and Malaysian authorities realized that they were dealing with an explosive situation which needed to be handled with great care. A small misstep on either side would jeopardize the relationship that both had come to treasure but which was increasingly under pressure.

To make the situation worse, former prime minister Tunku Abdul Rahman told the *Nation Review* in Bangkok on 6 May 1976 that "the communists now had full control of the Betong salient. There are no Thais in the district. There are only the CPM elements and some Malays. The cause of the demonstration has nothing to do with damages done to any Thai's property" (Pairatchakarn 1979, 72–73; Thomas 1977a, 309). While the protesting Thais considered the Chinese CPM members and sympathizers as Thai nationals deserving protection, Malaysian authorities saw them as outlaws to be suppressed.

If that statement by the former prime minister did not stir Thai feelings, nothing would. What Tunku implied was that the Thai government could not protect the nation's sovereignty. Fortunately, the former Malaysian premier's statements were confined to the English daily and not carried in the Thai daily newspapers, so the extent of hurt pride was limited.

The situation was so serious that the Foreign Relations Committee of the National Assembly was called in. Dr. Paitoon Kruakaew, the committee chairman, traveled south with his colleagues and made a controversial report to the full parliament supporting the positions taken by the organizers of the demonstrations in Betong. His report revealed some of the underlying problems inherent in the relations between the two countries, with implications for today's bilateral affairs.

The report accused the Malaysian forces of violating the original agreement in many instances. Rather than taking actions against the communists, the Malaysian security forces indiscriminately killed, wounded, and arrested Thai citizens (mostly of Chinese origin) who were innocent of the communist insurgency. It was a unilateral action with no Thai official taking part in the operations. As against the original intent of the 1970 agreement, it was not a hot-pursuit operation. The Malaysian forces stayed on Thai soil for fourteen days rather than seventy-two hours as stipulated. The people of Betong would like to see more Thai police and soldiers stationed in the area, the committee observed. It also pointed out that the Thai forces were attacked only when accompanying the Malaysian forces. It accused the Malaysians of "showing no trust and displaying an unfriendly attitude toward their Thai hosts" (Foreign Relations Committee Report, 11 June 1976).

In addition, the Committee made some disturbing observations with regard to the joint border operations. Tan Sri Ghazali Shafie, then the Malaysian Home Affairs Minister, had stated:

I fear that the Betong salient will be completely dominated by the Communists. Should this happen, that part of our border could be seriously threatened since the enemy will have an unencumbered base to train, plan, initiate action, and withdraw to safety with impunity. . . . To protect our national interest and indeed our survival, we will have to regard that part of Thailand as hostile, and the ramifications of such an attitude must not only be understood but also accepted by all. (*FEER*, 18 June 1976, 11)

The committee responded with the following:

The Committee wants to remind the Malaysian government that Thailand is now governed by a democratic regime and that the Thai people treasure and jealously guard their sovereignty. Whatever action is needed in the suppression of the communists (CPM) or to insure law and order on every square inch of the land should be the responsibility of the Thai government in accordance with the policy made and approved by the Parliament, which is, in turn, responsible to the people in general. (Foreign Relations Committee Report, 11 June 1976)

The Committee also suggested that any cooperation rendered by the Thai armed forces should be reciprocated in kind by the Malaysian security forces in preventing and suppressing "aid and assistance given to the Malay-Muslim separatist movement directly or indirectly." The chairman of the Committee ventured to offer his personal opinion with regard to the Agreement of 1970, under which the joint border operations were supposed to be governed, that it was tantamount to "turning over Thai sovereignty to Malaysia" (*Prachachart Daily*, 30 June 1976).

The Seni Pramoj government was overthrown in October of the same year. Parliament was dissolved, no opposition to government policies was tolerated, and the hysterical era of communist suppression began with the ascent of Thanin Kraivixian to prime minister. This civilian authoritarian government ruled without popular participation, brushing aside irritations that had caused so much apprehension and anxiety during the democratically elected government under Seni Pramoj. In fact the essential points in the agreement of 1970, which had been considered to be indications of "inequity," were ignored in a new agreement signed by Thanin and Dato Onn during the latter's visit to Thailand on 4 March 1977 (*The Bangkok Post*, 8 March 1977).

The present [1983] border relations between the two countries are governed by the 1977 agreement. And the official circles dealing with the thorny issue of the CPM are still very much apprehensive. If anything, the problem has gotten to be more complicated than ever. Thus, during an interview soon after he came to power, General Prem Tinsulanonda, the present Thai prime minister, was asked if the relations between Thailand and Malaysia "have deteriorated since joint military operations began." His reply was: "What leads outsiders to think they have deteriorated is that we have made some positive, bilateral adjustments." But he declined to elaborate on the "positive adjustments" (*Asiaweek*, 2 May 1980).

Obviously what the premier referred to were the points that were raised before during the Seni government. The rocky relations continue and the issue of the CPM has not been resolved. As late as 15 October 1983, General Harn Leenanonda, the well-known commander of the Fourth Army Region responsible for Thai-Malay border security until the end of the previous month, raised the issue of "inequity, insincerity, and hypocrisy" on the part of the Malaysian authorities in handling the border problems.

ETHNIC COMPOSITION AND PERCEPTIONS OF THREAT

Post-Vietnam Southeast Asia became more complex than the East-West confrontation that culminated in the protracted war of Indochina. A united Vietnam led to a revived dream of a "federation of the Indochina states" under the leadership of Hanoi. The Chinese leaders felt threatened by the ever increasing influence of the Soviet Union over Vietnam. While Laos remained rather oblivious of what was going on around her, Kampuchea became a bone of contention between China and Vietnam. The Chinese tried to strengthen their ties with the Khmer Rouge leaders in order to keep Vietnam occupied with her southwestern border rather than concentrating her forces along her northern border with China. The conflict turned into a crisis when Hanoi decided that the Kampuchean leadership under Beijing's influence was too much of a threat to Vietnam and invaded Kampuchea in early 1979. And that move by Hanoi exacerbated the already shaky conditions in the region.

Thailand and Malaysia's fear of communism has served as a mutual bond. During the postwar period this fear has undergone a transformation as the once unitary communist threat showed itself to be divided. With the Vietnamese troops stationed right up to the border, Thailand feels the immediate danger of being engulfed by the communist ideology and all that implies; her only comfort is the ever-widening rift between China and Vietnam. But by repositioning herself in alliance with the Chinese to offset the Vietnamese threat, Thailand inadvertently aroused fears in her southern neighbor because the latter considers Beijing the main supporter of the communist menace she has been facing. To the Malaysian leadership, being communist is synonymous to being Chinese. The communist threat is equivalent to the Chinese threat.

In the middle of 1975, immediately after the fall to the communists of the three Indochina countries, M. R. Kukrit Pramoj, the Thai prime minister at the time, was reported to have asked his military commanders how long the Thai armed forces could withstand an open invasion from the *east*. He was told that although the Thai defense apparatus would give the invaders stiff resistance, the prime minister should not expect the eastern defense line to stand "for more than one week." Then and there the erstwhile premier gave an order to his aides to "prepare for a trip to China."

Amidst the uncertainty of American policy in the region the Thais were forced to maneuver to insure their own security. If the Chinese leaders thought that keeping their influence over the Khmer Rouge and sustaining them was the way to apply pressure to the defiant Vietnamese, the Thai leaders were also quick to "borrow the Chinese hands" to squeeze the aggressive Vietnamese. Kukrit went to Beijing in July to explore the Chinese intent and strategy.

Thailand's rivalry with Vietnam over Cambodia, as it used to be called, has a very long history. For over two hundred years the unarticulated preference of both countries has been the neutrality of an independent buffer state between them. A lopsided influence of one would always make the other feel insecure. Thus, the taking over of Kampuchea by the Vietnamese soldiers not only brought the threat of communism closer to the Thais, but also, for the first time in two centuries, the two traditional adversaries became "neighbors" despite the differences between them.

But the very security strategy that Thailand has been following since the fall of Indochina gave the Malaysian leadership a jolt. Any opportunity for the regime in Beijing to exert its influence in the region is considered a threat to noncommunist Southeast Asia, particularly Indonesia and Malaysia. Both have gone through their respective bitter experiences with Beijing-inspired crises, in 1965 and 1969. The fragile ethnic composition in both countries justifies their paranoia over the China threat.

Because of the geographical proximity and cultural affinity the Thais have with the Chinese, racial integration and social acculturation work best in Thai society. Thus, even before the political rapprochement initiated by Kukrit in 1975, there was already a tendency to accommodation between the People's Republic of China and Thailand (Shee Poon Kim 1981, 310–24). The Kampuchean issue has given a greater sense of urgency to the efforts at consolidating that traditional tie.

Following Kukrit's move, both General Kriangsak and his successor, General Prem, have brought Bangkok and Beijing to an alliance that goes beyond the political. When Kriangsak visited the Chinese capital early in 1978, a request was made of the Beijing leadership to "stop supporting the Communist Party of Thailand" as a sign of good faith toward Southeast Asia as a whole. The issue of "logistical support" for the embattled Khmer Rouge was also raised. The Chinese, it turned out, needed to channel military hardware through Thailand and hoped for the latter's cooperation. Beijing obviously sensed Bangkok's anxiety over the mounting Vietnamese pressure along her eastern frontier. The Chinese response was typically noncommital and a distinction was drawn between government-to-government and party-to-party relationships. The Communist Party of China has "a moral obligation" to support its sister parties, whose members are mostly ethnic Chinese, in the region. The Thai visitors took the response as implying that the government of China was willing to consider the Thai request, subject to the Party's approval.

Actions speak louder than words. During a public discussion on Thai foreign policy on 15 November 1980, Sarasin Veeraphol, a China expert and an influential foreign policy formulator, said that the level of support for the CPT had been markedly reduced since Kriangsak's visit and since the Vietnamese invasion of Kampuchea. Thailand is satisfied with China's action—trust has deepened.

During his visit to Washington in October 1979, Kriangsak quashed wide speculation that Thailand had been cooperating with China in transporting military supplies to the Khmer Rouge guerrillas struggling against the occupying Vietnamese. But back in Southeast Asia, Thailand's southern neighbor began to feel that the intimate relationship between China and her mainland ASEAN partner was becoming "too close for comfort." Just as the Thai premier prepared to take off for Washington, in September, Houssain Onn of Malaysia went to Moscow hoping to enlist the Soviet Union's support in solving the stalemate over Kampuchea. Kuala Lumpur calculated that with the encouragement of Moscow, the Vietnamese would be more accommodating toward ASEAN and help reduce apprehension over its aggressive design; once an agreement was reached, the role of China would also be reduced. While Kriangsak's trip to Washington won Thailand renewed assurance of assistance in the event of a crisis involving an external threat, as well as a speedy shipment of arms already contracted, Houssein's trip to Moscow bore little tangible result.

Internal political developments in Thailand during 1981–82 further convinced the Thai leadership that its "China card" is the single most effective guarantee for security in the face of the Vietnamese threat. The spate of defections of members of the CPT signaled a breakdown, not only of morale, but also of party organization. The government's Communist Suppression Command sensed victory in its operations around the country, affording some reason to celebrate. The closure of the CPT's most effective propaganda organ, the Voice of the Thai People radio, at the request of Kriangsak, finally had its effect on the CPT. The Chinese had delivered.

Thailand has been drawn deep into the scheme of containment Beijing designed to counter Soviet influence in the area. It fits Thailand's own need for security and assurance amidst the turmoil in the region. It is reminiscent of what Thailand did when both the British and French were encroaching upon her during the nineteenth century: play one against the other. And the practical results are perceived, at least for the present, to be quite rewarding.

But Malaysia has had a different experience. The domestic threat from the communist insurgency is very much in evidence. In addition, whatever the Chinese did to assuage Thailand tended to have an adverse effect on Kuala Lumpur. While the continued "political and moral" support for the area's communist parties satisfies Thailand somewhat, Malaysia wants the link severed altogether. On the other hand, facing the Vietnamese and behind them the Russians, Thailand agrees with the Chinese leaders that if, as suggested, the link is severed, the Vietnamese and the Russians will undoubtedly fill the void. That argument was not and is not appreciated in Kuala Lumpur (*FEER*, 21 August 1981). The Malaysian leaders interpret this as only a ploy to maintain the link for a future communist design.

On the issue of closing the clandestine radio stations supporting the communist parties in the region, Malaysia pointed out that the Chinese had not shown them the same sincerity they had shown Thailand. "Long before the broadcasts from China ceased," Datuk Seri Mahathir said in Bangkok in August 1981, "the radio station informed everyone that they would broadcast on another wavelength in another name, which is very much the same thing. We feel that our relations with China have not really improved beyond the big step in 1974" (when Tun Abdul Razak, then prime minister, normalized diplomatic relations with China [*FEER*, 26 August 1981]). The Voice of Malaya Revolution (VMR) was closed down on 30 June in south China, and, on 1 July 1981, the Voice of Malayan Democracy (VMD) began its broadcast from a mobile unit believed to be in the area of the Bannang Satar district of Yala province, Thailand.

While Bangkok is currently preoccupied with the Kampuchean question and has actually declared that the communist threat within the Thai frontiers has been eradicated (*Nation Review*, 20 October 1981), Malaysia finds more evidence of Beijing's designs to eventually take over the country. These designs in major part hinge upon the unprecedented intimate bond between Bangkok and Beijing. The increasing reluctance of the Thais to cooperate with the efforts of their Malaysian counterparts to eradicate the CPM's Chinese elements along their common border is being perceived as a direct result of Thai-Chinese friendship. The gulf of mistrust between the two ASEAN neighbors widens even more.

The creation of the Voice of Malayan Democracy (VMD) with Chinese support coincided with the shift of policy to promote more of a Malay image in the insurgency campaign. Since the "Emergency," the CPM had portrayed itself as more a Chinese than a united multi-racial movement. However, in the wake of the phenomenal rise of Malay consciousness in the country, they thought it imperative to make the party appear more in tune with the rising tide. Thus emerged the Revolutionary Malay Nationalist Party (RMNP) on 15 June 1981, a mere two weeks before the VMD began broadcasts from Bannang Satar. This area is reportedly under the control of the Tenth Regiment of the CPM, which is dominated by individuals of Malay origin (Ruengyot 1980, 178; Thomas 1977a, 310). China is suspected to have a role in this development also.

From the Thai point of view, the more the communist insurgency against Malaysia is perceived to be "Malay," the easier for Thailand to extract cooperation from the Malaysian authorities to help suppress the Malay-Muslim separatists. So far Malaysia has been insisting that the two issues are separate. Indeed, one observer has suggested that the Chinese enticed Thailand to lessen her cooperation with the Malaysian forces in the suppression of the CPM. "Intelligence analysts here [in Kuala Lumpur] now believe that Chinese pressure on Vietnam's northern border was a payoff for the Thai break with Malaysian forces," wrote K. Das, who tends to reflect the official thinking of Kuala Lumpur (*FEER*, 14 August 1981).

While there is no direct evidence to link Thailand's reluctance with the Chinese actions against Vietnam, it is obvious that Bangkok has come to the conclusion that going along with the Chinese is more beneficial to the Thai national interest than cooperating with her southern neighor, which has repeatedly refused to reciprocate on the issue of the Malay-Muslim separatist movement.

A change of direction is needed in the border operation. More emphasis must now be put on the socioeconomic dimension of the problem. Economic cooperation in developing the border area should be intensified and the military alliance minimized. Thailand's problem with her Malay-Muslim population is of a social, economic, and political nature, much like those which have given rise to insurgency all around the country. By continuing to assist the Malaysian government's suppression efforts against the CPM, which has more a political reason for its existence, Thailand would have to divert her resources and energy away from her own immediate problems. Besides, once the CPM is wiped out in the area along the common border, what guarantee does Thailand have of Malaysian cooperation in solving Thailand's irredentist problem? This thinking was apparent in the refusal of Lieutenant-General Juan Wannrat, a former commanding general of the South, to go along with Ghazali Shafei, a former Malaysian minister of Home Affairs, currently its foreign minister, when the latter suggested in 1981 that joint border operations should take place again and often. Lieutenant-General Harn Leenanonda, Juan's successor, said much the same when he took over the southern command in October, 1981. Harn still insists on the point now (*FEER*, 19 June 1981; personal interview, 9 October 1981; *Nation Review*, 15 October 1983).

This gradual shift to accomodation of interests with China, resulting from altered perceptions of threat, has led to an increase of tension between Thailand and Malaysia. And it does have an implication for ASEAN's approach to the most intractable of all problems, Kampuchea, the issue that has drained most of Thailand's political vigor and diplomatic drive. We can trace the reasons behind the changes to the ethnic composition of the two ASEAN neighbors and their domestic experiences with their ethnic minorities.

MALAY ETHNIC NATIONALISM: THE THAI DILEMMA

If the issue of the CPM is considered the single foremost national security concern for Kuala Lumpur, so can the perpetual question of the ethnic Malay-Muslim separatist movement, in exactly the same area, be considered Thailand's "Achilles' heel." Now that the focus of national security efforts is shifted from other parts of the country to the South, the separatist issue has gained the government's special attention. High government officials have expressed their frustrations with a code phrase which, however, has been universally deciphered: "the root cause of separatism in the South is foreign-inspired. But for the purpose of preserving good relations with our neighbors, we cannot elaborate on that."

The very proximity of the South to the geographical world of the Malay people poses a problem for Bangkok. Throughout history, the South has remained an area of opposition, with centrifugal forces at work in various ways at different levels of the region's affairs. It "might best be considered a tributary territory separating the Thai and Malay social formations" (Elliott 1978, 64). Indeed, it is a demarcation line between the Buddhist mainland and the Malay-Muslim world of Southeast Asia. Thus, the centrifugal forces that are manifest in the case of the Malay Muslims of south Thailand can, at the same time, be viewed as a result of the centripetal tendency of the Malay geocultural phenomenon. The ethnic ties, cultural links, and historical bond exert themselves in defiance of political boundaries superficially imposed on them. As Syed Husin Ali put it:

The peninsular Malays (including the Malays of south Thailand) constitute but a minor portion of the people from the same stock, and the culture they inherit forms only part of a greater cultural heritage of the rest of the people in the area. What has set the Malays in this country quite apart from the rest socially and culturally has been the result of recent colonial history. (Ali 1966, 65)

The two conflicting views—centrifugal by the Thais and centripetal by the Malays—concerning the problems of the Malay Muslims of south Thailand have been the sources of many sensitive incidents and policy differences between the two governments. While the historical background spans many centuries, the modern point of reference is the end of the World War II. When the movement for Malayan independence began, the Malay Nationalist Party represented the strongest support for the inclusion in the emerging federation of four Malay-dominated provinces of south Thailand: Patani, Yala, Narathivat, and Stun. The nationalists proclaimed as policy the right of the Malays in the four southern provinces of Thailand to self-determination (Suhrke 1977, 201). But the British, having forced Thailand to return Kedah, Kelantan, Trangganu, and Perlis after a brief period of Thai rule during the war, felt it more urgent to win Thailand's favor and her willingness to export rice to help alleviate serious famine in the Far East. So they saw it as prudent to resist any Malay nationalist desire. London merely conveyed to Bangkok that "Whitehall expects a just solution of Patani's case" (Jones 1948, 4–5).

Independent Malaya, in 1957, did not include the four southern provinces, but the sentiment for their separation and the grass-roots support for it continue through the postwar period. Efforts at integration by the Thais invariably encounter stiff resistance and further fuel separatist tendencies. The further Malaysia moves along the road of national development through her "pro-Malay communal politics," the stronger is the effect the process has on the irredentist movement. Thus, the national unity that both nations desire for their own security and well-being, at the same time has an undesirable effect, unfortunately, on the ethnic minority issue in south Thailand.

During the last decade, even a small opposition party with a power base in the northern states of Malaysia was a cause of concern among Thai officials. Parti Islam (PI) leaders in Kelantan, for example, have been vociferous in their support of the Patani Muslims. In 1970, Datuk Mohammad Asri of Kelantan wrote in *The Muslim* of London that the struggle against Thai rule in southern Thailand was a "holy one" and deserved support from Muslims the world over (July 1970, 230). But he caused the most concern and drew violent reactions from the Thai press when he commented, while being chief minister of the state and minister for religious affairs of the federal government, that: "The request for autonomy with specific conditions for the four provinces as put forward by the freedom front seems credible if well received" (*The Straits Times*, 18 June 1974).

But both Malaysian domestic politics and the drastic changes which have taken place in the Muslim world in general have also transformed the perception of the Thais with regard to the "external dimension" of the Muslim separatist movement.

THE FEDERAL GOVERNMENT'S ROLE

Since 1978, the consolidation of power by the more moderate Malay faction (the United Malays National Organization—UMNO) in the northern states has brought the Kuala Lumpur government closer to the issue. No longer can the support be brushed aside as being just "locally inspired." This is due, to a large extent, to the rise of a strong Malay identity as a result of the indigenous Malays' participation in the national economy and in politics. Thanks to the New Economic Policy (NEP) launched in 1970 by Tun Razak, the lot of *bumiputras* (the ethnic Malays) has been consciously and systematically improved (Siddiqui 1980). Much as the flush of *merdeka* had induced conservative Malays to press the federal government to back the Patani cause (*Asiaweek*, 4 April 1980), the NEP and its pro-Malay emphasis have had effects among the Malays of south Thailand. Indeed, what used to be considered only as an opposition party's policy of support for the kinfolk across the border is now seen as the general policy of the federal government.

MUSLIM REFUGEES FROM BETONG AND WEANG

The "Muslim refugee" issue during the early part of 1981 demonstrated well how a "local problem" was blown up to national dimensions and captured world attention. Under pressure from Bangkok to withdraw by January 1980, the Malaysian Field Forces intensified their operations against the CPM (*Asiaweek*, 2 May 1980). The Chinese communist insurgents were forced to disband into small units and abandon their long-established sanctuaries in Waeng (Narathivat) and Betong (Yala). As a result, Malay Muslims, including elements and sympathizers of the Patani United Liberation Organization (PULO) moved into the area to fill the vacuum. The confrontation ensued after Malaysian forces withdrew, but did not explode into a crisis until March and April 1981 when Thai security forces as well as the CPM and the separatists became involved. Muslim villagers caught in the cross fire moved over the border into Kedah and Kelantan. At the height of the confrontation, 1,178 people entered "refugee camps" inside Malaysia, vowing not to return until their safety could be guaranteed (*Impact*, 24 April 1981).

The federal government in Kuala Lumpur reasoned that the "refugees" must be treated as such by federal authorities. Bangkok, suspicious of the PULO's desire to exploit the situation, and seeing it with its supporters in Malaysia as making a mountain out of a molehill, moved quickly to contain the damage and avoid international attention. But in the wake of other Indochina refugees flooding Malaysian shores, the issue was considered particularly sensitive by the Malaysian authorities. Given the fact that Vietnamese refugees with Chinese backgrounds were treated with tough measures, including the celebrated "shoot on landing" policy pronounced by the then Deputy Prime Minister Datuk Seri Mahathir, the Malay Muslims from southern Thailand could not be treated with too obvious leniency or the government would be accused of having a double standard, as well as of discrimination, by Malaysia's own racially mixed populace.

The Thai local authorities, meanwhile, argued that many Muslims from southern Thailand had crossed the border before and had been readily absorbed by their relatives in Malaysia without much protest. In that, this time, the Malaysian government was going to put them in camps and refused to disperse them, they saw sign of some ulterior motive. And when Kuala Lumpur went as far as announcing its plan to ask the United Nations High Commissioner for Refugees (UNHCR) to administer the camps, Bangkok strongly objected, and some local officials accused their Malaysian counterparts of "internationalizing the situation."

Since they constituted the strong power base of PI and a bastion for Islamic conservatism, the northern states of Malaysia and the border area had to be treated with great care. UMNO could not afford to risk offending local sentiment. Their leaders realized that UMNO still did not have strong enough support in the area once ruled by the opposition, which could very easily stage a comeback if there was an issue to stir up emotions (Kessler 1974, 273–313).

Thus, as against the dramatic policy toward the Vietnamese boat people of "shoot on landing," Mahathir said "the [Malay] refugees would not be returned against their wish and Malaysia would provide them shelter on purely humanitarian grounds." The official position, he explained, was nonacceptance of refugees, but he admitted there was no definite policy on the Malay Muslims as opposed to the other Indochinese refugees. "The final government policy would depend on the results of their study of the background of this mass exodus" (*Impact*, 24 April 1981).

Mahathir appeared to cover himself against charges that might have come from any quarter. Being from Kedah himself, he knows how strong is the sentiment and support for the kinfolk across the border. By declaring the assistance to be on humanitarian grounds only, he protected himself against the Thai accusation that the Malaysians were assisting the PULO and its sympathizers.

Back in Thailand, however, charges were made that the Malaysian authorities encouraged elements of the PULO to strike at the base areas of the CPM in Weang and Betong, who in turn informed the Thai authorities of the separatists' activities and movements. Paisal Sricharatchanya, of the *Far Eastern Economic Review*, observed:

Betong officials who observed the exodus in April claim they saw Malaysian militiary vehicles picking up the refugees once they had crossed the border. Border Patrol Police (BPP) sources claim that since late 1980, Muslim separatists have been wearing jungle fatigues and using tinned rations and equipment similar to those used by Malaysian forces. (*FEER*, 9 October 1981)

What concerned Bangkok most was the economic impact of the prolonged crisis. The very existence of the camps just inside the Malaysian border testifies to the lack of security in Thailand. Such an atmosphere discourages many thousands of Malaysian tourists and businessmen who have been important elements of the southern economy. Finally, in September 1980, the Thai government negotiated with Kuala Lumpur to settle the refugee issue. As a gesture of friendship and as a favor to an ASEAN partner, Kuala Lumpur decided to "absorb" the Malay Muslims who were left in the camps, just as had usually been the case previously with people from the border area.

The incident revealed how both national governments now are being brought into the area of conflict. Because both are determined to consolidate their grip over local affairs along their common border, there is greater likelihood of confrontation. In April 1980, the governor of Narathivat could express his hope that the defeat of PI in Kelantan would improve the situation as far as the support for PULO was concerned. As it turns out, the problem has become more complicated and could grow into an international conflict.

MUSLIM MINORITIES, MALAYSIA, AND THE MUSLIM WORLD

In addition to the internal development of Malaysia with regard to Malay ethnic consciousness and Islamic identity, the international atmosphere of the Muslim world in general has also been a cause of much concern for Bangkok. Indeed, as Islamic consciousness rose dramatically during the last decade due to the newfound confidence and influence of the Muslim nations, the issue of Muslim minorities everywhere is being taken up by various organizations including the Organization of Islamic Conference (OIC) and the Islamic Foreign Ministers Conference (IFMC).

Traditionally, Bangkok has relied on the two Muslim nations of ASEAN, Malaysia and Indonesia, to "support Thailand in the international circles against the activities of the separatist movement," as a top secret memorandum, drawn up by the Thai National Security in 1978, puts it. In February of that year, the same document stated that Prime Minister Kriangsak Chomanand had asked the Indonesian and Malaysian leaders to continue their support for Thailand in containing possible damages done by the propaganda efforts of the separatist elements at international forums.

Given the fact that PULO has been most vigorous in its public relations abroad, Bangkok can expect the two ASEAN partners, particularly Malaysia, to deny it the opportunity to voice its case in the Islamic forums. At the highest level of government, such "ASEAN solidarity" has so far produced no results. PULO, according to its own admission, has failed to capture any official attention from the various Muslim international bodies where both Malaysia and Indonesia were present. As an article in *Impact* (London) puts it:

To find a place on the agenda of the OIC of IFMC, an issue has to be formally proposed by a member state. Who should do that? Most countries were either too indifferent or too unknowing. The Malaysians, who the others supposed would know and say so if there was a problem which deserved their attention, felt that to do so would be violating the code of ASEAN "solidarity." Privately they would express their sympathy and even anguish, but officially no such problem existed. (April 1981)

What PULO could not accomplish officially it could, however, do through other means. One recent effort to gain attention was the circulation of an appeal during the Islamic Summit Conference held in Mecca and Taif in January 1981. The document found its way into the April 1981 issue of *The Journal of the Muslim World League* with the title "Patani Plea for Muslim Help" (47–49). PULO receives considerable support from the League, which is the Saudi Arabian government's official organ for rendering assistance to Muslims around the world. Instances of social, educational, and religious assistance have been documented. Whether the Summit Conference considered the plea of PULO or not cannot be ascertained due to the absence of an official communiqué on the matter. But the publication of the plea is an adequate testimony that support for it is growing in official and semiofficial quarters.

The Thai government is also concerned with Malaysian officials actively engaging in a campaign of soliciting support for the separatist cause. While Bangkok has yet to make an official complaint to Kuala Lumpur on the issue, it views the trend with alarm, and plans are being drawn to counter these efforts. Authorities in Bangkok and in the newly established Center for Administrative Coordination for the Border Provinces in Yala have expressed their private concern about "foreigners acting on behalf of the separatist in the Middle East." They point to the celebrated connection between Datuk Asri Muda of Kelantan and Tuan Mustapha of Sabah and their respective contributions to the causes of the Malays of southern Thailand and the Moro Muslims of the southern Philippines. Both men have been regarded as "surrogates" for Libya and other fundamentalist organizations in their support of the twin separatist movements in Southeast Asia. "In November 1977, when it was assumed that Datuk Asri was in London, our intelligence sources confirmed that he was in Mecca and Tripoli trumpeting the PULO's cause," Mr. Orachun Nuibandan, special assistant for security affairs to the governor of Narathivat, pointed out (interview, 12 October 1983). And the governor himself was quoted as saying that after the defeat of PI in Kelantan in early 1978, "the situation has improved." After his public statement in support of PULO in 1974, Asri has been closely watched by officials across the border.

Another example of middle-level Malaysian officials publically voicing their support for the Muslim separatist movement of southern Thailand is to be found in the *Journal of Muslim World League,* September 1978. It quotes Tan Sri Abdul Aziz bin Zain, president of the Muslim Welfare Organization of Malaysia, as saying to a gathering in Saudi Arabia:

The Malays in South Thailand had nourished a resentment to what they considered the forcible incorporation of their homeland into Thai-speaking Buddhist Thailand. For more than a century Thailand had been trying to assimilate their Malay subjects through their policy of natural integration which required a citizen to have Thai culture. These efforts were considered by the Muslims as an attempt to suppress their identity, Malay customs, Islamic religion and culture. And nothing concrete was done to help them overcome their economic, social, and educational problems. (36–37)

What the official was saying, of course, is in direct contradiction to what Thai authorities are projecting to the world. While it is realized in Bangkok that it is not a policy of the federal government in Kuala Lumpur to aggravate Thailand's problem with her ethnic Malays in the South, measures have been taken to contain damages done by such "propaganda on behalf of the separatists," as the 1978 NSC document on the matter puts it. The government's information dissemination effort must be more vigorous "in some influential Middle Eastern countries." Typically, it calls for "a psychological operation" to give the correct image of the Thai government's attitude and policy toward the "Thai Muslims along the southern border." Influential personages and officials of Muslim organizations should be invited to visit the South. But they "must not be allowed to travel as they wish," the secret document suggests. And finally, "diplomatic relations with the Muslim countries must be improved." An information office "should be established in Mecca because it is the center of Muslims from all over the world."

As Malaysia is going through her process of "reassessment of the Islamic ideological contribution to state formation" and Islam can be expected to give form and content to the evolution of the Malaysian polity during the rest of the century (Siddiqui 1981, 23), the Malay Muslims of southern Thailand have also been affected by the waves of emotion and excitement characteristic of such a national identity search. Through no conscious design of any government, the religious fever and nationalist sentiment that are generated could conceivably be sources of conflict and threaten the good neighborly relations between Thailand and Malaysia.

Thus the Thai government is waging its own "information campaign" in Middle Eastern countries, and has been prepared for the day when Malaysia cannot be expected to "support Thailand in the international community" on the issue of her Malay-Muslim minority. The Special Committee on the Study of the Situations in the Three Southern Border Provinces, in its report to the full Parliament in December 1979, put it this way: "Thailand will face many problems if and when political factions with nationalist leanings come to power inside Malaysia."

CONCLUSION

ASEAN has been singled out as an example of a regional organization that has achieved its goal far beyond expectations. It has attained a high degree of cohesiveness, economic cooperation, and cultural exchange. Outside powers now regard ASEAN as a single unit and have been convinced that it has a tremendous potential for development and trade. ASEAN has also impressed other countries as being viable as a political entity, and its solidarity has grown through the difficult period of change and uncertainty in Southeast Asia. It has taken many unified stands on various world issues at international forums. The record of ASEAN achievement has been impressive indeed.

But as pointed out earlier, all five ASEAN countries have problems among themselves that need to be resolved. In this paper we have examined three problems that affect the relations between Malaysia and Thailand which potentially could grow into major crises. Each problem raised is closely related to the ethnic composition of the two states, and they are becoming more complex, involving outside powers and other changes in the international arena.

First we took up the question of the CPM elements operating along the Thai border. Thailand is anxious to get the Malaysians to cooperate in the suppression of the Muslim separatists in return for her assistance in containing the CPM activities. But Malaysia is unwilling to reciprocate because of the ethnic affinity its own populace feels toward the Malay Muslims of southern Thailand.

Meanwhile the superpowers' rivalry in the region is having an impact on Thai-Malay relations. The more influence the Chinese have over Thailand in her confrontation with Vietnam over Kampuchea, the less secure the Malaysians feel about the Thais' policy toward the Chinese-dominated CPM. The Chinese refused to sever their relations with the CPM for fear of the Vietnamese and the Russians taking over the leading roles in the region. The Malaysians suspect the Thais of being too closely allied with the Chinese, who also have a design on Malaysia through her many ethnic Chinese. Their difference on this issue also jeopardizes Malaysia and Thailand's good neighborly relations.

Finally, there is the issue of the ethnic Malay-Muslim minority in southern Thailand. Increasingly, the Thai authorities are concerned with the Malay-Islamic identity and consciousness which have been growing in Malaysia. Such a development has direct implications for the Malay Muslims of southern Thailand and deepens their own sense of alienation from the Thai political and cultural milieu. Trust in the Malaysians' cooperation in supporting Thailand on this issue has declined. Thailand now is planning her own campaign of information to counter the activities of PULO and the support of other groups for the movement in the Middle East. Malaysian officials' direct support for the organization also has been noted with concern.

All three issues deserve careful analysis and serious deliberation by officials of both countries. Failure to address them would eventually lead to more problems that would threaten ASEAN as a whole.

REFERENCES

Ali, S. Husin. 1966. "A Note on Malay Society and Culture." In *The Cultural Problems of Malaysia in the Context of Southeast Asia*. Kuala Lumpur: Malaysia Society of Orientalists. Quoted by S. Siddiqui, 1961.

Boyce, P. 1968. *Malaysia and Singapore in International Diplomacy*. Sydney: Sydney University Press.

Chaweewan, W. et al. 1982. *A Survey of Perceptions of the Thais About the Joint Border Operations Along the Southern Border* (in Thai). Patani: Prince of Songklha University.

Elliott, D. 1979. *Thailand: Origins of Military Rule*. New York: Porter Publisher.

Forbes, A. D. W. 1982. "Thailand Muslim Minority: Assimilation, Secession, or Coexistence?" *Asian Survey* 22, no. 1 (November).

Hiranyato, Uthai. 1983. *The Communist Party of Malaya and the Southern Border Provinces of Thailand* (in Thai). Bangkok: Department of Local Administration.

Jones, Barbara. 1948. "Patani Appeals to UNO." *Eastern World* (April): 4–5.

Kessler, C. S. 1974. "Muslim Identity and Political Behaviour in Kelantan." In *Kelantan: Religion, Society and Politics in a Malay State*, edited by William R. Roff, 272–313. Kuala Lumpur: Oxford University Press.

Kroef, Justus M. von der. 1981. "ASEAN, Hanoi, and the Kampuchean Conflict: Between 'Kuantan' and a 'Third Alternative'." *Asian Survey* 21, no. 5 (May): 515–35.

Miller, H. 1959. *Prince and Premier*. Singapore: Donald Moore Ltd.

———. 1972. *Jungle War in Malaya*. London: Arthur Barker Ltd.

Niksch, L. A. 1981. "Thailand in 1980: Confrontation with Vietnam and the

Fall of Kriangsak." *Asian Survey* 21, no. 2 (February).

Pairatchakarn, S. 1979. *South Thailand: Thailand's or Malaysia's?* (in Thai). Bangkok: Pakarang Press.

Pitsuwan, Surin. 1982. "Islam and Malay Nationalism: A Case Study of the Malay-Muslims of Southern Thailand." Ph.D. diss., Harvard University.

Reungyot, Chantarakiri. 1980. *Situations in Three Border Provinces.* Bangkok: Wongpan Press.

Shee Poon Kim. 1981. "The Politics of Thailand's Trade Relations with the People's Republic of China." *Asian Survey* 21, no. 3 (March).

Siddiqui, S. 1980. "Some Aspects of Malay-Muslim Ethnicity in Peninsular Malaysia." Singapore, Institute of Southeast Asian Research.

_____ 1981. "Conceptualizing Contemporary Islam: Religion or Ideology?" Singapore, Institute of Southeast Asian Research. Manuscript.

Suhrke, A. 1977. *Ethnic Conflict in International Relations.* Edited by L. G. Noble. New York: Praeger.

Thomas, Ladd. 1977a. "The Malayan Communist Party." *Asian Affairs* (May-June), 306–16.

_____ 1977b. "The Malayan Communist Insurgents and Thai-Malaysian Relations." *Asian Affairs* (July-August), 371–84.

Ethnicity and State-Building in Indonesia: the Cultural Base of the New Order

BURHAN D. MAGENDA

INTRODUCTION

In recent years, studies on "ethnic identity" and "cultural mobilization" have gained a new direction in the social sciences, both in the Western World and the Third World. Earlier studies had mostly concentrated analysis on the local level, undoubtedly influenced by the anthropological approach in which the main emphasis was on the microlevel of societal interaction. It is in this category that one might put the works of Cohen, Mangin, and Southall,[1] among others.

While maintaining the cultural aspects of ethnic identity, the newer studies have focused on the relationship between the state and particular ethnic groups, especially on how economic development has strengthened the power of the state vis-à-vis society. Where the state is identified with particular ethnic groups, the problems have been viewed as "internal colonialism," adding economic antagonism to the analysis based on the Marxian dichotomy between the center and the periphery. In this category one can look at the studies of Casanova and of Hechter as well as the burgeoning literature on "ethnic nationalism" in the Western World.[2] In relating the processes of state-building and the growing ethnic consciousness in modern societies, recent studies have overcome the shortcomings of earlier ones such as those of Geertz and of Wallerstein.[3]

The basic premise of both Geertz and Wallerstein was that ethnic identity was a phenomenon temporary in nature. Once national integration and unity had been achieved under the institutions of the modern nation-state, such "primordial sentiments" would automatically disappear, to be replaced by new loyalty to the civil society. The persistence of ethnic identity in modern states can be seen as the common denominator of the increasing interest of present-day social scientists in "ethnic problems." In many ways it resembles the Marxian debates over the nature of the state in the 1970s, in which the notion of *class interests* has been challenged by the creation of the modern state apparatus. [4]

In this context, the main argument has rightly been put forward by Enloe in her description of the interaction between state-building and ethnic structures. [5] It is her opinion that state-building could be used by some ethnic groups to gain state power over other ethnic groups within the nation-state, supported by particular policies in various fields of government. Although her description was mostly drawn from Malaysia's example, her analysis could be used as the appropriate approach in explaining, difficult as it is, the complex relationship between state-building and the role of ethnicity in Third World countries.

Hence, Hechter and Enloe present us with two approaches to the study of ethnic identity in relation to the processes of state-building. Each has its merits and shortcomings, but both have greater explanatory power than previous studies. Moreover, both have seen ethnic problems as permanent in nature and becoming increasingly important aspects of the modern nation-state. In a way, their arguments can be seen as a revision of Marxian undermining of ethnic problems and emphasis on class consciousness per se. Recent studies have shown that ethnic identity and ethnic consciousness can become potent tools for political mobilization or, for that matter, political demobilization as well.

While one cannot deny the inherent disparity of class interests in a world dominated by states, it is fair to say that in most Third World countries the political mobilization of such interests, especially of the lower classes, has been difficult to achieve. Modern governments have offered other incentives to displace those for class mobilization, and if there is no such mobilization, simple repression is quite common. Hence the trend toward what O'Donnell calls the "bureaucratic-authoritarian state," in which the processes of economic development and state-building go hand in hand with the suppression of class interests and organized political groups. [6] In states where ethnic structures are more complex, cultural mobilization based on ethnic identity might be used by the state to prevent mobilization on class interests, thereby channeling the forces created by economic development in ways that guarantee, or at least strengthen, the power of the state.

It is in this theoretical analysis that Indonesia forms a unique object of study. It has the main elements of the above discussion: the processes of nation-building and state-building; the ethnic structures and other "primordial sentiments"; and the trend toward replacing popular mobilization based on class interests with disguised cultural mobilization. All these elements have been encouraged in the last fifteen years by an increasingly powerful state under the New Order government.[7]

THE PROBLEM

The persistence of a strong nationalist ideology has long provided the main resistance to any overt attempt at cultural mobilization. In what has become a classic study on Indonesian nationalism, Kahin explained how attempts at institutionalizing the so-called "primordial sentiments" have failed—for example, the creation of federal states in the Federal Republic of Indonesia in 1949–50—even with strong Dutch support.[8] Hence, despite the presence of "primordial sentiments," Indonesian polity was thought to be capable of containing any attempt at cultural mobilization which was viewed as detrimental to nationalist ideology.

Yet, while nationalism is and has always been the main ideology of Indonesians, the ethnic elements of the polity are becoming more and more evident. In a way, this shows that nationalism has become a force that can be taken for granted in modern Indonesia. Looked at in another way, the growth of ethnic identity could be characterized as the coming of age of Indonesian polity, which has passed from the period of nation-building, through mass mobilization and a search for ideologies, to the period of state-building and ethnic accomodation, accentuated by the processes of economic development.

Nationalism, thereby, is to be seen as the constraint which any argument for cultural mobilization in Indonesian polity has to take into consideration. Casanova's and Hechter's analyses offer us no explanation of the relevance of this constraint to the problems of Indonesian polity as viewed from ethnic perspectives. Moreover, the structures of ethnic groups in Indonesia are more complex than in Mexico or the Celtic communities, where the relationship of ethnic groups is always dichotomous. On the contrary, despite their position of dominance, the Javanese constitute merely the largest of many minority Indonesian ethnic groups, placing them in a unique position to play the role of unifying the ethnic polities—unlike the situations in other countries such as those described by Casanova, Hechter, or for this case, Enloe as well.

Within the Javanese ethnic group itself, there is a powerful stratum which has become the main cultural base of Indonesia's New Order: the *priyayi*. It is the aim of this paper to explain the dominant and unifying role in the New Order's polity of the Javanese *priyayi*, who combine the notions of cultural sphere, social class, and bureaucratic power in a single group that can be seen as the main controller of Indonesian politics.

Although the early argument will emphasize the traditional role of the priyayi as a social class in Javanese social structures, its actual role can only be understood by considering its dominance in the bureaucracy and the state apparatus in general, its cultural flexibility in accommodating different elements of Indonesia's "primordial sentiments," and its rise as an economic class, which constitute a breaking out from its traditional patterns.

By looking at this particular social class, Indonesia's concept of ethnic structures and cultural mobilization will show itself as having a unique character for study in the social sciences: the basis of Indonesian polity is neither a Marxian class nor Casanova's "ethnic majority," but a complex array of alliances in which the priyayi is the core.

TRADITIONAL AND COLONIAL LEGACIES

Originally, the priyayi were the *abdidalem* (officials) of the King in traditional Javanese kingdoms—they formed the social stratum between the King and the masses. Thereby they became a distinct social class, constituting a sort of aristocracy of profession.[9] They differed from the mandarins in Confucian tradition, where examination was the main criterion for acceptance. On the contrary, from the very beginning, the priyayi were flexibly recruited on the basis of personal loyalty. Promotion was given to any devoted *kawula* (subject) of the king.

It should be noted that the model priyayi was supposed to be superior in character. He was to be a *ksatria* (knight), free of selfish motives in his service to the King, and he was to follow certain spiritual training such as the period of *lara* (pain) and *nyuwita* (apprenticeship). Therefore, while preparing themselves to become kings' representatives in the regions, as well as kings' officials in the center, the priyayi had to show that they had absorbed key elements of basic Javanese philosophy. It was assumed that once they were mature in the cultural sphere they would be able to do the bureaucratic work assigned to them. Tradition thus had it that the priyayi were to combine the role of bearers of Javanese cultural tradition and social class, linking the ruler and the masses, and that of bureaucratic officers from whom the old and modern states were to get their new recruits.

In the colonial period, the priyayi enlarged their societal role with the encouragement of the colonial ruler. As Sutherland has made clear, the priyayi benefited from the colonial reformation in many ways, sometimes at the expense of the traditional rulers.[10] In the first place, the priyayi became the main beneficiaries of the expansion of the educational system under the early twentieth-century Ethical Policy. Thereby, the priyayi not only filled most of the colonial administration's posts, if not all, but also provided the Indonesian nationalist movements with most of their educated leaders. Secondly, the social mobility allowed by the nature of the priyayi as a social class rapidly enlarged the number of priyayi in comparison with both the rulers' immediate families, and even with the masses in general. In this context, the increasing numbers of the priyayi further strengthened its position as a distinctive social class, cementing them as the middle group between kings (states) and masses.

Beyond enlargement in numbers, the priyayi had also secured new sources of income as salaried officials of the colonial government. Whereas before they depended the king's variable patronage, the expansion of the colonial economy necessitated the creation of many new positions with regular salaries. Moreover, with the creation of the Administrative Schools for Natives (CSVIA), the priyayi could institutionalize its old *magang* (apprenticeship) tradition for training new recruits. The extent of this bureaucratization by the end of colonial rule was such that a prominent historian on Indonesia, the late Harry Benda, wrote about the creation of an Administrative State (*Beamtenstaat*) in Indonesia, manned by the priyayi.

Thanks to their education, the priyayi also became the first indigenous Indonesians to be Westernized, especially in terms of "life-style." Although the processes of Westernization also created strong reactions in the forms of Javanese cultural revivalism, such as the *Taman Siswa* educational movement, on the whole the priyayi had a head start in comparison with other social groups as far as adopting Western ways. This early association would help them in competing with other groups in dominating the state structure and in the latter-day process of modernization which involves dealing with the Western world.

While the priyayi as a social class had benefited most from colonial expansion of the administrative apparatus, it was not a monolithic group politically. Indonesian nationalist movements were led also by leaders of priyayic background or their equivalents from the Outer Islands. When the Dutch colonial government attempted certain political reforms, such as the creation of the pseudo-legislative *Volksraad* (People's Council), it installed many bureaucratic priyayi as members with the aim of competing with the noncooperating nationalists, often led also by politicians of priyayi origin. But on the whole, the bureaucratic structure was much more priyayinized than the nationalist movements.

The end of colonial rule endangered the dominant position of the priyayi. During the Japanese interregnum of 1942–45, the occupiers opened the way for political mobilization by the Islamic groups. Hence the Japanese period signaled the start of open competition between the priyayis and other social groups, and social classes as well, to dominate the state structure of modern Indonesia.

THE PRIYAYI AS STATE BUILDER

The victory of the priyayi over other groups and classes originated from its control over the new Indonesian Army, born after 1945. While Anderson has described at length the victory of state over society in modern Indonesian polity, he says less about the ethnic and class nature of the state-builder, the priyayi.[11] It was not until 1966 that the victory of the bureaucratic priyayis was assured against the challenge of other social groups and classes.

During the national revolution of 1945–49, their compromises of the colonial period had led to some "social revolutions" by the masses, organized mostly by radical leftist groups.[12] Such social revolutions occurred in areas where the economic suffering of the Japanese occupation was used by the radical movements to mobilize popular support, such as in the Tiga Daerah of north-central Java.

In each case, the revolt against the bureaucratic priyayis was organized and led by lower-class elements in Javanese society. They tried to polarize Javanese society along class lines, thereby challenging the traditional position of the bureaucratic priyayis as the bridge between the state and the masses. Moreover, serious attempts at replacing the priyayis as *the* bureaucratic class were also made by the political parties in the 1950s and early 1960s, halted only by the intervention of the army in 1958–59. In this sense, the army was the main savior of the priyayi's dominance, and thereby made it possible for them to consolidate their power after the New Order came into being in 1965 in Indonesia.

As Skocpol has rightly argued, state-building could only be started by the process of centralization.[13] The end of various regional revolts and rebellions in Indonesia (1960) marked the beginning of the state-building process, in which the army was the prime mover. The man behind the process, then Army Chief of Staff, General A. H. Nasution, did not come from Javanese priyayi background (although married to a woman from that background), but most army officers were of priyayi origin. Nasution was exceptional not only in terms of social and ethnic origins; he was also a graduate of a prewar colonial military academy, whereas most of his officers came mainly from the PETA—the armed force created by the Japanese in 1943–45.[14]

The PETA officers could fairly be said to represent the officers of the revolutionary "Generation of 1945," distinct from both the older generations of civilian leadership and the bureaucratic class of priyayi origin. Sukarno and his civilian contemporaries came from priyayi background and had been university-educated, the highest level of education open to Indonesians in the colonial era. Moreover, they had been exposed to modern ideologies such as Marxism and nationalism, and could communicate across ethnic and cultural lines, enabling them to become the proponents of the "modern Indonesian State." As did Sukarno, they lived in Indonesia's major cities where institutions of higher learning were located, or they went to the Netherlands to further their studies, as did Satta and Sjahrir. The cultural elements of their nationalism were less visible, although they had in no way altogether disappeared.

On the contrary, the PETA officers came from a rather different social background. Although they shared with Sukarno a deep commitment to Javanese cultural tradition, such as *wayang* (puppet shows) and the use of the Javanese language, to say the least, they mostly came from small *kawedanan* (districts), or at best, *kabupaten* (townships). Since they joined PETA in their late teens, most of them had barely finished elementary school, although some managed to complete second-class secondary schools (MULO). For them, modern ideologies were out of the question. Nationalism was not so much interpreting Renan's theory—as it was for Sukarno—as the real *semangat* (will) to defend the nation and its main element, the state.

For these officers, Javanese cultural nationalism is more likely to have a strong attraction than other ideologies. One may assume that the concept of "old glory" would count more with them than their predecessors in creating a modern state. The centralizing tendency of the Javanese traditional state was more likely to attract them than anything modern ideologies could offer. Such feelings were only to be deepened by their bitter experiences with regional issues. Theirs was the generation that was socialized politically by the suppression of regional (often Islamic) rebellions and the revolts of the Javanese masses.[15] The end result was to consolidate the mainstream of priyayi traditional doctrine: to lead the masses in traditional ways; to ensure the power of the Center; to suspect Islamic and communist ideologies, partly because of their alien nature, and partly because of their appeal to the masses.

The basic thrust of this trend could be seen in the choice of alliances made by the priyayi officers in building the state apparatus. The "negation of ideology" has become the main criterion for army leadership. The possibility of a revival of the "warlordism" of the 1950s was prevented by not appointing native sons to their own regions in the Outer Islands. Officers from devout Islamic backgrounds were not put in important commanding positions. Indeed, preference has been given to Christian minorities in the Outer Islands. Furthermore, officers with strong cultural affiliations to *priyayi kejawen* (Javanese religious practices) were given preference over officers from Islamic backgrounds.[16]

Since the priyayi officers were the central power behind the process of state-building, the priyayi civilian bureaucrats were given the task of creating the centralized-state bureaucracy. This task was made easier by the enactment of the law on local government in 1974, by which all regional appointees—such as governors and regents—have to be approved by the central government. This has permitted the priyayi bureaucrats to ally with the local aristocracies of the Outer Islands, making them a part of the centralized state apparatus.

In this context, cultural and class alliances have been created between the priyayi at the Center and the local aristocracies (*adat* chiefs) at the periphery. Both groups oppose those groups insisting on a strong emphasis on puritanical Islamic values, even though in terms of Islamic practices the local aristocrats of the Outer Islands are sometimes as pious as Muslims. Ideologically, both groups are hostile to the Islamic groups which were behind the strong anti-aristocratic movements in many parts of the Outer Islands in the 1950s. Therefore, through cultural similarities and class origins, the priyayis have been able to form strong alliances with the religious minorities and local aristocracies of the Outer Islands.

However, with the increasing number of *sentri* (pious Muslim) children graduated from universities in the 1970s, it was not possible anymore to deny them social mobility through the government bureaucracy. Moreover, with the dangerous influence of radical Islamic ideologies from the Middle East, the presence of state employees with *sentri* background could give the state necessary ammunition against the accusations of being "anti-Islam," as have been made by militant Islamic groups. The presence of substantial numbers of state bureaucrats with Islamic backgrounds has also been helpful to the state when it organized the government-backed Functional Group as its political arm. It is this group of Islamic bureaucrats that forms the leadership of *Majelis Dakwah Islamiya* (MDI—Islamic Dakwah movement), which has become the mass organization of the *Golkar*, the state party specializing in mobilizing Islamic support.

The strengthening of the state apparatus with members of Islamic background has also deprived the only Islamic party, the Unitary Development Party, of its potential for drawing leadership from modern educational institutions. Although the party can still depend on its traditional bases of leadership—the rural *kiyayis* (religious scholars) and the urban merchants—many of the more ambitious educated Muslims have joined the state, and by implication, the *Golkar*. Moreover, among the Javenese priyayi themselves, there has been a new trend toward demonstrating their "understanding of Islam," if only in formal practice. Many officials from priyayi backgrounds have undertaken the pilgrimage to Mecca, and some have gone as far as to organize what used to be a *sentri's* preoccupation, the Koranic recitation (*pengajian*) and *dalwah* (proselytization organizations). Priyayi officials who live in strong Islamic environments in the Outer Islands find themselves practicing Islam as piously as the *sentri*. Hence they become a population of "good Moslems but without Islamic ideology."[17]

CULTURAL WORLD VIEW

Although the priyayis who have become pious Moslems are still at the periphery of the priyayi group, and are relatively few, the point is that the priyayis have been able to enlarge their cultural horizon while retaining their traditional beliefs, an Islamic-tinged *kejawen*. By adapting to Islamic militancy, the priyayis hope to halt Islamic radicalism in Indonesia, and, with the help of bureaucrats of Islamic background, any ideological radicalization along Middle East lines.

It is in this context that one has to see the increasing Javanese cultural mobilization in Indonesia. The priyayi officials of the state have assumed that since Indonesia's New Order does not have strong ideological content, Javanese culture could play the role of a strong native culture against the influences of foreign cultures, be they Islamic, Western, or others. Hence, the notion of ideology is being replaced by cultural mobilization in which the Javanese culture is thought to be able to resist foreign cultures, both by its capacity to domesticate and by its ability to adopt new elements. The effect has been what Geertz once called "ideology as a cultural system" through which a particular culture, the Javanese *priyayi kejawen*, is being promoted to become the dominant culture. Hence, instead of the notion of dominant class, Indonesia's New Order has used the priyayi's cultural tradition as the dominant culture, and thus is also trying to legitimate the cultural base of the New Order in place of the old ideological competitions of the period of Guided Democracy.

The process of cultural mobilization of the dominant culture is quite apparent in the changing political communications in Indonesian politics and cultural life. One egalitarian legacy of the 1945 revolution was the use of the term *bung* (brother) in political speech, in a way analogous to the *citoyen* of the French Revolution. In recent years, the hierarchical nature of Javanese culture has presented itself in the increasingly common usage of *bapak* (father) or, at the least, *mas* and *mbak* (older brother or sister). While use of the Javanese language is rare in public places (both to avoid any ethnic backlash and because of the reluctance of the Javanese to speak Javanese in front of other ethnic groups), more and more non-Javanese officials are now accustomed to speaking Javanese, or are becoming familiar with common Javanese idioms.[18]

Mass communication is also being used to promote the *wayang's* characters. One of the most popular television programs has been the *Ria Jenaka*, in which satirical roles are played by the *punakawan*, the wise clowns of Javanese puppet theater. By adapting themselves to Indonesian language and big-city environments, Javanese comedians have been able to attract a non-Javanese audience. The most popular theatrical group in Jakarta today is the *Srimulat*, which actually devotes itself to satire against the priyayi's life-style. Their popularity shows that Javanese culture has its popular side and its egalitarian traditions, symbolized by the instant celebrity of *Srimulat* star Gepeng, prototype of the *wong cilik* (little people).[19]

The popularity of Javanese popular culture, such as *Srimulat* and *ludruk* (a revue-style theater featuring female impersonators), has been accompanied by a rising demand for Javanese "court culture." The priyayi-oriented celebration of the Javanese New Year (the first of *Sjuro*) with the *wayang* has become a tradition among Jakarta's elite. Cultural mobilization of the priyayi draws on other elements of the *kejawen* tradition: ceremonies including, for example, marriage, and exorcism.

It is also possible to look at cultural mobilization as a Javanese reaction to the tragedy of 1965–66—the anti-Communist massacres that took between half a million and one million lives of which more than 80 percent were Javanese from the provinces of central and eastern Java. It is common for the Javanese masses to be reminded that the Communist Party (PKI) was behind the coup that led to the massacres, and thus that the PKI was like the *Kurawa*, those "on the wrong side" in the war between cousins (*Mahabharata*) central to the *wayang* plays. For most, if not all Javanese, the massacre is the turning point culturally in what can be categorized as its civil war. The civil war brought about increasing polarization along class lines, which resulted in painful memories for the Javanese collectively. By abandoning class conflict and by coming back to their cultural heritage, the Javanese masses could be "guaranteed" that at least another civil war would never happen again.

In this context, mobilization of Javanese culture is also aimed at getting the cultural support of the Javanese lower classes, especially the peasants, in modern times often antagonists of the priyayi. If cultural mobilization could combine these two key groups in modern Indonesian history into a single bloc, a revival/reintegration of Javanese traditional polity based on the patron-client relationships and the concept of *manunggaling kawulo lan Gusti* (the unity of God and His subjects; between Servant and Master) could be effected.

Cultural mobilization has also been helpful in accommodating the changing environment of the Javanese masses. As problems of landlessness are becoming widespread—involving about eleven million Javanese families—migration to the cities has been the easiest way for Javanese laborers to try to solve their problems. In the big cities, such as Jakarta, the members of the Javanese lower classes are organized by their regional origins. Leadership in such regional associations has been taken over by priyayi officials from earlier lower-class leaders, thereby completing the hierarchical nature of cultural mobilization in urban environments. Hence, even in the independent atmosphere of Jakarta's metropolitan superculture, the priyayi officials have consolidated their traditional position of power over the *wong cilik*, enabling them to prevent the possibility of the emergence of leadership along class lines.

In the Outer Islands, priyayi patronage has also increased considerably, mostly because of the consolidation of the state apparatus. In the capitals of the provinces and regencies, there has always been a small community of Javanese priyayi of mostly official background. Some of them came as early as the dawn of the twentieth century, sent by the colonial government and remaining. But most of them came recently, as late as the early 1960s when the state apparatus started its nationwide expansion. In most cases, military officers have stayed on in provincial capitals after retirement. This group of retired officers has come to dominate the political life of particular provinces, and thereby has become the critical "elite linkage" to the priyayi officers in national-level politics. These priyayi officers also have acted as the leaders of the increasing number of lower-class Javanese migrating under government-sponsored transmigration projects and on their own initiative. Hence, cultural mobilization has taken place both in Jakarta and in the Outer Islands by which the old notion of priyayi leadership is assured in new settings.

However, it should be noted that the cultural environment of the Outer Islands is not always friendly to the lower Javanese classes, especially those of the *kejawen* persuasion. Many Javanese settlers were victims of indiscriminate killings by local populations in the aftermath of the 1965 coup, reminding them of the frailty of class solidarity in areas that still put strong emphasis on ethnic origins. As in the case of Javanese peasant in Java, cultural mobilization led by the priyayi could assure the Javanese settlers and laborers in the Outer Islands of their security in a rather hostile environment. Such hostility has appeared in the violence that has occurred in the settlement projects, necessitating the involvement of priyayi leaders to settle the problems with local Outer Island leaders through elite-cooperation mechanisms.

In addition to control through cultural mobilization and patron-client relationships, the priyayi has also used the flexibility of definition of its membership to expand. It should be noted that lower-class Javanese can become priyayi (*mriyayine*—of becoming a priyayi). University graduates of lower-class origins can rise socially, mostly through marriage to women of priyayi backgrounds. Since the Javanese family is bilateral, the children are mostly considered priyayi. This has also occurred with the younger officers of the armed forces, who by graduating from the military academies are able to marry women of priyayi or Javanese origins.[20]

As Moertono has observed, marriage was used by the traditional Javanese *kratons* (palaces) as an important method of dealing with peripheral powers, especially potentially rebellious ones.[21] Since the establishment of Indonesia's nation-state, the Javanese concept of *pasisir* (periphery) has been enlarged to include the non-Javanese cultural sphere. Territorial domination was never enough in itself for the Center's control over the region. Marriage has become one of the most important methods through which the brightest men of non-Javanese origins, who are in the cultural position of *durung Jawa* (not yet Javanese), are Javanized culturally to the position of *wis Jawa* (become Javanese). Hence, the cultural meaning of being Javanese is never applied to territory alone, but more importantly to the adoption of the cultural values of the priyayi. It is in this context that cultural mobilization has become the main effort of the Javanese priyayi in the recruitment of non-Javanese leaders, all the easier since any important appointment has to be approved by the state intelligence agency (BAKIN), one of the most Javanized sectors of Indonesia's state apparatus.

THE EMERGING PRIYAYI MERCHANTS

The consolidation of the priyayis as state officials and their incorporation of the Javanese lower classes through cultural mobilization have been accompanied by another important trend: the emergence of priyayi merchants or, if you will, capitalists. The cause of this has been priyayi domination over the state apparatus and thereby the re-creation of the traditional appanage system in a new capitalist context.

In the colonial era, the priyayi officials often depended on the Chinese traders for credit and short-term necessities in order to complement their salary. This was true especially for beginners in the colonial administration, who had to wait years before being appointed to positions of influence and (more importantly) financial power. Only on reaching the position of *asisten wedana* (subdistrict officer) could a priyayi bureaucrat expect financial independence.

The financial situation of the priyayi officials did not change much during the period of Liberal and Guided Democracy, although some priyayi officials did engage in business activities through the creation of new state enterprises. But the expansion of state enterprises during the Guided Democracy era combined with the later oil bonanza and huge foreign aid has opened the way for wide-ranging business activities by the priyayi officials under the New Order. It should be noted that even in the colonial period some priyayi were involved in commercial activities, either as banking clerks or officials of companies owned by the colonial state. However, the involvement was merely an extension of their role as state officials and not in a private capacity.

However, under the New Order, the priyayis as individuals have been involved massively in business activities. A debate over the nature of this emerging priyayi business class has arisen since the publication of Robert Robison's thesis. According to Robison, these priyayi are merely playing the role of clients to Chinese *cukongs* (monopolists) with whom they have economic relationships.[22] Robison is of the opinion that the priyayi are not able to become an "independent bourgeoisie" in contrast with the older Muslim merchant class.

In the climate of the priyayis' consolidation of power (bureaucratically, culturally, and politically), one might reject Robison's argument as being one-sided, at the least. In reality, it should be noted that the *cukong* depend on their priyayi connections in the state apparatus and indeed are an extension of priyayi power. Contrary to Robison's suggestion, priyayi merchants are the masters, while the Chinese *cukong* are merely their junior partners, if not their clients. Recent evidence suggests that the *hokie* (good luck) of the *cukong* disappears as soon as their priyayi masters lose their power or do not support them any more.[23] It is not surprising to find that the emergence of priyayi merchants has only taken place after the consolidation of the power of the state in which the priyayi officials have been the dominant group.

In this context, the emergence of priyayi merchants characterizes the last, and possibly the most difficult stage in the priyayis' consolidation of power. By engaging in economic life, priyayi merchants have made a cultural break with the old notion of *tanpa pamrih* (being without self-interest) and of aiming to achieve *kasampurnan* (perfection of life).

It should be remembered that the priyayi's absence from trade activities was a colonial policy aimed at separating the political power of priyayi bureaucrats from economic power, similar to British policy in Malay states. The effect had been the strengthening of foreign Orientals (Chinese, Arabs, Indians) in economic activities, with indigenous Muslim merchants playing supplementary roles. In the New Order, the expansion of the priyayis into commercial activities can be seen as necessary to their consolidation of power. The choice of Chinese *cukong* as partners may be seen as the lesser of two evils (from the priyayi officials' point of view): the indigenous Muslim merchants could, after all, challenge their political position, while the pariah Chinese *cukong* depended on them for protection.

Enloe has argued that the capitalist world-system tends to support a pattern of ethnic-state relations that strengthens the dominant ethnic group. Hence, the stability of the regime can best be guaranteed by giving the dominant group (here, the priyayi officials) a big stake in economic activities. International capitalists prefer to work with the major (dominant) ethnic group in a way that ensures the continuation of their dominance. Moreover, by becoming merchants themselves, by being tied to the capitalist world-system, the Javanese priyayi can gain additional external support should class antagonists reemerge (although the chance of this is still slim).[24]

CONCLUSION

Indonesian politics since the New Order might be seen as the process of consolidation of the Javanese priyayi's power over non-Javanese groups in Indonesia, as well as over the Javanese lower classes. In making secure their control of the state apparatus, the priyayi (led by priyayi military officers) have worked mainly with the help of people of similar cultural backgrounds in the Outer Islands, as well as with religious minorities. Anti-Islamic and anti-Communist ideologies have been the common denominator. Civilian priyayi have worked to develop alliances with the local aristocracies of the Outer Islands, and to some extent even with the university graduates of Islamic backgrounds.

The main pillar of priyayi solidarity is their world view, which to some extent is shared with their potent antagonists, the Javanese lower classes, especially the peasants. Being both adherents to *kejawan* tradition, Javanese priyayi and peasants are united by their cultural orientation, thereby making it less easy to develop organizations based on class interest. Moreover, the bitter collective memory of 1965–66 will work for a long time against any attempts at creating class solidarity at the village level. Meanwhile, the priyayis have been using their common cultural position to strengthen their position as the dominant group in Indonesian politics. In the last two decades, such consolidation has been supported by their involvement as merchants and traders.

The noted social historian Barrington Moore once wrote—with Japan in mind—that it was possible to embark on modernization processes in conservative ways, which meant without a change in the social structure.[25] If the analogy can be made, the Javanese priyayis seem to pursue that direction.

NOTES

1. The concept of ethnic identity is taken from Fredrik Barth, *Ethnic Groups and Boundaries: The Social Organization of Culture Difference* (Boston: Little, Brown & Company, 1969), 9–38. The concept of "cultural mobilization" is given by Crawford Young in his article, "The Temple of Ethnicity," *World Politics* (July 1983): 653–62. For an anthropological approach, see Abner Cohen, *Custom and Politics in Urban Africa: A Study of Hausa Migrants in Yoruba Towns* (Berkeley: University of California Press, 1969); William Mangin, *Peasants in the Cities: Readings in the Anthropology of Urbanization* (Boston: Houghton Mifflin, 1970); Aidan Southall, ed., *Urban Anthropology: Cross-Cultural Studies of Urbanization* (New York, London, and Toronto: Oxford University Press, 1973)

2. For the concept of "internal colonialism," see Pablo Gonzalez Casanova, *Democracy in Mexico* (Oxford University Press, 1970); Michael Hechter, *Internal Colonialism: The Celtic Fringe in British National Development, 1536–1966* (Berkeley: University of California Press, 1975). For the concept of "ethnic nationalism," see, for example, Werner Link and Werner J. Feld, eds., *The New Nationalism: Implications for Transatlantic Relations* (Elmsford: Pergamon Press, 1979); also Joseph Rothschild, *Ethnopolitics: A Conceptual Framework* (New York: Columbia University Press, 1981).

3. For a study on "national integration" and "nation-building" see Clifford Geertz, ed., *Old Societies and New States: The Quest for Modernity in Asia and Africa* (Glencoe: The Free Press, 1963); see also Immanuel Wallerstein, "Ethnicity and National Integration," *Cahiers d'Etudes Africaines* (October 1960): 129–39.

4. For details of Geertz's argument, see his article, "The Integrative Revolution: Primordial Sentiments and Civil Politics in the New States," in Geertz, ed., *Old Societies and New States*. For a thorough analysis of the State, see Erik Olin Wright, *Class, Crisis and the State* (London: New Left Books, 1978).

5. See Cynthia H. Enloe's article, "State-Building and Ethnic Structures: Dependence on International Capitalist Penetration," in Immanuel Wallerstein and Terence K. Hopkins, eds., *Processes of the World-System* (Beverly Hills and London: Sage Publications, 1980), 266–88. See also her book, Cynthia H. Enloe, *Ethnic Conflict and Political Development* (Boston: Little Brown, 1973).

6. See Guillermo O'Donnell, *Modernization and Bureaucratic Authoritarianism: Studies in South American Politics* (Berkeley: University of California, 1973).

7. For a good analysis of state and society in Indonesia, see Benedict R. O'G. Anderson, "Old State, New Society: Indonesia's New Order in Comparative

Historical Perspective," *Journal of Asian Studies* (May 1983): 477–95.

8. See George McT. Kahin, *Nationalism and Revolution in Indonesia* (Ithaca and London: Cornell University Press, 1952).

9. See Soemarsaid Moertono, *State and Statecraft in Old Java: A Study of the Latter Mataram Period, 16th to 19th Century*, Cornell Modern Indonesia Project (Ithaca and London: Cornell University Press, 1968), 93–94. See also Leslie H. Palmer, *Social Status and Power in Java* (London: The Athlone Press, 1960).

10. For this change, see Heather Sutherland, *The Making of a Bureaucratic Elite, The Colonial Transformation of the Javanese Priyayi* (Hong Kong and Kuala Lampur: Heinemann Educational Books, 1979), especially chaps. 2 and 4.

11. See Anderson, "Old State, New Society."

12. For "social revolutions," see Benedict R. O'G. Anderson, *Java in a Time of Revolution*, (Ithaca: Cornell University Press, 1972); Anthony Lucas, "The Bamboo Spears," Ph.D. diss., Australian National University, 1977.

13. See Theda Skocpol, *States and Social Revolutions: A Comparative Analysis of France, Russia, and China* (Cambridge and New York: Cambridge University Press, 1979).

14. For the history of the PETA, see Anderson, *Java*; also Nugroho Notosusanto, *The PETA Army in Indonesia* (Jakarta: Gramedia Press, 1978).

15. The Islamic rebellions were led by former guerrillas who were disappointed by their status after the Revolution. Peasant insurrections in Java never resulted in strong rebellions, possibly because of disastrous experiences since colonial times.

16. For the meaning of *kejawen* and *sentri* (see below), see Clifford Geertz, *The Religion of Java* (Glencoe: The Free Press, 1960).

17. It is interesting to compare this notion with present-day Malaysia where Mahathir Mohammed has tried to counter Islamic militarism by adopting the slogan of "Islamization of Malaysian life." The main difference is the existence of Javanese cultural tradition in Indonesia which works against *any* ideologies from abroad, including Islamic militancy. Moreover, the fortunes of various Islamic rebellions has worked against any serious radicalism among the majority of Islamic people in Indonesia. Islamic radicalism, then, is confined to the small groups of urban youths.

18. For Indonesian political communications, see Benedict R. O'G. Anderson, "The Languages of Indonesian Politics", in *Indonesia* vol. 1 (1966), 89–116. The necessary use of polite idioms derived from Javanese, is exampled with *"mohon"* (to ask) and *"menghaturkan"* (to say), instead of the usual Indonesian words, *"minta"* and *"mengucapkan"*.

19. The comedian Gepeng was recently sentenced to probation because of ownership of unlicensed arms. The Javanese have a saying in which one is reminded not to be surprised (*ojo kaget*) both in facing happiness and suffering.

20. The Military Academies are located in Magelang (the Army), Yogyakarta (the Air Force), Surabaya (the Navy), and Semarang (the Police).

21. See Moertono, *State and Statecraft in Old Java*, 108–9.

22. See Richard Robison, "Capitalism and the Bureaucratic State in Indonesia, 1965–1975," Ph.D. diss., Sydney University, 1978.

23. Yos Sutomo, an immensely rich timber merchant in East Kalimantan is currently being investigated on the charge of tax fraud. A big shot since the early 1970s, his vulnerability has been "found" only after he lost support at high levels of the state apparatus. For his role in East Kalimantan's timber boom, see the author's dissertation, "The Aristocracy in Provincial Politics in Indonesia: A Study of Its Relationship with the Bureaucracy, Ethnicity and Religion in Three Provinces of the Outer Islands," Cornell University, 1981.

24. See Enloe, in *Processes of the World-System*, 280–84. A booklet for foreign businessmen in London just recently advised its readers to seek partners of Javanese origins.

25. Moore was also of the opinion that strong leadership was needed to suppress the "reactionary elements" concentrated among the landed upper classes. Since the *priyayi* are salaried officials, Moore's argument could be applied well to Indonesia, where the dynamic elements of the *priyayi* use their bureaucratic power to "regularize" the upper classes. See Barrington Moore Jr., *Social Origins of Dictatorship and Democracy: Lord and Peasant in the Making of the Modern World* (Beacon Press: Boston, 1966), 441–42 and chap. 5 on Japan.

Ethnicity and Islam
in the Philippines

CESAR ADIB MAJUL

People are what they make of themselves, as well as what others make of them. They make their own history and in turn are determined by it, both as beneficiaries and as victims. Thus it is with the Muslims in the Philippines: a religious and ethnic community, they were required to become part of an emerging national state—a state whose present dominant majority had been in open conflict with them for three hundred years. Never truly integrated into the colonial society that Spain imposed until 1898, they neither participated in the Revolutions of 1896 and 1898 (which had acquired national overtones), nor in the national consensus—if such there was—that made possible the Philippine Commonwealth in 1935 and the Republic in 1946.

The Muslims' slow but progressive incorporation into the body politic was due more to Spanish and American colonial policies, later continued by the Philippine government, than to any choice on their part. The attitudes and position of Muslims vis-à-vis the national society have been determined largely by the inner dynamics of their particular cultures. The factors that enter are their traditional political and social structures, centuries of independence, a continuous history of warfare against colonial intrusion and dominance when other natives were willing and active instruments of colonial policies, the religious motive which colored the warfare, and the manner in which, eventually and inevitably, they were incorporated into a new body politic. Muslims have viewed the present governmental structure and distribution of power as an infringement upon a cherished traditional structure, often interpreting national laws as studied attempts to do away with their culture. They have deeply resented laws that they felt contradicted their own customary laws based, essentially, on the Qur'an.

National policy makers, too, in their view of and attitudes toward Muslims, work within a different cultural framework. It is difficult to convince Muslims that many of the new national laws are not based on values that have a basically Christian and Western ethical character; to argue that many of these values are secular may be even worse, for in general Muslims rationalize their actions within a religious framework. Unless they have been educated in Western-oriented schools, the concept of secular values has little significance for them, and they feel compelled to add some religious dimension to such values. Nor do Muslims in the Philippines ever admit that their own moral values might be inferior to those of any other origin. To add to the Philippine government's problems, when Muslims of other countries become involved the attitudes of the Muslim Filipinos begin to acquire new dimensions and complexity. The present Muslim movement in the Philippines—which aims at the formation of a more cohesive and creative *umma* (Islamic community) in different ways with various segments of the population, peaceful here and bloody there—involves, if not foreign Muslims' direct participation, at least some of their concerns. This is unavoidable, for the very concept of *umma* has transnational connotations.

But History moves on. Old values may emerge in new forms, some replacing others and becoming more accepted, while others are temporarily thrust into the background. There are national leaders who are consciously trying to emancipate themselves from colonial attitudes and past policies that have proved disruptive. Their goal tends to be the good of all rather than of special segments of the population. Along with Muslims who believe that an independent *umma* is the prerequisite to the good Islamic life, there are others who believe that a viable, strong and creative Muslim community is possible within a national community whose common cultural matrix is older than either Christianity or Islam in the Philippines. While there is an armed Muslim resistance against government authority, there are also Muslims in the Armed Forces of the Republic, with a few members of the *ulama* (religious teachers) even serving as chaplains. Whereas some traditional leaders are participating in the government, others stand aloof. Against oppressive military actions in Muslim areas are heard voices expressing sympathy toward Muslims—mainly from the youth in the universities and colleges. Only a very rash prophet would dare to predict what the play of all these conflicting forces will eventually bring forth.

In 1975, the estimated total population of the Philippines was slightly over 40 million. Of this number, at least 3 million (or 7 percent) were Muslims, constituting the second largest religious community in a predominantly Catholic country. At least twelve ethnolinguistic groups have been identified as Muslim. One source[1] gives the following:

Group	Estimated 1975 Population
1. Maguindanao	674,000
2. Maranao and Iranun	670,000
3. Tausug	492,000
4. Samal	202,000
5. Yakan	93,000
6. Jama Mapun	15,000
7. Palawan Muslim groups (Palawani and Molbog)	10,000
8. Kalagan	5,000
9. Kolibugan	4,000
10. Sangil	3,000

This list does not include those Badjao or Samal Laut (about twenty thousand) who profess Islam in varying degrees, the Muslim Subanun (in Zamboanga) and the Bukidnon Muslims. Neither does it include the many Muslim converts in Manila and Luzon who, with their families, easily number at least ten thousand. At present, there are thousands of Maranao and other Muslims from Mindanao and Sulu who have come to settle in Manila and its environs in order to get away from the armed conflict in their areas. However, the vast majority of Muslims continue to live in the Philippine South, that is, in the large island of Mindanao and the Sulu archipelago.[2]

According to Filipino scholars, the many languages and dialects spoken by Filipinos, both Christian and Muslim, all belong to the same linguistic family—the Malayo-Polynesian. Some Muslim languages, such as Maguindanao and Maranao, are mutually intelligible; in others, the differences (e.g., between Iranun and Marana, or between the Samal, Jama Mapun and Badjao) are minor matters of dialect. All of these are quite different from Tausug, which is closer to Tagalog and Visayan (whose speakers are often Christian). In Sulu, where the earlier language was Samal, Tausug is believed to have been "intrusive."

Muslims who have gone through the public schools, especially those with a secondary education, are literate in the English language. For many years, however, only a small percentage finished high school. Most of the present-day ulama among them know literary or classical Arabic, having graduated from Muslim educational institutions in the Arab world. With the help of occasional Egyptian teachers, they have taught hundreds of students this language, to the admiring surprise of Arab visitors who may know only colloquial Arabic. In colleges and universities, Muslim students who do not belong to the same linguistic group would normally converse in English or Tagalog, the latter being much like Pilipino, the national language. (Tagalog movies, which have spread out in Muslim areas and are a popular form of entertainment, seem to be generally understood.)

Muslim groups share many pre-Islamic beliefs. In addition, they often reveal marked differences—in aspects of their customary laws (*adat*), in costumes, dances and art forms. They all share a more or less similar social structure. Their political organization has been characterized by the *datu* system, a pre-Islamic institution found in other parts of the Malay world, including numerous pre-Hispanic non-Muslim settlements. The *datu* was a local or petty chief with executive and military functions; it was a position arrived at through descent, physical prowess, wealth, astuteness, or a combination of such attributes. With the advent of Islam, a few powerful datus eventually assumed the title of sultan, often claiming certain prerogatives over the other datus on the basis of Islam. Indeed, to bolster their right to rule, the major sultans claimed descent from the Prophet Muhammad, even though their right to own property was in fact based on pre-Islamic customary law. Often the sultans stood for the extension of the Shari'a, or religious law, as against datus who, as descendants of defeated chieftains, appeared as protectors of the *adat*. There were also the so-called "royal" datus: relatives of the sultan, or descendants of former sultans, they could be candidates for the sultanate and wielded great power. Most commercial benefits accrued to the interests of the royal datus, including the sultan. Today, there are still datus as well as claimants to various sultanates, but they are much diminished in their power and prerogatives. Most Muslims who have been able to attain national office have originated from these datu families.

In past centuries the Muslim groups represented, singly or in combination, various independent political aggregations. Although commercial rivalries and conflicting claims to the collection of tribute have often led to warfare between them, when faced with a common external threat they would cooperate militarily. It is noteworthy that in the past there were frequent marriages between members of their ruling families—for dynastic, economic and other political motives. Such marriage alliances extended to other parts of insular Southeast Asia, such as Ternate, Makassar, Brunei, etc. Nowadays, marriages between different social classes among Muslim Filipino groups are becoming more frequent, as accelerated transportation and other communication has drastically reduced their isolation. Both Manila, as the educational center and capital of the country, and Zamboanga City, a commercial center that is located strategically in the Muslim area, have served to improve contacts between members of different Muslim groups.

There are religious courts (*agama*), and marriage and divorce follow Islamic lines. This is not so true for laws of inheritance, where earlier *adat* elements often predominate or intervene. There are hundreds of Qur'anic schools (*maktab*) for little children, and *madrasa*, mostly privately owned and run, with curricula ranging from simple ones to those extending for many years. As in Indonesia and Malaysia, the *Shafi'i* school predominates among Muslim Filipinos.

By any definition of the term, Filipino Muslims are bona fide Muslims. The pious pray five times a day and observe strictly the fast during the month of Ramadan. Many of those who may be lax about their *salat* observance during other months of the year, perform it regularly during that period. Friday congregational prayers are normally well attended, with a higher percentage of women than is usual in the Arab world. Even those Muslims who are not very pious console themselves with the hope and prayer that they will improve in piety during their last years and that their relatives and friends will give them a Muslim burial and perform the funeral prayers for them. The *haj* (pilgrimage), regardless of one's financial condition, is a must, and for the last three decades pilgrims have numbered over a thousand each year. Some people, not satisfied with only three or four pilgrimages, are called professional hajis. Upon their return to their communities, hajis acquire some prestige, the more traditional among them, at least the older ones, wearing a white cap until their death.

Some Muslim groups believe that because of their earlier exposure to Islam they exemplify higher sophistication and orthodoxy than others with regard to Islamic externals and institutions. Whatever the regional prejudice on this matter, the influence of the *adat* in fact varies among groups, as well as among individuals within the group. Moreover, adherence to the externals of Islam—such as congregational prayers and celebration of the 'Id festivals—is more evident and organized in populated towns than in rural areas. Economic factors may be involved here since, in the old days, *Maulid* festivals were grand affairs, and it required a rich sultan to support them.

Not a few foreign Muslim visitors remark that they find among Muslim Filipinos certain practices that to them seem non-Islamic. Thus, while all the Islamic requirements for a marriage are strictly adhered to, different Muslim groups have added traditional elements to these requirements. The dowry, festivities, mutual visits of future relatives, and so on, though not ordained by the Qur'an, are part and parcel of the marriage ceremony. Traditional accretions to other events such as circumcision, funerals, etc., are common and normally differ among the various groups. But such accretions are not peculiar to Muslim Filipinos; they are found all over the Muslim world, as they are elsewhere. What is judged as superstitious by the learned men is another matter. The ulama, especially those who have studied abroad in Arab lands, continually instruct the faithful in avoiding what is anti-Islamic, or even simply un-Islamic, and adherence to practices believed to be genuinely Islamic. As a result, many "superstitious" practices evident twenty years ago have disappeared—at least publicly.

Nonetheless, Muslims in the Philippines all identify themselves as such. They pray together and are aware that their religion is distinct from that of other Filipinos. They recognize each other as members of a wider religious community transcending linguistic, regional, racial, tribal, and national barriers. Except for a few who have studied in advanced theological centers, or who are widely read, most are untroubled by such differences as those between Sunni and Shi'i, if they are aware of them at all. Their basic assumption of the oneness of the Islamic community often leads them to conclude that what especially characterizes Christianity are its innumerable sects. (Incidentally, most Muslim Filipinos are surprised to learn that there are Christian Arabs.)

Whatever their degree of participation in national life or in other institutions and associations, Islam is the major source of identification among Muslim Filipinos. They do not question that they are Muslim first and Filipino second—that is, if they care to mention the second at all. This identity is the culmination of historical forces of the last four or five centuries, reinforced by events in the last three or four decades.

THE CHRISTIAN FILIPINOS

Christians compose about 90 percent of the Philippine population, living primarily in Luzon, the Visayas, and Eastern Mindanao. Highly urbanized, their cities and towns are in the coastal areas and flat plains. They are mostly Catholics; the rest are Protestants or belong to "indigenous" churches. When the Americans came to the Philippines they found the Christians, like the Muslims, divided into dozens of different ethnolinguistic groups. They called the Christians "Christian tribes," the Muslim groups "Moro tribes," and those native inhabitants who lived in the mountains in the interior of the islands and who were neither Christian nor Muslim they called "Pagan tribes."[3]

Both Christians and Muslims belong to the wider Malay race and are physically indistinguishable. However, the Christians appear to have mixed more readily with Chinese settlers, and Chinese marrying into Filipino families have tended to adopt the religion of their brides—at the very least their children do. While there are instances of Christian women marrying Muslims, it is quite rare to have a Muslim woman marrying a Christian unless he converts to Islam.[4] Christians do identify themselves as Christians, but unlike most Muslims they have been influenced by modern or Western ideas, often "secular" ideas (called "liberal" by some) that mark their thinking in part. They generally value their Christian heritage and believe that this has opened their horizons to a desirable Western influence in both the political and scientific spheres. Their ethical framework is still the one nurtured within their families and their Christian schools.

Students of Philippine society have noted that all Christian groups there share a common cultural matrix that is pre-Hispanic and that this matrix is also common to Muslims. Growing awareness of its scope may have pragmatic consequences on the way all groups view the emerging national community. Although romantic attempts at resurrecting certain common nativistic elements believed once to have been shared by all are little more than wishful thinking, the following historical incident at the beginning of the Colony is revealing of these common cultural roots:

In 1603, the datus and their followers in the town of Dulag, Leyte, had become Christians. As such, they supported the Spaniards in the wars against the Muslims in the Philippine South. In retaliation, Datu Buisan, the sultan of Maguindanao, with fifty war vessels and about a thousand warriors, attacked Dulag, put the town and its church to the torch, took a few hundred captives as slaves for ransom, and acquired much booty. Before leaving, he left word that he was returning within a week and that he wanted to hold a conference with the datus, who had in the meantime fled to the interior of the island. As promised, Buisan returned, and the datus were there to greet him. Buisan returned their gold and ornaments as well as those prisoners the datus wanted released. Buisan scolded them for paying tribute to the Spaniards who were not, after all, invincible, and had failed to protect them against him. He asked them to ally themselves with him against the Spaniards, promising to return the next year with a larger armada and with their help to sweep the islands clear of all Spaniards. The following then took place: "The datus, many of whom were dissatisfied for a number of reasons, thought that there was much wisdom in this speech. They sat down with Buisan and entered into a blood compact with him. They slashed their wrists and let the blood drip into a bowl of brandy. Then they drank their mingled blood from the common bowl, and so became brothers. This done, Bwisan turned the prows of his fleet for home."[5]

This historical blood pact has significant implications. Muslims and Christians readily participated in a ritual that was pre-Islamic and pre-Christian. Muslims must have known that the drinking of blood as well as any alcoholic drink were *haram* or religious taboos. The Christian datus could not have failed to note that the ritual recalled a pagan past which they were turning away from. Thus it may reasonably be speculated that all the chiefs who participated in the pact must have recognized elements of a common ancestry and cultural history, and that they must have had a sense of the fact that, in the long run, the Spaniards were their common enemy. Not much, however, came of the above incident in practical terms. Intrusive forces made the history of the two groups involved take a turn they had tried to avoid; succeeding events even made them inveterate enemies. Spanish colonial policy eventually succeeded in its aim of dividing peoples in order to rule them more effectively.

ISLAM'S ARRIVAL IN THE PHILIPPINES

The Philippines was the last stop in the expansion of Islam in insular Southeast Asia. Due to the archipelago's geographical position, it was drawn into the international maritime trade from the Red Sea to the China Sea. From the ninth century C.E. up to the fifteenth century, this trade was generally under the control of Muslims. In the beginning of the tenth century, when they were temporarily barred from reentering China, many Muslim traders settled in Malaya. From here they learned of new products from the Indonesian islands, and accelerated their trade in spices. Arab and other Muslim merchants are known to have visited Borneo in the tenth century, and later Sulu, while some stayed on Jolo island. Ships owned or piloted by Muslims would often stop at islands in the Philippines on their way north to Chinese ports. In the fourteenth century, Muslim preachers, having the title of *makhdum*, came from neighboring Indonesian islands to Sulu as part of a religious movement. These *makhdumin*, some of whom were Sufis, taught the basic elements of Islam and erected simple mosques. They also indulged in trade, and if traditions are to be believed, were acquainted with China.

In the last few years of the fourteenth century, the Majapahit empire (centered in Java) attacked Sumatra in order to do away with what remained of the once glorious Srivijaya empire. As a result, many Muslim Sumatran princes sailed away to other parts of the Malay world. According to traditions, one of these princes, a *baguinda*, came to Jolo to establish a principality among Muslims; he became a rajah and married a local high-ranking lady. After many years, an Arab sharif settled in the principality, married a daughter of the *baguinda*, and after his death proclaimed himself a sultan. Historians calculate this event to have taken place around 1450. All Sulu sultans and royal datus have claimed descent from this sharif, who was reputed to be a descendant of the Prophet Muhammad.

The fourteenth century saw Malacca as the international emporium and most important pied-à-terre of Muslim traders in Southeast Asia. It had become, too, the most important theological center of the area. Sultan-sponsored preachers spread from it to nearby islands, undoubtedly affecting the Philippine South. However, in 1511, this fabled city fell to the Portuguese. In search of "pepper dear," they were instructed by their sovereign that if the Portuguese were to monopolize the trade in spices they must cut Islam out of it. Following a time-honored pattern, scions of the Malacca ruling family then sailed to other ports in nearby islands. Tradition again narrates how one of them sailed to the shores of Illana Bay, founding a principality among the Iranuns. He and his descendants spread their power southwards to the Cotabato area, establishing their capital at the mouth of the Pulangi (Rio Grande). Thus was the Maguindanao dynasty of Iranun origins born—all Maguindanao sultans have claimed descent from this sharif, who was also reputed to have Arab blood and to be a descendant of the Prophet Muhammad.

The Portuguese hope that the control of Malacca would lead to their control of all trade between the West and Southeast Asia was not fulfilled. Discrimination forced Muslim traders to patronize other ports more friendly to them. This explains the rise of Acheh ("the gateway to Makkah") in the north of Sumatra, and Brunei in the north of Borneo. In only a few years, Brunei emerged as a leading Malay naval and commercial power, forcing the Portuguese to deal with it as an independent state. By the 1520s, Muslim Borneo traders began to frequent the Philippines in increasing numbers. Also at this time, Manila had become a Muslim principality under rajahs and datus who were close relatives of Brunei's sultan. Brunei Muslim preachers were now to be found not only in the Philippines but as far away as the Moluccas.

From all accounts, Islam generally spread peacefully among those inhabitants in the Philippines who adopted it. There were various reasons for this. Aside from the spiritual dynamics of Islam which may have made it attractive, economic and political motives contributed to datus accepting it. Through it, they gained a larger share in the benefits of a commercial enterprise controlled by foreign Muslims, while participating in a richer and technologically superior culture. Economic changes brought about by the international maritime trade could not but affect the traditional animistic set of beliefs, and the ensuing spiritual vacuum would necessarily be filled by a more powerful force satisfying these emerging needs. Islam too, served to legitimize the independence of many coastal chiefs vis-à-vis former overlords. What is crucial to note is that during the first half of the sixteenth century, when confronted by the presence of Portuguese and Spaniards with economic and religious designs for colonialization, Islam served as a standard for resistance. It is no accident that at this time there was a resurgence of Islamic preaching by Brunei and Indonesian religious leaders in uncommitted Malay islands. The adoption of Islam by peoples in Sulu and Mindanao was manifold and profound in its effects: by adopting Islam, a segment of the population of the Philippines became part of a wider religious community extending from the Pillars of Hercules to the borders of China. These people in the Philippines gained from Islam a high sense of religious community, new laws, a more developed political organization, a new system of writing, and, above all, a new ethical outlook on life. Having adopted values that transcended their race and particular culture, they began to consider themselves as an historical people, yet assuming all the time that their history was not the result of their own making or efforts. Without this consciousness as well as all the benefits that Islam brought to the peoples of Sulu and Mindanao, they would easily have been swept away by Western colonialism and relegated to the limbo of conquered peoples.[6]

ENTER THE SPANIARDS: CONQUISTADORES, FRIARS, ET AL.

When the Spaniards first came to the Philippines in 1521 under the leadership of Magellan, the Malay world consisted of a constellation of principalities or petty kingdoms, mostly maritime, engaged in mutual trade. The empires of Srivijaya and Majapahit and the sultanate of Malacca had died out. Malacca was tenuously held by the Portuguese. Acheh and Brunei were on the rise. At least one sultanate could be identified in the Philippines—that of Sulu. Luzon and the Visayas were dotted with riverine and coastal settlements headed by rajahs, datus, and lesser chieftains. These settlements, called barangays after the boats which brought settlers to the different islands, were often relatively isolated, sometimes in actual conflict with one another. In fact, it was his unwise interference in the conflicts of datus in the Visayas that led to Magellan's death on Mactan island a few weeks after his arrival in the area, the military and proselytizing effects of his expedition soon fading from memory.

When the conquistador Miguel Lopez de Legazpi came to the Philippines in 1565, Luzon and the Visayas were still dotted with barangays, with populations ranging anywhere from two dozen families to a hundred. Their beliefs can be categorized as animistic. The Manila settlement, ruled by a Muslim rajah and a court, was an exception. While there is no evidence that most of the inhabitants of his principality were Muslims, it is clear that some of them were beginning to be exposed to Qur'anic teachings and were refraining from eating pork. Circumcision was also becoming common, but this may not have had the same religious connotations for all people. Nor was there evidence of Islam in the settlements around Laguna Bay which were in intimate trading relations with Manila. As trading center on the largest island and the most populous settlement in the north of the archipelago, Manila became the focus for Spanish covetousness.

The rationale for the Spanish conquest of the Philippines was clear and unequivocal: reduction of the natives into vassalage to the Spanish king, while increasing his domains and revenues. The natives were also to be converted to Catholicism. To these ends, Legazpi was provided with ships and about two hundred soldiers and six missionaries. Two years later, two hundred soldiers from Mexico were added, along with much-needed supplies. In Luzon and the Visayas, each and every barangay had to be reduced to submission. If gifts, flattery of the datus, and friendly persuasion failed, they resorted to force. The Manila settlement gave the fiercest resistance, but eventually it too fell to the superior Spanish artillery. Practically every barangay around Laguna Bay resisted—but to no avail. Never presenting a united front, one by one they fell. An attempt by Tagalog and Pampanga datus to join forces never materialized. The same thing happened when defeated but disgruntled datus from the Manila area tried to get help from the Brunei sultan.

The situation in the Philippine South was entirely different. There the Spaniards found three relatively well-organized sultanates: those of Sulu, Maguindanao, and Buayan. They had progressed beyond the barangay level, and represented a central authority supported by various datus. The Sulu sultan exercised power over various islands and points in Zamboanga. The Buayan sultanate, centered in the upper valley of the Pulangi in the Cotabato, claimed suzerainity over thirty settlements. Consequently, the fall of one settlement to the Spaniards, even if it represented the sultan's seat, did not spell the defeat of the sultanate. The Sultan and the datus and warriors could simply trek to the interior of the island and wait for the Spaniards to tire and return to their original bases. They might then go back to their former capital and rebuild it. In any case, they never considered themselves conquered and once again assumed an attitude of insolent defiance toward the Spaniards. It was a stance that would persist for more than three hundred years.

JOINING OF THE COLONIAL POLITICAL AND RELIGIOUS COMMUNITIES

In order to consolidate their territorial gains and propagate Catholicism, the Spanish colonial government began a program of integrating various barangays into single units, thus beginning a process of urbanization. The idea was to put their inhabitants within hearing distance of church bells (*"bajo las campanas"*). Located in the center of the pueblo or town were the church, parish and convent, municipal offices, and jail. As an inducement for families to move to the pueblo, their datus were requested to move their residences to choice lots in the pueblo center. Such forced relocations inevitably caused suffering, and there were natives, known as *remontados*, who fled to the mountains in the interior of the islands. Friar persuasion and assurances did much to moderate opposition to such a movement; indeed, friars often defended the natives from a rapacious soldiery.

At the beginning of the seventeenth century—about forty or fifty years after the arrival of the *adelantado* Legazpi—two communities, theoretically distinct but actually coinciding, arose. The first was a colonial political entity in which the natives were subjects of the Spanish monarch. At its head was a Spaniard who was both governor and captain general: the first title stood for his position as chief administrator and executive, while the latter emphasized his military powers. The colony was divided into separate provinces and these in turn were divided into pueblos with their surrounding barrios. The second community was an ecclesiastical, or religious community. At its pinnacle was the archbishop who, like the governor, resided in Manila. This community was divided into various bishoprics, each coinciding with two or more provinces. Each pueblo, which was also a parish, had its priest, usually a Spanish friar with civil functions as well. The governor exercised royal prerogatives in ecclesiastical matters, with no separation between church and state. (In time, conflicts of state functions would trouble the colony, confusing native Christians.)

At this juncture, it should be noted that the Muslims in the Philippine South were never integrated into any of the above Spanish-imposed communities, up to the very last day of Spanish rule—in spite of the existence of Spanish fortified places in parts of Sulu and Mindanao. Instead, the Muslims developed their own independent political and social history. Their contacts with the colony were usually those of war and conflict.

Those natives who were eventually Christianized and integrated into colonial society came to be called *indios* by the Spaniards; the undefeated Muslims were called Moros. The term *infieles* was reserved for isolated mountain tribes whose eventual conversion was believed to be only a matter of time. Filipino was the term for Spaniards born in the colony—now called the Filipinas.

Thus the indio called himself so, since this is what he was called by his conquerors. In letters to Spanish officials, especially when he was defending himself, or desired some favor, the indio would usually profess his loyalty to the Spanish king and declare that he was a good Christian—identifying himself as a Christian subject of the Spanish king. While he might mention his town or barrio, or even his linguistic affiliation, these were less important. Muslims,on the other hand, when asked what they were would invariably say "Islam." In some cases, when confronted by Spaniards regarding their identity, they might say "Moro" in order to be better understood.[7]

THE MORO WARS

The long series of armed conflict between the Spaniards and Muslims came to be called the Moro Wars. Frustrated at the failure of several of their expeditions, the Spaniards did not hesitate to use their full resources in men and materials. They developed a fierce hatred of the Filipino Muslims and their institutions. It may be recalled here that when the Spaniards arrived with Legazpi in 1565, it was less than a hundred years since the Moorish kingdom of Granada had fallen. There were still hundreds of thousands of Moriscos in Spain under the watchful eyes of the Inquisition. Spaniards brought their native conflicts to the Philippines, transporting their frustrated crusading spirit to a different clime, against another race.

To conquer the Muslims, the Spaniards did not hesitate to recruit more and more indios. Appealing to recently acquired religious sensibilities and political commitments, they assured the indios that the Moros were enemies of their faith and that to fight them was a religious duty. Nor did they fail to mention that booty would be available. Thus the indios formed the bulk of the infantry, serving as spearmen and bowmen, rowers and camp followers. From all indications they fought well, and there are few reports of desertions. However, defeating the sultanates in pitched battles, and burning their settlements, did not necessarily mean conquest. Eventually many Spanish forts were abandoned, due to continuous harassment. The sultans would proclaim this as a Muslim victory and return arrogantly to their old settlements.

Regular punitive expeditions against Muslims inevitably engendered negative and hardening attitudes, which were reinforced by devices such as the Moro-moro plays. These were plays introduced by Jesuits, following the 1637 expedition against the redoubtable Iranun sultan Qudarat of Maguindanao—an expedition that was led by the Spanish governor himself and resulted in the wounding and retreat of the sultan. The Spaniards celebrated their victory with a Te Deum, fireworks and other festivities in Manila, including the so-called Moro-moro plays. These were essentially morality plays presented in the public *plaza*; the Moros were depicted as dirty, treacherous, ugly, and superstitious fanatics. Their Christian opponents were portrayed as well-groomed knights who exemplified the virtues of bravery, gallantry, and honor. These plays usually ended with the defeat of a sultan or his conversion to Christianity, or a *mora* princess marrying a brave

Christian officer—and embracing his faith.

In time such plays became part of the standard repertoire in all town fiestas honoring their patron saint—that is, put on at least once a year if the town could afford it; and the parish priest saw to it that the town could afford it. The Moro-moro plays were often still enacted during the American occupation, even up to the eve of the Japanese invasion of the country. With music, dances, and a great deal of pageantry, the plays served not only as entertainment, but as educational techniques to foster hatred of Muslims. Generation after generation was nurtured on these plays, including the older Filipino generation of today. Enlightened Filipinos have opposed their reenactment, despite romantic cultural revivalists who have seen the plays only as "part of the national cultural heritage"—a semiconscious revelation of some of the underlying problems that still remain in the attitudes of the religious communities toward each other.[8]

In the last two or three decades of Spanish rule in the Philippines, official Spanish policy moved away from converting Muslims. With liberal and republican ideas beginning to filter into the thinking of government officials in the mother country, the idea became to transform Muslims into Spanish subjects. Although the new policy actually moderated the resistance of many datus who had become impoverished in the wars, Spanish friars insisted on pointing out to Spanish colonial officials that the Muslims would accept Spanish sovereignty only if they became Christians. To justify conversion, the friars claimed that the Moros were not truly Muslims, and that whatever Islamic characteristics they displayed were only superficial. In brief, the Moros were to be treated as savages to be civilized.

At bottom, the Spanish ecclesiastical stand was a bid not only for government support for missionary activities but also for recognition of the important function of the Spanish priests in bringing about greater political cohesion for the colony—in that Catholicism was a major instrument in making the Moros more docile (the word often used is *manso*, domesticated). Thus, consciously or not, these Spanish priests revealed how religion could serve the purposes of colonial domination.

Fearing that the British might enter into a treaty with the Sulu sultan, or extend their possessions in the north of Borneo to include Sulu, the Spanish government decided to impose its sovereignty over Sulu by force in the campaign of 1876. The issue was political: one colonial power was trying to offset the designs of another. But Spanish ecclesiastical authorities wanted to get into the picture too, to enhance their own missionary aims. In pulpit and press, the friars proclaimed that the campaign was a just and holy war against "the wicked sons of the Qur'an." A public subscription of at least 250,000 pesetas was raised, with contributions from friar orders, towns, a few Chinese merchants, and children from catechism schools. The ensuing defeat of the Sulu sultan forced him to sign a treaty with the Spaniards, as did datus in Mindanao. At this time, conversions among Muslims were insignificant, since the few converts had to transfer to Christian settlements away from their relatives and roots, and to Muslims, as we have seen, the treaties with the Spanish were temporary truces to be disregarded whenever feasible. In effect, the major Muslim sultanates survived the Spanish presence in the archipelago, but as mere shadows of their former selves. This is how the Americans found them in 1898.

EFFECTS OF THE MORO WAR

The Moro Wars had many long-lasting effects. Traditional commercial activities of the Muslims were disrupted. The commercial policies of the Dutch, who later came to occupy the Indonesian islands and wanted all trade to be done through them or their agents, aggravated this problem. As early as the seventeenth century, the Spanish adopted a policy of depopulation: in all expeditions against the Muslims, any sea craft seen was captured or destroyed; Muslim settlements and orchards were burned. In the next century, Muslims were taken as slaves, and even branded. Analogously, Muslims attacked Christian towns and settlements, burning churches, taking prisoners for ransom or for sale to the slave markets of Makassar and Batavia, until the Dutch stopped that practice. Tributes to the Spanish king fell to as low as 20 percent. Fields were abandoned and many farmers went to live in the comparative safety of the mountains. The peaceful inhabitants there, mostly defenseless since the Spaniards did not allow them to carry arms, saw the Muslims as inveterate pirates and cruel slavers. In turn the Muslims despised the indios as colonial instruments and as merchandise.

The wars also tended to increase the centralized powers of the sultans as opposed to those of the datus. *Ulama* or *panditas* became more important, reminding the faithful of their Islamic duty to fight invaders who were trying to take away their faith. Patriotism as love and defense of the land, protection of the family and possessions, and loyalty to the sultan and datus became lumped together as Islamic duties. Warriors who died in battle were considered martyrs. Islam began to provide the ingredients for a sort of "nationalism" and it was on the basis of their common religion that conflicts between Muslim sultans were often moderated. In 1656, the concept of *jihad* was used by Qudarat, a well-known *pandita*, to convince the sultans of Sulu, Brunei, Makassar, and Ternate to present a united front for the defense of the faith and the Shari'a. Thus, the wars played a not inconsiderable role in reinforcing and stiffening Islamic attitudes.

Their increasing isolation, too, forced the Muslims to depend more and more on their own resources, even though they learned new fighting techniques—such as trench warfare, believed to have been taught to them by the Dutch. But the sultanates never recovered their original commercial prosperity, nor did they evince significant agricultural expansion or improvement. Moreover, medical ignorance and poor sanitation affected their population growth.

The primary result of the wars was the separation of the Philippine people into two mutually antagonistic religious communities. It is an antagonism which has left scars that remain up to the present.

INTERNAL EVENTS IN THE COLONY

The Spaniards did not do away with the datus or native aristocracy in the islands they conquered. Unlike other indios, they were generally allowed to keep their local names. From their ranks the Spaniards appointed the heads of the barrios (*cabezas de barangay*), and the heads of towns (*gobernadorcillos*), the highest posts to which an indio could aspire. These offices were usually hereditary, and when partial elections were eventually introduced, it stood to reason that those elected would come from the same class. Holders of such offices were called *principales*; collectively, *principalia*. Exempted from tribute, forced labor and other indignities, they enjoyed privileges such as reserved seats at the front rows of churches. Charged with the collection of taxes, they served as intermediaries between the government and the people, a role in which the friar parish priests were their competitors.

In effect, the colonial government reinforced the position of the old datus vis-à-vis their "subjects." In the past, relations between the datus and their followers had been less rigid and localized: persons dissatisfied with their datus could transfer their loyalty to another datu if they wished, or sail to another island to form a new barangay under a new emerging datu line. Under Spanish rule, however, the *principalia* were Spanish-supported and legitimized so that they came to constitute a completely separate class in native society.

For more than two hundred years, the indio population was viewed as a society under the tender care of friars who saw to it that they were not contaminated by alien influences, but held firmly under the beneficent Laws of the Indios. The indios grew and multiplied and stood as silent witnesses to the chronic squabbles between colonial officials and priests. Kept in a childlike position of dependency, they were not even subject to the Inquisition Board, which was only for Spaniards. A poor ignorant child could not, by definition, be an apostate or a heretic.

But things must change. The British invasion and occupation of Manila in 1762, though it lasted less than two years, led many *principales* to conclude that Spain was not, after all, invincible. Spanish officials leading the resistance in the province appealed for native support against "Protestant heretics" who were out to take Catholicism away from them. During the previous century the same argument had been used when there had been a threat from a Dutch fleet. After the British withdrawal, the government tried to increase agricultural production, and to introduce some manufacturing so as to end the colony's dependence on the Mexican subsidy that paid for the salaries of colonial officials. Commercial policies all around the world were also changing, and by the middle of the nineteenth century, the colony was beginning to develop an export economy. Land conflicts began, and the issuance of royal titles to land, while intended to resolve land disputes, enabled many *principales* to get titles to formerly public land. The economic base of the *principalia* class was thus strengthened. Some would even own houses in Manila. Political changes in Europe eventually led to Manila's becoming a free port with better roads and other improved forms of communication. It was becoming a highly urbanized center with seats of higher learning and foreign companies, hospitals and sanitary facilities; and inoculation against smallpox, a major source of fatalities, was introduced, increasing the population.

Of great importance to the colony was the royal educational decree of 1863. It provided for the establishment of a primary school in every town, a system of secondary education for larger population centers, and for a normal school in Manila to produce primary school teachers. Before this decree, the only schools available for the children of indios were catechism schools, where they were taught religion in their native languages. The friars who controlled all education never encouraged the teaching of Castillian Spanish; Sunday sermons were conducted in the language of the region in which they were held. The pontifical university in Manila was only for Spaniards, and only after 1850 was there a program which accepted the sons of Spaniards by native women—that is, Spanish mestizos. However, it should be mentioned that there were seminaries to produce native secular priests. Here, Latin and Spanish were taught. Most if not all of the native priests in such seminaries came from *principalia* families.

In 1870, natives who had completed their primary education were permitted to enter secondary school. Of 1883 such students in Manila, 1421 were mestizos and indios, the rest Spaniards. By 1876, indios were enrolling in the colleges or university, taking courses in medicine, law, sanitation and engineering—not to mention advanced courses in the arts and humanities, some background for which was provided at the secondary level. For complex reasons, indios were at this time discouraged from becoming secular priests, so they went avidly for the professions. Clearly, the vast majority of these ambitious natives came from the *principalia* class. Eventually, a new class emerged: the *ilustrados*.[9] It was mainly from this class, more than two hundred years later, that the Reform Movement developed.

By virtue of their educational and professional attainments, as well as their social origin and position in native society, the *ilustrados* began agitating for reforms in the colony that would enable them to occupy positions in the government hitherto denied to indios. They requested representation of the colony in the Spanish *Cortes*; the right to occupy positions in the civil bureaucracy by competitive exams; the right to be officers in the Army; the expulsion of the friars and the holding of the parishes by a native secular clergy; and the abolition of military rule in the colony. The ilustrados' so-called reform movement represented the effort of a segment of the native population to get a better share of the colonial benefits while having a hand in defining the colony's destiny. It was an assertion of native leadership. Since, by definition, Filipinas was for the Filipinos, the movement meant that the indio wanted to be transformed into a Filipino. Some of them were actually calling themselves so—to the dismay of Spaniards and friars.

The ilustrados initially talked of "assimilation"—that is, they wanted to have the colony become a province of Spain, like Andalusia or Galicia. They met with fierce opposition from within and without the colony, even to the point of being persecuted for their ideas. The ideas then filtered down to the humbler strata of native society, until they developed with a secret organization fighting for separation from Spain.

THE ORIGINAL CONCEPT OF A FILIPINO NATIONAL COMMUNITY AND THE PHILLIPPINE REVOLUTION OF 1896 AND 1898

Here the work and ideas of José Rizal (1861–96) are relevant. Living in Europe to avoid persecution, imbued with many of the liberal ideas spreading through Spain and France, Rizal was deeply affected by Rousseau and the French Revolution. He understood that independence as such would not necessarily bring about the good life. To him, from a moral point of view, a native tyranny was essentially the same as that of a colonial oppressor. Realizing that the native was a member of two communities that exploited him, he conceived of an alternative community transcending both personal interests and religious commitments, where exploitation would be absent—a national community where "national sentiment" would hold sway. But this community still had to be created, since the Filipino "was only an individual, he is not a member of a nation." Because of his ideas, his organization of a society to help generate national consciousness, and his suspected role as leader, Rizal was executed by firing squad in 1896. The uprising itself did not fare well, its leadership eventually falling into the hands of *principales* who in 1897 entered into a treaty with the Spanish government.

When the United States entered into war with Spain in 1898, and the U.S. Fleet appeared in Manila Bay, revolutionary leaders returned from exile and recommenced the revolution with American encouragement. Before 1896, complaints of severity of tribute, forced labor, agrarian disputes, abuses by Spanish colonial officials and friars, and unnecessary provocation of a few disgruntled *principales* had led to uprisings against the Spanish government, but they were isolated and short-lived. The Revolution of 1898 produced a revolutionary government, then a republic with a well thought-out constitution. With a Congress and Army that represented various provinces, regions, and linguistic groupings, it had many of the elements of a national struggle. The Americans, however, had no intention of letting the Filipinos rule themselves. Rather, their plan was to defeat Spain and to possess the Philippines as an American colony; American military superiority decided the issue in the Filipino-American War which was fought from 1899 to 1901.

It is important to note that Muslims in the Philippine South did not participate in the Revolution of 1896 and 1898, considering the whole affair a war between Christians. Nevertheless, in 1898, in an effort to present a common front against Spain, and possibly America in the future, the revolutionary government contacted Mindanao datus, appealing to a common "ancient liberty" and "common God."[10] In his address to Congress one month before the onset of hostilities between Filipino and American soldiers, the President of the Republic proposed that the government be empowered "to negotiate with the Moros of Sulu and Mindanao for the purposes of establishing national solidarity upon the basis of a real federation with absolute respect for their beliefs and traditions." Such appeals, declarations, and proposals, however, fell on deaf Muslim ears. As Spanish troops withdrew from their strongholds in Mindanao, Muslim warriors came in to fill the vacuum. Many Christian Filipinos in formerly Spanish-protected settlements were captured as slaves, and datus who wanted to eliminate the revolutionary representatives tried to capture Zamboanga. Only the timely arrival of American troops averted a massacre by Muslims of a relatively defenseless population. When American officers told the Sulu sultan that there was a revolution of Filipinos against Spaniards, he remarked that the Filipinos in Luzon were simply doing what they, the Sulus, had been doing for centuries. He and other Moro datus had absolutely no intention of supporting a Filipino government which to them was just as Christian as that of the Spaniards. They had neither forgotten nor forgiven Filipinos who, as allies of the Spaniards, had ravaged their lands in the past. They were, however, willing to enter into separate treaties with the Americans who, they believed, would allow them to keep their independence and gain certain material benefits. In this they were mistaken.

UNCLE SAM IN MOROLAND

The claim of the United States to Muslim lands in the Philippines was based on the Treaty of Paris, by which, in December 1898, Spain ceded the Philippine Archipelago. In less than a year, American troops were slowly occupying Muslim settlements, initially without opposition. They found a people with a different way of life from those in Luzon and the Visayas, and a religion utterly foreign to them. It was quite unlike Manila with its educated class already exposed to Western ways. There it was not difficult for the American authorities eventually to transform their military government to a civil one, with many positions occupied by Filipinos—the *ilustrados*—with political parties and a national assembly. They could not, however, deal with the unurbanized Muslims in this way. Their inclination at first was to treat the Muslims as savages, somewhat like American Indians—it is no accident that many of the soldiers and officers sent to pacify the Muslims were well-known Indian fighters. Time slowly modified their attitude to one of grudging respect, if not some sort of romantic fondness.

American officers did not interfere with the datu system or with Muslim religious beliefs. However, some wished that the Muslims would become Christians so as to become easier to communicate with, and hence to govern. Military officers tended to pamper friendly datus while treating those antagonistic to them more harshly. The Sulu sultan was given money and gifts to keep him quiet, but he and the sultans of Mindanao had lost much of their power and prestige. The decline of any sultanate invariably led to an increase in the power and independence of other datus. And, because the American Army prohibited the time-honored practice of slavery and exacting tribute, and because the presence of American soldiers represented foreign Christian troops, not a few of these datus rose up in revolt. Some notable battles took place, but Moro forts and trenches were no match for superior artillery—dum-dum bullets and the famed .45 caliber pistol. Such battles ended as sheer massacres.

The whole area of the traditional sultanates was reorganized into one Moro province, which American military officers administered until 1913. In 1920, its administration was turned over to Christian Filipino officials. When the Filipino Commonwealth was established in 1936, a commissioner for Mindanao and Sulu was appointed by the

Filipino President. By this time, units of the Philippine Constabulary and Philippine Scouts, mostly Christians from the north, were in Moroland to maintain peace and order. This gradual administrative and coercive integration of Muslims into the emerging Filipino political society occurred in response to pressure on American officials by Filipino politicians, who were preparing to inherit the colonial mantle themselves.

In 1898, not a few American officers believed they were coming to Christianize the Filipinos. To their surprise they found hundreds of churches, priests and nuns already there. Some officers believed they could introduce "Anglo-Saxon civilization" to the Muslims if they could gradually eliminate the Moro "habits of life." There was even one maverick officer who believed that more orthodox Islamic institutions had to be introduced in order to do away with what he considered negative, non-Islamic customs. He succeeded in having the Sublime Porte in Istanbul send a learned Muslim to Mindanao to upgrade Muslim instruction—to the discomfiture of his brother officers. The fact is that although officially the Americans never interfered in the religious lives of Muslims, by and large they discouraged Arabs and other foreign Muslims from visiting Moroland. American Protestant missionaries interested in converting Muslims never got official encouragement or support. One of these had the grand dream of converting the Moros to Christianity and then use them to convert the Muslims of the Indonesian islands, and even possibly those in India![11] Such American noninterference in Islam played a considerable role in winning the general good will of Muslims. A time would come when Muslims would look to the Americans to protect them from integration into a Christian Philippines.

To help hasten the political integration of Moroland into the colonial society, and on the premise that Christian Filipinos were more sophisticated along modern administrative lines than the Muslims, Americans soon introduced them as civil officials and clerks in Muslim areas. To permit Muslim farmers to learn relatively more advanced agricultural techniques from Christians, and to encourage interpersonal relations among them, they initiated a process of bringing Christian farmers and settlers to traditional Muslim areas. Well intentioned but unwise, this move was to bring about in a few years the unintended results of conflict and bloodshed.

Meanwhile, the Filipino nationalistic movement agitating for eventual independence was accelerating. Filipino national leaders were preparing to take control of all internal affairs. Drafting a constitution largely patterned after that of the United States, and getting the U.S. president to approve it, they were able to head the Commonwealth government of 1936 and received a promise of full independence in ten years.

Except for a very few prominent Muslims who had something to gain, the vast majority of traditional Muslim leaders did not want anything to do with the goals and institutions of the Filipino leaders. They petitioned American officials to keep their provinces separate from the rest of the country and under American rule—until such time as they could be granted their own, separate, independence. In this they had the sympathy of some Americans. Thus the Bacon bill, which provided that Mindanao and Sulu be retained under American rule and separate from Luzon and the Visayas, was presented to the U.S. Congress in 1926. It brought forth an outcry from Filipino national leaders, who charged Americans with the imperial policy of "divide and rule" and sinister economic interests in Mindanao. The bill never passed Congress.

The Commonwealth government viewed Mindanao as a "land of promise," to be exploited for the national gain. President Manuel Quezon spoke of its "colonization and economic development," as well as of the overpopulation in some of the provinces, Luzon and the Visayas (another aim may have been to contrast Japanese ambitions in Mindanao). Accordingly, the government began encouraging Christian settlers to go to Mindanao, including some areas that were considered traditional Muslim lands. Aided by the government, these settlers came with implements and work animals. Soon they would have towns among them, with schools and churches, changing the demographic situation in Cotabato and Lanao.[12]

Quezon, who loved public speeches, often declared that the hand of the law would fall equally on all citizens, whether Christian or Muslim, and that sultans, datus and humble Moros were all equal before the law. But such statements did not get the expected sympathetic response. Traditional Muslim leaders interpreted them to mean that the government intended to do away with them, while ordinary Muslims, conditioned to treat their traditional leaders with some awe, must have felt embarrassed by the whole thing.

Neither were Muslim parents and their religious leaders enthusiastic about the public education fostered by the government. The government wanted a system that was uniform all over the country, a curriculum that would foster civic virtues and a moral code with national overtones, in order to instill among the children a sense of national consciousness and loyalty to an emerging national community soon to be independent. Unfortunately, in many of the history books the heroes extolled and set up as models were those of the North; most had been participants in the Revolution of 1896 and 1898, with whom Muslims did not identify. References to Muslims were mostly about their role in the Moro Wars, where they were portrayed as rapacious and fearsome pirates. Furthermore, animals used as illustrations for lessons in arithmetic or language proficiency were often those abhorred by Muslims as unclean. This insensitivity to Muslim history and beliefs made many Muslim families shun government schools for their children. Many saw in the public primary educational system not only a ridiculing of Muslim beliefs, but a subtle attempt to gradually wean the children from Islam.

Although Muslims participated to some extent in national elections and a few were elected to office, the majority of Muslims stood outside the national mainstream. Very few held high government posts even in their own provinces. No comprehensive economic program was devised for the Islamic regions in spite of evidence of the breakdown of law and order in some areas. Just as Muslim participation in the formation of the Commonwealth government was minimal, so were efforts to bring them into the mainstream of national life. Muslims studying for the professions in Manila or other big centers of population could almost be counted on the fingers of one hand, while there were hundreds of Filipino physicians, lawyers, and engineers. The fact is that national leaders were now most concerned with "politics" and with jockeying for choice positions that would soon become available with independence. In foreign policy their concern was focused principally on Japanese designs on their country—"the pearl of the Orient seas."

During the Japanese occupation of the country in World War II, there generally was no cooperation with or sympathy for the Japanese among Muslims. Resistance of various Muslim groups took the form of pitched battles, damaging ambushes, and terrible retaliations from the occupying soldiers. Hundreds of Muslim families evacuated to remoter areas. Muslim and Christian joined in guerrilla units under American patronage, and cooperation was the rule. Some Muslim officials appeared to cooperate with Japanese authorities while they were secretly in contact with guerrilla units, and some Muslims from traditional families became famous as guerrilla leaders. In spite of Japanese efforts, none could be induced to make a public proclamation of hatred against Americans.

The eventual defeat of Japan brought some important consequences to Muslims. With firearms and ammunition left behind by both Japanese and American forces, Muslim datus began having armed men around them, not only for prestige and out of habit, but with an eye to future use. Rehabilitation brought a large amount of cash, helping to bring about a money economy as against a former barter one. Hundreds of Muslims were now able to go on the haj and extra money was available for building mosques and for invitations to Muslim teachers to come from Indonesia.[13]

With independence in 1946, some prominent Muslims—mainly those who had gained prominence as guerrilla leaders—were invited to join the opposing political parties. But it was not till after 1950 that the highest political offices in the provinces of Sulu, Cotabato, and Lanao were open to elections. As could be expected, Muslims were generally indifferent to the independence ceremonies in Manila and other parts of the country. They simply wanted to be left alone. Nor did the government, wracked by post-independence politics, have the inclination, the will, or the time to listen to Muslim aspirations and expectations.

In the meantime, more Christian settlers kept coming to Lanao and Cotabato. From 1953 to 1957, during President Magsaysay's administrations, the coming of settlers accelerated. Settler colonies, consisting of thousands of ex-soldiers, ex-Communists, ex-prisoners, etc., were established in the midst of Muslim settlements and in lands traditionally under the sway of the old sultans. Many of these lands were declared public lands simply because Muslims did not have government titles to them. According to Muslim theory, the land belonged to God, to be held in trust by the community. In actual operation, most of the land was held communally under the general supervision of the datus—a situation the Spaniards found in Luzon when they first came. As long as there was still available land to occupy nearby, land conflicts with the settlers were moderate; but a time would come when there would be landless Muslims as well as landless Christians. Christian settlers often had to pay different members of the same Muslim family for the same lot of land. While this situation arose from different concepts of land tenure, the Christians attributed it to Muslim greed. The new government's laws encouraging Muslims to get titles to their land allowed some traditional leaders to get access to communal land, but the majority of common people failed to take advantage of the law. A widespread understanding of the so-called Torrens title was particularly slow among Islamic populations, for the cultural reasons already mentioned.

Moreover, Muslim farmers looked with frustration and resentment, if not envy, at the superior implements and agricultural efficiency of the settlers. Apprehensive at the rise of settler towns in their midst, they noted that these towns had better roads, sanitation, schools, as well as government-sponsored irrigation projects. It was only in 1972, when martial law was declared, for example, that a real irrigation project was started in Muslim lands. In short, Muslims concluded that government discrimination was intentional, and that government help was only for Christians—to them, still, the Filipino government was a Christian one.

While land conflicts were on the rise in Cotabato, Sulu was having a problem with law and order. Although Sulu did not have a settler problem, it was overcrowded and there were land conflicts among Muslims themselves. Unemployment was rife and it had one of the lowest literacy rates in the country; outlaw bands made it dangerous to travel in the interior of Jolo. Finally, in 1954, the lower house of the Philippine Congress formed a special committee, headed by a Muslim, to engage in a thorough study and make recommendations for solving the so-called Moro Problem. The committee reported that the majority of the Muslims they interviewed did not identify themselves with the government; that they did not consider themselves Filipinos; and that their areas were economically depressed. Policies and programs to make Muslims feel that they belonged to the national society were thus deemed necessary.

Of their many recommendations—for all cultural minorities—the only one to be implemented was the establishment of the Commission of National Integration (CNI), in 1957. The CNI concentrated on offering scholarships to members of cultural minorities (mostly Muslims), to study in colleges and universities. Although it did not fully accomplish all of its goals, it was able to grant scholarships to about eight thousand students (again, mostly Muslims). Slightly less than 20 percent of these were able to get a formal degree; but all were exposed to higher education and to urban life. While the CNI believed that the return of these scholars to their own areas might help bring about the socioeconomic uplift of Muslim communities, what actually happened was that their education and literary sophistication helped make them more conscious of their Islamic identity and more vocal in their aspirations. Eventually, in 1975, the CNI was abolished.

In 1961, Datu Ombra Amilbangsa—a former pretender to the Sulu sultanate and now a member of the Philippine Congress—presented a bill in the Lower House providing for the independence of Sulu. Most members of Congress as well as the Press viewed it as a curiosity; probably it was meant to dramatize publicly the worsening situation in Sulu. Given the thinking of many Tausugs and Samals in Sulu, it must have engendered some expectations among them. It did stimulate many discussions in Sulu.

In 1963, the Philippine Senate formed its own committee to study the problems of the cultural minorities. This committee concluded that the land problem in Mindanao was *the* root problem; that government officials paid more heed to the land claims of Christian settlers; and that often local politicians, government agents, and rich parties would all connive in the disposition of agricultural lands—to the detriment of farmers who were poor and ignorant. In 1971, the Senate committee on national minorities once again pointed out that the growing discontent in Mindanao was due to land problems. It blamed the Commonwealth government and the ensuing Republic for their policy of bringing settlers from Luzon and the Visayas to traditional Muslim lands, without enabling Muslims to legitimize their hold on them or get titles. It added ominously that the natives in the land "are no longer willing to be pushed around."

The concern of national leaders for Muslims' chronic complaints and their position in the national society was due not only to reports of rising disorders in Sulu and Mindanao. By now, Muslim traditional leaders (some of whom had become members of Congress), Muslim professionals, and student bodies, had begun to use the media as well as Congress to voice the aspirations and complaints of their people. The fact was that after World War II, there was a resurgence of Islamic awareness in the Philippines. It began slowly, but by the sixties its results were becoming more manifest in the national scene.

ISLAMIC RESURGENCE

Immediately after the War, hundreds of Muslims took the opportunity to go on the haj; soon the number would average at least a thousand ea^h year. Isolated for many years from other Muslims, the hajis returned with greater enthusiasm for their universal brotherhood and with increased religious fervor. Teachers came from Indonesia and from Egypt, teaching Islam and the Arabic language in the madrasa and mosques. Maktabs and madrasas increased. During the Nasser regime, hundreds of Muslim Filipinos were granted scholarships to study in Islamic theological centers in Egypt, especially at Al Azhar—some of these scholars drifting to professional schools and even to the military academy. With their return, a new and more "enlightened" ulama emerged. Madrasas sprung up with better curricula, and the quality of the khutbas in mosques was upgraded. There was less distrust of the public school system and young Muslims flocked to secondary schools, many then qualifying as scholars of the CNI. Foreign Muslim visitors visited Muslim villages, reassuring Muslims of their concern. The increase in the number of independent Muslim countries also raised the pride of Muslims. A small professional class of Muslims was growing up and Muslim student organizations were proliferating. Muslim leaders, whether politicians or ulama, were being invited to Islamic conferences abroad. Money from philanthropic Muslims abroad helped to build new mosques or improve old ones. Islamic literature from abroad became more available. All of this encouraged higher attendance at Friday prayers, lessening of practices believed to be un-Islamic, increasing adoption of Arab names rather than local ones, and more local Islamic conferences and associations. In brief, a more intensified sense of the *umma* began to prevail. All the while, Muslims began to delve deeper into their history, with a heightened sense of dignity and pride.

This Islamic resurgence had its impact on the behavior and actions of Muslim traditional leaders. Many Muslim politicians, especially sensitive to the religious sensitivities of their constituencies, were themselves quite pious by upbringing and inclination, and saw themselves as Muslim leaders of Muslims. Others made an effort to show that they, too, had Islamic consciousness: often their first action when elected was to go on the haj to reassure their followers of their Islamic commitments. An unchanging feature of Muslim leaders, pious or not, was their unfailing loyalty to their communities and origins—origins in which Islam had played an important part. Working in two different political systems—the traditional one in their communities and the national one with its different set of rules— these Muslim leaders were often quite astute. Their goals were to get the government to declare a moratorium on the continuing influx of settlers to traditional lands, more appointed positions for Muslims at the national level, more autonomy for their religious laws, more diplomatic recognition of Muslim countries with more Muslims as Filipino-accredited diplomats, and more economic improvements in the way of agricultural aid and establishment of industries in their areas. To their request for an institution of higher learning in their provinces, the government responded with the Mindanao State University—which became operative in Lanao in 1962. The majority of its students, however, have always been Christians from other provinces.

But there were problems facing Muslim aspirations. For one thing, the demographic factor in Cotabato and Lanao was increasingly against them, and, as a developing country, there were other poor regions in the Philippines that also merited attention. National leaders were, as usual, involved in "politics," to the neglect of pressing national problems. Muslim politicians belonging to opposing political parties served to confuse, if not divide, the people. Moreover, many national leaders belonging to the dominant majority had not emancipated themselves from the Moro-moro.

THE 1968 JABIDAH MASSACRE

In 1967, certain quarters of the Philippine military created Merdeka— a secret project to recruit young Muslims in Samal areas of Sulu and train them for a special force. At the end of the year the recruits, numbering possibly 180, were transferred to Corregidor Island at the entrance to Manila Bay. The project, renamed Jabidah, intensified the training of the recruits in jungle warfare and guerrilla tactics. In March 1968, some of these young Muslims were killed. One of the trainees, shot in the leg, managed to swim away from the island and be rescued by fishermen. Muslim politicians visited him, heard the story of the massacre in all its grisly details, and exposed it to the public.

The opposition party raised an uproar, and Congress then started an investigation. While the real reason for creating Jabidah was never fully told, the ostensible justification given to the recruits was the invasion of Sabah in North Borneo—which the government had often claimed belonged to the old Sulu dominions and therefore should now be a part of the Republic. Enemies of the President imputed other more sinister motives to the Jabidah project, in which about twenty-eight Muslim trainees were killed for an alleged mutiny. The exposure in the media generated international reactions. Muslim students, professionals, families, politicians, and associations raised questions as to the killing of Muslims by government troops without benefit of investigation or trial. Khutbahs dealt with the issue. There was a well-planned Muslim demonstration before the Presidential palace attended by various Muslim organizations and supported by Muslim politicians. The result of all this was a sudden government moratorium on discussions of the massacre—giving "national unity" as the excuse. Muslims, however, concluded that they were mere pawns and that the government was utterly insensible to the loss of Muslim lives.

Nothing could have been better designed to bring together diverse elements of the Muslim population. After the Jabidah Massacre, radical students began to reassess their position in the national society, trying to find more effective ways to enhance Muslim security and integrity.[14] Ominously, a few months later there were rumors of young Muslim Filipinos sailing to North Borneo for training under foreign patronage.

THE MIM AND SUCCEEDING EVENTS

Capitalizing on Jabidah, Udtog Matalam, one of the most prominent Maguindanao datus, announced the formation of the Muslim Independence Movement (MIM): its goal the independence of Sulu and Mindanao. A famed guerrilla leader against Japan who had once been appointed governor of Cotabato, his action revived memories of past freedom. In reaction, many isolated Christian settlers transferred to more populated Christian centers, upsetting their leaders—who had plans of their own. To allay fears of the Christians in Mindanao, the datu changed the name of his movement to the Mindanao Independence Movement (still MIM). After a few months, armed groups of nonresident Visayans were seen in increasing numbers in Christian settlements; Muslim trainees from abroad were also returning. Armed outlaw bands—the Christians were known as Ilagas, the Muslims as Blackshirts and Barracudas—began roaming the countryside of Cotabato, and pitched battles took place. The government sent additional military and constabulary units to Lanao and Cotabato. Age-old tensions between Muslim and Christian communities erupted in killings. Schools were closed, farms were abandoned, and economic life was at a standstill in many areas. By the end of 1970, thirty thousand Muslims, Christians, and members of the cultural minorities in the area left for safer places.

MASSACRES AND INTERNATIONAL MUSLIM CONCERN

Increasingly, battles between Ilagas and Muslim armed bands became the order of the day, and the early months of 1971 saw more and more towns in Cotabato placed under constabulary control. Officially, constabulary units were instructed to prevent any conflict between warring bands. However, it was clear that when these bands met, it was the constabulary that normally attacked the Muslim band, and that when the Ilagas attacked a Muslim settlement, the constabulary would arrive late. Muslim leaders suspected that there was collusion between Christian politicians, settlers, and officers of the constabulary but could do little to prevent it. After the June 1971 Ilaga massacre of about seventy innocent and helpless Muslims in a mosque in Manili, Cotabato, some Muslim leaders began to cry "genocide." In July, a group of Muslims—representing politicians, scholars, ulama, professionals, and student leaders—framed a manifesto in which they pledged before God to preserve their communities and lands. The government saw this manifesto, which was published in one of the leading newspapers, as a veiled threat to its authority.

In August, the famous Buldon battles took place. The Iranuns faced a superior army force and gave a good account of themselves—not without some aid from their close kin, the Maranaos. The infamous Tacub massacre—where about forty innocent and unarmed Maranaos were killed by Army units—took place during the November elections of the same year. There was a perfunctory investigation of the massacre: in less than two months, charges were dropped against officers believed to be guilty. In retrospect it appears that this was done so as not to alienate the Army, since the President was already planning to establish martial law the next year. By the end of 1971, the number of Muslim and Christian refugees went over the hundred-thousand mark.

During the final half of 1972, there was a noticeable decline in Muslim "massacres," or battles between Muslim and Ilaga groups. One explanation may be that they had been meant primarily to drive

Muslims away from certain areas so that Christian candidates could win in the November elections. Once this was accomplished, the Ilagas, who were financed by these politicians, proved an embarrassment to their patrons. Their ensuing extortion of Christian traders led to their being disliked, and not a few were finished off by angry Christian settlers. In any case, the November elections were fateful for Muslims, especially those in Cotabato and Lanao. Political power—which in many areas had once been under the sway of datus or sultans—was now under the administration of Christian governors and mayors. This process seemed irreversible.

International Muslim concern for Muslim Filipinos had been consistent. After the Jabidah Massacre, groups in Malaysia and Kuwait as well as religious institutions in Egypt began to make official inquiries. After the Manila Massacre, Mu'ammar Qadhafi sent one of his ministers to visit President Marcos to express his concern; and after the Buldon battles, he declared publicly that if "the genocide still went on," he would assume responsibility for protecting Muslim Filipino lives. He also sent money for food and medicines for Muslim refugees, and financed the trip of mutilated Muslim children for medical treatment abroad. However, it was the Supreme Council of Al Azhar which, after expressing grave concern over the situation of Muslim Filipinos in a message to President Marcos, cabled the Chairman of the 3rd Islamic Conference of Foreign Ministers then meeting in Jeddah (29 February–4 March 1972). The following July President Marcos invited a combined Egyptian-Libyan delegation to tour the South to see that there was no genocide. After visiting some trouble spots, the head of the Libyans declared that although he did not believe that the "war" in the South was essentially a religious one, that was how the Muslims viewed it. He did maintain, however, that it was a war between religious communities. The 4th Islamic Conference asked the Philippine government to help Muslim refugees return to their lands. It created a "Fund to help the Muslims" and a Committee of Four to visit the Philippines. Up to the present, the Islamic Conference had expressed its deep concern each year. Curiously, in December 1971, three religious dignitaries from the Soviet Union–two from Tashkent and one from Moscow—came to visit Muslims in Manila and in the South.

International Muslim pressure was only one of the things occupying the mind of President Marcos. On 21 September 1972, he declared martial law. Among the many reasons given—such as communist subversion, a rightist conspiracy, widespread student unrest and demonstrations, the increasing impotence of the government to implement much desired reforms, and so on—was what he termed a Muslim secessionist movement in the South.

Muslims generally interpreted martial law as meaning greater military repression, and given their recent experiences, the Army's move to confiscate all arms met with fierce resistance. The Muslim fear of being exposed unarmed to military units and Christian settlers probably motivated the Marawi uprising in October 1972—by all indications an isolated incident—in which many soldiers died.

After the declaration of martial law, the Moro National Liberation Front (MNLF) was forced to come out in the open. Led by young university students and professional—some of whom had been trained abroad after the Jabidah Affair—its overall chairman was Nur Misuari, a young instructor at the University of the Philippines. Its military arm was the Bangsa Moro Army (BMA). Some members of the MNLF's central committee were former students of Al Azhar and were related to prominent datus. Others, such as Nisuari, came from humble origins. Crossing as they did regional and linguistic lines, the MNLF was able in March 1973 to launch simultaneous attacks on at least twelve municipalities in Cotobato. This demonstration of the MNLF's ability to coordinate its scope of operations worried Army quarters, accustomed as they were to the operations of outlaws, private armies of traditional warlords, or disgruntled Moro armed bands. [15] Large-scale fighting between about a thousand MNLF men and government troops in Jolo town, in February 1973, resulted in the complete destruction of the town and the orderly retreat of the MNLF. Another result was the visit of the Saudi Arabian Foreign Minister to Manila, who reported that the continued troubles of the Muslims were mainly due to the Army rather than to the President. Consequently, the Philippines was grudgingly removed from the oil-embargo blacklist.

It was in the first few years of martial law that the government initiated a serious attempt to solve the so-called Moro Problem, coinciding with the rise of the MNLF and mounting international pressure. Top government officials, inspired by their sincere desire to bring about the declared "new society," were harnessed. A massive socioeconomic program was devised to elevate Muslim education and standards of living, but there was as always a perennial lack of funds. A bank was created to cater to Muslim needs and even adopt a Muslim system of banking; barter trading with Sabah was allowed. A Southern Philippines Development Administration—with many Muslims in its administration—was formed, and so on. The idea in all this was that such economic programs would eventually satisfy Muslims and slowly integrate them into the mainstream of national life. Assurances were made to Muslims that their faith would be respected, even through the building of mosques—often called cultural centers so as to fulfill the constitution's requirement of the separation of church and state. An Institute of Islamic Studies was established at the University of the Philippines, offering degrees and a few scholarships for deserving Muslim students. The teaching of Arabic was to be authorized in schools where there was a demand for it. The President, in his many speeches before Muslims, emphasized the role of Muslims in the colonial struggle and Islam's part in the Philippines' cultural heritage. In talks before Muslim groups he would narrate how a Muslim soldier in Bataan had once saved his life during the Japanese invasion. He would even claim that his ancestors were Muslims but that the Spanish Conquest had obliterated this heritage. This remark in particular would draw appreciative smiles from his audience even though it was well recognized as simply a symbolic gesture.

Of greatest importance was the formation of a Presidential commission to draft a code of Muslim Personal Laws. Presented to the President in August 1975, it was not until February 1977 that he signed it, nor has it yet been fully implemented. One reason is that ulama who can serve as judges in the Shari'a courts do not have degrees in national law, while Muslims who have graduated from the law schools do not know enough about the Shari'a. Training institutes are handling this not insoluble problem, and it is hoped that any time now the government will appoint the judges as well as a mufti. [16]

All of the above economic, educational and social measures have been presented to the Islamic Conference of Foreign Ministers as tangible efforts by the Philippine government to show that it wants to solve the problems of Muslims. Yet, there is still a major question that needs settling: that of autonomy and of the future role of the MNLF.

PROBLEMS OF AUTONOMY FOR MUSLIMS

The first formal contact between the MNLF and the government took place in Jeddah in January 1975. The Philippine Panel invited the MNLF leadership to return to the country to see for themselves government efforts to help the Muslims and to participate in them. The MNLF's condition for continuing the talks was that the government should grant autonomy to the islands of Sulu, Mindanao, Palawan, and Basilan as one political unit "within the framework of Philippine sovereignty and territorial integrity." It was now willing to modify its former demand for secession to that of a significant autonomy. The government panel, however, declaring that it was not empowered to grant this, tried to enter into a truce arrangement with the MNLF to reduce bloodshed between Filipinos. Little came of the talks other than a willingness to meet again.

Eventually, in December 1976, in Tripoli, Libya, a truce was declared between a new government panel and the MNLF. Of significance was a general agreement on certain principles of autonomy. However, various government actions in presenting the problem of autonomy to the provinces for plebiscite—among them the claim that the MNLF did not truly represent all Muslims but that other sectors or factions had to be considered as well—led the MNLF to accuse it of insincerity and lack of adherence to the Tripoli Agreement. Eventually the truce was broken and once again the MNLF was talking of secession. From all indications the present form of autonomy that has been declared in Regions IX and XII does not fully satisfy even the expectations of those Muslims cooperating with the government. Thousands of Muslim refugees have still not returned to their former homes and farms. In Sabah alone there are about two hundred thousand Samal and Tausug refugees being cared for by the Malaysian government; there may be even more Maguindanao refugees scattered throughout Mindanao. There is still sporadic fighting between MNLF and Army units—although a few thousand former MNLF fighters, including commanders, have decided to return to the fold of the law. Peace is still distant from Moroland.

OBSERVATIONS AND FUTURE PROSPECTS

One of the most striking phenomena of the postwar Philippines is the conscious and determined efforts of its Muslim ethnic minorities to preserve their cultural identity. The Islamic resurgence aims at a further cohesion of the *umma* which will retain local traditional values and institutions as well as transcend regional and linguistic lines. This of course has political consequences: one can assume that in general Muslims, especially most of the old leaders, would prefer to be independent of the Philippine state. However, if this is not feasible, the alternative is some kind of meaningful autonomy. Unlike the Communists whose aim is the control of the Philippine government, most Muslims want to get as far away from it as possible and be left to their own devices. There are, of course, Muslims—educated in Manila or with national positions that benefit them and their families—who have a concept of a wider community. These too do not deny their roots, but often do their best to help their communities of origin.

Within its limited resources, the government has found it imperative to meet many of the demands of Muslims for economic improvement and guarantees for the preservation of Islam. The land conflict, however, has not been solved. The Muslim demand to reclaim all traditional lands is in conflict with the expanding territorial needs of the Christian majority. So far, the government has not returned the bulk of Muslim refugees to their former farms and villages, which are now occupied by Christians from other provinces. Relocating these refugees to other lands will give rise to additional problems.

Clearly, government concessions to Muslims have come about because Muslims have agitated and fought for them, especially the MNLF. International Muslim concern has also played its part in moderating the repressive military actions against Muslims. The MNLF's recognition by the Islamic Conference of Foreign Ministers as the organization representing the Muslim struggle has led some Muslim traditional leaders to try to control it. So far to no avail: the Conference still recognizes Nur Misuari as its Chairman. At present, it is far from convinced that the kind of autonomy given to Muslim regions follows the principles drawn up in the Tripoli Agreement of 1976. Not only does this strengthen the MNLF hand, but it can be used by Muslims administering the regions as an argument for greater administrative and executive powers. However, the rivalry and fragmentation that exists in the Muslim leadership in the Philippines often allows the government to play one against the other. Regional prejudice too is common—among Christians as well as Muslims. But then, this is not a Philippine monopoly!

Return of most if not all of Muslim refugees, implementation of more meaningful autonomy in accordance with the Tripoli Agreement, creation of industrial projects in Muslim areas with a Muslim majority representation, development of a strong professional group among Muslims, greater representation in the upper echelons of the national govenment: measures such as these may slowly bring about the desired peace. But of the greatest importance is withdrawing the present Army units and substituting Muslim units under regional government control. Muslims view the present military units in their lands as an Army of occupation, by definition oppressive. The common soldier coming from other provinces often enough views all Muslims as enemies. When Muslim families mourning the loss of loved ones take revenge on individual soldiers, army retaliation is usually out of proportion to these killings of soldiers in isolated incidents. Muslim soldiers would possibly be more understanding of Muslim civilians and more sensitive to their difficulties and problems. The Pata island incident in February 1981, where about 120 government soldiers were killed—presumably by MNLF units—is a case in point regarding the nature of the continuing conflict. According to rebel sources, the soldiers were killed because of their abuses of Muslim women, the strafing of homes of peaceful civilians, the confiscation of food, and the desecration of mosques. In a massive retaliation involving at least fifteen thousand government troops, from five hundred to a thousand innocent civilians were killed, farms and plantations were deliberately destroyed, and civilians were not allowed to go to their farms or to fish. Muslim officials cooperating with the government objected to the treatment of all Muslims as enemies or rebels. They saw the Pata incident as a repetition of the Moro Wars; only instead of Spaniards, this time the soldiers were Filipinos.[17]

To insist that religious attitudes do not play a part in the conflict between Muslims and Christians in the Philippine South reflects either ignorance of some salient facts or hypocrisy. When the MNLF leaders speak of protection of their communities, they call their communities "Muslim." Their program contains demands for Islamic institutions involving education and legal matters. Most Muslim leaders, whether cooperating with the government or advocating secession, think within an Islamic framework. The same is true for Christian Filipino government officials: in their dealings with Muslim problems and demands they work within a Christian framework. Even when influenced by liberal or secular ideas to the point that they are not committed to a particular religion or sect, their upbringing and values belong to a system different from the Islamic. When a Filipino academic said: "The problem with the Muslims is that they are different from the rest of us and do not want to become like us," he was assuming that national identity is to be defined by his particular group. The fact is that historical factors have led to the present situation, where many of the elements of the emerging national culture have been defined by the culture of the majority.

Although the Philippines is an independent state, the formation of a national community along lines defined by its founding fathers—such as the national hero José Rizal—is still in process. As the Filipinos are trying to become more and more of a national community, making Muslims in the Philippines think more and more as Filipinos is only one problem.[18] Another problem is to make Christian Filipinos think more and more as Filipinos, that the values of their religious community need not be those of the national community. For the Philippines is a pluralistic society and will continue to be so indefinitely. Eventually, the emerging national community can come up with a national culture different from both the dominant majority and the cultural minorities. As a national culture, it might contain elements of all cultures or it might transcend elements of these particular cultures. And one of these elements is precisely that principle which asserts that no particular culture ought to be suppressed in favor of another one. Indeed, this is a value and moral principle that can lead to the good life of all citizens and do away with divisive forces in a national society. The alternative is continued bloodshed and unnecessary suffering.

NOTES

1. Peter G. Gowing, *Muslim Filipinos—Heritage and Horizon* (Quezon City: New Day Publishers, 1979), 2. The figures given are rough estimates, since it is difficult to arrive at exact figures. For political purposes, government figures tend to be very conservative while those given by Muslims tend to be quite high. In a public speech in June 1974, President Marcos stated that the Muslim population was 1.5 million, while Muslim sources claimed at least 3 million; by 1980, the corresponding claims were for 3 and 5 million respectively. Complete agreement on the yearly rate of increase is lacking. At the time of writing, the total Muslim population may be estimated at anywhere between 4 and 4.5 million.

2. The Maguindanao, the largest Muslim group, are mostly concentrated in the Cotabato region in Mindanao, consisting of various provinces. They are basically an agricultural people practicing wet-rice planting. The Maranao live in the two Lanao provinces, principally in the area around Lake Lanao. They cultivate upland rice and corn and are justly famous for their brasswork and weaving. As spirited traders, there is practically no place in the country where they are not found selling their wares. Their close kin, the Iranun (or Ilanun), inhabit the Lanao region around Illana Bay and the northern part of Cotabato. They practice agriculture and, to a lesser extent, fishing—in the past they were well-known as seafarers. The Tausug and Samal are found in the Sulu archipelago; many have settled in Basilan island and in Zamboanga del Sur. The Tausug of the interior of Jolo Island practice agriculture and have fine orchards, while the coastal Tausug, with the Samal, engage in fishing and barter. The Yakan, concentrated in Basilan Island, grow upland rice and root crops. They rarely fish, leaving this activity to the Samal living on the coast of their island. The Jama Mapun, who mainly live by fishing, confine themselves to the island of Cagayan de Sulu. The Palawani live in the southern part of Palawan Island, while the Molbog (Melebuganon) are in the nearby Balabac Island which is just off Sabah in the north of Borneo: both Palawan Muslim groups engage in fishing and barter. The Kalagan, spread on the shores of the Davao Gulf; the Kolibugan, confined mainly to Zamboango del Sur; and the Sangil, in Davao, parts of Cotabato and the Sarangani islands, are involved mainly in fishing and, to some extent, trading.

3. Initially, the Americans adopted the Spanish classification.

4. This is based on personal observation. There seem to be no statistics on this matter.

5. Horacio de la Costa, "A Spanish Jesuit among the Magindanaus," *Proceedings of the International Conference of Scholars (Nov. 25–30, 1960, Manila)*. Manila: The Philippines Historical Association, 83–84.

6. Cesar Adib Majul, *Muslims in the Philippines* (Quezon City: University of the Philippines Press, 1973), 78.

7. In 1565, the Spaniards initially tended to call all the natives they met Moros. Later on, when they found out that not all of them were Muslims, they used the term *indio* for those who were not Muslims. Eventually this term came to denote any native who had become Christian. It was only in the

nineteenth term that the term began to have any derogatory connotation. In the last decade or so of Spanish rule in the Philippines, some educated indios began referring to themselves as Filipinos, and were referred to as such by a few Spaniards. Educated natives who were in Spain were also called Filipinos to indicate their place of origin. However, for about three hundred years, the term Filipino was reserved for Spaniards who were born in the Philippines; they were also referred to as *insulares* to distinguish them from *peninsulares*—Spaniards who were born in Spain. The term Moro, used earlier in Spain to refer to the Moors, was originally a religious classification. However, with time this term began to acquire a fearful connotation in the Philippines. Because of this, starting in the fifties, some prominent Muslims started a campaign to have themselves called Muslims instead of Moros. Now, many Muslims, especially those advocating a separate nationality, have reverted to calling themselves Moros and their homeland Moroland (*Bangsa Moro*).

8. All the combatants in the Moro wars were imbued with religious motives. Spanish friars were known not only to have accompanied troops but to have engaged in active fighting. There is a report of one friar who complained that there were also fanatical *panditas* on the opposing side.

9. The term *ilustrado* referred to persons who had some formal education and were literate in the Castillian language. Often it was used to refer to any member of the *principalia* and their families. Strictly speaking, it would refer to an educated member of the *principalia* families. However, in time, members of the humbler classes would have this title by virtue of educational merits.

10. One letter blamed the Spaniards for sowing religious discord between Muslims and Christians, pointing out that a combination of Muslims with the "people of Luzon" would make it quite difficult for foreigners to dominate Filipinos.

11. He asked for the aid of Frank Carpenter, the first—and last—American governor of the Moro Province, to direct such a project, and thus "have the privilege of beginning the end of the Moslem regime." Carpenter was not at all interested, or amused.

12. In one basin of Lanao where there were only about twenty Christian families in 1918, on the eve of the Japanese invasion there were about about eight thousand Christian settlers who had come on their own in the early part of the century, and whom the Muslims had had to help with seeds, animals, and implements; not a few of them had been adopted by datus and ended up as Muslims.

13. For a good summary of the effects of the Japanese Occupation in Moroland, see Gowing, *Muslim Filipinos*, 179–83.

14. One of the leaders in the demonstration before Malacañang Palace was Nur Misuari, who was later to become chairman of the Control Committee of the Moro National Liberation Front (MNLF). At that time, he was a political science student at the University of the Philippines; later on he became an instructor in the same university.

15. At this time the MNLF probably had about fifteen thousand armed men and could count on twice this number if supported by the datus who had armed

men of their own. In Sulu and Mindanao, the Army numbers were about the same, though not all of the soldiers were in Muslim areas.

16. Before martial law in 1972, the government used to pass bills that would be effective for a period of ten years, allowing Muslims and other cultural minority groups to be exempted from the provisions of the Civil Code relating to marriage. This was to legalize Muslim marriage rites as well as divorce. That such bills were meant to be temporary in character was based on the premise that eventually, with more education, Muslims would do away with their traditional institutions. What government officials failed to note was that such temporary provisions as well as the official premises were deeply resented by Muslims. In any case, with or without the bills, Muslims normally follow their religious and traditional practices regarding marriage. The new Code on Muslim Personal Laws now accepts these laws as part of the national laws, but, naturally, applicable only to Muslims.

17. Negative stereotyped attitudes toward Muslims are normally absent from university students. This may be due to having Muslim classmates, visiting their communities, the development of a new concept of what a national society or community ought to be, and an absence of the Moro-moro play syndrome. The blaming of any terrorist activity on Muslims by military authorities is often met by skepticism. However, this skepticism may also be attributable to the absence of government credibility in many of its proclamations, as, for example, that the MNLF has become Communist-oriented, and so on.

18. Last year the Philippine government declared its policy of progressively integrating the Muslim madrasa system into the national educational system. This will involve the upgrading of the curricula to include communication skills in Pilipino and English as well as courses to help the graduates serve as agents for the social improvement of their respective communities. But Arabic is to be retained as the basic language of instruction and the emphasis of the madrasa would still be the enhancement of Islamic institutions and culture. The Minister of Education promised government aid to improve the teaching staffs and instructional facilities and eventual accreditation of students' work in the madrasa. This means that there will be formal governmental recognition of the madrasa system, which at present is considered part of the informal educational system. Problems in recognition involve the nature of madrasa ownership, differences in the number of years offered, qualifications of the teaching staff, etc. Right now, there are about 1000 madrasas (including some maktabs) with an enrollment of at least 150,000 Muslim students. Eighty percent of the schools were probably created after the 1960s.

REFERENCES

De los Santos, Joel. 1975. "The 'Christian Problem' and the Philippine South." *Asian Studies* 13, no. 2 (August): 27–43.

Filipinas Foundation, Inc. 1975. *An Anatomy of Philippine Muslim Affairs: A Study in Depth on Muslim Affairs in the Philippines*. Manila: Filipinas Foundation. [Contains economic data and discusses Muslim-Christian attitudes.]

George, T. J. S. 1980. *Revolt in Mindanao: The Rise of Islam in Philippine Politics*. Kuala Lumpur: Oxford University Press. [Discusses thoroughly events in the secessionist movement in the Philippines.]

Glang, Alunan C. 1969. *Muslim Secession or Integration?* Manila: R. P. Garcia. [Anticipated many problems in the country and discusses nature of Muslim leadership.]

Gowing, Peter G. 1973. "Muslim Filipinos between Integration and Secession." *South East Asia Journal of Theology* 14, no. 2: 64–77.

_____ 1977. *Mandate in Moroland: The American Government of Muslim Filipinos, 1899–1920*. Quezon City: Philippine Center for Advanced Studies, University of the Philippines. [Comprehensive account of American rule.]

_____ 1979. *Muslim Filipinos—Heritage and Horizon*. Quezon City: New Day Publishers. [Contains a comprehensive account of the cultures of Muslim Filipinos as well as an account of historical and contemporary events.]

_____ and Robert McAmis, eds. 1975. *The Muslim Filipinos*. Manila: Solidaridad Publishing House. [Contains valuable historical, sociological, and anthropological data on Muslim Filipinos. A good handbook.]

Guerrero, Leon Ma. 1972. *Encounter of Cultures: The Muslims in the Philippines*. Manila: National Media Production Center for the Department of Foreign Affairs. [Discusses the differences and conflicts of two cultures.]

Kiefer, Thomas M. 1972a. "The Tausug Polity and the Sultanate of Sulu: A Segmentary State in the Southern Philippines." *Sulu Studies* 1: 19–64.

_____ 1972b. *The Tausug: Violence and Law in a Philippine Moslem Society*. New York. [One of the best sociological studies ever made on the Tausug.]

Mahmoud, Mohammed Fatthy. 1974. "The Muslims in the Philippines: A Bibliographic Essay." *Asian Studies* 12, nos. 2–3 (August-December).

_____ 1975. "Muslims in the Philippines: How they Perceive their Problems." DPA diss., College of Public Administration, University of the Philippines. [Muslim aspirations, feelings toward the government and other Filipinos.]

Majul, Cesar A. 1971. *Muslims in the Philippines: Past, Present and Future Prospects*. Pamphlet. Manila: Converts to Islam Society of the Philippines. [Anticipates and warns of further massacres of Muslims and exposes weaknesses of the Muslim community.]

_____ 1972. *The Historical Background of the Muslims in the Philippines and the Present Mindanao Crisis*. Pamphlet. Manila: Converts to Islam Society of the Philippines. Also published by Ansar ul Islam, 2nd National Symposium, Marawi City, 1972. Paper read before the Second National Conference of the Philippine Muslim Lawyers League, Manila, December 15–18, 1971. [Anticipates foreign concern about the Mindanao crisis, points out the religious dimensions in Muslim-Christian conflict, and appeals to

Muslim lawyers to ask the government for formal recognition of Muslim personal laws.]

_____ 1976a. "The Education of the Muslims in the Philippines: History, Present Situation, and Problems." Paper prepared for the First International Conference on "Muslim Education in the Modern World: Challenge and Response," held in Mecca, Saudi Arabia, March 31–April 8, 1977. Manuscript (104 pages).

_____ 1976b. "Some Social and Cultural Problems of the Muslims in the Philippines." *Asian Studies* 14, no. 1 (April): 83–99.

_____ 1976c. "Towards a Social Policy for the Muslims in the Philippines." *Philippine Political Science Journal* no. 4 (December): 1–17.

_____ 1977. "The General Nature of Islamic Law and its Application in the Philippines." *Philippine Law Journal* (Quezon City) 52, no. 4 (September): 374–94.

_____ 19–. "Cultural Diversity, National Integration and National Identity in the Philippines." In *Development in Southeast Asia: Issues and Dilemmas.* Inauguration Conference of Southeast Asian Social Sciences Association. Hong Kong. Also published in pamphlet form by *Convislam,* 1972.

_____ *Muslims in the Philippines.* 2d ed. Quezon City. [Deals with the history of Muslim Filipinos from early times to the eve of the American occupation.]

Mastura, Michael. 1972. "Maguindanao Hopes and Fears from the Constitutional Convention." *Solidarity* 7, no. 4 (April): 18–24.

Moro National Liberation Front, Central Committee, Office of the Chairman. 1974. "The Rise and Fall of Moro Statehood: Our Plight and Determination to Survive." Manuscript (50 pages).

_____ n.d. "Cultural Genocide in the Philippines." Speech delivered by Nur Misuari, Chairman, Central Committee of the MNLF, before the International Congress on Cultural Imperialism sponsored by the Lelio Basso Peace Foundation, Algiers, Algeria, October 11–15, 1977. Found in *The Moro People's Struggle,* published by the Alliance for Philippine National Democracy (UGNAYAN), United States.

Philippines, Republic of the. *Code of Muslim Personal Laws of the Philippines.* [Published in various pamphlets by government and private individuals. The Code was approved by Presidential decree on February 4, 1977, more than a year after it was presented by the Presidential Commission.]

Tamano, Mamimtal A. 1973. "How to solve the Muslim Problem Without Bullets." *Solidarity* (Manila) 8, no. 6 (December): 17–26.

_____ 1975. "The Expectations of Muslims as Philippine Citizens." *Solidarity* 10, no. 6 (July-August 1975): 30–34.

Tavakoley, Mohammed Kazen. 1979. "The Image of the Moros among the Christians in Selected Areas of Southern Negros Islands, Philippines." Master's thesis, Silliman University, Dumaguete City, Philippines. [Deals with the nature of Christian attitudes of some Visayans toward Muslims and attributes most of them to colonial experiences.]

Afterword

BENEDICT R. O'G. ANDERSON

A certain solitude surrounds each contribution to this volume. It is not merely that the authors come from four continents and grew up in many different cultural and academic traditions. The truth is that, in different ways, all are deeply engaged, morally, as well, perhaps, as politically, with the fates of particular minority communities. Hence the single-mindedness of anyone facing an emergency. Yet their contributions also continuously engage one another, bound as they are within the covers of this volume; and it is to this silent, mutual interrogation that these concluding pages are addressed.

It is immediately striking that more than half the contributors on South and Southeast Asia are themselves "representatives," in one form or another, of local minorities, whereas no such representatives appear for Latin America and Oceania. Doubtless this difference goes some way to explaining the paradoxical lack among the Asianists of the apocalyptic tone evident at times among the Americans. But in itself it also underlines, unobtrusively, the signally different implications of nationalism and ethnicity in the two main regions under study.

All four indigenous South and Southeast Asian contributors are, or have been, members of the "national" intellectual elites of their countries. Cesar Majul was for many years Dean of the Law Faculty at the University of the Philippines; Burhan Magenda is a leading political scientist at the University of Indonesia; Surin Pitsuwan, currently a member of the Thai parliament, was earlier a well-known political scientist at Bangkok's Thammasat University; and, though long since at Harvard, Stanley Tambiah originates from the cultivated late-colonial liberal intelligentsia of Ceylon. Moreover, Majul and Pitsuwan speak for minorities which are religious more than ethnic. The Moros of the Philippines include a variety of distinct, and historically antagonistic, "ethnic groups"; the Muslims of Thailand include both "ethnic Thais" and "ethnic Malays." Furthermore, these minorities have ready access to allies, more or less reliable, on the peripheries of the states they occupy: the Moros in East Malaysia, and the Muslims of Thailand in Western Malaysia. Still more important, they belong, more so than ever in the age of the airplane, the telex, and OPEC, to the vast, resurgent world of Islam, which is in no danger of extinction. Hence, whatever their unpleasant local fates, their central identification—as Muslims—is not catastrophically threatened. With some qualifications, much the same can be said of the Tamils in Ceylon. There is no question of Tamil civilization being destroyed, and the looming presence of India probably guarantees that whatever the current horrors being perpetrated by the Sinhalese-dominated regime in Colombo, some form of political accommodation will eventually be reached. Indonesia is in the fortunate position of having no single "ethnic majority," but rather dozens of significant minorities; and though the Javanese are the largest and most influential of these minorities, the sheer size and complexity of the country, no less than the broad multiethnic base of the nationalist movement of 1900–1950, ensure against ethnocide (except in the terrible instance of recently occupied East Timor). Even in the case of the Akha, a small, recently-arrived upland ethnic minority in Northern Thailand, the experience described by Cornelia Ann Kammerer is by no means wholly alarming. The Thai state has only recently become a national state, and the Thai elite wears its nationalism fairly lightly. The Akha appear as marginal, rather than profoundly subjected, to the "national polity."

It is also true that almost all the nationalisms of this region are of recent origin, the oldest going back no further than the 1880s. They were thus the heirs of the popular (and populist) nationalism of mid-nineteenth-century Europe—and not merely ideologically. Broad popular bases were essential in the struggle against the powerful, centralized, bureaucratic, high-capitalist colonial regimes of the first half of the twentieth century. Still more important, these nationalisms unified their supporters on the basis of a profound rejection of alien, white rule. Even in the case of the Philippines, which for obvious reasons shared much with the histories of the Latin Americas, it is striking how quickly and immediately, after the revolution of 1896–98, the very idea of *indio* (nationless "native") simply vanished.

The contrast with the Spanish Americas could not be more striking in almost every respect. The authors writing on this region have good reason to speak of ethnocide and perhaps even to regard the local nation-states as intrinsically murderous. It is worth reflecting on the reasons for the difference, and for the special moral stance the authors take up (even the North Americans among them).

The crux of the difference surely derives from the fact that the southern American nation-states were, and are, *creole* nation-states, where the dominant groups have always been descendants of white immigrants, and speaking the languages of Europe, no matter what indigenous ancestries they have come, over time, to claim. Three centuries of Spanish (and Portuguese) rule prior to the moment of independence had largely crushed the indigenous civilizations—which, in addition, had no external, let alone "universalist" connections. (Compare the Philippines, where the Spanish confronted, already in the sixteenth century, the outriders of the vast transcontinental Islamic civilization.) The indigenous populations, if not exterminated, were brutally subjugated to Christianity, Hispanization, and peonage.

It was precisely the fact that the creoles were Europeans and thus shared language, culture, and religion, no less than technological, mercantile, and military skills, with the metropole that enabled them to develop the first world-historical wave of nationalism in the period 1770–1820—well before Europe itself. But this originality also meant that the local nationalisms, genuine as they were, had sparse social and cultural roots. Moreover, the world-historical period in which they arose was one in which a third-rate imperial power like Spain did not exercise the bureaucratic, military, or economic power necessary to force (except perhaps in Mexico) any full-scale popular mobilization in the colonies. Accordingly, the nationalists of the Americas, especially the southern Americas, not only had little need of indigenous allies, but, as latifundists, lawyers, and middle-ranking imperial officials, stood directly to gain by maintaining the social status quo minus the thin layer of peninsular functionaries. For creole nationalists it was always impossible genuinely to cast themselves as anti-European or anti-white; nor could they look back through the centuries for unambiguous links to Cuzco or Teotihuacan in the way that Indonesians could attach themselves to a long-forgotten Borobudur or Thais to the burnt shell of Sri Ayutthaya. (The difficulty can be compared, perhaps exaggeratedly, to the task of Boers seeking ancestors in the Zulu conquerors Tshaka and Dingaan.)

But this need to indigenize American nationalism seems only to have appeared as a conscious project well after political independence was achieved. Doubtless, in part it presented a response to the worldwide change in the idea of nationalism produced by the *volkisch* European nationalism of the later nineteenth century. But since by then the real aborigines of the Americas had been, if they were not exterminated, radically crushed and marginalized, and since the ascendancy of creoles and mestizos was based on this historic obliteration, "indigenization" almost everywhere was necessarily constructed in bad faith and as a kind of political theater.

In the memorable Brazilian film *How Tasty was My Darling Frenchman,* we are presented with an exemplary (not least in its Chinese-box ironies) sketch of this willed *indigenismo*. It purports to tell the story of a young Frenchman, emblem of European Enlightenment, who falls in with a small tribal community in savage eighteenth-century Brazil. Taken for a god, he comes to accept the fate of gods within the tribe's cosmology: after a period of adoration, he is killed and eaten by his worshipers for their own salvation. Thus is the white immigrant "absorbed" by native America. Yet the director does not fail to tell us that shortly after the events depicted the tribe was completely exterminated—so that the "actors" of both immigrant and aborigines in the film are, like himself, creoles and mestizos. It is as if the building of America required two erasures.

One could argue that, in addition, a crucial role has also been played by the one creole society largely to escape the above-mentioned double-bind. In what came, after the 1770s, to be known as the United States of America, the indigenous populations were, as everywhere else in the New World, sequestered, decimated, exploited, and culturally lobotomized. But the sheer size of the country, its immense commingling of European populations, its Protestant fragmentation, its calm links with the English world-lords of the nineteenth century, and its sheer economic dynamism, produced a messianic nationalism in which *indigenismo* played little part. With a sacred Constitution, a God-given world-mission, a mythic Frontier, and an ideology profoundly, if unconsciously, creole, it thought nothing, even dreamed nothing, about the societies over which it triumphantly trampled. They were fortunate that the aborigines they encountered had built no awe-inspiring monuments (as had the Mayas, Aztecs, and Aymaras further south). Already by the end of the nineteenth century it was extending its imperial power into the southern Americas. Can one doubt that under these circumstances the criollo ruling classes of the south, even where they collaborated with the northern giant, tried to preserve some dignity as "fellow-creoles?" Were they not at least Christians, if Catholics, at least European language-speakers, if Hispanics, at least Liberals, if not grandchildren of Adam Smith?

In the encounter with the North, virtually everywhere the South bunkered down behind its Spanish and Portuguese ancestry, accepting without too many qualms that it was, indeed, a "Latin" America. It was thus exceptionally fortunate that this volume contains a fine, dispassionate account by Theodore Macdonald of the confrontation of the Nicaraguan Sandinistas with both American imperialism and aboriginal Miskito society. We are, of course, shown the shady cynicism with which the Reagan Administration has attempted to exploit the cultural apprehensions of Nicaragua's Pawnees. But Macdonald shows remorselessly that the Sandinista revolutionaries are the unwitting heirs of ladino nationalism; that the Miskitos, whether they speak English or Miskito, block the Hispanic, criollo project; and that, with—perhaps—the best will in the world, Daniel Ortega and his colleagues simply have no idea of what to do with the Miskito aborigines, except to Hispanicize, museumize, socialize, and patronize them. That a regime which, in contrast to so many others in the southern Americas, genuinely believes itself liberationist, should nonetheless quite unselfconsciously align itself with "Latin America" shows better than anything else why, as so many contributors to this volume insist, the "indigenes" are sensibly reluctant to throw away the few cards they still hold, and underwrite criollo revolutions.

But it would be "Tasty" to overlook a final interrogation in this volume: that posed, in exemplary fashion, by Alain Babadzan in his study of *Kastom* and nation-building in the South Pacific. For what he offers us is an ironical picture of ethnic liberation, i.e., if you like, the future of the Miskitos as a "nation," with a necessary presence at the United Nations General Assembly in Manhattan. In a world in which the only profoundly legitimate form of political organization is the nation-state, no matter how "mini," we can be sure that an independent Miskitia would have its well-dressed Foreign Ministry, its national anthem and flag, its folklorica, its civic education, its museums, and its "kastom." Babadzan's ironies find their mark: he is surely not wrong to underline the sentimentality and formalism of Oceanic nationalism, and the way in which it is exploited by culturally mestizo elites. But is there not here also a sort of Rousseauian nostalgia for noble savagery? For tradition, as against Tradition? Does not his own work suggest that every wounded ethnicity is a Kastom-nation in the making? We are not now, and never were, living in Eden. Nationalism is the most profound cultural and political force of our time. It is, in itself, neither better nor worse than older forms of political imagining. Like all imaginings, it consists, in equal parts, of fabrication and intervention, memory and amnesia, solidarity and murder. But it has profoundly to be reckoned with—and on a planetary scale. Precisely this, it seems to me, is what this fractious, fragmented book encourages us to undertake, with sympathy, but without illusions.

Authors

Benedict R. O'G. Anderson: director, Cornell University Southeast Asia Program, and Aaron L. Binenkorb professor of international studies

Alain Babadzan: visiting professor, department of ethnology, University of Paris X, Nanterre

Shelton H. Davis: former director of the Anthropology Resource Center in Boston; currently employed as an anthropologist in the World Bank, Latin America and Caribbean Environmental Division

Serge Gruzinski: research associate, Centre National de Recherche Scientifique (CNRS), Paris

Remo Guidieri: professor of anthropology, University of Paris X, Nanterre

Cornelia Ann Kammerer: Ph.D. in anthropology, University of Chicago, 1986; currently conducting a follow-up research project sponsored by the Joint Committee on Southeast Asia of the Social Science Research Council and the American Council of Learned Societies

Theodore Macdonald: projects director, Cultural Survival, Cambridge, Mass.; research associate, department of anthropology, Harvard University

Buhran Magenda: department of political science, University of Indonesia, Djakarta

Cesar Adib Majul: professor of Islamic philosophy and dean of the Institute of Islamic Studies (retired), University of the Philippines

Francesco Pellizzi: associate in Middle American ethnology at the Peabody Museum, Harvard University; editor of *RES: Journal of Anthropology and Aesthetics*

Surin Pitsuwan: currently a member of the Thai parliament; formerly of the department of political science, Thammasat University, Bangkok

Stanley J. Tambiah: professor of anthropology, Harvard University; curator of South Asian ethnology at the Peabody Museum

Serge Thion: research associate, Centre National de Recherche Scientifique (CNRS), Paris

Stefano Varese: visiting fellow at the Stanford University Humanities Center

DATE DUE

DEC 0 6 2004			
NOV 0 8 2004			